basic
Japanese

Learn to Speak Everyday Japanese
in 10 Carefully Structured Lessons

WITHDRAWN

SAMUEL E. MARTIN & ERIKO SATO

TUTTLE Publishing
Tokyo | Rutland, Vermont | Singapore

The Tuttle Story: "Books to Span the East and West"

Most people are surprised to learn that the world's largest publisher of books on Asia had its humble beginnings in the tiny American state of Vermont. The company's founder, Charles E. Tuttle, belonged to a New England family steeped in publishing. And his first love was naturally books—especially old and rare editions.

Immediately after WW II, serving in Tokyo under General Douglas MacArthur, Tuttle was tasked with reviving the Japanese publishing industry. He later founded the Charles E. Tuttle Publishing Company, which thrives today as one of the world's leading independent publishers.

Though a westerner, Tuttle was hugely instrumental in bringing a knowledge of Japan and Asia to a world hungry for information about the East. By the time of his death in 1993, Tuttle had published over 6,000 books on Asian culture, history and art—a legacy honored by the Japanese emperor with the "Order of the Sacred Treasure," the highest tribute Japan can bestow upon a non-Japanese.

With a backlist of 1,500 titles, Tuttle Publishing is more active today than at any time in its past—inspired by Charles Tuttle's core mission to publish fine books to span the East and West and provide a greater understanding of each.

Published by Tuttle Publishing, an imprint of Periplus Editions (HK) Ltd.

www.tuttlepublishing.com

Copyright © 2012 by Periplus Editions (HK) Ltd.

Library of Congress Cataloging-in-Publication Data

Martin, Samuel E. (Samuel Elmo), 1924–2009.
  Basic Japanese : learn to speak everyday Japanese in 10 carefully structured lessons / Samuel Martin, Eriko Sato. — 1st ed.
     p. cm.
  ISBN 978-4-8053-0962-9 (pbk.)
1. Japanese language—Textbooks for foreign speakers—English. 2. Japanese language—Spoken Japanese. 3. Japanese language—Self-instruction. I. Sato, Eriko. II. Title.
  PL539.5.E5M27 2012
  495.6'82421—dc23   2012003345

Distributed by

North America, Latin America & Europe
Tuttle Publishing
364 Innovation Drive
North Clarendon, VT 05759-9436 U.S.A.
Tel: 1 (802) 773-8930; Fax: 1 (802) 773-6993
info@tuttlepublishing.com
www.tuttlepublishing.com

Asia Pacific
Berkeley Books Pte. Ltd.
61 Tai Seng Avenue #02-12
Singapore 534167
Tel: (65) 6280-1330; Fax: (65) 6280-6290
inquiries@periplus.com.sg
www.periplus.com

First edition
16 15 14 13 12   10 9 8 7 6 5 4 3 2 1   1205MP
Printed in Singapore

TUTTLE PUBLISHING® is a registered trademark of Tuttle Publishing, a division of Periplus Editions (HK) Ltd.

Contents

About This Book

Basic Japanese introduces the structure of Japanese through authentic, commonly heard Japanese sentences, useful contemporary Japanese vocabulary, and natural conversation. This book is particularly suited for those who wish to quickly build their knowledge of sentence structures and their communicative skills in Japanese.

Each lesson starts with a section of Basic Sentences, which offers ten to twenty sentences serving as typical examples of essential sentence structures. These structures are explained thoroughly in the Structure Notes section later in the lesson. Basic Vocabulary lists thematically sorted vocabulary words and phrases that are relevant to the contextual theme of the lesson. The thematic grouping of the vocabulary is to help learners make associations to contexts more easily. The Conversation section offers an authentic dialog, in which you can learn basic, everyday discourse devices, such as natural ways of responding and acknowledging as well as appropriate ways of ending sentences in the context. Exercises are provided to strengthen your understanding of the content of the lesson.

Lesson 1 is mainly on sound systems, and not many grammatical facts are covered. However, the subsequent lessons introduce gradually more complex structures and facts about usage, so one can start with simple sentence structures and eventually learn complex sentences including conditionals, passives, and causatives by the time all ten lessons have been completed.

Basic Japanese is an extensive revision of *Essential Japanese*, by Samuel E. Martin, first published in 1957 and long a standard text for learning Japanese. Although Samuel Martin passed away in 2010 and was unable to review and approve the new changes, *Basic Japanese* maintains all the exciting linguistic insights of *Essential Japanese*, while incorporating linguistic changes that have taken place over the past several decades in terms of structure, vocabulary, and socio-cultural norms that are essential for communication in Japan today. Furthermore, all Japanese sentences (except those embedded in the English paragraphs) are presented in both kana/kanji and Romanization, and all sections except the Structure Notes and Exercise are recorded in the accompanying audio CDs to help users learn the language as a whole. Illustrations, culture notes, and usage tips are provided in sidebars wherever they may help learners to put themselves in the communicative contexts. Here are some tips for getting the most out of *Basic Japanese*:

The sentences in Basic Sentences are laid out so you will see Japanese sentences on the left and English translations on the right. It will be helpful if you cover the English translations as you read (and hear) the Japanese sentences and look at the translations only when needed. Some items in each sentence are underlined, showing that they bear grammar/usage points that will be discussed in Structure Notes.

It is advisable that you not write down the answers in Exercises so you can use this section repeatedly for reviewing and reinforcing your understanding. Answers are provided in a smaller font after the questions.

Many vocabulary words are presented outside of the Basic Vocabulary section, and you are advised to learn words from all the sections in each lesson. For example, Structure Note 3.1 lists relative time expressions such as **ashita** 'tomorrow', **kinō** 'yesterday', **raishū** 'next week', and **kotoshi** 'this year'. Furthermore, all Japanese sentences except in Exercise are accompanied by English translations, so you can expand your vocabulary as you work through them. A glossary is provided at the end of the book for the learner's convenience.

The authors are grateful to Cal Barksdale, Nancy Goh, Tan Cheng Har, and other editors and staff at Tuttle for their dedication and professionalism, as well as Akiko Saito for providing numerous illustrations, Taeko Kamei for her photographs, and Rui Tamura and Azuma Tanaka for helping to record the audio CD.

About the Japanese Language

The origins of the Japanese language are incompletely known, and multiple theories have been proposed over the past few centuries connecting Japanese to North Asian languages, South Asian Languages, and languages in other areas. Currently, it is thought that the strongest theory among them is one of the North Asian ones, which places Japanese with Altaic languages such as Turkish and Mongolian based on the typological similarities, for example, sequential suffixation (agglutinating morphology), Subject-Object-Verb order, and vowel harmony in native vocabulary. Around the fourth and the fifth centuries AD, Chinese characters and vocabulary started to be brought to Japan. The Japanese developed *man'yōgana*, in which a limited set of kanji were used to write Japanese words with their phonetic contribution. Eventually, in Heian Period (794–1185), hiragana and katakana were developed from some of the kanji characters included in *man'yōgana*. Most content words, such as nouns, adjectives, and verbs, have a Chinese origin due to the strong influence of China in history. However, modern Japanese also includes an increasing number of loan words from English. The Japanese language is obviously extremely complex in terms of its lexicon and writing systems, but its unique structural features also surprise many speakers of English. The following are only some of its unique features.

Word order and particles
The basic word order in English is subject-verb-object, whereas in Japanese it is subject-object-verb. The word order is rigid in English in most cases but can be very flexible in Japanese, so long as the verb is placed at the end of the sentence. For example, the English sentence *Ken called Yumi* can be either *Ken-ga Yumi-o yonda* or *Yumi-o Ken-ga yonda* in Japanese.

Postpositions
English prepositions such as *from, in, on, at,* and *with* correspond to postpositions in Japanese. Instead of saying *from New York,* they say something like *New York from,* or **Nyū Yōku kara**. Japanese and English are mirror images in this respect.

Dropping pronouns
The Japanese are not lazy people, but they like to drop personal pronouns such as 'I,' 'you,' and 'he.' The use of the second person pronoun **anata** 'you' is almost forbidden in conversations. To ask, 'Is it yours?' in speaking to Ms. Yamada, the Japanese will say, **Sore wa Yamada-san no desu ka** 'Ms. Yamada, is it Ms. Yamada's?'

Verb morphology

Japanese verbs and adjectives can be followed by numerous suffixes, one after another, just as if you are creating a necklace by putting beads together. For example, **tabe** is the shortest pronounceable form of the verb 'to eat.' However, **tabe-ru** means 'will eat,' **tabe-sase-ru** means 'will make someone eat,' **tabe-sase-rare-ru** means 'will be made to eat,' **tabe-sase-rare-tai** means 'want to be made to eat,' and **tabe-sase-rare-taku-nai** means 'do not want to be made to eat.' This feature of language is called agglutination, and it is one of the reasons many scholars think Japanese belongs to the Altaic language family.

Counters

Another feature that exists in Japanese but not in English is a category of suffixes called counters. Counters are placed after numerals in order to express the quantity or amount of people and things, and the choice of counters varies depending on the shape, size, and type of the item. For example, **go-nin no hito** means 'the five people'; **go-hiki no inu** means 'the five dogs'; **go-dai no kuruma** means 'the five cars.' **Nin**, **hiki**, and **dai** are the counters for these respective types of items.

Honorifics

The Japanese language has rich and extensive honorific systems that express respect, humility, and politeness. These systems govern speech styles through the choices of suffixes, prefixes, (pro)nouns, verbs, adjectives, and phrases that are determined based on the relationship among the speaker, the listener, and a third party with respect to the social grouping and social hierarchy. For example, a simple question like 'Will you go?' can be **Iku no**, **Ikimasu ka**, or **Irasshaimasu ka** depending on how close or distant the speaker feels to the person. English does not have such verbal suffixes for expressing politeness or respect. However, this does not mean English speakers are rude. English speakers use different strategies for expressing politeness. For example, they tend to use a longer phrase for expressing politeness: they may say 'I'm wondering whether it is okay for me to leave now' instead of 'Is it okay to leave now?' for politely asking for permission to leave. Or, they may elaborate on a statement with the addition of kind comments or brief explanations for conveying politeness in a variety of speech functions such as asking for permission, requesting, apologizing, thanking, and refusing invitations.

In this lesson you will learn some everyday phrases and sound structures of the Japanese language.

Sound It Out in Japanese!
日本語で言ってみよう！
Nihongo de Itte Miyō!

 **Basic Sentences**

[cue 01-1]

1. 「こんにちは。」   "Hello! (*literally*, As for today…)"
   "**Kon'nichi wa.**"

   「ああ，こんにちは。」   "Oh, hi!"
   "**Ā, kon'nichi wa.**"

2. 「先生，おはようございます。」   "Professor, good morning! (*lit.*, It is
   "**Sensei, ohayō gozaimasu.**"   early.)"

   「ああ，山田さん。おはよう。」   "Oh, good morning, Ms. Yamada!'
   "**Ā, Yamada-san, ohayō.**"

   > …ございます **…gozaimasu**

   Remember that you must add **gozaimasu** after **ohayō** 'good morning'
   and **arigatō** 'thank you' when you say these to your superior.

3. 「こんばんは。」   "Good evening! (*lit.*, As for this
   "**Konban wa!**"   evening…)"

   「ああ，こんばんは。」   "Oh, good evening!"
   "**Ā, konban wa!**"

4. 「(どうも)ありがとうございます。」 "Thank you (very much)."
   "**(Dōmo) arigatō gozaimasu**."

   「いいえ。」 "Not at all. (*lit.*, No.)"
   "**Īe**"

5. 「ありがとうございました。」 "Thank you (for what you have done)."
   "**Arigatō gozaimashita**."

   「どういたしまして。」 "You're welcome."
   "**Dō itashimashite**."

6. 「お元気ですか。」 "How are you? (*lit.*, Are you well?)"
   "**Ogenki desu ka**."

   「はい, おかげさまで。」 "Yes, I'm fine, thank you. (*lit.*, Thanks
   "**Hai, okage-sama de**." to you and others.)"

7. 「さようなら。」 "Goodbye!"
   "**Sayōnara!**"

   「さよなら。」 "Goodbye!"
   "**Sayōnara!**"

8. 「お母さん, おやすみなさい。」 "Good night, mom! (*lit.*, Please rest
   "**Okāsan, oyasuminasai**." well.)"

   「ああ, おやすみ。」 "Oh, good night!"
   "**Ā, oyasumi**."

9. 「あのう, (ちょっと)すみません。」 "Excuse me."
   "**Anō, (chotto) sumimasen**."

   「はい。」 "Yes."
   "**Yes**."

ちょっと **chotto**

Chotto means 'a little bit' and is used with a variety of verbs and
adjectives, but it also functions just to make one's expression soft and
friendly. It can be used by itself to get attention or softly refuse something or express dislikes.

10. 「 (どうも) すみませんでした。」 "I'm (very) sorry. (I have committed a
    "**(Dōmo) Sumimasendeshita**." discourtesy.)"

    「いいえ。」 "No, (don't worry)."
    "**Īe**."

すみません **Sumimasen**

Sumimasen is one of the most frequently used words in Japanese. Depending on the context, it is used to catch attention or apologize. It is also used to thank someone when one receives overwhelming generosity or kindness from him/her.

11. 「あ, ごめんなさい。」
"**A, gomen nasai.**"

"Oh, I'm sorry."

「うん, だいじょうぶ。」
"**Unn, daijōbu.**"

"Nothing. I'm fine."

12. ちょっと失礼ですが…
Chotto shitsurei desu ga...

Excuse me, but... (I have a question or request).

13. ちょっと待って (ください)。
Chotto matte (kudasai sai).

Please wait a moment.

14. 「ゆっくり (話してください)。」
"**Yukkuri (hanashite kudasai).**"

"(Please talk) slowly."

「はい。」
"**Hai.**"

"Sure."

15. もう一度 (言ってください)。
Mō ichido (itte kudasai).

(Please) (say it) again.

16. お願いします。
Onegai shimasu.

Please (do so). (I'll make a request of you.)

17. では(or じゃ), 失礼します。
"**De wa (or Ja), shitsurei shimasu.**"

Well, I'll say goodbye. (Excuse me.)

18. 「じゃ, また。」
"**Ja, mata.**"

"So long! (Well, (see you) again!)"

「ええ, じゃ, また。」
"**Ē, ja, mata.**"

"Okay, see you!"

19. 「はじめまして。スミスです。よろしく。」
"**Hajimemashite. Sumisu desu. Yoroshiku.**"

"Hi! I'm Ms. Smith. Nice to meet you!"

「はじめまして。田中です。こちらこそよろしく。」
"**Hajimemashite. Tanaka desu. Kochira koso yoroshiku.**"

"Hi! I'm Mr. Tanaka. Nice to meet you, too!"

CULTURE NOTE Puzzling Japanese Phrases

Beginner students of the Japanese language are often puzzled by simple, daily expressions when they see their literal translations. This is mainly due to socio-cultural differences between Japan and other countries, especially in the West, although structural differences in the language are also responsible. Many Japanese phrases were derived from locutions that express modesty and respect. For example, when the Japanese introduce themselves to others, they say **yoroshiku onegai shimasu** at the end. Phrase books will offer a conventional translation, like 'Nice to meet you,' but the literal translation is very different. Literally, **yoroshiku** means 'well,' 'appropriately,' or 'favorably.' **Onegai** means 'wish' or 'request.' **Shimasu** means 'will do.' So, the entire phrase literally means something like 'I request (you to act) in favor (of me)' or 'please be kind to me.' You may wonder why Japanese people say something that implies their helplessness at the very moment they introduce themselves, but the phrase actually expresses their modesty, their respect for the person they're speaking to, and their willingness to have a good relationship with him or her. And while the literal translation of the phrase is awkward, understanding the culture, understanding the idea of the phrase, and learning exactly when the phrase is used—by whom, to whom, and for what purpose—is the key to success in acquiring the language. Conventional English translations may be useful for you at the outset, but in a later context they will eventually confuse you. So, when you learn Japanese, think in Japanese, not in English!

 **Basic Vocabulary**

LISTEN

[cue 01-2]

FAMILIAR JAPANESE WORDS

折り紙 **origami**	origami
着物 **kimono**	kimono
空手 **karate**	karate
すし **sushi**	sushi
刺身 **sashimi**	sliced raw fish
すき焼き **sukiyaki**	sukiyaki (beef stew)
うどん **udon**	udon noodle
うなぎ **unagi**	eel
アニメ **anime**	anime, animation
マンガ/漫画 **manga**	comic books
ドラマ **dorama**	TV drama series
オタク **otaku**	otaku (people with obsessive interest in their hobby)
J-POP **jei poppu**	Japanese pop (music), J-pop

FAMILY

お父さん **otōsan**	father
お母さん **okāsan**	mother
お兄さん **onīsan**	older brother
お姉さん **onēsan**	older sister

CULTURE NOTE Manga

In Japan, people of all ages read **manga**, or comic books. At restaurants in the business district, it's common to see office workers in suits reading manga during their lunch breaks. Most cyber cafés in Japan offer their clients shelves of manga. There are popular long-running manga magazines like *Shonen Jump*, and some super-popular manga—for example, *Nana* by Ai Yazawa—have been turned into anime and/or movies. Manga's history can be traced back to the twelfth century, but the modern style of manga has flourished since World War II, with themes varying from action-adventure to romance, history, comedy, science fiction, fantasy, mystery, and horror, among others. Manga are studied by scholars, and there are even manga museums (for example, the Kyoto International Manga Museum). One reason for the appeal of manga is that they are very much accessible to anyone. They can influence people's lives, giving them courage, offering enlightenment, and releasing stress. Near 40 percent of the total sales of books and magazines in Japan are from manga publications. In fact, many supplementary teaching materials take the form of manga, teaching kanji, proverbs, history, and other subjects. Manga can be a good study tool for learners of Japanese like you, because they introduce kanji with the aid of a pronunciation guide (**furigana**), vocabulary words, colloquial phrases, onomatopoeia, and other features in illustrated contexts.

ANIMALS

犬 **inu**	dog
猫 **neko**	cat
兎 **usage**	rabbit
猿 **saru**	monkey
馬 **uma**	horse

LANDSCAPE

山 **yama**	mountain
川 **kawa**	river
海 **umi**	ocean, sea
池 **ike**	pond
湖 **mizuumi**	lake

Structure Notes

1.1. Pronunciation

Every language has a system of sounds, and no two systems are exactly alike. The same organs are used in pronouncing the sounds of Japanese and those of English, but they are used in somewhat different ways. These organs are parts of the mouth, the tongue, the nose, and the throat. You will find it helpful to learn a bit about how these organs are used to make the sounds of English and those of Japanese. Many of the sounds in these two languages are so similar that you can use English sounds for the Japanese ones without being misunderstood, but there are some English pronunciation habits that you must avoid if you are to speak understandable Japanese. And if you don't want your Japanese to have a marked American accent, you will want to pay close attention to the slight differences between even those sounds that are most alike in the two languages.

1.2. Rhythm

English is spoken in a SYNCOPATED fashion—we bounce along, rushing syllables in between heavy stresses, keeping an irregular rhythm and tempo based on our stress system. Each normal English syllable is spoken with one of four stresses—and there's even an extra one, especially loud, to show unusual emphasis. If you listen to the word *windshield wiper* you will notice that the first syllable ('wind-') is more heavily pronounced than the others; the last syllable ('-er') is the weakest; and for some speakers there is a difference in stress between the remaining syllables ('-shield-' and '-wipe-'). Those Americans who hear no difference in stress between '-shield-' and '-wipe -' may hear the somewhat stronger stress on the syllable 'new' in the phrase "a new windshield wiper" (with the strongest stress still on the syllable 'wind-').

Japanese, on the other hand, speak in a METRONOMIC fashion—as if there were a musician's metronome evenly beating out each syllable. Instead of putting a heavy stress on some syllables and various weaker stresses on the others, the Japanese gives each syllable a moderate and even stress. And instead of rushing syllables in between the heavy-stressed ones, speeding up the weaker syllables, slowing down for the stronger ones, the Japanese speaker allows about the same amount of time for each of his syllables, regardless of the apparent prominence of the syllable. To the ears of an American, accustomed to hearing distinctive stresses, not all Japanese syllables are heard evenly strong. This is because not all Japanese syllables are equally PROMINENT. The prominence of a syllable is conditioned by a variety of factors, such as stress, vowel color, pitch, voicing, etc. Of these factors, stress is the most important in English, but the least important in Japanese. Of course, those syllables that have voiceless or dropped vowels in Japanese will sound weakly stressed to an untrained American ear. So the first English habit to overcome in speaking Japanese is syncopation. Try to time your Japanese syllables evenly, giving them an equal stress.

1.3. Syllables

Now, what is a Japanese syllable? An English syllable, as noted above, is a sound or group of sounds accompanied by one of four stresses. A Japanese syllable isn't that sort of thing at all. It's a sound or group of sounds that take up a certain relative space of time. In other words, one of those metronome beats. A Japanese syllable may consist of a SHORT VOWEL (**e** 'picture', **o** 'tail'), or A CONSONANT + A SHORT VOWEL (**te** 'hand', **ta** 'field', **yo** 'world'), or A CONSONANT + Y + A SHORT VOWEL (the first syllable of **kyonen** 'last year'). Note that the sounds **sh**, **ch**, **ts** are in each case single consonants even though we write them with two letters.

In addition, a syllable may consist of a consonant when followed by another consonant (other than **y**) or a pause. For example, the first **k** of **yukkuri** 'slowly', the first **s** [a spelling abbreviation for what is really **sh** of **irasshaimashita** '(you) came', the first **n** of **kon'nichi** 'today', and both instances of the **n** in **konban** 'this evening'. The syllabic consonants are further discussed in note 1.9.

Finally, a syllable may consist of EITHER HALF OF A LONG VOWEL. In other words, what we write as **ā, ē, ī, ō, ū** are really just abbreviations for **aa, ee, ii, oo, uu**—two syllables each. Long vowels are further discussed in note 1.6.

Below are some of the words occurring in the Basic Sentences, with the syllable divisions indicated by hyphens.

はい	**hai**	*ha-i*
ちょっと	**chotto**	*cho-t-to*
おはよう	**ohayō**	*o-ha-yo-o*
こんにちは	**kon'nichi wa**	*ko-n-ni-chi-wa*
こんばんは	**konban wa**	*ko-n-ba-n-wa*
さようなら	**sayōnara**	*sa-yo-o-na-ra*

[cue 01-3]

1.4. Voicing

In the throat there are two pieces of muscular tissue that can be vibrated with a flow of air from the lungs like a couple of heavy rubber bands. They are called vocal cords. When vocal cords vibrate, we say the sound has VOICING or is VOICED. When these cords are somewhat relaxed at the sides of the throat, we say the sound is VOICELESS or UNVOICED. You can feel the vibration of the vocal cords by placing your hand on your throat. Or put your hands over your ears and you will notice a buzz whenever a sound is voiced.

In most languages, some of the sounds are typically voiced and others are typically voiceless. For instance, in English the initial sounds of these pairs differ in that the ones on the left (**k**, **ch**, **t**, **s**, **p**, **f**, **th**) are voiceless, and those on the right (**g**, **j**, **d**, **z**, **b**, **v**, **th**) are voiced:

Voiceless	Voiced
Kay	gay
cheer	jeer
toe	dough
seal	zeal
pay	bay
fan	van
thin	then

There are similar pairs of voiced and voiceless sounds in Japanese:

[cue 01-4]

Voiceless	Voiced
金 **kin** gold	銀 **gin** silver
血 **chi** blood	字 **ji** graphic character, letter
十 **tō** ten	どう **dō** how
そう **sō** so, right	象 **zō** elephant
パン **pan** bread	番 **ban** guard, watchman

In English, the sounds we call VOWELS, those made without any close contact between the tongue and top of the mouth, are always voiced, unless we are softly whispering. In Japanese, vowel sounds are often unvoiced when they come between voiceless consonants. Virtually every speaker of Japanese pronounces the vowels written **i** and **u** as unvoiced between voiceless consonants, and some drop these vowels completely. At the end of a word and after a voiceless consonant, these vowels are also frequently unvoiced or dropped, so that the final syllable of **ohayō gozaimasu** 'good morning' and **genki desu** 'I'm fine' sound AS IF there were no **u** there at all. The other vowels, those we write **a**, **e**, and **o**, are usually pronounced voiced. But unaccented **ka** and **ko** at the beginning of a word are often unvoiced when followed by the same syllable: **kakanai** 'does not write,' **koko** 'here.' And **ha** and **ho** are often unvoiced when followed by a voiceless consonant and the same vowel: **haka** 'grave,' **hokori** 'dust,' and **hosoi** 'slender.'

1.5. Vowels

There is a striking difference between the way a Japanese pronounces his vowels and the way an American pronounces his. Japanese vowels seem to stand still. English vowels often slide off from their starting points in one of three directions: with the tongue moving front and up (as in *key, bay, shy,* and *toy*); with the tongue moving back and up and the lips rounding (as in *now, know,* and *who*); with the tongue relaxing toward a central position (as in *yeah, ah, law, uh,* and *huh*; with many speakers also in *bad, bed, bid,* and *bud*; with some Southern and Western speakers also in *bat, bet, bit,* and *butt*).

A vowel takes its characteristic color from the way the tongue, mouth, and lips are held. Vowels are often described in terms of the tongue's position in three top-to-bottom levels (HIGH, MID, LOW) and three front-to-back positions (FRONT, CENTRAL, BACK). If we ignore the off-glides mentioned above, and think only about the points of departure, we can illustrate these positions for American vowels with such words as these:

	Front	Central	Back
High	beat, bit		boot, book
Mid	bait, bet	but, cut	boat, paw
Low	bat	father, cot	caught

Note: Some speakers do not distinguish *caught* from *cot*.

For many American speakers all nine possible positions are used. The Japanese speaker, however, fills only five of the spaces as in the following words:

LISTEN
[cue 01-5]

		Front	Central	Back
High		いびき **ibiki** snoring	---	つづく **tsuzuku** continues
Mid		せめて **semete** at least	---	こども **kodomo** child
Low		---	あなた **anata** you	---

In English, we spell the same vowel sound many different ways (*dough, toe, slow, so, sew,* etc.) and the same letter may indicate a number of different vowels (*line, marine, inn, shirt,* etc.). In Romanized Japanese, the same symbol is normally used for each occurrence of the same vowel. You should learn these symbols and the sounds they stand for, and not confuse this simple use of these letters with their many English uses. The use of the letters may be remembered as: **i** as in *ski*, **e** as in *pet*, **a** as in *father*, **o** as in *so*, **u** as in *rhubarb*. In both English and Japanese, the lips are relaxed for vowels in the front and center of the mouth, and somewhat rounded for those in the back. Many Japanese round their lips very little, however, and you will probably notice that the Japanese **u** involves less of this lip-rounding than the American equivalent. (Actually, much of the American lip-rounding is part of the off-glide.) After the consonants **s**, **ts**, and **z**, the Japanese **u** is sometimes pronounced in a HIGH CENTRAL position.

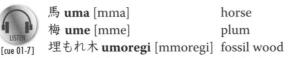

[cue 01-6]

進む	**susumu**	advances
車	**kuruma**	wagon
靴	**kutsu**	shoes
続く	**tsuzuku**	continues
盗む	**nusumu**	steals, swipes
牛乳	**gyūnyū**	milk

In ordinary conversation when the Japanese syllable **u** comes before **ma**, **me**, or **mo**, it is often pronounced as if it were the syllable **m**:

[cue 01-7]

馬 **uma** [mma]　　　　　horse
梅 **ume** [mme]　　　　　plum
埋もれ木 **umoregi** [mmoregi] fossil wood

Notice that Japanese does not utilize the MID CENTRAL position on the vowel chart. This is one of the most common of English vowels; it is sometimes indicated by the phonetic symbol ə (the schwa or 'inverted e'). For many English speakers, this is the most common vowel in weak-stressed syllables; so the American who forgets that Japanese has no weak-stressed syllables tends to replace various Japanese vowels with this relaxed central vowel. For **anata** 'you,' many Americans will say **anata**, overstressing the syllable **na** and sliding over the other syllables. Be careful to avoid weak stresses, and you will not confuse the Japanese with this mid-central vowel.

1.6. Vowels in sequence

In Japanese, any vowel may be followed by any other vowel. Each is pronounced in a short, clear, evenly stressed fashion. Here are some examples of vowel sequences:

[cue 01-8]

はい	**hai**	yes
家	**ie**	house
上	**ue**	top
甥	**oi**	nephew
青い	**aoi**	is blue

Note that there is a syllable, an even space of time, for each vowel: **ha-i**, **i-e**, **u-e**, **o-i**, **a-o-i**.

Now, in English we do not have vowels in sequence. Each vowel is followed either by a consonant or by one of those three off-glides mentioned in 1.5: the y-glide in *key*, *bay*, *by*, and *boy*; the w-glide in *now*, *know*, and *new*; the h-glide in *ah*, *yeah*, *law*, and *huh*. When we Americans hear a Japanese vowel sequence, we are apt to reinterpret this as one of our combinations of vowel + glide. We hear Japanese **hai** like English *high* and Japanese **mae** like English *my*. The difficulty is that English *high* and *my* rhyme, but Japanese **hai** and **mae** do not. The following chart will give you an idea of the difference in pronunciation between the two English words on the one hand and each of the Japanese words on the other:

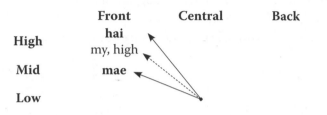

Note that there are some Tokyo speakers who do sound their **ai**'s much like their **ae**'s. Such speakers rhyme the words **kaeru** 'return' and **hairu** 'enter'. Speakers of Standard Japanese, however, try to keep these sequences distinct.

Just as we hear Japanese **ai** and **ae** alike, we tend to hear Japanese **au** and **ao** the same. Listen carefully to the difference between these pairs:

買う **kau**	buys
会う **au**	meets
顔 **kao**	face
青 **ao**	blue

[cue 01-9]

Do **kau** and **au** seem to sound like English *cow*? Do **kao** and **ao** seem to sound like English *ow*? The following chart will give you an idea of the difference in pronunciation. As you can see, this chart is a mirror image of the one above.

	Front	Central	Back
High			kau
Mid			cow
Low			kao

Since any vowel can follow any other vowel in Japanese, it is natural that a vowel can follow itself. These double vowels are sometimes called LONG VOWELS because, being two syllables, they take twice as long to pronounce as the short ones. In the Hepburn Romanization of Japanese, which this book uses, the double vowels are usually written with a macron (-) over the simple vowel, except in the case where there is a morphological boundary, as in **oishi-i** 'delicious.' Instead of a macron, some people use a circumflex accent (^ —like a small inverted V).

It is extremely important to master the difference between the short (simple) vowels and the long (double) ones early in your study of Japanese. So many words are distinguished by vowel length alone that, unless you are careful with these distinctions, your Japanese will be like a faulty telephone connection, likely to break down at any moment. English vowels are neither long nor short, by Japanese standards, but they often SOUND long, because of the off-glides. Remember to make your SHORT vowels SHORTER and your LONG vowels LONGER than the equivalent English vowels. Here are some examples of long and short vowels:

[cue 01-10]

田 **ta**	field	さあ **sā** [sa-a]	well
絵 **e**	picture	ええ **ē** [e-e]	yes
木 **ki**	tree	いい **ii** [i-i]	is good
帆 **ho**	sail	法 **hō** [ho-o]	law
府 **fu**	metropolitan prefecture	封 **fū** [fu-u]	seal

In ordinary conversation, most Japanese do not distinguish the vowel sequence **ei** from **ee** (=**ē**). In some parts of Japan, however, the distinction is still maintained. To an American ear, both sequences sound about like the vowel in *bay*. You should practice making the **ē** sound clear and long without the off-glide of the equivalent English sound. Examples:

[cue 01-11]

| 丁寧 **teinei** | polite | 経営 **keiei** | management |
| おねえさん **onēsan** | older sister | テーブル **tēburu** | table |

1.7. Consonants

In the structural system of every language, a given sound is made in somewhat different ways, depending on what sounds precede and follow it. If you hold your hand very close to your mouth and say the word *pan* clearly and naturally, you will feel a slight puff of breath; on the other hand, if you say *span* or *ban*, you will not feel the puff of breath. A more effective demonstration is to light a match and hold it close. Those consonants with a puff of breath will put the match out; those without will merely make it flicker. This puff of breath

PAN
SPAN
BAN

is called ASPIRATION; consonants accompanied by it are said to be ASPIRATED. English **p**, **t**, **ch**, and **k** (often spelled with the letter **c** as in *cat*) are aspirated in initial position, but not after the consonant **s**. Compare the two words in each of the following pairs:

pin and *spin*
tick and *stick*
charge and *discharge*
key and *ski*

In final position, English **p**, **t**, and **k** may be either aspirated or unaspirated, or not released at all.

Now in Japanese, the consonants **p**, **t**, **ch**, and **k** are usually somewhat aspirated as in English, but the aspiration is not so heavy. The Japanese consonants are UNASPIRATED when they are double (that is, long). Since the corresponding English double consonants are aspirated as in *hip pocket*, *part-time*, *night chief*, and *bookkeepers*, you should give special attention to suppressing the puff of breath when you make the Japanese double consonants.

Another characteristic of Japanese double consonants, including **ss**, **ssh**, as well as **pp**, **tt**, **tch**, **kk**—is the special TENSENESS with which they are pronounced. It is as if the Japanese speaker tightened up his throat in order to hold on and get in that extra syllable represented by the first of the consonants.

Listen to the difference between the single and double consonants in the following examples, then imitate them, being very careful to hold the first of the double consonants for a full syllable's duration and then release it tight and clear with no puff of air.

LISTEN
[cue 01-12]

Single Consonant	Double Consonant
ペン **pen** pen	一遍 **ippen** one time
糸 **ito** thread	一途 **itto** a way, a course
過去 **kako** past	括弧 **kakko** parentheses; brackets
火災 **kasai** fire	喝采 **kassai** applause
遺書 **isho** will, testament	一緒 **issho** together
一 **ichi** one	一致 **itchi** accord, agreement, unity

Just as the difference between long and short vowels is very important to make your Japanese understandable, so is the difference between long and short consonants.

One other point about aspiration. In English we do not aspirate a consonant after **s**. But in Japanese, when the syllable **su** is reduced to just a syllabic **s** (as in **Ikaga desu ka**.), a following **p**, **t**, or **k** still has the slight aspiration it would have in initial position. Notice the difference in pronunciation between English *ski*, one syllable, no aspiration—and Japanese **suki** 'likes'—two syllables, with **u** unvoiced or dropped, but with slight aspiration of **k**.

Consonants are usually described in terms of the WAY they are pronounced (voiced, voiceless; aspirated, unaspirated; etc.) and the PLACE they are pronounced. In general, Japanese uses about the same places in the mouth as English—**b**, **p**, and **m** are made with the lips, and **k** and **g** with the back of the tongue against the soft part of the roof of the mouth. However, **t**, **d**, and **n** are all made farther front than the English equivalents. For these sounds in English, most of us touch the front of the tongue or the tip (or both) against the ridge BEHIND the teeth, or even farther back than that. But in Japanese, the tongue is pushed forward against the teeth themselves. This gives the Japanese sounds—called DENTAL consonants—a sharper quality; the English sounds—called ALVEOLAR consonants (after the alveolar ridge behind the teeth)—sound dull and indistinct to a Japanese. Notice the difference between sounds in certain Japanese and English words:

LISTEN
[cue 01-13]

English (alveolar!)	**Japanese** (dental!)
toe	十 **tō** ten
dough	どう **dō** how
no	能 **nō** No (Japanese classical ballet)

The Japanese consonants **s**, **z**, **sh**, **ch**, and **j** are also pronounced somewhat more FRONT than many American speakers pronounce the English equivalents. Since the American sounds are farthest front in words like *see*, *zeal*, *sheep*, *cheap*, and *jeep*, it may help to think of the sounds in these words. Some Japanese give the **j** a sound rather like that used by the French in *Jacques* or by some Americans in *azure*, *garage*, and *rouge*. (At the beginning of a word, many Japanese pronounce **z** as if it were spelled **dz**; in slow over-precise speech, you may hear the **dz** version even in the middle of a word.)

Be careful how you pronounce the Japanese. English **f** is made with the lower lip against the upper teeth. The Japanese place both lips close together (as if about to make a **p** or a **b** or as if about to whistle) and then let the air come out in a puff between. A Japanese **f**, then, is an **f** WITHOUT ANY TEETH. Occasionally you will hear a Japanese use an ordinary **h** instead of this **f**.

Japanese voiced consonants (**b**, **d**, **z**, **j**, **g**, **m**, **n**) are more fully voiced than

English initial voiced consonants. In English we start off somewhat lazily with the voicing, giving our vocal cords an instant to warm up. It is only between vowels, *rabbit, lady, dizzy, tiger, coming,* and *inning,* that we voice these sounds all the way through. Japanese warm their vocal cords up an instant before they start to make the sound and this gives their voiced consonants a bit more prominence than ours.

The Japanese consonant **g** has two pronunciations. In Southern Japan it is usually pronounced like **g** in English *go* (but of course never like **g** in *gem* because that sound would be written *j*). In Northern Japan, many people pronounce the **g** always like the English sound in *sing* or *singer*. In Tokyo, there is a compromise. The general rule is: initial in a word, pronounce as in *go*; within a word, pronounce as in *singer*. There are a few exceptions to this rule. The particle **ga** is always pronounced with the **ng** sound, and the element **go** meaning 'five' is usually pronounced like English *go* even within a word, but these are of minor importance.

You may have trouble with this **ng** sound. It is made with the tongue in the same position as for **g**, but with the nasal passage open, the way it is for **m** or **n**. Notice that this is NOT the same sound as that used by most English speakers in the word *finger*—that is, by those speakers who do not rhyme this word exactly with *singer*. It is as if we should spell the former word *fingger* to show that we make first the back nasal sound (**ng**) and then the back non-nasal sound (**g**). Since you are not used to using this **ng** sound at the beginning of a stressed syllable in English, you may want to practice it in the following way. Hold the tip of your tongue down with your finger or one of those flat tongue-depressors doctors use. Then try to say the sound **n** as in *nine*. You will feel the tip of your tongue try to come up, but keep it down and make the back part of the tongue do the work. You have then made the **ng** sound. All you have to do after that is to train the tip of your tongue so you will not have to hold it down with a tongue de-pressor while making this sound. The Japanese **g** in the middle of a word, then, is an **n** made with the

back of the tongue. If you find this sound too difficult, just use your English **g** in all positions. You will not quite be talking Standard Japanese, but then neither do lots of Japanese! Here are some examples of the two kinds of **g**:

[cue 01-14]

g- [g]	-g [-ng]
学校 **gakkō** school	小学校 **shogakkō** primary school
銀 **gin** silver	金銀 **kingin** gold and silver
蛾 **ga** moth	…が **... ga*** but [subject particle]
15 **jū-go*** fifteen	銃後 **jūgo** non-combatant (status); behind the guns
1,005 **sen-go*** 1005	戦後 **sengo** postwar

* Exceptions!

The word **gogo** 'p.m., afternoon' shows both kinds: [**go-ngo**].

Another sound that may cause you trouble is **ts**. Unlike Japanese **t** (dental!), this sound usually starts at the alveolar ridge like an English **t**. It normally occurs only before the vowel **u**, and between the **t** and the **u** there is a slight hiss represented by the **s**. This sound does not occur initially in English, except for a few rare words like *tsetse fly*. However, you sometimes hear it in rapid speech: *ts cool today* (for *it is cool today*), *ts all right with me* (for *it is all right with me*). You may tend to slide over the **t** and only pronounce the **s**; this will cause confusion, because **tsu** and **su** distinguish a number of words, for example:

[cue 01-15]

s	ts
隅 **sumi** inside corner, angle	罪 **tsumi** guilt
する **suru** does	釣る **tsuru** fishes
住む **sumu** resides	つむ **tsumu** spindle
粕 **kasu** dregs	勝つ **katsu** wins
すずき **suzuki** sea bass	つづき **tsuzuki** continuing; sequel

Notice that the vowel **u** gets unvoiced or dropped when there is a following voiceless consonant:

[cue 01-16]

s	ts
好き **suki** [s-ki] likable	月 **tsuki** [ts-ki] moon
進む **susumu** [s-su-mu] advances	包む **tsutsumu** [ts-tsu-mu] wraps up
すすき **susuki** [s-su-ki] pampas grass	つつき **tsutsuki** [ts-tsu-ki] pecking, biting

After you have practiced on the difference between **tsu** and **su** for a while, you might try these tongue-twisters:

[cue 01-17]

すすみつづけました **susumi-tsuzukemashita** continued to advance
つつみつづけました **tsutsumi-tsuzukemashita** continued to wrap up

The thing to remember about the syllable **tsu** is: DON'T OMIT THE **t**.

In addition to the simple consonants are the combinations **ky**, **gy**, **py**, **by**, **my**, **ny**, and **hy**. (There is also **ry**, for which see below, 1.8.) These are pronounced somewhat as are the corresponding English sounds in *cute*, *gew-gaw* or *regular*, *rebuke*, *music*, and *Hugh*, provided you distinguish *Hugh* from *you*). In English, these combinations are usually followed by a vowel corresponding to Japanese **u**, but in Japanese they are also followed by **a** and **o**. For example, **byōin** [byo-o-i-n] 'hospital' and **biyōin** [bi-yo-o-i-n] 'beauty shop' sound similar but differ in that the former has the combination of **b** and **y** whereas these consonants are in separate syllables in the latter. Here are some examples:

[cue 01-18]

客車 **kyakusha** [kya-ku-sha]	passenger car
郵便局 **yūbinkyoku** [yu-u-bi-ng-kyo-ku]	post office
急行 **kyūkō** [kyu-u-ko-o]	express (train)
逆 **gyaku** [gya-ku]	reverse
実業家 **jitsugyōka** [ji-tsu-gyo-o-ka]	businessman
牛肉 **gyūniku** [gyu-u-ni-ku]	beef
八百 **happyaku** [ha-p-pya-ku]	eight hundred
発表 **happyō** [ha-p-pyo-o]	presentation
ピューと **pyū to** [pyu-u-to]	with a hiss (like a bullet)
三百 **sanbyaku** [sa-m-bya-ku]	three hundred
病気 **byōki** [byo-o-ki]	ill
ビューロー **byūrō** [byu-u-ro-o]	bureau
山脈 **sanmyaku** [sa-m-mya-ku]	mountain range
明晩 **myōban** [myo-o-ba-N]	tomorrow evening
ミューズ **myūzu** [myu-u-zu]	muse
ニャー **nyā** [nya-a]	meow
尿 **nyō** [nyo-o]	urine
牛乳 **gyūnyū** [gyu-u-nyu-u]	milk
百 **hyaku** [hya-ku]	farmer
標準 **hyōjun** [hyo-o-ju-N]	standard
ヒューズ **hyūzu** [hyu-u-zu]	fuse

1.8. Flapped *r*

The sound that seems to cause Americans most distress is the Japanese **r**. This is a sound called a flap. You make it by lifting the tip of the tongue backwards, then quickly and decisively bringing it down with a brief flick against the alveolar ridge (behind the teeth). Many Americans have this sound in the middle of words like *Betty*, *letter*, *latter*, and *cottage*. Some Englishmen use this sound for the **r** in *very*, *merry*, and *berry* so that the Englishman's *berry* often sounds like the American *Betty*. This **r** will sound a little bit like a **d** to you. The differences between the Japanese **r** and **d** are primarily two: length—the **r** is brief, the **d** somewhat longer; and position of contact—the **r** is against the alveolar ridge with the very tip of the tongue, but the **d** is against the teeth with somewhat more of the tongue. You might begin to practice this sound in medial position, being careful not to make it like an American **r**—nor to trill it lengthily like an Italian **r**—and at the same time keep it distinct from the Japanese **d**:

[cue 01-19]

Japanese d (TEETH!)	Japanese r (RIDGE! BRIEF!)	American r
肌 **hada** skin	鱈 **tara** cod fish	*horror*
届ける **todokeru** delivers	蕩ける **torokeru** is enchanted	*Tory*
袖 **sode** sleeve	それ **sore** that	*Cory*
---	蟻 **ari** ant	*sorry*
---	する **suru** does	*true*

Be sure you are putting the **r** at the beginning of the syllable: **sorosoro** [so-ro-so-ro] 'leisurely.' Once you have acquired the sound, try practicing it initially:

[cue 01-20]

Japanese d (TEETH!)	Japanese r (RIDGE! BRIEF!)	American r
抱く **daku** embraces	楽 **raku** comfort	*rock*
電柱 **denchū** telephone pole	連中 **renchū** gang	*wrench*
毒 **doku** poison	六 **roku** six	*rogue*
---	りんご **ringo** apple	*ring*
---	留守 **rusu** absence	*roots*

Once you're able to make the initial **r**, you're ready to tackle the combination **ry**. This sound is made by putting the back part of the tongue in position to make the **y** sound, then very swiftly moving just the tip of the tongue up to make the flap for the **r**. You might practice the words first without the **r**, making the **y** good and strong; then go over them inserting the **r** lightly, without damaging the **y**. Do not make the **r** and then add an extra syllable just to get the **y** in. Examples:

[cue 01-21]

略 **ryaku** [rya-ku] abbreviation
琉球 **Ryūkyū** [ryu-u-kyu-u] Ryukyu (Islands)
省略 **shōryaku** [sho-o-rya-ku] abbreviation, omission
上流 **jōryū** [jo-o-ryu-u] upper reaches (of a river)
大統領 **daitōryō** [da-i-to-o-ryo-o] president

1.9. Syllabic nasal

There is one more sound that may cause you some trouble. This is the syllabic nasal. The Japanese write this sound with the same symbol, but it is pronounced in different ways, depending on the sounds around it. For example, the **n** sounds in **tan-i** 'academic credits' and **tani** 'valley' sound completely different. The Hepburn Romanization writes the syllabic nasal sometimes **m**, sometimes **n** and sometimes **n'** or **n-** (**n** followed by an apostrophe or a hyphen). The sound may be written **m** if it is followed by **p**, **b**, or **m**—any lip sound other than **f** or **w**; it is written **n'** or **n-** if it is followed by a vowel (**a**, **e**, **i**, **o**, **u**) or by **y**; and it is written just **n** before other consonants (including **f** and **w**) and at the end of a word.

The pronunciation of the syllabic nasal varies according to its surroundings, but it is always pronounced with the nasal passage open and it always takes a full syllable's time. There are four main pronunciations:

1. a long (syllabic) **m** (before **p**, **b**, and **m**)
2. a long (syllabic) **n** (dental!, before **t**, **ts**, **d**, **n**, **ch**, and **j**)
3. a long (syllabic) **ng** (before **k** and **g**)
4. long nasalization **N** (elsewhere (before vowel, **y**, **w**, **r**, **s**, **sh**, **z**, **h**, **f**, or at the end of a word))

You will have little difficulty with the first two pronunciations. Just remember to hold the nasal for a full syllable's time. Here are some examples:

[cue 01-22]

1. a long (syllabic) **m**
见物 **kenbutsu** [ke-m-bu-tsu]   sightseeing
金髪 **kinpatsu** [ki-m-pa-tsu]   blond (hair)
三枚 **sanmai** [sa-m-ma-i]   three sheets (of paper)

[cue 01-23]

2. a long (syllabic) **n**
ちゃんと **chanto** [cha-n-to]   just, precisely
心痛 **shintsū** [shi-n-tsu-u]   anguish, heartache
今度 **kondo** [ko-n-do]   this time; next time
こんにちは **kon'nichi wa** [ko-n-ni-chi-wa]   hello, good afternoon
建築 **kenchiku** [ke-n-chi-ku]   construction, building
三時 **sanji** [sa-n-ji]   three o'clock

The third pronunciation may cause you some difficulty. The combination **nk** is pronounced about as in *banker*, but the **ng** sound of the **n** is held for a full syllable. The combination written in the Hepburn Romanization as **ng** is pronounced with that **ngg** sound of *fingger* in some parts of Japan, but in the Standard Language it is pronounced like two **ng** sounds in a row: **ngng**, with the first held for a full syllable and the second beginning the following syllable. Get out your tongue-depressor again, and keep the tongue tip down a little longer.

Cf. **nangai** 'how many floors' and **nagai** 'is long.'

[cue 01-24]

3. a long (syllabic) **ng**

元気 **genki** [ge-ng-ki]	good health
三角 **sankaku** [sa-ng-ka-ku]	triangle
インキ **inki** [i-ng-ki]	ink
今月 **kongetsu** [ko-ng-nge-tsu]	this month
金魚 **kingyo** [ki-ng-ngyo]	goldfish
文学 **bungaku** [bu-ng-nga-ku]	literature
りんご **ringo** [ri-ng-ngo]	apple

The fourth pronunciation you will probably find the most difficult. The basic part of this sound is just nasalization—such as the French put on some of their vowels in words like *garçon*, *Lyons*, or *chanson*. Some Americans use simple nasalization in place of the **nt** in words like *plenty*, *twenty* [ple'y, twe'y]. If you like, you may think of this as an **n** with the tongue not quite touching the top of the mouth anywhere. This sound is heard most distinctly at the end of a word:

[cue 01-25]

4. long nasalization **N**
(At the end of a word)

パン **pan** [pa-N]	bread
新聞 **shinbun** [shi-m-bu-N]	newspaper
日本 **Nihon** [ni-ho-N]	Japan
金 **kin** [ki-N]	gold
ペン **pen** [pe-N]	pen

(Before **s**, **sh**, **z**, **h**, **f**, and **r**)

検査 **kensa** [ke-N-sa]	investigation
新式 **shinshiki** [shi-N-shi-ki]	new style
万歳 **banzai** [ba-N-za-i]	hurrah!
時間表 **jikanhyō** [ji-ka-N-hyo-o]	timetable
日本風 **Nihonfū** [ni-ho-N-fu-u]	Japanese style
管理 **kanri** [ka-N-ri]	management

Before y, w, and vowels

Before vowels, **y**, and **w**, the syllabic nasal takes on some of the color of the following sound. For example, in **hon'ya** [ho-N-ya] 'bookshop,' the **N** sounds like a nasalized **y**, anticipating the following, non-nasal **y**. In **hon wa** [ho-N-wa] 'as for the book,' the **N** sounds like a nasalized **w**, anticipating the following, non-nasal **w**. Before **i** or **e**, the syllabic nasal may also sound like a nasalized **y**: **Nihon e** [ni-ho-N-e] 'to Japan,' **ten-in** [te-N-i-N] 'clerk.' Here are some more examples:

[cue 01-26]

パン屋 **pan'ya** [pa-N-ya]	bakery, bakeshop
婚約 **kon'yaku** [ko-N-ya-ku]	engagement (to be married)
神話 **shinwa** [shi-N-wa]	myth
電話 **denwa** [de-N-wa]	telephone
禁煙 **kin'en** [ki-N-e-N]	No Smoking
千円 **sen'en** [se-N-e-N]	1000 yen
金色 **kin'iro** [ki-N-i-ro]	gold color
単位 **tan'i** [ta-N-i]	unit
南欧 **nan'ō** [na-N-o-o]	Southern Europe

1.10. Accent

In English, accent refers to the way in which stress levels occur. In Japanese, the accent is the way in which PITCH LEVELS occur. When the vibrating vocal cords are drawn out long and tight, the pitch is high. When they are relaxed and shortened, the pitch is low. In English we use different pitch levels to indicate certain general types of phrases—like question (?), statement (.), suspension (...), continuation (,), and so forth. This use of pitch is called INTONATION. Japanese has intonation, too, but it is usually restricted to the last voiced syllable of a phrase. Note that in English the intonation contour extends over much more of the phrase, but the Japanese intonation occurs only with the last syllable or two. In addition to intonation, Japanese uses pitch to differentiate words and phrases from each other, like we use stress in English. It is this use of pitch that we call accent.

In different parts of Japan there are different accent patterns. More than a half of the Japanese population speaks with accent patterns rather like those of Standard Japanese—that is, the speech of Tokyo. The principal exception is Western Japan (Kyoto, Osaka, Kobe; also parts of Shikoku and southern Kyushu). There, the accent often seems just the opposite from that of Standard Japanese. Where the Tokyo speaker goes up in pitch, the Kyoto speaker often goes down. In some parts of Japan (places in northern Kyushu and in northeastern Honshu), the accent is not distinctive at all; all words have the same pattern. If you are planning to talk Japanese in Western Japan, you can completely ignore the accent marks in this section. And even if you are going to talk Japanese in Tokyo, you will be fairly well understood, even without the accent distinctions. The Japanese of today are used to hearing their language spoken with a variety of accent patterns. The important thing is that you should always imitate the persons you hear speaking Japanese and mimic their accents, wherever you may be. However, if you wish to put the final polish on your knowledge of Standard Japanese, you may want to devote some attention to the accent.

What the accent mark represents in Standard Japanese is THE LAST SYLLA-BLE BEFORE A FALL IN PITCH. In **yukkuri** 'slowly,' there is a fall of pitch right after the syllable **ku**. In Tokyo speech EVERY SYLLABLE UP TO THE FALL OF PITCH IS HIGH EXCEPT THE FIRST OF THE PHRASE. Of course, if the first syllable is itself the last before the fall, it is high. The relative pitches in **yukkúri** 'slowly' and **Génki desu** 'I'm fine' look as below, where L stands for a low pitch and H stands for a high pitch:

[cue 01-27]

ゆっくり
yukkúri
[yu-k-ku-ri]
L H H L
'slowly'

げんきです。
Génki desu.
[ge-n-ki-de-s]
H L L L L
'I'm fine.'

You will be able to hear this fall of pitch most clearly when it occurs on the first of a vowel sequence—like the long vowels **ā, ē, ī, ō, ū**, or the sequences **ai, ei, oi, ui**— or when it occurs on a vowel followed by the syllabic nasal. This is because we tend to hear each of these double-syllables as just one syllable and we are used to hearing a fall of pitch WITHIN a syllable in English: *He saw Jóhn. Look at the bóy. Sáy. Hí! Mé. Nó. Yóu.* Listen to these examples:

[cue 01-28]

どういたしまして。
Dō itashimashite. [dó-o-i-ta-shi-ma-sh-te]
Not at all.

日本にいます。
Nihon ni imasu. [ni-hó-n-ni-i-ma-s]
He's in Japan.

青い着物をきています。
Aoi kimono o kite imasu. [a-ó-i-ki-mo-no-o-ki-te-i-ma-s]
She's wearing a blue kimono.

The range of pitch is somewhat wider in English than in Japanese. When we have a fall, it descends from higher to lower pitches than the corresponding Japanese fall. To our ears, the Japanese rises and falls in pitch are very light and often difficult to catch. They are nonetheless an important part of Japanese speech. In

Standard Japanese there is just one accent—one fall of pitch—within a phrase. But a given sentence may either be broken up into a number of small phrases or read all in one big phrase. It's possible to say the sentence meaning 'Not at all; you're welcome' slowly and deliberately as three phrases: **dō itashi mashite**. It is more usual to say it as just one phrase: **dōitashimashite**. When two or more smaller phrases are said together as a larger phrase, the accent of the first phrase stays, but the accent of the later phrases disappears. Instead of **shitsúrei itashimáshita** you will more often hear **shitsúrei itashimashita** 'excuse me,' instead of **arígatō gozaimásu** you will hear **arígatō gozaimasu** 'thank you.' Since the accent mark represents the last syllable before a FALL in pitch, it never occurs right before a pause. Before a pause, you cannot tell whether a word has a final accent or no accent at all; when you add a particle (such as the topic particle **wa**) it immediately becomes clear:

[cue 01-29]

鼻。 **Hana.** Nose.
鼻は。 **Hana wa...** As for the nose...

花。 **Haná.** Flower.
花は。 **Haná wa...** As for the flower...

The term *final accent* refers not only to an accent on the very last syllable, but also often to one on the next-to-last syllable, provided the last syllable is the second of a vowel sequence—like **kinō** [ki-nó-o] 'yesterday,' **chihō** [chi-hó-o] 'region,' **senséi** [se-n-sé-i] or [se-n-sé-e] 'teacher,' **kudasái** [ku-da-sá-i] 'please (give),' or is the syllable nasal-like **Nihón** [ni-hó-n] 'Japan,' **hón** [ho-n] 'book.' In these cases, the intonation often extends over the last two syllables.

When a vowel becomes unvoiced or dropped (like **u** in **arimásu** 'something exists,' **désu** 'something equals something,' and **itashimásu** 'I do'), the intonation usually covers the preceding syllable and the accent really disappears: **arimasu** [a-ri-ma-s]. The accent appears again, however, if the word is followed by another word as in **Arimásu ka** 'Are there any?' and **Arimásu ga...** 'There are, but....' Here are some examples of the accent on various syllables. Listen for the pitch falls. Remember, the single phrases may be joined together into longer phrases and the later accents dropped.

いいですか。
Íi desu ka.
[cue 01-30]　Is it all right?

だめです。
Damé desu.
It's no good, it won't do.

結構です。
Kékkō desu.
No, thank you.

忘れました。
Wasuremáshita.
I've forgotten (it).

分れましたか。
Wakarimáshita ka.
Did you understand?

好きですか。嫌いですか。
Sukí desu ka. kirai désu ka.
Do you like it or not?

ちょっと来てください。
Chótto kíte kudasai. (Chótto kite kudasai.)
Please come here a minute.

いくらですか。
Íkura desu ka.
How much is it?

窓を開けてください。
Mádo o akete kudasái.
Please open the window.

戸を閉めてください。
To o shímete kudasái.
Please close the door.

戸を開けてください。
To o akete kudasái.
Please open the door.

 **Conversation**

Annie (A) is talking with Professor Tanaka (T) on campus. She sees Makoto (M), whom she hasn't seen for six months.

A.　まことさん！
Makoto-san!
Makoto!

M.　ああ，アニーさん。お元気ですか。
Ā, Anī-san. Ogenki desu ka.
Oh, Annie! How are you?

A.　元気です。まことさんは？
Genki desu. Makoto-san wa?
Yes, I'm fine. How about you, Makoto?

M.　おかげさまで。元気です。
Okage-sama de. Genki desu.
I'm fine, too.

A.　田中先生，こちらはまことさんです。
Tanaka-sensei, kochira wa makoto-san desu.
Profesor Tanaka, this is Makoto.

M.　はじめまして。伊藤まことです。よろしくお願いします。
Hajimemashite. Itō Makoto desu. Yoroshiku onegai shimasu.
Hello! I'm Makoto Ito. Very pleased to meet you.

T.　田中です。こちらこそよろしく。
Tanaka desu. Kochira koso yoroshiku.
I am (Ms.) Tanaka. Nice to meet you, too.

はじめまして **Hajimemashite**

Many of you might have wondered why the Japanese say **hajimemashite** when they see someone for the first time. **Hajimemashite** sounds like the **hajime** that is used at a karate dojo, doesn't it? **Hajimemashite** is a derived form of the verb **hajimeru**, which means 'begins.' It is the first phrase when you "begin" conversation with someone new. It is difficult to translate into English, but its function is to clarify that this is the first time for one to talk to the person and also to convey one's willingness to get to know the person. Don't try to translate this phrase to English, but remember when to use it.

Exercises

I. For each of the following situations, pick the Japanese sentence which best fits.

1. You accidentally step on someone's foot getting to your seat in a movie theater.
   (a) すみません。 **Sumimasen.**
   (b) おはよう。 **Ohayō.**
   (c) じゃ，失礼いたします。 **Ja, shitsurei itashimasu.**
   (d) お願いします。 **Onegai shimasu.**

2. You don't quite understand what someone has just said.
   (a) 失礼します。 **Shitsureishimasu.**
   (b) もう一度。 **Mō ichido.**
   (c) ありがとうございます。 **Arigatō gozaimasu.**
   (d) いいえ。 **Īe.**

3. The person is talking too fast.
   (a) はい。 **Hai.**
   (b) すみません。 **Sumimasen.**
   (c) ゆっくり話してください。 **Yukkuri hanashite kudasai.**
   (d) じゃ，また。 **Ja, mata.**

4. You are about to go to bed.
   (a) ありがとう。 **Arigatō.**
   (b) じゃ，また。 **Ja, mata.**
   (c) おやすみなさい。 **Oyasumi nasai.**
   (d) すみません。 **Sumimasen.**

5. The teacher gave you a dictionary. You say:
   (a) どうもありがとうございます。 **Dōmo arigatō gozaimasu.**
   (b) こんにちは。 **Konnichi wa.**
   (c) おかげさまで。 **Okagesama de.**
   (d) 失礼します。 **Shitsurei shimasu.**

II. Choose the correct item.

1. dog
   a. 兎 **usagi** b. 猿 **saru** c. 犬 **inu** d. 猫 **neko**

2. mountain
   a. 湖 **mizuumi** b. 山 **yama** c. 馬 **uma** d. 池 **ike**

3. ocean

 a. 空手 **karate**   b. 海 **umi**   c. 馬 **uma**   d. すき焼き **sukiyaki**

4. older brother

 a. お母さん **okāsan**   c. お兄さん **onīsan**

 b. お父さん **otōsan**   d. お姉さん **onēsan**

III. Circle the one you hear.

[cue 01-32]

1. **koko** here   **kōkō** high school
2. **tori** bird   **tōri** street
3. **otto** husband   **oto** sound
4. **kin'en** no smoking **kinen** commemoration
5. **kámi** god   **kamí** hair
6. **kin** gold   **gin** silver

LESSON 2

In this lesson you will learn how to identify people and things around you. You will learn many ways to refer to items, using the Japanese equivalent of the copular verb 'to be.'

What? Where? Who?
何？どこ？だれ？
Nani? Doko? Dare?

 **Basic Sentences**

[cue 02-1]

1. <u>あれ</u>は<u>富士山</u>です。
   <u>**Are wa** Fujisan **desu**</u>.

   That one over there is Mt. Fuji.

2. 「<u>それ</u>は<u>何</u>です<u>か</u>。」
   "<u>**Sore**</u> wa <u>**nan**</u> desu <u>**ka**</u>."

   "What is that (the thing you are holding)?"

   「<u>これ</u>はカメラです。」
   "<u>**Kore**</u> wa kamera desu."

   "This is a camera."

3. 「<u>あの</u>人は<u>だれ</u>ですか。」
   "<u>**Ano**</u> hito wa <u>**dare**</u> desu ka."

   "Who is that person?"

   「マイクさんです。マイクさんは学生です。」
   "**Maiku-san desu. Maiku-san wa gakusei desu.**"

   "He is Mike. Mike is a student."

4. 「この傘はだれ<u>の</u>ですか。」 "Whose is this umbrella?"
   "Kono kasa wa dare <u>no</u> desu ka."

   「それは<u>私</u>のです。」 "That's mine."
   "Sore wa <u>watashi</u> no desu."

5. 「田中さんの傘は<u>どれ</u>ですか。」 "Which is Ms. Tanaka's umbrella?"
   "Tanaka-san no kasa wa <u>dore</u> desu ka."

   「私のはあれです。」 "Mine is that one over there."
   "Watashi no wa are desu."

6. 「銀行は<u>どこ</u>ですか。」 "Where is the bank?"
   "Ginkō wa <u>doko</u> desu ka."

   「あそこです。」 "It's over there."
   "Asoko desu."

7. 「パソコンはどこ<u>にあります</u>か。」 "Where is the computer?"
   "Pasokon wa doko <u>ni arimasu</u> ka."

   「机の<u>上</u>にあります。」 "It's on the top of the desk."
   "Tsukue no <u>ue</u> ni arimasu."

8. 「マイクさんはどこにいますか。」 "Where is Mike?"
   "Maiku-san wa doko ni imasu ka."

   「銀行にいます。」 "He is at the bank."
   "Ginkō ni imasu."

9. 「アンさん。アンさんは日本<u>の</u> "Ann, do you like Japanese food?"
   食べ物<u>が好き</u>ですか。」
   "An-san. An-san wa Nihon no tabemono <u>ga suki</u> desu ka."

   「ええ，大好きです。」 "Yep, I love it."
   "Ē, daisuki desu."

10. 「日本のアニメは<u>どう</u>ですか。」 "What do you think of Japanese anime?"
    "Nihon no anime wa <u>dō</u> desu ka."

    「素晴らしいです。」 "(It) is wonderful."
    "Subarashii desu."

[cue 02-2]

IN MY ROOM

部屋 **heya**	room
テーブル **tēburu**	table
ソファー **sofā**	sofa
ベッド **beddo**	bed
椅子 **isu**	chair
机 **tsukue**	desk
パソコン **pasokon**	computer (*lit.*, personal computer)
テレビ **terebi**	TV
リモコン **rimokon**	remote control
スタンドライト **sutandoraito**	floor/table/desk lamp
充電器 **jūdenki**	battery charger, charger
鉛筆 **enpitsu**	pencil
ペン **pen**	pen
時計 **tokei**	clock, watch
カメラ **kamera**	camera
本 **hon**	book
新聞 **shinbun**	newspaper
雑誌 **zasshi**	magazine

PLACES

駅 **eki**	train station
郵便局 **yūbinkyoku**	post office
銀行 **ginkō**	bank
病院 **byōin**	hospital
映画館 **eigakan**	movie theater
レストラン **resutoran**	restaurant
喫茶店 **kissaten**	coffee shop
ネットカフェ **netto kafe**	
	cyber café
ATM **ei tī emu**	ATM
スーパー **sūpā**	supermarket

PEOPLE

人 **hito**	person, people
友達 **tomodachi**	friend
学生 **gakusei**	student
先生 **sensei**	teacher

SCHOOLS

学校 **gakkō**	school
高校 **kōkō**	high school
大学 **daigaku**	college, university
大学院 **daigakuin**	graduate school

CULTURE NOTE ➤ Netto Kafe

Internet cafés in Japan are called **netto kafe** or **nekafe**, and are found in most major cities. They are actually very complex. In addition to desktop computers, Internet access, and drinks, they offer tons of comic books, magazines, and DVDs for the customers to read and watch as much as they want during their stay. They are usually open 24/7, and the customers are charged by time. They offer some private rooms in different sizes so the customers can read or watch undisturbed by others. Some **netto kafes** have comfortable reclining chairs, massage chairs, and shower rooms as well as billiards, karaoke, and darts. It is possible for homeless people to live in **netto kafes** in Japan, because a one-night stay could cost as little as ten dollars, and such people are called **etto nanmin** 'net refugee.'

COUNTRIES

日本 **Nihon/Nippon**	Japan
アメリカ **Amerika**	The United States of America
イギリス **Igirisu**	England
中国 **Chūgoku**	China
韓国 **Kankoku**	South Korea
オーストラリア **Ōsutoraria**	Australia
フランス **Furansu**	France
ドイツ **Doitsu**	Germany
スペイン **Supein**	Spain
インド **Indo**	India
フィリピン **Filipin**	The Philippines
ロシア **Roshia**	Russia

PEOPLE

日本人 **Nihonjin**	Japanese
アメリカ人 **Amerikajin**	American
中国人 **Chūgokujin**	Chinese
韓国人 **Kankokujin**	Korean
フランス人 **Furansujin**	French

LANGUAGES

日本語 **Nihongo**	Japanese
英語 **Eigo**	English
中国語 **Chūgokugo**	Chinese
韓国語 **Kankokugo**	Korean
フランス語 **Furansugo**	French

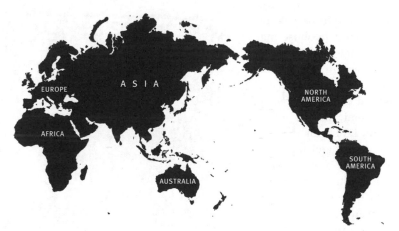

EUROPE   ASIA   NORTH AMERICA   AFRICA   AUSTRALIA   SOUTH AMERICA

Structure Notes

2.1. Nouns and pronouns

Nouns are words that name people, places, things, and concepts such as **hito** 'person,' **Yamada** '(Ms.) Yamada,' **zasshi** 'magazine,' and **uchi** 'house.' Nouns often precede a particle like **wa**, **ga**, **no**, and **ni**, or occur before the word **desu** 'is (equals).'

Pronouns refer to people and things. Personal pronouns refer to people. **Watashi** means 'I' or 'me.' In a formal situation **watakushi** is used instead of **watashi**. Women also say **atashi** in an informal situation. Men often say **boku** for 'I, me'; a rougher term is **ore**. The pronoun 'you' in Japanese is **anata**, and a rougher term is **anta**. **Kimi** is a slightly intimate term for 'you'; a condescending form is **omae** (sometimes used to small children). However, you should remember to avoid using these second-person pronouns (you) as much as possible: you can drop the pronoun or use the name or the title of the person. **Kare** means 'he' or 'him' and **kanojo** means 'she' or 'her', but again, you can use the name or the title of the person as much as possible.

Demonstrative pronouns can be conveniently used for referring to items that both the speaker and the listener can see. For referring to things, use **kore**, **sore**, or **are**. For referring to locations use **koko**, **soko**, or **asoko**. (See 2.15. for related words.)

これ	**kore**	this one
それ	**sore**	that one near you
あれ	**are**	that one over there
どれ	**dore**	which one
ここ	**koko**	this place, here
そこ	**soko**	that place (near you), there
あそこ	**asoko**	over there
どこ	**doko**	where

「先生，これは先生の傘ですか。」
"Sensei, kore wa sensei no kasa desu ka."
"Professor, is this your umbrella?"

「いいえ，それはマイクさんの傘です。」
"Īe, sore wa Maiku-san no kasa desu."
"No, it's Mike's."

2.2. Prenouns

The words **kono**, **sono**, and **ano** are prenouns, or more commonly called demonstrative adjectives. These words precede a noun and modify its meaning, much as a noun is modified by a phrase consisting of a noun followed by the particle **no**: **kono gakkō** 'this school', **watashi no gakkō** 'my school.'

この	**kono**	this
その	**sono**	that
あの	**ano**	that over there
どの	**dono**	which

2.3. Place words (relative location)

Words such as **ue** 'topside' and **naka** 'inside' are used along with reference nouns as in **tēburu no ue** 'on the top of the table.' They are often used for situations we would express in English with prepositions like *in*, *on*, *under*, *behind*, *above*, and *between*.

前	**mae**	in front
後ろ	**ushiro**	behind
右	**migi**	right
左	**hidari**	left
上	**ue**	up
下	**shita**	below
そば	**soba**	beside, near
近く	**chikaku**	near(by)
中	**naka**	inside
外	**soto**	outside
隣	**tonari**	next door, next position
間	**aida**	between (two places)

Here are some example sentences.

駅は銀行の後ろです。
Eki wa ginkō no ushiro desu.
The train station is behind the bank.

充電器はテーブルの下にあります。
Jūdenki wa tēburu no shita ni arimasu.
The charger is under the table.

2.4. Adjectival nouns

The word **suki** 'likable' is a special kind of noun called an adjectival noun (or copular noun, nominal adjective). It acts as an adjective describing a noun, but it patterns like a noun, being placed before some form of the copula **da/desu** 'is (equals).' Here are a few examples:

好き(だ)	**suki (da)**	(is) likable, liked
嫌い(だ)	**kirai (da)**	(is) dislikable, disliked
きれい(だ)	**kirei (da)**	(is) neat, pretty, clean
シック(だ)	**shikku(da)**	(is) chic, stylish
派手(だ)	**hade (da)**	(is) showy
静か(だ)	**shizuka (da)**	(is) quiet
まじめ(だ)	**majime (da)**	(is) serious, studious
簡単(だ)	**kantan (da)**	(is) easy
駄目(だ)	**dame (da)**	(is) not good

Notice that the literal translation of **suki desu** and **kirai desu** is '(something) is liked' and '(something) is disliked,' but we freely translate them '(somebody) likes (something)' and '(somebody) dislikes (something).'

2.5. Untranslated English words

In English we seldom say just 'book.' We say 'a book,' 'the book,' 'some books,' or 'the books.' In Japanese, the situation is just the other way around. Since the Japanese have another way of implying that they've been talking about the noun, by making it the topic with the particle **wa**, as in **hon wa** 'the book, the books,' they don't need a word to translate 'the.' And they usually leave it up to the situation to make it clear whether there are several things in question or just one, unless they want to focus your attention on the number itself, in which case the number word indicates just how many you are talking about. The Japanese, like everyone else, do not always bother to express things they think you already know. This doesn't mean they lack ways to say things we do; it just means they leave implied some of the things we are used to saying explicitly. Americans tend to use **watashi** and **anata** too much. Remember to omit pronouns when the reference is clear.

2.6. Particles

In English, we usually show the relations between words in the way we string them together. The sentences 'Jon loves May' and 'May loves Jon' both contain the same three words, but the order in which we put the words determines the meaning. In Japanese, relations between words are often shown by little words called particles. This lesson will introduce you to several of these particles: **wa**, **ga**, **ka**, **no**, and **ni**.

2.7. は *wa*

The particle **wa** sets off the TOPIC you are going to talk about. If you say **Watashi wa gakusei desu** 'I am a student,' the particle shows you are talking about **watashi** 'I'—what you have to say about the topic then follows. A pidgin-English way of translating this particle **wa** is 'as for': **Shinbun wa koko ni arimasu** 'As for the newspaper, it's here.' But it is better not to look for a direct translation for some of these particles—remember they just indicate the relationship between the preceding words and those that follow.

2.8. が *ga*

The particle **ga** shows the subject. In **Eiga ga suki desu** 'I like movies,' the particle **ga** shows that **eiga** 'movies' is the subject of **suki desu** 'are liked.' The difference between the particles **wa** and **ga** is one of emphasis. In English we make a difference in emphasis by using a louder voice somewhere in the sentence. We say 'I like MOVIES' or 'I LIKE movies,' depending on which part of the sentence we want to bring out. In Japanese, the particle **ga** focuses our attention on the words preceding it, but the particle **wa** releases our attention to focus on some other part of the sentence. So, **eiga ga suki desu** means 'I like MOVIES,' but **eiga wa suki desu** means 'I LIKE movies.' When there is a question word in the sentence (like **dare** 'who,' **dore** 'which one,' **dono** 'which,' and **doko** 'where'), the attention usually focuses on this part of the sentence, so the particle **wa** is not used: **Dono tatemono ga eki desu ka** 'Which building is the train station?' Since our attention is focused on 'WHICH building,' the answer is **Ano tatemono ga eki desu** 'THAT building is the train station.' If the question is **Ano tatemono wa nan desu ka** 'What is that building?,' our attention is released from **ano tatemono** 'that building' by the particle **wa** and concentrates on 'WHAT,' so the answer is **Ano tatemono wa eki desu** 'That building is a TRAIN STATION,' or just **Eki desu** 'It's a train station.' Some sentences have both a topic—or several successive topics—and a subject:

> あなたは日本のアニメが好きですか。
> **Anata wa Nihon no anime ga suki desu ka.**
> Do you like Japanese anime?

> あなたは日本のアニメは好きですか。
> **Anata wa Nihon no anime wa suki desu ka.**
> Do you LIKE Japanese anime?

Because the difference in meaning between **wa** and **ga** is largely one of emphasis, you can often take a sentence and change the emphasis just by substituting **wa** for **ga**. The particle **wa** can be thought of us an "attention-shifter": the words preceding it set the stage for the sentence, and serve as scenery and background for what we are going to say. This can lead to ambiguity. The sentence **Tarō wa Hanako ga suki desu** (literally, 'Taro as topic, Hanako as emphatic subject, someone is liked') can mean either 'Taro likes Hanako' (It's HANAKO that Taro likes') or 'Hanako likes Taro' (It's HANAKO that likes Taro). The situation usually makes it clear which meaning is called for. If you have both **wa** and **ga** in a sentence, the phrase with **wa** usually comes first: the stage is set before the comment is made.

Sometimes two topics are put in contrast with each other: **Kore wa eigakan desu ga, sore wa ginkō desu** 'This is a movie-theater, but that is a bank.' (The particle **ga** meaning 'but' is not the same particle as the one indicating the subject.) In this case, the emphasis is on the way in which the two topics contrast—in being a theater on the one hand, and a bank on the other.

2.9. か *ka*

The particle **ka** is placed at the end of a sentence to show that it is a question. It is as if we were pronouncing the question mark:

あの家です。
Ano ie desu.
It's that house.

あの家ですか。
Ano ie desu ka.
Is it that house?

A common way of asking a question in Japanese is to give two or more alternatives, one of which the answerer selects.

あの人は日本人ですか。中国人ですか。
Ano hito wa Nihonjin desu ka. Chūgokujin desu ka.
Is he Japanese or Chinese? (Literally, 'Is he Japanese. Is he Chinese?')

Alternative questions are further discussed in Note 7. 8.

2.10. の **no**

The particle **no** shows that the preceding noun "modifies" or "limits" the noun following. The particle **no** is often equivalent to the English translation *of*, but sometimes it is equivalent to *in* or other words.

私の本 **watashi no hon**	my book
日本語の本 **Nihongo no hon**	Japanese (language) books
私の友達 **watashi no tomodachi**	my friend
部屋の中 **heya no naka**	the inside of the room
家の外 **ie no soto**	the place outside the house
ここの学校 **koko no gakkō**	the schools of this place, the schools here
東京の銀行 **Tōkyō no ginkō**	banks in Tokyo
アメリカの新聞 **Amerika no shinbun**	American newspapers
日本の会社員 **Nihon no kaishain**	company employees in Japan

The expression NOUN + **no** is sometimes followed directly by the copula **desu** 'is (equals),' as in:

「これはだれのですか。」 「石田さんのです。」
"Kore wa dare no desu ka." **"Ishida-san no desu."**
"Whose is this?" "It's Ms. Ishida's."

2.11. に *ni*

The particle **ni** indicates a "general sort of location" in space or time, which can be made more specific by putting a place or time word in front of it. The phrase **heya ni** means 'at the room, in the room.' To say explicitly 'in(side) the room,' you insert the specific place word **naka** 'inside': **heya no naka ni**. Notice the difference between **gakkō ni imasu** 'he's at school, he's in school' and **gakkō no naka ni imasu** 'he's in(side) the school (building).'

A NOUN PHRASE + **ni** is not used to modify another noun, and it does not occur before **desu** 'is (equals)'; it is usually followed by **arimasu** '(a thing) is (exists)' or **imasu** '(a person) is (exists in a place).' To say 'the people in the room,' you connect **heya no naka** 'the inside of the room' with **hito** 'the people' by means of the particle **no: heya no naka no hito**.

The particle **ni** is also used figuratively:

友達に言いました。
Tomodachi ni iimashita.
He said TO his friend.

It sometimes shows "purpose":

散歩に行きました。
Sanpo ni ikimashita.
He went FOR a walk.

It is also used to indicate a "change of state" and after an adjectival noun, to show "manner":

先生になりました。
Sensei ni narimashita.
He became a teacher, he turned into a teacher.

ネットカフェにしました。
Netto kafe ni shimashita.
They made it into an Internet café.

きれいに書きました。
Kirei ni kakimashita.
He wrote neatly.

Occasionally, a particle like **ni** will be used in an expression that calls for an unexpected equivalent in the English translation:

だれに日本語を習いましたか。
Dare ni Nihongo o naraimashita ka.
Who did you learn Japanese FROM?

2.12. Words meaning 'is'
In this lesson we find three different Japanese words translated as 'is' in English: **desu**, **arimasu**, and **imasu**. The word **desu** is the COPULA and it means 'equals.' Whenever an English sentence containing the word *is* makes sense if you substitute *equals* for *is*, the Japanese equivalent is **desu**.

あれは富士山です。
Are wa Fujisan desu.
That is Mt. Fuji. (That one = Mt. Fuji)

あの人は私の友達です。
Ano hito wa watashi no tomodachi desu.
That person is my friend. (That person = my friend)

それは私のです。
Sore wa watashi no desu.
That's mine. (That = mine)

Preceding the word **desu**, there is always a noun or a phrase consisting of NOUN + **no** or some other particle, but never **wa**, **ga**, **o** (discussed in 3. 6.), **de** (discussed in 3. 5), or **ni**.

When an English sentence containing the word *is* makes sense if you reword it as '(something) exists,' the Japanese equivalent is **arimasu**:

ATMがあります。
ATM ga arimasu.
There is an ATM.

When the English sentence can be reworded '(something) exists in a place' or '(something) is located,' the usual Japanese equivalent is also **arimasu**:

リモコンはそこにあります。
Rimokon wa soko ni arimasu.
The remote control is there.

But often, especially if the topic is itself a place, for example, a city, a building, a street, a location, either **desu** or **(ni) arimasu** may be used:

映画館はあそこです。/映画館はあそこにあります。
Eigakan wa asoko desu./Eigakan wa asoko ni arimasu.
The movie theater is over there.

お台場はどこですか。/お台場はどこにありますか。
Odaiba wa doko desu ka./Odaiba wa doko ni arimasu ka.
Where is Odaiba?

When an English sentence containing the word *is* makes sense reworded as '(somebody) exists (in a place)' or '(somebody) stays (in a place)' or '(somebody) is located,' the Japanese equivalent is **imasu** 'stays':

「あの人はどこにいますか。」   「外にいます。」
"Ano hito wa doko ni imasu ka."   **"Soto ni imasu."**
"Where is he?"   "He's outside."

There are other uses of these two verbs, **arimasu** and **imasu**, which we will examine later. It may help to think of tag meanings for these words as follows: **desu** 'equals,' **arimasu** 'exists,' **imasu** 'stays.' Note that 'exists' is the usual way of saying '(somebody) has (something)':

プリンターはありますか。

Purintā wa arimasu ka.

Do you have a printer?   (Does a printer exist?)

2.13. Inflected words

Words like **desu**, **arimasu**, and **imasu** are called inflected words, because their shapes can be changed (inflected) to make other words of similar but slightly different meaning. In English, we change the shapes of inflected words to show a difference of subject—'I am, you are, he is; I exist, he exists,' as well as a difference of time—'I am, I was; you are, you were.' In Japanese, the shape of an inflected word stays the same regardless of the subject: **Gakusei desu** can mean 'I am a student, you are a student, he is a student, we are students, you are students, they are students' depending on the situation. If you want to make it perfectly clear, you can put in a topic: **Watashi wa gakusei desu, anata wa gakusei desu, ano hito wa gakusei desu.**

2.14. Dropping subject nouns

In English, every normal sentence has a subject and a predicate. If there is no logical subject, we stick one in anyway: 'IT rains' (what rains?), 'IT is John' (what is John—it?). Sentences that do not contain a subject are limited to commands—'Keep off the grass!'—in which a sort of 'you' is understood, or to a special style reserved for postcards and telegrams, for example, 'Arrived safely. Wish you were here.' In Japanese, the normal sentence type contains a predicate, **Arimasu** 'There is (some),' **Kamera desu** '(It) is a camera'—and to this we may add a subject or a topic, but it isn't necessary unless we wish to be explicit. Since the topic of a sentence is usually obvious in real conversation, the Japanese often doesn't mention it at all, or occasionally throws it in as an afterthought.

A predicate may consist of a simple verb, **arimasu**, **imasu**, or of a noun plus the copula, **Kyōshi desu** 'It's (I'm) a teacher,' but it cannot consist of the copula alone. The Japanese can talk about the equation A = B, that is **A wa B desu** as in **Kore wa kamera desu** 'This is a camera,' by dropping the topic (A) and just saying = B, that is **B desu** as in **Kamera desu** '(It) is a camera.' But they never say just = (**desu**) or give a one-sided equation like A = (B). Something has to fill the blank before the word **desu**, in all cases.

2.15. Words of relative reference and question words

Notice the related shapes and meaning of the following classes of words:

わたし	あなた	あの人	だれ
watashi	**anata**	**ano hito**	**dare**
I	you	he, she	who

これ	それ	あれ	どれ
kore	**sore**	**are**	**dore**
this one	that one near you	that one over there	which one

この	その	あの	どの
kono	**sono**	**ano**	**dono**
(of) this	(of) that	(of) that there	which

こんな	そんな	あんな	どんな
konna	**sonna**	**anna**	**donna**
like this	like that one near you	like that one over there	what sort of

ここ	そこ	あそこ	どこ
koko	**soko**	**asoko**	**doko**
here	there	over there	where

こう	そう	ああ	どう
kō	**sō**	**ā**	**dō**
in this way	in that way	in that way there	in what way, how

The words in the column with **watashi** are used to refer to something near the speaker. The words in the column with **anata** refer to something near the person you are talking with, or to something you have just mentioned. The words in the column with **ano hito** refer to something at a distance from both you and the person you are talking with. For some situations, either those in the column with **anata** or those in the column with **ano hito** may be heard, since the reference is a relative matter. Be sure to keep **dare** 'who' and **dore** 'which' distinct. Instead of **konna**, **sonna**, **anna**, and **donna**, we often hear the more colloquial **kō iu**, **sō iu**, **ā iu**, and **dō iu**. (Note that **iu** 'says' is often pronounced as if spelled **yū** or 'you.')

その中にカメラがあります。
Sono naka ni kamera ga arimasu.
Inside it, there is a camera.

どんな本ですか。
Donna hon desu ka.
What sort of book is it?

どうですか。
Dō desu ka.
How is it?

あの人はだれですか。
Ano hito wa dare desu ka.
Who is that person?

2.16. Words for 'restaurant'

There are a number of different words for various types of restaurant in Japan. You will often hear the word **resutoran**, from the English word of French origin. Other words include old-fashioned **shokudō** 'dining room/hall,' **kissa** or **kissaten** 'a kind of French-type café,' and specialized restaurants or shops that end in **ya** 'store,' as in **sushiya** 'a sushi restaurant,' **sobaya** 'a noodle restaurant,' **yakinikuya** 'a table-top BBQ restaurant,' **yakitoriya** 'a grilled chicken restaurant,' and **izakaya**, a friendly bar that serves home-style dishes and alcoholic beverages. **Ryōtei**

is a rather high-class traditional Japanese restaurant. In addition, there are many American-style fast-food restaurants that serve hamburgers, donuts, and fried chicken.

2.17. Words for 'toilet'

As in English, there are various oblique ways of talking about toilets in Japanese. Probably the most current polite terms are **otearai** 'lavatory' and **(o)toire** 'toilet,' but women may say **keshōshitsu** 'powder room.' So when asking where it is, you may say **O-tearai wa doko ni arimasu ka**.

2.18. 何 *nani/nan* 'what'

The word meaning 'what' is usually expressed by **nan** before a word beginning with **t**, **d**, or **n**, and **nani** before other words. However, **nan-** 'how many' never has the shape **nani-**.

> 何ですか。
> **Nan desu ka.**
> What is it?

> 何と言いましたか。
> **Nan to iimashita ka.**
> What did (he) say?

> 何の本ですか。
> **Nan no hon desu ka.**
> What book is it?

> 何がありますか。
> **Nani ga arimasu ka.**
> What is there? What do you have?

何をしていますか。
Nani o shite imasu ka.
What are you doing?

CDが何枚ありますか。
Shī dī ga nan-mai arimasu ka.
How many CDs do you have?

本が何冊ありますか。
Hon ga nan-satsu arimasu ka.
How many books are there?

 Conversation

[cue 02-3]

Emi (E) is a member of a rock band formed in her college. She shows a photo of the members to Masahiro (M).

M: これは恵美さんですか。
Kore wa Emi-san desu ka.
Is this you, Emi?

E: ええ。**Ē.** Yes.

M: ぜんぜん違いますね。
Zenzen chigaimasu ne.
Look so different.

E: そうですか。**Sō desu ka.** Really?

M: この人はだれですか。**Kono hito wa dare desu ka.**
Who is this person?

E: 洋介です。ギタリストです。**Yōsuke desu. Gitarisuto desu.**
Yosuke. He is a guitarist.

M: かっこいいですね。同じ大学の学生ですか。
Kakko ii desu ne. Onaji daigaku no gakusei desu ka.
He is cool, isn't he? Is he a student in the same college?

E: ええ。**Ē.** Yes.

M: じゃあ、この人は？**Jā, kono hito wa?** Okay, then. Who is this person?

E: ベーシストの拓也です。**Bēshisuto no Takuya desu.**
He is Takuya, the bassist.

M: ドラマーはだれ？**Doramā wa dare?** Who is the drummer?

E: 私。**Watashi.** Me.

Exercises

*Do it aloud; don't write the answers down.

I. For each situation illustrated below, choose which word the speaker would use, *kore*, *sore*, *are*, or *dore*.

| 1 | 2 | 3 | 4 |

II. Fill in the blanks with the appropriate particles.

1. あの建物＿＿何ですか。**Ano tatemono ＿＿ nan desu ka.** What is that building?

2. 私＿＿学生です。**Watashi ＿＿ gakusei desu.** I'm a student.

3. 私＿＿本です。**Watashi ＿＿ hon desu.** It's my book.

4. 新聞はテーブル＿＿下にあります。**Shinbun wa tēburu ＿＿ shita ni arimasu.** The newspaper is under the table.

5. どれ＿＿あなたのですか。**Dore ＿＿ anata no desu ka.** Which one is yours?

III. Choose the appropriate item in the parentheses.

1. (あれ・あの) は富士山です。**(Are, ano) wa Fujisan desu.** That's Mt. Fuji.

2. (これ・この) カメラはだれのですか。**(Kore, kono) kamera wa dare no desu ka.** Whose camera is this?

3. 「それは何ですか。」「(それ・これ) はカメラです。」 **"Sore wa nan desu ka." "(Sore, kore) wa kamera desu."** "What is that?" "It's a camera."

4. 郵便局は (あれ・あそこ) にあります。 **Yūbinkyoku wa (are, asoko) ni arimasu.** The post office is over there.

5. 銀行は (あれ・あの) です。 **Ginkō wa (are, ano) desu.** The bank is that one over there.

IV. Fill in the blanks with one of the words です *desu*, あります *arimasu*, or います *imasu*.

1. あなたは学生＿＿＿＿か。**Anata wa gakusei ＿＿＿＿ ka.** Are you a student?

2. 銀行はどこ＿＿＿＿か。**Ginkō wa doko ＿＿＿＿ ka.** Where is the bank?

3. ホテルはどこに＿＿＿＿か。**Hoteru wa doko ni ＿＿＿＿ ka.** Where is the hotel?

4. 犬はどこに＿＿＿＿か。**Inu wa doko ni ＿＿＿＿ ka.** Where is the dog?

5. 机の下には雑誌が＿＿＿＿。**Tsukue no shita ni wa zasshi ga ＿＿＿＿.** There is a magazine under the desk.

Answers:
I   1. あれ are 2. それ sore 3. これ kore 4. どれ dore
II 1. は wa 2. は wa 3. の no 4. の no 5. が ga
III 1. あれ are 2. この kono 3. これ kore 4. あそこ asoko 5. あれ are
IV 1. です desu 2. です desu 3. あります arimasu 4. います imasu 5. あります arimasu

LESSON 3

Actions! Actions! Actions!

これして！それして！あれやって！
Kore Shite! Sore Shite! Are Yatte!

In this lesson you will learn how to express your daily activities. It introduces basic forms of verbs as well as particles that are needed to complete the meaning of the verb.

🎧 Basic Sentences

[cue 03-1]

1.	昨日大阪から友達が来ました。 **Kinō Ōsaka <u>kara</u> tomodachi <u>ga</u> kimashita**.	My friend came from Osaka yesterday.
2.	土曜日に友達とビデオゲームをしました。 **Doyōbi ni tomodachi <u>to</u> bideo gēmu <u>o</u> shimashita.**	I played a video game with my friend on Saturday.
3.	今メールを書いています。 **Ima mēru o <u>kaite imasu</u>.**	I'm writing an email now.
4.	あしたは家族でレストランに行きます。 **Ashita wa kazoku <u>de</u> resutoran <u>ni</u> ikimasu.**	We will go to a restaurant as a family.
5.	月曜日から金曜日まで働きます。 **Getsuyōbi <u>kara</u> Kinyōbi <u>made</u> <u>hatarakimasu</u>.**	I work from Monday to Friday.

6.	うちからオフィスまで歩きます。 **Uchi <u>kara</u> ofisu <u>made</u> arukimasu.**	I walk from home to my office.
7.	公園に行きます。公園で歩きます。 **Kōen <u>ni</u> ikimasu. Kōen <u>de</u> arukimasu.**	I go to the park. I walk in the park.
8.	いっしょに日本語を勉強しましょう。 **<u>Issho ni</u> Nihongo o benkyō shi<u>mashō</u>.**	Let's study Japanese together.
9.	ボストンに住んでいます。ボストンで働いています。 **Bosuton <u>ni</u> sunde imasu. Bosuton <u>de</u> hataraite imasu.**	I live in Boston. I work in Boston.
10.	週末は掃除を<u>して</u>，洗濯を<u>して</u>，散歩をします。 **Shūmatsu wa sōji o <u>shite</u>, sentaku o <u>shite</u>, sanpo o shimasu.**	On weekends I do cleaning, laundry, and take a walk.
11.	先週は仕事を<u>しませんでした</u>。 **Senshū wa shigoto o <u>shimasen deshita</u>.**	I did not work last week.
12.	朝ごはんを食べてから新聞を読みます。 **Asa-gohan o tabe<u>te kara</u> shinbun o yomimasu.**	I eat breakfast and then read the newspaper.
13.	駅には歩いて行きます。スーパーには自転車で行きます。 **Eki ni wa arui<u>te</u> ikimasu. Sūpā ni wa jitensha <u>de</u> ikimasu.**	I walk to the train station. I ride a bike to the supermarket.
14.	高校で教師をしています。 **Kōkō de kyōshi <u>o shite</u> imasu.**	I teach at a high school.
15.	日本の高校はアメリカの高校と違うでしょう。 **Nihon no kōkō wa Amerika no kōkō <u>to</u> chigau deshō.**	Japanese high schools are different from American high schools.

 **Basic Vocabulary**

[cue 03-2]

TRAVELING

観光 **kankō**	sightseeing
空港 **kūkō**	airport
駅 **eki**	train station
交番 **kōban**	koban

TRANSPORTATION

車 **kuruma**	car
タクシー **takushī**	taxi
バス **basu**	bus
地下鉄 **chikatetsu**	subway
電車 **densha**	train
自転車 **jitensha**	bicycle
オートバイ **ōtobai**	motorcycle
スクーター **sukūtā**	scooter
飛行機 **hikōki**	airplane

交番 **Kōban**

A **kōban** is a neighborhood police station, usually found in a small building or in a portion of a large building, where a small contingent of police officers take turns responding to emergencies, giving directions to passersby, and patrolling the neighborhood by bicycle. In large cities, you find **kōban** every few blocks or so. The existence of **kōban** has greatly contributed to public safety in Japan.

ACTIONS

行く・行きます **iku/ikimasu**	goes
帰る・帰ります **kaeru/kaerimasu**	returns
来る・来ます **kuru/kimasu**	comes
歩く・歩きます **aruku/arukimasu**	walks
乗る・乗ります **noru/norimasu**	gets on...
降りる・降ります **oriru/orimasu**	gets off...
食べる・食べます **taberu/tabemasu**	eats
見る・見ます **miru/mimasu**	watches
読む・読みます **yomu/yomimasu**	reads
書く・書きます **kaku/kakimasu**	writes
働く・働きます **hataraku/hatarakimasu**	works

勤める・勤めます **tsutomeru/tsutomemasu**   works, gets (is) employed
する/します **suru/shimasu**   does

Fun activities

コスプレ **kosupure**   cosplay
ビデオゲーム **bideo gēmu**   video game
コンピューターゲーム **konpyūtā gēmu**   computer game
ボーリング **bōringu**   bowling
ビリヤード (or 玉突き) **biriyādo** (or **tamatsuki**)   billiards
ダーツ **dātsu**   darts
カラオケ **karaoke**   karaoke

Days of the week

月曜日 **Getsuyōbi**   Monday
火曜日 **Kayōbi**   Tuesday
水曜日 **Suiyōbi**   Wednesday
木曜日 **Mokuyōbi**   Thursday
金曜日 **Kinyōbi**   Friday
土曜日 **Doyōbi**   Saturday
日曜日 **Nichiyōbi**   Sunday

Spouses

家内 **kanai**   one's own wife
妻 **tsuma**   one's own wife
奥さん **okusan**   someone else's wife
主人 **shujin**   one's own husband
ご主人 **goshujin**   someone else's husband

Work

仕事 **shigoto**   job
会社 **kaisha**   company
教師 **kyōshi**   teacher (plain form, cf. 先生 **sensei**)

医者 **isha**   doctor

Structure Notes

3.1. Time words (relative time expressions)

In the preceding lesson we found that place words like **ue** 'topside' and **naka** 'inside' are a kind of noun in Japanese. Time words are a similar sort of noun. Such words are **kyō** 'today', **kyonen** 'last year', and **mainichi** 'every day'. The general question word used to ask the time is **itsu** 'when'. Here are some time words you will find useful:

昨日	今日	あした/明日	毎日
kinō	**kyō**	**ashita/asu**	**mainichi**
yesterday	today	tomorrow	every day
先週	今週	来週	毎週
senshū	**konshū**	**raishū**	**maishū**
last week	this week	next week	every week
先月	今月	来月	毎月
sengetsu	**kongetsu**	**raigetsu**	**maitsuki**
last month	this month	next month	every month
去年	今年	来年	毎年
kyonen	**kotoshi**	**rainen**	**maitoshi/mainen**
last year	this year	next year	every year
先学期	今学期	来学期	毎学期
sengakki	**kongakki**	**raigakki**	**maigakki**
last academic term	this academic term	next academic term	every academic term

Here are some example sentences with relative time expressions:

いつ大阪に行きますか。
Itsu Ōsaka ni ikimasu ka.
When are you going to Osaka?

来年行きます。
Rainen ikimasu.
I'll go there next year.

私は昨日ステーキを食べました。
Watashi wa kinō sutēki o tabemashita.
I ate steak yesterday.

3.2. Nouns with and without particles

Most nouns usually occur followed by a particle of some sort or by the copula—**kono hon wa...**, **gohan o...**, **byōki desu**. Some nouns occur either with or without a particle, with only a slight difference in meaning. The time words listed in note 3.1 can be followed by the particle **wa** or used alone without the particle:

毎日は仕事をしません。
Mainichi wa shigoto o shimasen.
I don't work EVERY day.

毎日仕事をします。
Mainichi shigoto o shimasu.
Every day I work.

When you use the particle **wa**, you are making the time word the topic of your sentence. Often you are CONTRASTING what happens at THAT time (**... wa**) with what happens at other times. When a noun is used without a particle, it usually modifies either the whole sentence or the verb phrase at the end; this we can call the ADVERBIAL USE of a noun.

3.3. Particles から *kara,* まで *made,* and へ *e*

After place words, the particle **kara** means 'from,' the particle **e** means 'to,' and the particle **made** means 'to, as far as, up to.' If you want to say 'from Kobe to Osaka' you can say either **Kobe kara Osaka made** or **Kobe kara Osaka e**, but there is a slight difference of meaning. When you use the particle **e**, you are primarily interested in the two endpoints; when you use **made**, you are also interested in the space, time, or means of travel between the two points. This difference of meaning is so subtle, however, that you can just remember that either **made** or **e** means 'to' when reference is to a place.

Many speakers in Eastern Japan often replace the particle **e** with the particle **ni**. So you will also hear **Kobe kara Ōsaka ni ikimashita** 'I went from Kobe to Osaka.' You can say either **Uchi e kaette benkyō shimashita** or **Uchi ni kaette benkyō shimashita** 'I went (back) home and studied.'

After **kore** 'this,' **sore** 'that,' or a time word, the particle **kara** has the meaning 'after, since,' for example, **sore kara** 'after that' and **kore kara** 'after this, from now on.' Compare them with **koko kara** 'from here.' In a similar way, the particle **made** means 'until': **sore made** 'until that (happens)' and **kore made** "until now (this)." Compare them with **koko made** 'up to here, as far as this place.'

(**Kara** with verbal expressions is discussed in notes 3.10 and 4.12. **Made** with verbal expressions is discussed in note 5.18.)

ご飯を食べて，それから映画を見ました。
Gohan o tabete, sore kara eiga o mimashita.
I had dinner and after that watched a movie.

これから毎日勉強します。
Kore kara mainichi benkyō shimasu.
From now on I'm going to study every day.

これまでマンガを読みませんでした。
Kore made manga o yomimasen deshita.
Until now I haven't been reading comic books.

昨日から病気なんです。でも，あしたからまた働きます。
Kinō kara byōki na n desu. Demo, ashita kara mata hatarakimasu.
He's been sick since yesterday. But he'll work from tomorrow (on) again.

明日の晩までその仕事をしています。
Asu no ban made sono shigoto o shite imasu.
We'll be doing that job until tomorrow night.

3.4. Particle ね *ne*

The particle **ne** is frequently tacked on at the end of a sentence to soften its tone. It implies that the speaker wants the hearer to agree with him, or that he wants what he is saying to agree with what the hearer might think. It is often translated by a rhetorical question (one to which an answer really isn't expected) such as '...isn't it,' '...doesn't he,' '... wasn't it,' or by something like '... you know,' '... you see.'

「中村さんは銀行員ですね。」
"Nakamura-san wa ginkōin desu ne."
"Mr. Nakamura is a bank clerk, isn't he?"

「はい，そうです。」
"Hai, sō desu."
"Yes, he is."

「また飛行機がおちたんだってね。」
"Mata hikōki ga ochita n datte ne."
"I heard that an airplane crashed again."

「ええ，昨日の新聞にありましたね。」
"Ē, kinō no shinbun ni arimashita ne."
"Yep, it was in yesterday's newspaper, wasn't it?"

「じゃあ，ホテルを予約しておきますね。」
"Jā, hoteru o yoyaku shite okimasu ne."
"Okay, I'll reserve a hotel room, okay?"

「ああ，どうも。」
"Ā, dōmo."
"Oh, thank you."

「まあ，きれいですね。」
"Mā, kirei desu ne."
"My, isn't it pretty?"

「そうですね。」
"Sō desu ne."
"Yes, indeed."

「また遊びに来てくださいね。」
"Mata asobi ni kite kudasai ne."
"Please come to visit us again, okay?"

「ああ，ありがとうございます。」
"Ā, arigatō gozaimasu."
"Oh, thank you."

「何が要りますか。」
"Nani ga irimasu ka."
"What do I need?"

「そうですね。ちょっと調べます。」
"Sō desu ne. Chotto shirabemasu."
"Well, let me see. I'll check it out."

「何か心配していますね。」
"Nanika shinpai shite imasu ne."
"You must be worrying about something."

「え, どうしてわかるんですか。」
"E, dōshite wakaru n desu ka."
"What? What makes you think that?"

We all know people who can't say three words without inserting something like 'I mean,' 'you know,' or 'you see': 'Well, you see, it was Friday, you see, and, you know, that movie, you see, it was new, I mean, I hadn't seen it, so....' In a similar fashion, some Japanese overwork the particle **ne**, inserting it after every few words. This seems to be particularly true of the speech of women, as in **Kyō ne**, **sūpā ni ne**, **ittara ne**, **Yamada-san ga ne**, **Tanaka-san to hanashiteta no yo** 'When I went to the supermarket today, (I saw) Ms. Yamada talking with Ms. Tanaka.' For the foreign student, it is advisable to avoid using the particle except at the end of a sentence, as above.

3.5. Particle で *de*
The particle **de** has two quite different meanings. One is 'by means of':

車で来ましたか。
Kuruma de kimashita ka.
Did you come by car?

筆で名前を書きました。
Fude de namae o kakimashita.
I wrote my name with a brush.

Another meaning is '(an action happens) at (a place)':

学校で勉強します。
Gakkō de benkyō shimasu.
I study at school.

You have already learned that the particle **ni** means 'at' in the sense of a location in space:

学校にいます。
Gakkō ni imasu.
I'm at school.

The difference in usage between **ni** and **de** depends on whether you use a verb that means something about existence—'exists, lives, stays'—or something about activity—'talks, works, studies, eats, sleeps.' There are very few verbs of the inactive sort; you have had **imasu** 'stays, (a person) exists (in a place),' **arimasu** 'exists,' and **sunde imasu** 'is living, residing.' With other verbs you will usually hear **de** for 'at,' but occasionally a Japanese will use **ni** if his attention is focused on the person's existence rather than his action. In general, you will be doing best to remember that 'at' corresponds to **ni** with the verbs **imasu**, **arimasu**, and **sunde imasu** (also **tomarimasu** 'stops or stays at'); with other verbs—alone or in a phrase with **imasu**, like **hataraite imasu**—'at' corresponds to **de**.

「夏休みには何をしますか。」
"Natsuyasumi ni wa nani o shi-masu ka."
"What will you do during summer vacation?"

「レストランでバイトをします。」
"Resutoran de baito o shimasu."
"I'll work part-time at a restaurant."

叔母が先週からうちに泊まっています。うちで母の手伝いをしてくれています。
Oba ga senshū kara uchi ni tomatte imasu. Uchi de haha no tetsudai o shite kurete imasu.
My aunt has been staying at our house since last week. She is helping my mother.

まだ東京に住んでいるんですか。大阪で働きませんか。
Mada Tōkyō ni sunde iru n desu ka. Ōsaka de hatarakimasen ka.
Are you still living in Tokyo? Wouldn't you want to work in Osaka?

Note that the nouns that express events such as meetings, conferences, and concerts are marked by the particle **de** even though the verb is **arimasu**.

会議は品川であります。ホテルは品川にあります。
Kaigi wa Shinagawa de arimasu. Hoteru wa Shinagawa ni arimasu.
The meeting will take place in Shinagawa. The hotel is located in Shinagawa.

3.6. Particle を *o*

The particle **o** (written **wo** in some spelling systems, but pronounced **o**) shows that the preceding word is the direct object of the verb.

何を見ていますか。
Nani o mite imasu ka.
What are you looking at?

本を読みました。
Hon o yomimashita.
I read a book.

The meaning of **o** is the OPPOSITE of that of **ga**, which is the particle indicating the subject of the verb, of the copula, or of the adjective (as we shall see later). Notice the following sentences:

ここでだれが何をしましたか。
Koko de dare ga nani o shimasu ka.
Who does what here?

だれがだれを見ましたか。
Dare ga dare o mimashita ka.
Who saw who?

誠が幸平を見ました。
Makoto ga Kōhei o mimashita.
Makoto saw Kōhei.

幸平が誠を見ました。
Kōhei ga Makoto o mimashita.
Kōhei saw Makoto.

Either **ga** or **o** can be replaced by the topic particle **wa**. That is, you can take either the subject or the object and make it the topic you are going to talk about.

誠は幸平を見ました。
Makoto wa Kōhei o mimashita.
Makoto saw Kōhei.

誠は幸平が見ました。
Makoto wa Kōhei ga mimashita.
It was Kōhei who saw Makoto.

幸平は誠を見ました。
Kōhei wa Makoto o mimashita.
Kōhei saw Makoto.

幸平は誠が見ました。
Kōhei wa Makoto ga mimashita.
It was Makoto who saw Kōhei.

Notice the shift of emphasis when one of the phrases is made the topic and released from the focus of attention. The most common focus of attention in both English and Japanese is on something other than the subject. We say 'Makoto saw Kōhei.' with a slightly heavier stress on 'Kōhei.' That is the most COLORLESS way we can say it. In a similar way, the Japanese will say **Makoto wa Kōhei o mimashita**. But in English we always have to have a subject. A Japanese sentence is complete without a subject—**Gohan o tabemashita** 'I've eaten dinner' (heaviest stress on 'dinner'). In this case, it is quite common to shift the emphasis over to just the verb itself, by taking the object and turning it into a topic: 'I've eaten dinner' (heaviest stress on 'eaten'), as in **Gohan wa tabemashita**.

The particle **o** is also used to show the place where a verb of motion takes place:

道を歩きます。
Michi o arukimasu.
(He) walks (in) the street

空を飛びます。
Sora o tobimasu.
(He) flies (in) the sky.

公園を (or で) 散歩します。
Kōen o (or de) sanpo shimasu.
(He) strolls (in) the park.

うちを出ます。
Uchi o demasu.
(He) leaves the house.

Verbs that can take a direct object or a noun marked by the particle **o** are called transitive verbs. Note that not all transitive verbs in English are also transitive verbs in Japanese. The following are examples of transitive verbs in Japanese with a sample direct object in the parentheses.

（コーヒーを）飲む **(kōhī o) nomu**	drinks (coffee)
（本を）読む **(hon o) yomu**	reads (a book)
（手紙を）書く **(tegami o) kaku**	writes (a letter)
（日本語を）話す **(Nihongo o) hanasu**	speaks (Japanese)
（音楽を）聞く **(ongaku o) kiku**	listens (to music)
（晩ご飯を）作る **(bangohan o) tsukuru**	makes (dinner)
（靴を）買う **(kutsu o) kau**	buys (shoes)
（はさみを）使う **(hasami o) tsukau**	uses (scissors)
（皿を）洗う **(sara o) ara(w)u**	washes (dishes)

（ピアノを）習う **(piano o) nara(w)u**　　　learns (how to play the piano)
（数学を）教える **(sūgaku o) oshieru**　　　teaches (mathematics)

3.7. Particle と *to*, meaning 'with' and 'and'

In **ginkō to depāto no aida** '(the place) between the bank and the department store,' the particle **to** means 'and.' This is an exhaustive 'and' that means you have listed everything in a series. There is also an inexhaustive 'and' that means you have listed only some of the things in a series; this is the particle **ya**. In an exhaustive listing of two or more things, each noun is followed by the particle **to** except the last, which is followed by whatever particle is appropriate to link the phrase up with the rest of the sentence.

> 肉と魚と野菜とご飯を食べました。
> **Niku to sakana to yasai to gohan o tabemashita.**
> We ate meat and fish and vegetables and rice (and that's all).

> 肉や野菜を食べました。
> **Niku ya yasai o tabemashita.**
> We ate meat and vegetables (among other things).

In the phrase **watashi to issho ni** 'together with me,' the particle **to** means 'with.' You can say **watashi to kimashita** 'he came with me,' but with verbs of motion it is more usual to add the phrase **issho ni** 'together,' as in **watashi to issho ni kimashita**. Notice that just **issho ni** often corresponds to 'with me' or 'with you' or 'with us.'

> 父と話しました。
> **Chichi to hanashimashita.**
> I spoke with my father.

> 彼女と一緒に旅行しました。
> **Kanojo to isshoni ryokō shimashita.**
> I went on a trip with my girlfriend.

> （私と）一緒に行きませんか。
> **(Watashi to) issho ni ikimasen ka.**
> Why don't you come with me?

Occasionally, the particle **to** is used in expressions that call for an unexpected equivalent in the English translation:

私はあなたと違います。
Watashi wa anata to chigaimasu.
I'm different FROM you.

ここはあそこと違いますね。
Koko wa asoko to chigaimasu ne.
It's different here FROM (what it is) there, isn't it?

3.8. Expressions for accompaniment

Tanaka-san to issho ni ikimasu means 'goes with Mr. Tanaka'; **Makoto o tsurete ikimasu** means 'brings Makoto along.' You use an expression of the latter type, or an expanded form, **Makoto o tsurete issho ni ikimasu**, when the person you are 'bringing along' is younger or socially inferior to you. If the person is your equal or superior, then you say he 'comes along with' you: **Yamada-san wa (watashi to) issho ni ikimasu** 'Ms. Yamada is going along (with me).' The noun **issho** means something like 'a group (as contrasted with a single person),' so **issho ni** means 'in a group; with others'; **issho desu** means 'are together.' **Issho** refers to either people or things; **(to) tomo ni** is a less colloquial synonym.

家族で一緒に公園へ行きました。
Kazoku de issho ni kōen e ikimashita.
I went to the park with my family.

主人と一緒に料理をしました。
Shujin to issho ni ryōri o shimashita.
I cooked with my husband.

今度一緒に映画を見に行きませんか。
Kondo isshoni eiga o mi ni ikimasen ka.
How about going to see a movie together next time?

3.9 Verbs, polite moods

You have heard forms like **ikimasu** 'goes,' **ikimashita** 'went,' and **ikimashō** 'let's go.' These are various moods of the same verb. Each verb, adjective, and the copula as well, can be changed in shape to correspond to different categories we call "moods." (Compare the English forms *go, went, gone, going.*)

In Japanese, each verb, like each adjective and the copula, has two sets of forms: "polite" and "plain." So far we have seen only the polite forms of verbs and the copula. In the next lesson we have some of the plain forms of these, and plain and polite forms of the adjectives. In normal polite conversation, it is customary to end a sentence with one of these polite forms. For a further discussion on the use of polite and plain forms, see the next lesson.

In this lesson, you'll find forms like **shite** 'doing,' **hanashite** 'talking,' **kaette** 'returned and,' **kite (kudasai)** '(please) come,' **aruite (ikimasu)** '(goes) on foot,' **tsurete (kimasu)** 'brings along,' **tabete (kara)** '(after) eating,' **(kuruma ni) notte (ikimau)'** (goes) riding (in a car).' These forms are called gerunds or **te**-forms. The use of gerunds is discussed in 3.10. You need not worry about how they are formed until the next lesson. Just learn them as they occur.

Below is a list of some verbs, and the copula, many of which you have seen by now in this book. Examine the list, but no need to memorize it.

| Meaning | Polite | | | Plain |
	Imperfect	Perfect	Tentative	Gerund
eats	たべます **tabemasu**	たべました **tabemashita**	たべましょう **tabemashō**	たべて **tabete**
sees, looks	みます **mimasu**	みました **mimashita**	みましょう **mimashō**	みて **mite**
stays, exists	います **imasu**	いました **imashita**	いましょう **imashō**	いて **ite**
exists	あります **arimasu**	ありました **arimashita**	ありましょう **arimashō**	あって **atte**
walks	あるきます **arukimasu**	あるきました **arukimashita**	あるきましょう **arukimashō**	あるいて **aruite**
goes	いきます **ikimasu**	いきました **ikimashita**	いきましょう **ikimashō**	いって **itte**
swims	およぎます **oyogimasu**	およぎました **oyogimashita**	およぎましょう **oyogimashō**	およいで **oyoide**
talks	はなします **hanashimasu**	はなしました **hanashimashita**	はなしましょう **hanashimashō**	はなして **hanashite**
returns	かえります **kaerimasu**	かえりました **kaerimashita**	かえりましょう **kaerimashō**	かえって **kaette**
rides, gets on	のります **norimasu**	のりました **norimashita**	のりましょう **norimashō**	のって **notte**
reads	よみます **yomimasu**	よみました **yomimashita**	よみましょう **yomimashō**	よんで **yonde**
calls	よびます **yobimasu**	よびました **yobimashita**	よびましょう **yobimashō**	よんで **yonde**
dies	しにます **shinimasu**	しにました **shinimashita**	しにましょう **shinimashō**	しんで **shinde**

	Polite			Plain
Meaning	Imperfect	Perfect	Tentative	Gerund
buys	かいます **kaimasu**	かいました **kaimashita**	かいましょう **kaimashō**	かって **katte**
wins	かちます **kachimasu**	かちました **kachimashita**	かちましょう **kachimashō**	かって **katte**
comes	きます **kimasu**	きました **kimashita**	きましょう **kimashō**	きて **kite**
does	します **shimasu**	しました **shimashita**	しましょう **shimashō**	して **shite**
equals, is	です **desu**	でした **deshita**	でしょう **deshō**	で **de**

You will notice that the mood we call the polite imperfect ends in **-masu** for all the verbs (**-su** for the copula); the polite perfect ends in **-mashita** for all the verbs (**-shita** for the copula); and the polite tentative ends in **-mashō** for all the verbs (**-shō** for the copula). The verb forms that appear before these polite endings are called infinitives (or pre-**masu** forms), and they all end in the vowel **-e** or **-i**. See 4.3 and 4.8 for more about infinitives. The plain gerund ends in **-te** or **-de** (no ending for the copula), and there are certain changes in the verb stem itself.

3.10. Use of the gerund (or *te*-form)

The gerund is often called the **te**-form. It is used before **kudasai** 'please' to make a polite request, for example:

> もう一度言ってください。
> **Mōichido itte kudasai.**
> Please say it again.

The gerund is used with the particle **kara** to mean 'after (do)ing.' For example:

> ご飯を食べてから新聞を読みました。
> **Gohan o tabete kara shinbun o yomimashita.**
> After eating, I read my newspaper.

The gerund is also used alone at the end of a clause to mean 'does/did/will do ... and...', for example:

> オフィスへ行って, メールを読みます。
> **Ofisu e itte, mēru o yomimasu.**
> I go to the office and read my e-mails.

The gerund is used in verb phrases with some form of the verb **imasu** to mean 'is (do)ing,' expressing a kind of "process" or "continuing action" and focising on the fact that the action lasts for a while. For example:

> 今ご飯を食べています。
> **Ima gohan o tabete imasu.**
> I'm eating now.

The simple verb form, on the other hand, focuses our attention on the action itself, either a specific act (**Nani o tabemasu ka** 'What do/will you eat?'; **Sakuban benkyō shimashita** 'Last night I studied') or a series thought of as a set of specific acts (**Mainichi hatarakimasu** 'Every day I work') rather than as a set of continuing actions taking up a space of time (**Mainichi hataraite imasu** 'Every day I'M WORKING'). The exact difference between **shigoto o shimasu** and **shigoto o shite imasu** is just as subtle as that between 'I work' and 'I'm working,' and in many situations either phrase would seem appropriate. Sometimes the difference between the simple verb and the GERUND + **imasu** seems to lie in a slightly different focus of emphasis. In the sentence **Ichiji kara niji made hatarakimashita** 'I worked from 1 o'clock to 2 o'clock,' the principal emphasis is on the fact that I worked and the time is incidental additional information. But in the sentence **Ichiji kara niji made hataraite imashita** 'From 1 o'clock to 2 o'clock I was working,' the emphasis, while perhaps really focused on the DURATIVE nature of the action, that is, on the word **imashita**, seems to be more on the time and what I was doing during the time.

The gerund is also used in certain phrases with other verbs:

> 歩いて行きます。
> **Aruite ikimasu.**
> He walks (He goes walking).

> 車に乗って来ます。
> **Kuruma ni notte kimasu.**
> He comes by car (riding in a car).

> マイクをつれて行きましょうか。
> **Maiku o tsurete kimashō ka.**
> Shall I bring Mike along (Shall I come bringing Mike)?

Notice that the gerund has no perfect, imperfect, or tentative meaning of its own but takes on the mood of the following (or final) verb.

旅行しています。
Ryokō shite imasu.
I am traveling.

旅行していました。
Ryokō shite imashita.
I was traveling.

旅行していましょう。
Ryokō shite imashō.
Let's keep traveling.

公園へ行って散歩しましょう。
Kōen e itte sanpo shimashō.
Let's go to the park and take a walk.

公園へ行って散歩しました。
Kōen e itte sanpo shimashita.
I went to the park and took a walk.

公園へ行って散歩しませんか。
Kōen e itte sanpo shimasen ka.
Won't you go to the park and take a walk?

3.11. Use of the imperfect, perfect, and tentative moods

The imperfect mood (sometimes called the present tense or non-past tense) indicates that an action has not been completed: it may or may not have begun, but it must be a definite, decided action. In the following sentence, we use the imperfect because I'm still sick today:

昨日から病気です。
Kinō kara byōki desu.
I've been sick since yesterday.

In the following sentence, perhaps you haven't even started to go yet, but it's definite that you will go:

どこへ行きますか。
Doko e ikimasu ka.
Where are you going?

On the other hand, the perfect mood (sometimes called the past tense) shows that the action has been completed:

田中さんは病気でした。
Tanaka-san wa byōki deshita.
Mr. Tanaka was sick (but he's well now).

どこへバスで行きましたか。
Doko e basu de ikimashita ka.
Where did you go by bus?

The tentative mood (sometimes called suggestive, future, probable future, or presumptive) is used when an action isn't quite definite. You're not sure about it—maybe it will be, probably it will be, perhaps it has already been—or you're suggesting it for consideration.

田中さんは病気でしょう。
Tanaka-san wa byōki deshō.
Mr. Tanaka must be sick. (I'm not sure, it isn't definite, but what do you think?)

どこへ行きましょうか。
Doko e ikimashō ka.
Where shall we go? (It hasn't been definitely decided where we will go, but we will probably go some place, so what shall we consider?)

This sometimes corresponds to English *let us*:

歩いて行きましょう。
Aruite ikimashō.
Let's walk. (It isn't definite that we will walk, but I'm suggesting it.)

3.12. Negatives

The polite imperfect negative of a verb is made by changing **-masu** to **-masen**. The polite negative of the copula **desu** is the phrase **ja arimasen**. Or, often, **ja nai desu**; and **arimasen** is often **nai desu**. **Ja** in negative forms is often **de wa** in formal contexts. Do not confuse this with the word **arimasen** all by itself; this is the negative of **arimasu** and means 'there isn't any.'

The most common type of attention-focus for a negative sentence in Japanese is on the negation itself 'there ISN'T any bread.' If you want to say 'There isn't any BREAD' (that is, 'It's BREAD that we lack (rather than something else)'), then you say **Pan ga arimasen**.

The polite perfect negative is a phrase, **-masen deshita** (for the copula **ja arimasen deshita**), and similarly the polite tentative negative is **-nai deshō** (for the copula **ja nai deshō**).

There is bread.
パンがあります。
Pan ga arimasu.

This is bread.
これはパンです。
Kore wa pan desu.

There is no bread.
パンはありません。
Pan wa arimasen.
（パンはないです。）
(Pan wa nai desu.)

This isn't bread.
これはパンじゃありません。
Kore wa pan ja arimasen.
（これはパンではありません。）
(Kore wa pan de wa arimasen.)
（これはパンじゃないです。）
(Kore wa pan ja nai desu.)
（これはパンではないです。）
(Kore wa pan de wa nai desu.)

There was bread
パンがありました。
Pan ga arimashita.

That was bread.
それはパンでした。
Sore wa pan deshita.

There was no bread.
パンはありませんでした。
Pan wa arimasen deshita.
（パンはなかったです。）
(Pan wa nakatta desu.)

That was not bread.
それはパンじゃありませんでした。
Sore wa pan ja arimasen deshita.
（それはパンではありませんでした。）
(Sore wa pan de wa arimasen deshita.)
（それはパンじゃなかったです。）
(Sore wa pan ja nakatta desu.)
（それはパンではなかったです。）
(Sore wa pan de wa nakatta desu.)

There won't be any bread (I bet).
パンはないでしょう。
Pan wa nai deshō.

That (probably) won't be bread.
それはパンじゃないでしょう。
Sore wa pan ja nai deshō.
（それはパンではないでしょう。）
(Sore wa pan de wa nai deshō.)

3.13. Words for 'work'

You have seen two ways to say 'I work.' **Shigoto o shimasu** means 'I do my job'; **hatarakimasu** means 'I work (often, but not necessarily, at something physical).' These two words can frequently be used in each other's place, with no great change of meaning. There is another word meaning 'is employed' or 'works'—**tsu-tomemasu**. This has a somewhat more refined connotation.

どこで働いていますか。
Doko de hataraite imasu ka.
Where do you work?

どこに勤めていますか。
Doko ni tsutomete imasu ka.
Where are you employed?

3.14. Verbal nouns (…する …*suru*)

There are some nouns, like **shutchō** 'a business trip,' **shōkai** 'introduction,' and **benkyō** 'study,' that can be followed directly by a form of the verb **suru/shimasu** 'does.' These constitute a class of nouns we call "verbal nouns." (They are also called **suru**-verbs more commonly.) Sometimes the particle **o** is inserted with expressions of this type, especially if the noun has something modifying it:

先月大阪に出張しました。
Sengetsu Ōsaka ni shutchō shimashita.
Last month I went to Osaka for a business trip.

友達に紹介しましょう。
Tomodachi ni shōkai shimashō.
Let me introduce you to a friend.

日本語を勉強しました。
Nihongo o benkyō shimashita.
I studied Japanese.

その勉強をしました。
Sono benkyō o shimashita.
I did that study.

The following are additional examples of verbal nouns followed by **suru**:

料理 **ryōri** cooking	料理する **ryōri suru** cooks
掃除 **sōji** (room) cleaning	掃除する **sōji suru** cleans
洗濯 **sentaku** laundry	洗濯する **sentaku suru** does laundry
予約 **yoyaku** reservation	予約する **yoyaku suru** reserves
契約 **keiyaku** contract	契約する **keiyaku suru** signs a contract
研究 **kenkyū** research	研究する **kenkyū suru** conducts research
卒業 **sotsugyō** graduation	卒業する **sotsugyō suru** graduates
準備 **junbi** preparation	準備する **junbi suru** prepares
旅行 **ryokō** trip	旅行する **ryokō suru** travels
結婚 **kekkon** marriage	結婚する **kekkon suru** marries

失礼 **shitsurei** rudeness   失礼する **shitsurei suru** is excused
メール **mēru** email, text   メールする **mēru suru** emails, texts
ツイート **tsuīto** tweet   ツイートする **tsuīto suru** tweets
チャット **chatto** chat   チャットする **chatto suru** chats
ログイン **rogu in** log on   ログインする **rogu in suru** logs on
ログアウト **rogu auto** log out   ログアウトする **rogu auto suru** logs out

3.15. Going in vehicles

To say 'I went by train,' you can say either of the following sentences:

電車で行きました。
Densha de ikimashita.
I went there by train.

電車に乗って行きました。
Densha ni notte ikimashita.
I went riding on a train.

The verb **norimasu** 'gets on board, rides,' like the verbs **imasu**, **arimasu**, and **sunde imasu**, takes the particle **ni**, here implying a change of position. **Doko de fune ni norimashita ka** 'Where did you board the ship?' Notice the difference between **Mainichi densha ni norimasu** 'He rides the train every day,' and **Mainichi densha ni notte ikimasu** 'He goes (there) on the train every day.' To get off (or out of) a vehicle, you use the verb **orimasu (orite): Kuruma o orimashita** 'I got out of the car.' **(Basu o) doko de orimashō ka** 'Where shall we get off (the bus)?' **Orimasu!** 'Coming out! Getting off!'

3.16 'As soon as'

A common way to say 'as soon as' is to use the gerund followed by **kara** 'after ...ing,' and then begin the next clause with **sugu** 'right away, immediately.' **Gohan o tabete kara sugu sanpo ni ikimashita** 'I went for a walk as soon as (right after) I ate dinner.' Sometimes the gerund is followed directly by the next clause without the particle **kara**, **Heya ni haitte sugu sensei ni hanashimashita** 'As soon as I entered the room, I spoke to the teacher.'

🎧 Conversation

[cue 03-3]

Takeshi (T) and Shizuka (S) are talking.

T: 昨日は仕事をしましたか。 **Kinō wa shigoto o shimashita ka.**
Did you work yesterday?

S: いいえ, 休みでした。 **Īe, yasumi deshita.** No, I didn't have to work.

T: ああ, そうですか。 **Ā, sō desu ka.** Oh, really.

S: ええ。仕事は月曜日から木曜日までなんです。
Ē. Shigoto wa Getsuyōbi kara Mokuyōbi made na n desu.
Right. My job is from Monday to Thursday.

T: ああ, いいですね。じゃあ, 家にいたんですか。
Ā, ii desu ne. Jā, ie ni ita n desu ka.
That's nice! Then, were you at home?

S: いいえ。昨日は大阪から友達が来ていたんです。
Īe. Kinō wa Ōsaka kara tomodachi ga kite ita n desu.
No. I had a friend visiting me from Osaka yesterday.

T: 友達とどこかへ行ったんですか。 **Tomodachi to dokoka e itta n desu ka.**
Did you go somewhere with your friend?

S: ええ。いっしょにディズニーシーに行きました。
Ē, isshoni Dizunīshī ni ikimashita.
We went to Disney Sea together.

T: 何で行きましたか。 **Nani de ikimashita ka.** How did you go there?

S: 車で行きました。 **Kuruma de ikimashita.** We went there by car.

T: あしたも休みですね。 **Ashita mo yasumi desu ne.**
You don't have to work tomorrow, either, right?

S: ええ。あしたは秋葉原に行きます。パソコンを買うんです。
Ē. Ashita wa Akihabara ni ikimasu. Pasokon o kau n desu.
Right. I'll go to Akihabara tomorrow. I'm buying a PC.

T: 僕も行きたいな。**Boku mo ikitai na.** I want to go there, too.

S: じゃあ，秋葉原の駅の前で待ち合わせをしましょう。
Jā, Akihabara no eki no mae de machiawase o shimashō.
Okay, then let's meet in front of the Akihabara train station.

Exercises

I. Fill in the blanks with either *de* or *ni*. Do it all aloud.

1. 山田さんはどこ＿＿＿働いていますか。**Yamada-san wa doko ＿＿＿ hataraite imasu ka.**

2. 銀行＿＿＿勤めています。**Ginkō ＿＿＿ tsutomete imasu.**

3. 会社にはバス＿＿＿行きますか。**Kaisha ni wa basu ＿＿＿ ikimasu ka.**

4. 電車＿＿＿乗ります。**Densha ＿＿＿ norimasu.**

5. 家は東京＿＿＿あります。主人と東京＿＿＿住んでいます。**Ie wa Tōkyō ＿＿＿＿ arimasu. Shujin to Tōkyō ＿＿＿ sunde imasu.**

II. Fill in the blanks with either *ga* or *o*.

1. 私はアメリカの映画＿＿＿好きです。**Watashi wa Amerika no eiga ＿＿＿ suki desu.**

2. もうご飯＿＿＿食べましたか。**Mō gohan ＿＿＿ tabemashita ka.**

3. 何＿＿＿ありますか。**Nani ＿＿＿ arimasu ka.**

4. だれ＿＿＿部屋の中にいますか。**Dare ＿＿＿ heya no naka ni imasu ka.**

5. 何の勉強＿＿＿しましょうか。**Nan no benkyō ＿＿＿ shimashō ka.**

6. だれ＿＿＿私のクッキーを食べましたか。**Dare ＿＿＿ watashi no kukkī o tabemashita ka.**

7. どの本＿＿＿買いましたか。**Dono hon ＿＿＿ kaimashita ka.**

III. Fill in the blanks appropriately by using verbs and the copula in negative.

1. 「刺身を食べましたか。」 「いいえ，食べ＿＿＿＿＿＿。」
   "Sashimi o tabemashita ka." **"Īe, tabe＿＿＿＿＿＿＿."**

2. 「今日は勉強しますか。」
    "Kyō wa benkyō shimasu ka."

    「いいえ，_____。」
    "Īe, _____."

3. 「今は働いていますか。」
    "Ima wa hataraite imasu ka."

    「いいえ，今は働_____。」
    "Īe, ima wa hata_____."

4. 「あの人は病気でしょうか。」
    "Ano hito wa byōki deshō ka."

    「いいえ，病気____でしょう。」
    "Īe, byōki_____deshō."

5. 「あの人は先生ですか。」
    "Ano hito wa sensei desu ka."

    「いいえ，先生_____。」
    "Īe, sensei_____."

Answers:
I   1. で **de** 2. に **ni** 3. で **de** 4. に **ni** 5. に **ni,** に **ni**

II 1. が **ga** 2. を **o** 3. が **ga** 4. が **ga** 5. を **o** 6. が **ga** 7. を **o**

III 1. …ませんでした **...masendeshita** 2. 勉強しません **benkyō shimasen** 3. …らいていません **...raite imasen** 4. …じゃない **...ja nai** or …ではない **...de wa nai** 5. …じゃありません **...arimasen** or …ではありません **... de wa arimasen**

What's the Weather Like?
天気はどう？
Tenki wa Dō

In this lesson you will learn how to describe weather and climate, how to conjugate adjectives and verbs, and the important distiction between plain forms and polite forms.

🎧 Basic Sentences

[cue 04-1]

1.	今日は<u>暑い</u>です。昨日も<u>暑かったで</u> す。明日はどうでしょう。 **Kyō wa <u>atsui desu</u>. Kinōmo <u>atsukatta</u> <u>desu</u>. Asu wa dō deshō.**	It's hot today. Yesterday was hot also. I wonder how the weather will be tomorrow.
2.	雨が<u>降るから</u>，うちにいましょう。 **Ame ga <u>furu kara</u>, uchi ni imashō.**	Because it will rain, let's stay home.
3.	雨が<u>降ったから</u>，うちにいました。 **Ame ga <u>futta kara</u>, uchi ni imashita.**	Because it rained, I stayed home.
4.	天気がよくなったから，外に<u>遊びに</u> 行きました。 **Tenki ga yoku natta kara, soto ni <u>asobi ni</u> ikimashita.**	Because the sky cleared up, I went out for fun.

5.	山田さんは優しい<u>し</u>, 頭がいい<u>し</u>, きれいだ<u>し</u>。 **Yamada-san wa yasashii <u>shi</u>, atama ga ii <u>shi</u>, kirei da <u>shi</u>.**	Ms. Yamada is kind, smart, and pretty....
6.	冬になる<u>と</u>雪がよく降ります。 **Fuyu ni naru <u>to</u> yuki ga yoku furimasu.**	When the winter comes, it snows very often.
7.	今もまだ雪が<u>降り</u>つづいています。 **Ima mo mada yuki ga <u>furi</u>-tsuzuite imasu.**	It is still continuing to snow now.
8.	「日本<u>では</u>雪が降りますか。」 **"Nihon <u>de wa</u> yuki ga furimasu ka."**	"Does it snow in Japan?"
	「場所によって違います。」 **"Basho ni yotte chigaimasu."**	"It is different depending on the place."
9.	「スキーを<u>したことがあります</u>か。」 **"Sukī o <u>shita koto ga arimasu</u> ka."**	"Have you (ever) skied?"
	「いいえ, ありません。」 **"Īe, arimasen."**	"No, I haven't."
10.	「ここは洪水に<u>なることがあります</u> か。」 **"Koko wa kōzui ni <u>naru koto ga ari- masu</u> ka."**	"Do floods occasionally occur here?"
	「はい, あります。」 **"Hai, arimasu."**	"Yes, they do."
11.	いつ庭掃除をする<u>つもり</u>ですか。 **Itsu niwa-sōji o suru <u>tsumori</u> desu ka.**	When do you intend to clean the garden?
12.	<u>だんだん</u>涼しくなってきましたね。 **<u>Dandan</u> suzushiku natte kimashita ne.**	It is gradually getting cooler.
13.	「そちらの天気はどうですか。」 **"Sochira no tenki wa dō desu ka."**	"How is the weather there (in your place)?"
	「今日は<u>曇っています</u>よ。」 **"Kyō wa <u>kumotte imasu</u> yo."**	"It's cloudy today (here)."
14.	兄はもう<u>結婚しています</u>。 **Ani wa mō <u>kekkon shite imasu</u>.**	My big brother is already married.

15.	田中さんはまだ来ていませんね。 **Tanaka-san wa mada <u>kite imasen</u> ne.**	Mr. Tanaka has not come yet.
16.	傘を持っていった方がいいよ。 **Kara kasa o <u>motte itta</u> hō ga ii yo.**	It's better to bring an umbrella.
17.	テレビがつけてあります。 **Terebi ga <u>tsukete arimasu</u>.**	The TV is turned on.

 **Basic Vocabulary**

[audio cue 04-2]

WEATHER

晴れ **hare**	clear sky
曇り **kumori**	cloudy sky
風 **kaze**	wind
雨 **ame**	rain
小雨 **kosame**	drizzle
雪 **yuki**	snow
霧 **kiri**	fog
雷 **kaminari**	thunder
日 **hi**	the sun

SKY

空 **sora**	sky
青空 **azora**	blue sky
曇り空 **kumori-zora**	cloudy sky
夕焼け空 **yūyakzora**	the sky at sunset

TEMPERATURE & HUMIDITY

寒い **samui**	is cold
暑い **atsui**	is hot
暖かい **atatakai**	is warm
涼しい **suzushii**	is cool
蒸し暑い **mushi-atsui**	is hot and humid

SEASONS

春 **haru**	spring
夏 **natsu**	summer
秋 **aki**	fall
冬 **fuyu**	winter
梅雨 **tsuyu**	rainy season

WEATHER-RELATED ITEMS

傘 **kasa**   umbrella
レインコート **reinkōto**   raincoat
レインブーツ **reinbūtsu**   rain boots
手袋 **tebukuro**   gloves
ミトン **miton**   mittens
マフラー **mafurā**   scarf
レッグウォーマー **reggu wōmā**
                                         leg warmer

ISLANDS IN JAPAN

北海道 **Hokkaidō**   Hokkaido
本州 **Honshū**   Honshu
九州 **Kyūshū**   Kyushu

四国 **Shikoku**   Shikoku
沖縄 **Okinawa**   Okinawa

COLORS

赤 **aka**   red color
赤い **akai**   is red
青 **ao**   blue color
青い **aoi**   is blue
黒 **kuro**   black color
黒い **kuroi**   is black
白 **shiro**   white color
白い **shiroi**   is white
ピンク **pinku**   pink
オレンジ **orenji** orange

CULTURE NOTE ▶ Weather in Japan

Japan consists of four major islands: Honshu, Hokkaido, Kyushu, and Shikoku, and nearly 7,000 islands in all, including numerous tiny islands where no one can live. The total land area of Japan is 145,902 square miles (380,000 square kilometers), only 1/25 of the total area of the United States. Most of the land is mountainous, and the flat portion where people can live is very limited. Japan is a small country, but it is long. Japan can be seen as a chain of islands that goes northeast to southwest and measures about 1,700 miles (3,000 kilometers) in length,. Japan's northern end is near 45° N., about the same as Montreal, Canada, and its southern end is near 20° N., about the same as the southern part of Florida. As might be expected, the climate is very different across the country. Everywhere in Japan except Hokkaido has a rainy season, called **tsuyu**. In Tokyo, it rarely snows, but its summer is quite muggy. Hokkaido is dry, but its winter is severe. Most of the northern areas suffer from high accumulations of snow in winter. Kyushu and the southern islands including Okinawa have very mild winters but very hot summers.

SHAPES, SIZES, AND QUALITIES

丸・円 **maru/en**	circle
丸い **marui**	is round
四角 **shikaku**	square
四角い **shikakui**	is square
大きい **ōkii**	is big
小さい **chīsai**	is little
長い **nagai**	is long
短い **mijikai**	is short
いい **ii**	is good
悪い **warui**	is bad
だめ(だ) **dame (da)**	(is) no good, won't do

VERBS

晴れる・晴れます **hareru/haremasu**	(the sky) gets clear
曇る・曇ります **kumoru/kumorimasu**	(the sky) gets cloudy
降る・降ります **furu/furimasu**	(rain or snow) falls
寝る・寝ます **neru/nemasu**	goes to bed, sleeps
遊ぶ・遊びます **asobu/asobimasu**	enjoys oneself
休む・休みます **yasumu/yasumimasu**	rests
急ぐ・急ぎます **isogu/isogimasu**	hurries
開く・開きます **aku/akimasu**	(something) gets opened
開ける・開けます **akeru/akemasu**	opens (something)
こわれる・こわれます **kowareru/kowaremasu**	(something) gets broken
こわす・こわします **kowasu/kowashimasu**	breaks (something)

Structure Notes

4.1. Adjectives

There are three classes of inflected forms in Japanese: verbs, adjectives, and the copula. You have observed the similar inflections of the verbs (**shimasu**, **shimashita**, **shimashō**) and the copula (**-desu**, **-deshita**, **-deshō**). Adjectives also have inflections for the same categories:

暑いです **atsui desu**	it's hot
暑かったです **atsukatta desu**	it was hot
暑いでしょう **atsui deshō**	it will (probably) be hot

The negative of adjectives is a phrase consisting of the plain INFINITIVE + **ari-masen** (or **nai desu**) 'does not exist.'

暑くありません **atsuku arimasen**	it's not hot
暑くないです **atsuku nai desu**	it's not hot
暑くありませんでした **atsuku arimasen deshita**	it was not hot
暑くなかったです **atsuku nakatta desu**	it was not hot
暑くないでしょう **atsuku nai deshō**	it will (probably) not be hot.

This is discussed further in 5.11.

4.2. Plain and polite forms

For the same inflectional category, like imperfect or perfect, a Japanese verb, adjective, or copula may have two forms: a plain form and a polite form. In familiar speech, only the plain forms occur. But in polite speech, the plain forms are limited in occurrence to some place other than at the end of the sentence. So, in the polite style of talking, you will say both of the following sentences:

雨が降りました。
Ame ga furimashita.
It rained.

雨が降ったから，うちにいました。
Ame ga futta kara, uchi ni imashita.
Because it rained, I stayed home.

Occasionally you will hear a polite form used somewhere other than at the end of the sentence. For instance, someone may say:

雨が降りましたから，うちにいました。
Ame ga furimashita kara, uchi ni imashita.
Because it rained, I stayed home.

In fact, before the particle **ga** meaning 'but, and,' the polite form is the usual thing. And before the particle **keredomo** 'but, however,' many people prefer to use the polite form.

The moods that occur at the end of a sentence are limited to the imperfect, perfect, and tentative. But within a sentence, there are a number of other moods, such as the gerund (see 3.9) and the infinitive (see 4.3, 4.5, 4.6, and 4.8). Here are some examples of the use of plain and polite forms within sentences:

寒いと 関節が痛みます。
Samui to kansetsu ga itamimasu.
When it's cold, my joints hurt.

疲れたから, もう寝ます。
Tsukareta kara, mō nemasu.
I'm tired, so I'll go to bed now.

父は心臓病で亡くなりましたが, 母は癌でなくなりました。
Chichi wa shinzōbyō de nakunarimashita ga, haha wa gan de nakunarimashita.
My father died of heart disease, but my mother died of cancer.

英語の教師だったけれども, 英語を話す国に行ったことはありません。
Eigo no kyōshi datta keredomo, eigo o hanasu kuni ni itta koto wa arimasen.
I was an English teacher, but I have never been to any English-speaking countries.

4.3. Shapes of the plain forms

Any Japanese inflected form may be broken up into a "stem" and an "ending." (Some call stems "roots," referring to the form without any endings.) Japanese verbs fall into two main classes: consonant verbs and vowel verbs. The consonant verbs are those with a stem that ends in a consonant; the vowel verbs are those with a stem that ends in a vowel. Vowel stems end only in **-e** or **-i**:

> (1) **-i** as in 見る **mi-ru**　　sees
> (2) **-e** as in 食べる **tabe-ru**　eats

Consonant stems end in one of the following nine sounds (verbs are usually mentioned by the plain imperfect form: **kau** 'buys'):

> (1) **-t[s]** as in 勝つ **kats-u**　wins
> (2) **-r** as in 乗る **nor-u**　rides
> (3) **-[w]** as in 買う **ka-u**　buys
> (4) **-s** as in 貸す **kas-u**　lends
> (5) **-k** as in 書く **kak-u**　writes
> (6) **-g** as in 泳ぐ **oyog-u**　swims
> (7) **-b** as in 呼ぶ **yob-u**　calls
> (8) **-m** as in 読む **yom-u**　reads
> (9) **-n** as in 死ぬ **shin-u**　dies

You will notice certain peculiarities in the above list of stem-final consonants. Verbs like **kau** 'buys' are said to be consonant verbs, but the consonant with which they end, **w**, just doesn't occur in Japanese except before the sound **a** (as in **watashi** 'I'). This means that for some of the endings, like the imperfect, these **w**-ending-stem verbs don't display this stem-final consonant at all. That is why we put the **w** in brackets—to show that it disappears before every vowel except **a**. You will notice another sound in brackets—the **s** of the verb **katsu** 'wins.' This verb stem basically ends in just **-t**, but the sound **t** does not occur before the sound **u** in Japanese, so that before an ending beginning with **u**, the **t** is replaced by **ts**. In a similar way, since the combination **ti** does not normally occur in Japanese, before the infinitive ending **-i**, the **t** becomes **ch—kach-i** 'wins.' Since the sound **si** does not occur, the infinitive of **hanas-u** 'speaks' turns out to be **hanash-i** 'speaking.' There is only one verb with a stem ending in **-n**, **shinu** 'dies,' and this is often replaced by a euphemism **nakunaru** 'passes away.' The verb **shinu** is included in our list only for completeness. Here are some models showing the formation of the plain forms:

	Stem (root)	Imperfect	Perfect	Gerund	Infinitive	English
Vowel Verbs	**tabe**	たべる **tabe-ru**	たべた **tabe-ta**	たべて **tabe-te**	たべ **tabe**	eats
	mi	みる **mi-ru**	みた **mi-ta**	みて **mi-te**	み **mi**	sees, looks
Consonant Verbs	**kat**	かつ **kats-u**	かった **kat-ta**	かって **kat-te**	かち **kach-i**	wins
	nor	のる **nor-u**	のった **not-ta**	のって **not-te**	のり **nor-i**	gets on
	kaw*	かう **ka-u**	かった **kat-ta**	かって **kat-te**	かい **ka-i**	buys
	kas	かす **kas-u**	かした **kashi-ta**	かして **kashi-te**	かし **kash-i**	lends
	kak	かく **kak-u**	かいた **kai-ta**	かいて **kai-te**	かき **kak-i**	writes
	oyog	およぐ **oyog-u**	およいだ **oyoi-da**	およいで **oyoi-de**	およぎ **oyog-i**	swims
	yob	よぶ **yob-u**	よんだ **yon-da**	よんで **yon-de**	よび **yob-i**	calls
	yom	よむ **yom-u**	よんだ **yon-da**	よんで **yon-de**	よみ **yom-i**	reads
	shin	しぬ **shin-u**	しんだ **shin-da**	しんで **shin-de**	しに **shin-i**	dies

*The **w** at the end of a consonant verb is pronounced and heard only if it is followed by the vowel **a**.

The endings, then, are as follows:

Imperfect: **-ru** after a vowel stem, **-u** after a consonant stem
Infinitive: (-ZERO) after a vowel stem, **-i** after a consonant stem
Perfect: **-da** after **-g**, **-b**, **-m**, and **-n** stems; **ta** after all other stems
Gerund: **-de** after **-g**, **-b**, **-m**, and **-n** stems; **-te** after all other stems

The ZERO ending is an ending that has no shape at all. Notice that multiple verbs might have exactly the same form, for example, the gerund forms of **katsu** 'wins' and **kau** 'buys' in the above table are both **katte**. Often the pitch accents are different in such cases, but you can always distinguish them by the context in which each is used.

4.4. Learning the forms

Now, how should one go about learning these inflectional forms? You have read a description of how they are put together, and that may be of some help to you. But in order to be able to make up the forms for a new verb you hear, you will want to compare it with a verb you already know and make its forms by analogy, using the old verb for a model. You can take the verbs used in the lists here for your models. Learn their forms well, and then make forms for other verbs on their patterns.

When you come across a new verb, the first thing you want to know is: is it a consonant verb or a vowel verb? Unless the verb ends in **-eru** or **-iru** in the imperfect, there is no doubt about it, but if the verb does end in **-eru** or **-iru**, you don't know whether it is a consonant verb or a vowel verb until you check one of the other forms, such as the infinitive or the perfect.

In this book we will show two imperfect forms, plain and polite, in the Basic Vocabulary section, so that you can clearly tell whether any of the **-eru** and **-iru** verbs are consonant verbs or vowel verbs: if you get the same form after removing **-ru** and **-masu**, the verb is a vowel verb. For example, take **taberu** and **tabemasu** 'eats,' and remove **-ru** and **-masu** from **taberu** and **tabemasu**, respectively. You get exactly the same form, which is **tabe**. This means that **taberu** is a vowel verb. Do the same for **kaeru** and **kaerimasu** 'returns.' After removing **-ru** and **-masu**, you get **kae** and **kaeri**, which are different. This means that **kaeru** 'returns' is a consonant verb. No need to be alert all the time. You just need to be alert if you see a verb that ends in **-eru** or **-iru**. The following are pairs of consonant verbs and vowel verbs whose plain imperfect forms are exactly the same.

Vowel Verb	Consonant Verb
iru/imasu stays, exists（いる）	**iru/irimasu** is necessary（要る）
kiru/kimasu wears on body（着る）	**kiru/kirimasu** cuts（切る）
neru/nemasu sleeps（寝る）	**neru/nerimasu** kneads（練る）
kaeru/kaemasu changes（変える）	**kaeru/kaerimasu** returns（帰る）

Most verbs with the imperfect ending in **-eru** or **-iru** are vowel verbs, so it is a good idea to memorize a small list of **-eru/-iru** ending "consonant" verbs. The following list is not exhaustive, but is helpful.

散る/散ります	**chiru/chirimasu**	falls, scatters
入る/入ります	**hairu/hairimasu**	enters
走る/走ります	**hashiru/hashirimasu**	runs
減る/減ります	**heru/herimasu**	decreases
要る/要ります	**iru/irimasu**	is necessary
煎る/煎ります	**iru/irimasu**	roasts
帰る/帰ります	**kaeru/kaerimasu**	returns
限る/限ります	**kagiru/kagirimasu**	limits
蹴る/蹴ります	**keru/kerimasu**	kicks
切る/切ります	**kiru/kirimasu**	cuts
参る/参ります	**mairu/mairimasu**	goes
混じる/混じります	**majiru/majirimasu**	mixes
ねじる/ねじります	**nejiru/nejirimasu**	twists
練る/練ります	**neru/nerimasu**	kneads
握る/握ります	**nigiru/nigirimasu**	grasps, takes hold
茂る/茂ります	**shigeru/shigerimasu**	grows thick
仕切る/仕切ります	**shikiru/shikirimasu**	divides
知る/知ります	**shiru/shirimasu**	knows
しゃべる/しゃべります	**shaberu/shaberimasu**	chats
滑る/滑ります	**suberu/suberimasu**	slides
照る/照ります	**teru/terimasu**	shines

4.5. Irregular verbs

There are only a few common verbs that have considerable irregularities of inflection. The verbs **kuru (kimasu)** 'comes' and **suru (shimasu)** 'does' are irregular in the plain imperfect itself. (We would expect something like ***ki-ru** and ***shi-ru** if the verbs were regular.) Nearly everywhere else these verbs behave the way you would expect a vowel verb ending in **-iru** to behave:

Imperfect	Perfect	Gerund	Infinitive
ku-ru	ki-ta	ki-te	ki(-zero)
su-ru	shi-ta	shi-te	shi(-zero)

The verb **ik-u** 'goes' is irregular only in the way the stem changes the **-k** to **-t** instead of **-i** before the **t**-endings. (We might have expected a form like *i-ita instead of the actual **it-ta**, if the verb were regular.) There is one other verb that is irregular in the imperfect only. This is the verb **i(w)-u** 'says, tells.' We write this form **iu**, but it is often pronounced **yū**.

Imperfect	Perfect	Gerund	Infinitive
ik-u	it-ta	it-te	ik-i
i-u (yū)	it-ta	it-te	i-i

Note that the perfect and gerund forms of **iu** 'says,' **iku** 'goes' and **ir-u** 'is necessary' are the same: **itta**, **itte**. You can tell them apart only by the rest of the sentence. (But some people pronounce **yutta** and **yutte** for 'said' and 'saying.') There are some verbs whose **masu**-forms lacks **r**. For example, the polite imperfect form of **kudasaru** is not **kudasarimasu** but **kudasaimasu**. Similarly, the polite imperfect form of **irassharu** 'to exist' is not **irassharimasu** but **irasshaimasu**.

4.6. Adjectives and the copula
Adjectives in Japanese end in:

-ai like **akai**	is red
-oi like **aoi**	is blue
-ui like **warui**	is bad
-ii like **ōkii**	is big

They are inflected simply by adding certain endings to the vowel before the **-i**, which is the imperfect ending itself:

Imperfect	Perfect	Gerund	Infinitive
-i	-katta	-kute	-ku

The copula is somewhat irregularly inflected, so the forms are best learned as separate words rather than being broken into stem and ending. The adjective **ii** 'is good' has an alternate form **yoi** 'is good.' The other forms are all based only on the form **yoi**.

	Imperfect	Perfect	Gerund	Infinitive
is red	赤い **aka-i**	赤かった **aka-katta**	赤くて **aka-kute**	赤く **aka-ku**
is blue	青い **ao-i**	青かった **ao-katta**	青くて **ao-kute**	青く **ao-ku**
is bad	悪い **waru-i**	悪かった **waru-katta**	悪くて **waru-kute**	悪く **waru-ku**
is big	大きい **ōki-i**	大きかった **ōki-katta**	大きくて **ōki-kute**	大きく **ōki-ku**
is good	いい・よい **i-i/ yo-i**	よかった **yo-katta**	よくて **yo-kute**	よく **yo-ku**
is nonexistent	ない **na-i**	なかった **na-katta**	なくて **na-kute**	なく **na-ku**
equals, is	−だ **-da**	−だった **-datta**	−で **-de**	---

Here are some examples of inflected forms of adjectives and the copula used in sentences:

山田さんは優しいし，頭がいいし，悪いところがないし，きれいだし。
Yamada-san wa yasashii shi, atama ga ii shi, warui tokoro ga nai shi, kirei da shi.
Ms. Yamada is kind, smart, no bad qualities, pretty...

10年前はまだ家も安かったし手続きも簡単だった。
Jūnen mae wa mada ie mo yasukatta shi tetsuzuki mo kantan datta.
Ten years ago, houses were still cheap and (purchase) procedures were simpler.

昨日は雨が降って寒くて最悪の天気で本当に困った。
Kinō wa ame ga futte samukute saiaku no tenki de hontō ni komatta.
Yesterday, it rained, it was cold, and it was the worst weather, and we were in real trouble.

急に涼しくなって海岸も人がいなくなって静かになってしまいましたね。
Kyū ni suzushiku natte kaigan mo hito ga inaku natte shizukani natte shi-maimashita ne.
It became cooler all of a sudden, people disappeared from the beaches, and it became completely quiet.

今日は天気がよくて風がなくて洗濯物を干すには最高の日でよかった。
Kyō wa tenki ga yokute kaze ga nakute sentakumono o hosu ni wa saikō no hi de yokatta.
Today, the sky was clear, no strong wind, and so it was an ideal day for hanging out the wash.

4.7. Uses of the plain imperfect and perfect

Both imperfect and perfect are used before the particle **kara** with the meaning 'because':

そこにあるから **soko ni aru kara**   because it's there
そこにあったから **soko ni atta kara**   because it was there

Notice the difference in meaning between GERUND + **kara** and PERFECT + **kara**:

友達が来てから，いっしょにご飯を食べました。
Tomodachi ga kite kara, issho ni gohan o tabemashita.
After my friend came, we had dinner together.

友達が来たから，いっしょにご飯を食べました。
Tomodachi ga kita kara, issho ni gohan o tabemashita.
Because my friend came, I had dinner with him.

Before **keredomo** 'however, but,' both imperfect and perfect occur:

私は学校へ行ったけれども勉強しませんでした。
Watashi wa gakkō e itta keredomo benkyō shimasen deshita.
I went to school, but I didn't study.

私は学校へ行くけれどもあまり勉強しません。
Watashi wa gakkō e iku keredomo amari benkyō shimasen.
I go to school, but I don't study very much.

Before the particle **to** meaning 'when,' only the imperfect occurs:

春になると，お天気がよくなります。
Haru ni naru to, otenki ga yōku narimasu.
When it gets to be spring, the weather gets nice.

子どもは先生を見ると，すぐ部屋の中へ入りました。
Kodomo wa sensei o miru to, sugu heya no naka e hairimashita.
As soon as they spotted the teacher, the children went into the room.

雪が降ると，うちにいて遊びます。
Yuki ga furu to, uchi ni ite asobimasu.
When it snows, we stay home and enjoy ourselves (here).

Before the phrases **koto ga suki desu** 'likes to,' **koto ga dekimasu** 'can,' and **tsumori desu** 'intends to,' only the imperfect occurs:

泳ぐことが好きです。
Oyogu koto ga suki desu.
I like to swim.

泳ぐことが好きでした。
Oyogu koto ga suki deshita.
I used to like to swim.

泳ぐことが好きでしょう。
Oyogu koto ga suki deshō.
You must like to swim.

山へ行くつもりです。
Yama e iku tsumori desu.
I intend to go to the mountains.

山へ行くつもりでした。
Yama e iku tsumori deshita.
I intended to go to the mountains.

山へ行くつもりでしょう。
Yama e iku tsumori deshō.
You must be planning to go to the mountains.

Before the phrase **koto ga aru** 'there exists the fact of,' either imperfect or perfect is used, depending on the meaning. If you use the imperfect, the meaning is 'sometimes':

公園へ行って散歩することがあります。
Kōen e itte sanpo suru koto ga arimasu.
I sometimes go to the park and take a walk.

秋にも寒いことがあります。
Aki ni mo samui koto ga arimasu.
It is sometimes cold in autumn, too.

If you use the perfect before **koto ga aru**, the meaning is 'has ever done, once did':

> 日比谷公園へ散歩に行ったことがありますか。
> **Hibiya-kōen e sanpo ni ittakoto ga arimasu ka.**
> Have you ever been (gone) to Hibiya Park for a walk?

> そこへ行ったことはありません。
> **Soko e itta koto wa arimasen.**
> I've never been there.

> 神戸へ旅行したことがあります。
> **Kōbe e ryokō shita koto ga arimasu.**
> I once took a trip to Kobe.

> もうそこへ行ったことがありましたが，前の旅行は冬でした。
> **Mō soko e itta koto ga arimashita ga, mae no ryokō wa fuyu deshita.**
> I had already been there (once), but the trip before was (in) winter.

4.8. Uses of the infinitive

The infinitive is a noun-like form of verbs and adjectives. There is no copula infinitive, except in the impersonal style (**de ari**), where the copula is always a phrase.

Verb and adjective infinitives are used before various particles just as nouns are.

> 鞄を取りに行きました。
> **Kaban o tori ni ikimashita.**
> I went to pick up the suitcase.

> 遅くまで勉強しました。
> **Osoku made benkyō shimashita.**
> I studied till late.

For emphatic contrast, a verb infinitive is sometimes followed by the particle **wa** and some form of the verb **suru**:

> 泳ぎはしませんでしたが，遊びはよくしました。
> **Oyogi wa shimasen deshita ga, asobi wa yoku shimashita.**
> I DIDN'T do any swimming, but I DID do a lot of playing.

Similarly, an adjective infinitive is followed by **wa** and a form of the verb **aru**:

小さくはありましたけれども，悪くはありませんでした。
Chīsaku wa arimashita keredomo, waruku wa arimasen deshita.
It WAS small, but it WASN'T bad.

The adjective infinitive often modifies other verb and adjective forms without any particle—this is similar to the ADVERB use of nouns without particles:

寒くなりました。
Samuku narimashita.
It got cold.

早く歩いてください。
Hayaku aruite kudasai.
Please walk fast.

髪を短くしました。
Kami o mijikaku shimashita.
I made my hair short.

The infinitive **yoku** (**-ii** 'is good') has three slightly different meanings: 'well; often; a lot':

よくなりました。
Yoku narimashita.
He got well.

雨がよく降ります。
Ame ga yoku furimasu.
It rains a lot.

ここは台風がよく来ます。
Koko wa taifū ga yoku kimasu.
Typhoons often come here.

The meanings 'often' and 'a lot' are similar to English 'a good deal' as in 'it rains a good deal' and 'she goes to the movies a good deal.'

The verb infinitive is easy to find: just remove the **-masu** from the polite forms such as **tabe-masu, nomi-masu, shi-masu,** etc. The verb infinitive is used to make compound verbs. For example, you can add the verb **tsuzukeru** 'continues something' to any verb infinitive to make a compound verb with the meaning 'continues to do something':

話しつづける **hanashi-tsuzukeru**	continues talking
飲みつづける **nomi-tsuzukeru**	goes on drinking
見つづける **mi-tsuzukeru**	keeps on looking

Another kind of compound verb is made with the verb **naosu** 'repairs, fixes, cures' added to the infinitive; this means 'does something again (correcting one's error)':

書きなおす **kaki-naosu**	writes again, corrects
読みなおす **yomi-naosu**	reads again (correctly this time)

Somewhat similar are compound verbs made by attaching **kaeru** 'changes something' (do not confuse **kae-ru** with **kaer-u** 'returns') to an infinitive:

乗りかえる **nori-kaeru**	changes trains ('ride-changes')
言いかえる **ii-kaeru**	rephrase

Still another kind of compound verb is made by adding either **hajimeru** 'begins something' or **dasu** 'puts something out; starts something' to an infinitive:

読みはじめる **yomi-hajimeru**	begins to read
走りだす **hashiri-dasu**	starts to run

A special type of compound is made by adding **sugiru** 'is in excess' to a verb infinitive (or to just the stem of an adjective, or to a copular noun):

食べすぎる **tabe-sugiru**	eats too much
働きすぎる **hataraki-sugiru**	overworks
遅すぎる **oso-sugiru**	is too late
大きすぎる **ōki-sugiru**	is overly large
静かすぎる **shizuka-sugiru**	is too quiet

The following sentenes have compound verbs:

三日前から雨が降りだして, 今もまだ降りつづけています。
Mikka mae kara ame ga furi-dashite, ima mo mada furi-tsuzukete imasu.
It started to rain three days ago, and it is still raining now.

誠は言いだしたら全然人の話を聞かない。
Mokoto wa ii-dashitara zenzen hito no hanashi o kikanai.
Makoto does not listen to anyone once he starts saying something.

食べすぎないようにしなくてはいけません。
Tabe-suginai yō ni shinakute wa ikemasen.
You must try not to overeat.

品川で乗りかえてください。
Shinagawa de nori-kaete kudasai.
Please change trains at Shinagawa.

考えなおして，働きはじめました。
Kangae-naoshite, hataraki-hajimemashita.
I reconsidered, and started working.

マンガを読みすぎました。
Manga o yomi-sugimashita.
I read comic books too much.

Finally, the verb infinitive is the source of many derived nouns:

休み **yasumi** 'vacation' from **yasumu** (rests)
はなし **hanashi** 'story' from **hanasu** (speaks)
はじめ **hajime** 'beginning' from **hajimeru** (begins)
泳ぎ **oyogi** 'swimming' from **oyogu** (swims)
通り **tōri** 'street' from **tōru** (passes)

There are a few nouns derived from adjective infinitives like **chikaku** 'vicinity' from **chikaku** 'being near,' as in **Ginkō wa chikaku ni arimasen** 'There is no bank in the vicinity.'

A special kind of noun is derived by adding the noun **kata** 'manner' to the infinitive. The meaning of these nouns is 'way or manner of (do)ing':

食べ方 **tabekata**   way of eating
話し方 **hanashikata**   way of talking
歩き方 **arukikata**   way of walking
読み方 **yomikata**   way of reading
書き方 **kakikata**   way of writing
仕方 **shikata**   way of doing, means

Here are some example sentences:

犬のような食べ方をしないで箸かフォークで食べなさい。
Inu no yō na tabekata o shinaide hashi ka fōku de tabenasai.
Don't eat like a dog, but eat with chopsticks or a fork.

この漢字の読み方と書き方を教えてください。
Kono kanji no yomikata to kakikata o oshiete kudasai.
Please teach me how to read and write this kanji.

「もう間に合わないね。」
"Mō maniawanai ne."
"We cannot make it anymore. (It's too late.)"

「仕方ないよ。」
"Shikata nai yo."
"There's nothing we can do (so let's give up)."

4.9. The plain negative

The plain form of the verb **arimasu** 'exists' is **aru**. The negative form of this is not a verb at all, but the adjective **nai**, 'is non-existent (= does not exist).' The adjective **nai**, then, is the plain adjective form corresponding to the polite verb form **arimasen**. The plain negative of other verbs are also adjectives derived from the verb stems by the addition of the suffix -(a)nai—this is discussed in 5.11. Here are some examples of the adjective **nai**:

車がないから電車に乗って行きます。
Kuruma ga nai kara densha ni notte ikimasu.
I don't have a car, so I go by train.

傘がなかったから濡れてしまいました。
Kasa ga nakatta kara nurete shimaimashita.
As I did not have an umbrella, I got wet.

ここに置いておいたのに財布がなくなりました。
Koko ni oite oita no ni saifu ga nakunarimashita.
I placed it here, but my wallet disappeared (became nonexistent).

うっかりしていて財布をなくしました。
Ukkari shite ite saifu o nakushimashita.
I was absent-minded and lost my wallet (made it nonexistent).

Note that **naku-suru** is also treated as **nakus-u**, a consonant verb.

4.10. Particle も *mo*

The particle **mo** means 'even' or 'also.' After numbers it is sometimes equivalent to 'as little as' or 'as much as.' When there are two phrases in a row, each ending in **mo**, the translation is 'both... and..' if the predicate is affirmative and '(n)either... (n)or..' if the predicate is negative.

今日も雨ですね。
Kyō mo ame desu ne.
Today is also a rainy day. (It is raining again today.)

簡単な漢字も書けなくなってしまいました。
Kantan na kanji mo kakenaku natte shimaimashita.
I became unable to write even easy kanji characters.

お酒は一杯も飲めません。
Osake wa ippai mo nomemasen.
I cannot drink even a glass of sake.

靴を5足も買ったんですか。
Kutsu o go-soku mo katta n desu ka.
You bought as many as five pairs of shoes?

ビールもワインも好きです。
Bīru mo wain mo suki desu.
I like both beer and wine.

ビールもワインもウイスキーも好きです。
Bīru mo wain mo uisukī mo suki desu.
I like beer, wine, and whiskey.

ビールもワインも好きじゃありません。
Bīru mo wain mo suki ja arimasen.
I don't like either beer or wine.

4.11. Expressing the time of the event 'when ...' (…と *...to,* …時 *...toki,* …間 *...aida*)

The particle **to** occurs after the plain imperfect with the meaning 'when, whenever, if.' Another way to say 'when,' with reference to some specific time, is to use either the imperfect (with present meaning) or the perfect (with past meaning) and follow this with the noun **toki** 'time.' If you mean 'during the interval of ...,' you can use the word **aida** 'interval' preceded by either the imperfect or the perfect (depending on the meaning) in the progressive form. **Aida** or **toki** can be followed by **wa, ni,** or **ni wa.**

窓の外を見ると雪が降っていた。
Mado no soto o miru to yuki ga futte ita.
When I looked outside through the window, it was snowing.

春になると花が咲く。
Haru ni naru to hana ga saku.
When it is spring, flowers blossom.

忙しいとあまり食べませんが，暇だとつい食べ過ぎてしまいます。
Isogashii to amari tabemasenga, hima da to tsui tabe-sugite shimaimasu.
If I'm busy, I don't eat much, but if I'm doing nothing, I tend to overeat before I know it.

道をわたる時には右と左をよく見てください。
Michi o wataru toki ni wa migi to hidari o yoku mite kudasai.
When crossing a street, look to your right and left carefully.

電車の中で変な荷物を見た時はすぐに車掌に言ってください。
Densha no naka de hen na nimotsu o mita toki wa sugu ni shashō ni itte kudasai.
When you see a strange package in a train, please let the conductor know as soon as possible.

小さい時から泳ぎは得意でした。
Chīsai toki kara oyogi wa tokui deshita.
I've been good at swimming since I was little.

洗濯をしている間に掃除もします。
Sentaku o shite iru aida ni sōji mo shimasu.
While doing laundry, I also clean.

冬の間は何もしません。
Fuyu no aida wa nani mo shimasen.
I don't do anything during the winter.

4.12. Particle から *kara* meaning 'since' and 'because'

The particle **kara** after a noun usually means 'from' in a physical sense: **Kobe kara** 'from Kobe.' From this it is extended to mean 'from' or 'after' or 'since' in a temporal sense: **kinō kara** 'from yesterday, since yesterday,' **sore kara** 'from that, after that,' **Nihon e kita toki kara** 'from the time I came to Japan, since I came to Japan.' After a GERUND also, it has the meaning of 'after':

ご飯を食べてから，テレビを見ました。
Gohan o tabete kara, terebi o mimashita.
After eating, we watched TV.

However, after the plain imperfect or perfect, this particle means 'since' in the causal sense of 'because':

雨が降ったから，行けませんでした。
Ame ga futta kara, ikemasendeshita.
Because it rained, I could not go there.

You will find it convenient to translate this **kara** as 'so,' since the word *so* fits into English syntax at about the same point that **kara** fits into Japanese syntax. The main difference is that we often pause BEFORE *so*, but the Japanese pause AFTER **kara**. The above Japanese sentence is repeated here with an English translation with *so*:

雨が降ったから，行けませんでした。
Ame ga futta kara, ikemasendeshita.
It rained, so I could not go there.

In English, we say things like 'I HAVE BEEN ill since last night. I've BEEN in Japan since last year,' using a present perfect even though we are still ill or in Japan at the time we are talking. In Japanese, the imperfect is used for these situations: **Sakuban kara byoki desu. Kyonen kara Nihon ni imasu.** Here are some examples of the uses of **kara** in a variety of contexts, in conjunction with gerund, perfect, and imperfect forms of verbs, adjectives, and the copula:

昨日気温が急激に下がってから池の水が凍ってしまいました。
Kinō kion ga kyūgeki ni sagatte kara ike no mizu ga kōtte shimaimashita.
As soon as the temperature dropped drastically, the pond froze.

お父さんが帰ったからゲームは隠した方がいいよ。
Otōsan ga kaetta kara gēmu wa kakushita hō ga ii yo.
As your dad has gotten home, it is better to hide the game.

今日は寒いから厚いジャケットを着た方がいいですよ。
Kyō wa samui kara atsui jaketto o kita hō ga ii desu yo.
It is cold today, so it is better to wear a thick jacket.

雪が降ったから学校が休校になった。
Yuki ga futta kara gakkō ga kyūkō ni natta.
As it snowed, the school was closed.

梅雨だから、雨がよく降る。
Tsuyu da kara, ame ga yoku furu.
Because it is rainy season, it rains a lot.

4.13. Multiple particles

Sometimes a word is followed by more than one particle. In such cases, the meaning of the last particle restricts the meaning of the entire phrase leading up to it. For example, in the phrase **Nihon de wa**, the particle **wa** sets off **Nihon de** 'in Japan' as the topic. In **koko ni mo arimasu** 'there's some here too,' the particle **mo** gives a special 'also' meaning to the phrase **koko ni** 'in this place.' In **Tokyo kara no densha** 'the train from Tokyo,' the particle **no** makes the entire phrase modify **densha** (what kind of a **densha**? the sort about which you can say **Tōkyō kara**).

Particles that occur after other particles are usually only the topic particle **wa**, the subject particle **ga**, the object particle **o**, and the intensive particle **mo**; these particles have somewhat more general meanings than those of **to** 'with,' **ni** 'at, to,' **e** 'to,' **de** 'at' **made** 'till,' **kara** 'from,' etc. The particles **wa**, **ga**, **o**, and **mo** never occur in sequences with each other—their meanings are mutually exclusive.

> 田中さんとは最近話していません。山田さんともあまり話していません。
> **Tanaka-san to wa saikin hanashite imasen. Yamada-san to mo amari hanashite imasen.**
> I haven't talked with Mr. Tanaka lately. I haven't talked with Mr. Yamada much, either.

> 居酒屋にはよく行きます。カラオケボックスにもよく行きます。
> **Izakaya ni wa yoku ikimasu. Karaoke bokkusu ni mo yoku ikimasu.**
> We often go to an *izakaya* bar very often. We also often go to a karaoke box, too.

> １２課からが難しいんです。12課からをよく勉強してください。
> **Jūni-ka kara ga muzukashii n desu. Jūni-ka kara o yoku benkyō shite kudasai.**
> Lesson 12 and the rest are the difficult parts. Please study Lesson 12 and after carefully.

4.14. こと *koto*

The word **koto** means 'thing (that you can't touch or see)'; there is another word **mono** that usually means 'thing (that you can touch or see).' **Mono** is also a humble word for 'person' (= **hito**); a vulgar synonym (in both meanings) is **yatsu**. (**Kono yatsu**, **sono yatsu**, **ano yatsu**, and **dono yatsu** are usually abbreviated to **koitsu**, **soitsu**, **aitsu**, and **doitsu**, respectively.)

Sometimes the word **koto** means 'act' or 'fact.' In this lesson there are two special expressions with **koto**: **(iku) koto ga arimasu** 'there exists the fact of (my going) = (I) sometimes (go)' and **(itta) koto ga arimasu** 'there exists the fact of my having (gone) = I have (gone), I once (went).' Note that the difference in meaning between these two expressions is carried by the mood of the verb in front of

koto: the perfect (**itta**) is used with the meaning 'once did, ever did' (negative 'never did'); the imperfect (**iku**) is used with the meaning 'sometimes does' (negative 'never does'). If you want to put either expression entirely in the perfect, you change the mood of the verb **arimasu**: **iku koto ga arimashita** 'there existed the fact of my going = I sometimes went,' **itta koto ga arimashita** 'there existed the fact of my having gone = I had once gone.'

The relationship between the plain forms of the verb (**iku** and **itta**) and the word **koto** is that of modifier to modified, with the meaning 'which (does or is).' That is, a **koto** WHICH **iku** or **itta**, a **koto** ABOUT WHICH YOU CAN SAY **iku** or **itta**. The plain inflected forms in Japanese can modify a noun (like **koto**) directly, without any particle. Nouns, on the other hand, have to be followed by the particle **no** (or a modifying form of the copula **na** or **no**, see 5. 3) to modify another noun. The modifier relationship is further discussed in 5. 1. More examples of expressions with **koto**:

「その本を読んだことがありますか。」
"Sono hon o yonda koto ga arimasu ka.
"Have you (ever) read that book?"

「いいえ, ありません。」
"Īe, arimasen."
"No, I haven't."

シカゴには行ったことがありません。去年まではニューヨークにも行ったことがありませんでした。
Shikago ni wa itta koto ga arimasen. Kyonen made wa Nyū Yōku ni mo itta koto ga arimasen deshita.
I haven't been to Chicago yet. Until last year I had never even been to New York.

「あの人の声が嫌だと思うことはありませんか。」
"Ano hito no koe ga iya da to omou koto wa arimasen ka."
"Don't you sometimes (ever) dislike his voice?"

「時々ありますね。」
"Tokidoki arimasu ne."
"I sometimes do."

ここでは冬はあまり寒くありませんが, 雪が降ることもあります。
Koko de wa fuyu wa amari samuku arimasenga, yuki ga furu koto mo arimasu.
The winter is mild here, but it occasionally snows.

アメリカでは日本のテレビを見ることはありません。
Amerika de wa Nihon no terebi o miru koto wa arimasen.
In America we never have the chance to watch Japanese TV programs.

Another use of the noun **koto** is in the phrases **koto ga suki desu** 'likes to' and **koto ga kirai desu** 'dislikes to.' The basic meaning of these phrases, preceded always by a plain imperfect form, is 'the fact (of doing something) is liked' and 'the fact (of doing something) is disliked.' Here are some additional examples of these phrases:

人の悪口を言うことが好きなんですか。
Hito no warukuchi o iu koto ga suki na n desu ka.
Do you like to speak ill of others behind their back?

人の名前を覚えることが苦手です。
Hito no namae o oboeru koto ga nigate desu.
I'm not good at remembering people's names.

A further use of **koto** is in the phrase **koto ga dekimasu** 'can (do something), is able to.' The basic meaning of this expression is something like 'the fact (of doing something) is produced,' but it is the usual way to say 'can.' If the verb is **suru**, the whole phrase is often abbreviated to **dekiru**: **benkyō (suru koto ga) dekiru** 'can study,' **yasuku (suru koto ga) dekiru** 'can make it cheaper.' This is not the expression used to translate the English 'can' that is used for 'may' in the sense of permission, as in 'Father says I can go.' That expression is translated by a special phrase discussed in note 8.6. Instead of PLAIN IMPERFECT + **koto ga dekimasu**, sometimes you will hear a noun derived from the infinitive + **ga dekimasu**; the meaning then is something more specific like 'knows how to' rather than the general meaning 'is able to' (which includes the specific meaning).

まだ泳ぐことができません。妹もまだ泳ぎができません。
Mada oyogu koto ga dekimasen. Imōto mo mada oyogi ga dekimasen.
I still cannot swim. My little sister cannot swim either.

まだ車を運転することができません。兄もまだ車の運転ができません。
Mada kuruma o unten suru koto ga dekimasen. Ani mo mada kuruma no unten ga dekimasen.
I still cannot drive a car. My big brother cannot do so either.

もう少し早く印刷することができませんか。
Mō sukoshi hayaku insatsu suru koto ga dekimasen ka.
Could you print them a bit earlier?

安くできませんか。
Yasuku dekimasen ka.
Can you make it cheaper?

4.15. つもり *tsumori*

Tsumori is a noun with the meaning 'intention.' Preceded by the plain imperfect (like **suru** 'does') and followed by some form of the copula (like **desu** 'is'), this noun makes a phrase with the meaning 'it is (someone's) intention to (do something) = someone plans to do something.'

明日天気がよければ庭掃除をするつもりです。
Asu tenki ga yokereba niwa-sōji o suru tsumori desu.
If the weather is good, I plan to clean my garden tomorrow.

いつになったら片付けるつもりですか。
Itsu ni nattara katazukeru tsumori desu ka.
When do you intend to put (them) away?

If you want to change the tense of the expression 'it WAS somebody's intention to do something, someone planned to do something,' you just change the mood of the copula: **suru tsumori deshita**.

昨日は勉強するつもりでしたけれども、天気がよかったので友達と公園に行きました。
Kinō wa benkyō suru tsumori deshita keredomo, tenki ga yokatta node tomodachi to kōen ni ikimashita.
I had intended to study yesterday, but the weather was nice, so I went to the park with my friends.

However, sometimes you will hear **shita tsumori desu** 'it is my intention to have (done)' 'I have tried to':

きれいに書いたつもりです。
Kirei ni kaita tsumori desu.
I have tried to write neatly.

4.16. More adverbs

You have seen some nouns used without particles to modify predicates or whole sentences in 3.2. Here are some more adverbs you will want to know, some of which cannot function as nouns:

少し **sukoshi**	a little, some, a bit
ちょっと **chotto**	a little, some, a bit
毎晩 **maiban**	every evening
毎朝 **maiasa**	every morning
最近 **saikin**	lately
たくさん **takusan**	lots
大変 **taihen**	very (*lit.*, awfully, terribly)
たいてい **taitei**	usually
普通 **futsū**	usually
時々 **tokidoki**	sometimes
度々 **tabitabi**	often
だんだん **dandan**	gradually
なかなか **nakanaka**	quite, rather, completely, at all
随分 **zuibun**	very (much)
とても **totemo**	completely, quite
相当 **sōtō**	rather, considerably
大分 **daibu**	mostly, for the most part
結構 **kekkō**	quite

父は朝はたいていごはんを食べますが, 時々パンを食べます。
Chichi wa asa wa taitei gohan o tabemasu ga, tokidoki pan o tabemasu.
My father usually eats rice in the morning, but he sometimes eats bread.

大変お世話になりました。
Taihen o-sewa ni narimashita.
You have helped me a lot.

漢字がなかなか書けませんでしたが, 最近書けるようになりました。
Kanji ga nakanaka kakemasen deshita ga, saikin kakeru yō ni narimashita.
I could not write kanji very easily, but I recently learned to write them.

随分上手に話せるようになりましたね。単語も相当知っているようだし。
Zuibun jōzu ni hanaseru yō ni narimashita ne. Tango mo sōtō shitte iru yō da shi.
You have learned to speak quite well, haven't you? You seem to know a lot of vocabulary.

度々申し訳ありませんが, ちょっと質問がありまして。
Tabitabi mōshiwake arimasen ga, chotto shitsumon ga arimashite.
I'm sorry to keep bothering you, but I have some questions.

普通はとても優しくていい人なのですが，怒ると結構わがままなことを
言います。

Futsū wa totemo yasashikute ii hito na no desu ga, okoru to kekkō wag-amama na koto o iimasu.

Normally, he is a kind and nice person, but once he gets angry, he says quite
selfish things.

4.17. More gerund expressions

The verbs **motsu** 'holds, has, owns' and **toru** 'picks up, takes' are used in several
expressions meaning 'brings, takes, carries (things)': **motte iku** 'holds and goes =
takes'; **totte iku** 'picks up and goes, carries (off)'; **motte kuru** 'holds and comes
= brings'; **totte kuru** 'picks up and comes, carries (over).' Remember, to take or
bring PEOPLE requires the verb **tsureru**, as in **hito o tsurete kuru** 'brings someone (else),' and it is generally used only when the person being brought is socially
inferior to the one bringing. Here are some more examples:

今日は雨がふりそうだから傘を持っていった方がいいよ。

Kyō wa ame ga furi sō da kara kasa o motte itta hō ga ii yo.

It looks like rain today, so it's better to bring an umbrella.

隣の息子は夜中に友達をたくさんうちに連れて来て大騒ぎをする。

**Tonari no musuko wa yonaka ni tomodachi o takusan uchi ni tsurete kite
ōsawagi o suru.**

My next-door neighbor's son brings many of his friends to his home and make
a big noise at night.

あ，お箸をわすれた。ちょっと持って来て。

A, ohashi o wasureta. Chotto motte kite.

Oh, I forgot chopsticks. Could you bring them?

In English, when someone goes on an errand and returns, we mention his GO-
ING and DOING THE ERRAND; we usually skip saying he came back: 'He went
and got his laundry.' 'He went and met Taro (and came back).' 'I'm going to go fix
the car.' 'Let's go buy that book.' The Japanese usually skip the part about going,
and mention DOING THE ERRAND and COMING back:

あの部屋が空いているか見て来ましょうか。

Ano heya ga aite iru ka mite kimashō ka.

Shall I go and see whether that room is unused.

悪いけど牛乳買って来てくれない？

Warui kedo gyūnyū katte kite kurenai?

Could you go and buy milk?

4.18. Gerund (*te*-form) + いる *iru*

In Lesson 2, we found that the verb **iru (imasu)** means 'stays, (a living being) exists (in a place)':

私は日本にいます。 **Watashi wa Nihon ni imasu.** I am in Japan.

In Lesson 3, we found that a gerund (**te**-form) plus the verb **iru** means '(somebody or something) is doing something':

「今お母さんは何をしているの。」
"Ima okāsan wa nani o shite iru no?"
"What is your mother doing now?"

「隣のおばさんとしゃべっているよ。」
"Tonari no obāsan to shabette iru yo."
"She is chatting with the lady in the next-door."

With intransitive verbs—those that do not ordinarily take a direct object, like 'goes, comes, gets tired, gets cloudy, clears up, becomes,' there is another meaning for GERUND + **iru**. With intransitive verbs denoting a single, specific act, like 'gets to be something, becomes, goes, comes, changes (into),' the most usual meaning of this construction is the present RESULT of an action that has ALREADY taken place. So **tsukarete imasu** usually doesn't mean 'is getting tired,' but more often it means just 'is tired' (is in a state resulting from having become tired). The idea is that you got tired and then exist.

今疲れていますから後にしてください。
Ima tsukarete imasu kara ato ni shite kudasai.
I'm tired now, so could we talk about it later?

兄はもう結婚しています。
Ani wa mō kekkon shite imasu.
My big brother is already married.

子どもはもう寝ています。
Kodomo wa mō nete imasu.
The children are already asleep.

父は出張で今仙台に行っています。
Chichi wa shutchō de ima Sendai ni itte imasu.
My father has gone to Sendai for a business trip.

林さんは大阪に住んでいます。
Hayashi-san wa Ōsaka ni sunde imasu.
Mr. Hayashi lives in Osaka.

マイクさんはまだ来ていませんよ。
Maiku-san wa mada kite imasen yo.
Mike has not come yet.

Remember that with the construction GERUND + **iru**, the subject can be either a living being or an inanimate object. With **iru** all by itself, the subject is ordinarily limited to a living being. Here are more examples.

ご飯はもうできています。
Gohan wa mō dekite imasu.
The meal is already ready.

空が晴れていますね。
Sora ga harete imasu ne.
The sky is clear, isn't it?

今日は曇っていますね。
Kyō wa kumotte imasu ne.
It's cloudy today.

霧がかかっています。
Kiri ga kakatte imasu.
It's foggy.

雷がなっています。
Kaminari ga natte imasu.
It is thundering.

絵がかかっています。
E ga kakatte imasu.
A picture is hung.

However, with an inanimate object, GERUND + **iru** is possible only if the verb is an intransitive verb. If it is transitive, the construction GERUND + **aru** is used instead of GERUND + **iru**.

絵がかけてあります。
E ga kakete arimasu.
A picture is hung.

4.19. 遊ぶ *asobu*

The verb asobu means 'enjoys oneself.' It is used for English 'plays, has fun, goes on a pleasure trip, pays a (social) call, visits (for pleasure),' and other expressions. Here are some examples:

去年北海道に遊びに行きました。
Kyonen Hokkaidō ni asobi ni ikimahsita.
Last year I went to Hokkaidō.

子どもが公園で遊んでいます。
Kodomo ga kōen de asonde imasu.
The children are playing at the park.

今晩遊びに来ませんか。
Konban asobi ni kimasen ka.
Won't you come to visit (us) this evening?

 **Conversation**

[cue 04-3]

Alison (A) is talking with Makoto (M) at her house.

A. ここのところ毎日雨ですね。 **Koko no tokoro mainichi ame desu ne.**
It has been raining every day lately.

M. ええ。日本では６月は梅雨ですから６月になると雨がよく降るんです。
Ē. Nihon de wa rokugatsu wa tsuyu desu kara rokugatsu ni naru to ame ga yoku furu n desu.
Right. June is a rainy season in Japan, so it rains very often in June.

A. ああ, そうですか。 **Ā, sō desu ka.** Oh, really.

M. 毎日雨なんて嫌ですよね。 **Mainichi ame nante iya desu yo ne.**
It's so annoying when it rains every day, don't you think?

A. そうですか。私は雨が好きなんです。
Sō desu ka. Watashi wa ame ga suki na n desu.
Really? I love rain.

M.   え？ちょっと変わっていますね。 **E? Chotto kawatte imasu ne.**
What? You are weird.

A.   大雨や雷は嫌いですが，しとしと雨が降るのは好きなんです。
**Ōame ya kaminari wa kirai desu ga shitoshito ame ga furu no wa suki na
n desu.**
I hate heavy rain, thunder, and so on, but I love quiet rain.

M.   どうしてですか。 **Dō shite desu ka.** Why?

A.   何か心が落ち着いて部屋の中で仕事がよくできるんです。
Nani ka kokoro ga ochitsuite heya no naka de shigoto ga yoku dekiru n desu.
I somehow feel calm and can work in the room better.

M.   ああ，確かに。天気がいいと家やオフィスにいるのが嫌になりますからね。
Ā, tashika ni. Tenki ga ii to ie ya ofisu ni iru no ga iya ni narimasu kara ne.
Oh, that's right. If the weather is good, we don't feel like staying at home or at the office, that's why.

Exercises

I. Match the illustrations and phrases:

Example: <u>さむいです</u>
samui desu

1. _____ です
   _____ **desu**

2. _____ です
   _____ **desu**

3. _____ です
   _____ **desu**

II. Fill in the blanks with properly inflected forms of the verbs and adjectives.

1. 何を＿＿＿＿＿＿＿＿いますか。
   Nani o＿＿＿＿＿＿＿＿imasu ka.
   What are you EATING?

2. 日本の映画を＿＿＿＿＿＿＿＿ことがありますか。
   Nihon no eiga o＿＿＿＿＿＿＿＿koto ga arimasu ka.
   Have you ever SEEN a Japanese film?

3. そこで＿＿＿＿＿＿＿＿ことがありますか。
   Soko de＿＿＿＿＿＿＿＿koto ga arimasen ka.
   Do you SWIM there?

4. 駅で横田さんに＿＿＿＿＿＿＿＿つもりでした。
   Eki de Yokota-san ni＿＿＿＿＿＿＿＿tsumori deshita.
   I intended to MEET Miss Yokota at the train station.

5. 雪が＿＿＿＿＿＿＿＿からバスが遅れました。
   Yuki ga ＿＿＿＿＿＿＿＿ kara basu ga okuremashita.
   Because it SNOWED, the bus was delayed.

6. 地下鉄に＿＿＿＿＿＿＿＿来ました。
   Chikatetsu ni ＿＿＿＿＿＿＿＿ kimashita.
   I came here by (TAKING THE) subway.

7. お酒を＿＿＿＿＿＿＿＿に行ってきます。
   Osake o ＿＿＿＿＿＿＿＿ ni itte imasu.
   I'll go to BUY some liquor.

8. あまり早く＿＿＿＿＿＿＿＿と疲れますよ。
   Ammari hayaku ＿＿＿＿＿＿＿＿ to tsukaremasu yo.
   If you WALK too fast, you get tired.

9. 暇＿＿＿＿＿＿＿＿と，ついテレビを見てしまいます。
   Hima ＿＿＿＿＿＿＿＿ to, tsui terebi o mite shimaimasu.
   When I AM at leisure, I tend to WATCH TV too much.

10. アメリカに＿＿＿＿＿＿＿＿ときも日本語を話しました。
    Amerika ni ＿＿＿＿＿＿＿＿ toki mo Nihongo o hanashimashita.
    Even when I LIVED in America, I spoke Japanese.

11. 姉はもう結婚＿＿＿＿＿＿＿＿ います。
    Ane wa mō kekkon ＿＿＿＿＿＿＿＿ imasu.
    My sister is married.

12. 松本さんはまだ＿＿＿＿＿＿＿＿いませんか。
    Matsumoto-san wa mada ＿＿＿＿＿＿＿＿imasen ka.
    Hasn't Mr. Matsumoto COME yet?

III. Explain the difference between the two sentences in each set.

1. a. 父は東京へ行きます。**Chichi wa Tōkyō e ikimasu.**
   b. 父は東京へ行っています。**Chichi waTōkyō e itte imasu.**

2. a. 晩ご飯を食べてうちに帰ります。**Bangohan o tabete uchi ni kaerimasu.**
   b. 晩ご飯を食べにうちに帰ります。**Bangohan o tabe ni uchi ni kaeri masu.**

3. a. 香港に行くことがあります。**Honkon ni iku koto ga arimasu.**
   b. 香港に行ったことがあります。**Honkon ni itta koto ga arimasu.**

4. a. きれいに書くつもりでした。**Kirei ni kaku tsumori deshita.**
   b. きれいに書いたつもりです。**Kirei ni kaita tsumori desu.**

5. a. カメラを壊しました。**Kamera o kowashimashita.**
   b. カメラが壊れました。**Kamera ga kowaremashita.**

Answers:
I 1. あたたかい **atatakai** 2. あつい **atsui** 3. すずしい **suzushii**
II 1. 食べて **tabete** 2. 見た **mita** 3. 泳ぐ **oyogu** 4. 会う **au** 5. 降った **futta** 6. 乗って **notte**
7. 買い **kai** 8. 歩く **aruku** 9. だ **da** 10. 住んでいた **sunde ita** 11. して **shite** 12. 来て **kite**
III 1. a. My father will go to Tokyo. b. My father has gone to Tokyo. 2. a. I'll eat dinner here, and then go home. b. I'll go home to eat dinner. 3. a. I sometimes go to Hong Kong. b. I have been to Hong Kong. 4. a. I intended to write neatly. b. I think I wrote neatly. 5. a. I broke the camera. b. The camera broke down.

Because It's for Business
これはビジネスだから
Kore wa Bizinesu Dakara

In this lesson, you will learn words and phrases useful in a business context in Japan. You will also learn a variety of clauses that can be used as a modifier for a noun or a modifier for the main sentence.

Basic Sentences

[cue 05-1]

1.	あそこに立っている人はパートの山本さんです。 **Asoko ni tatte iru hito wa pāto no Yamamoto-san desu.**	The person who is standing over there is Ms. Yamamoto, a part-time employee.
2.	昨日ここへ来たのはだれですか。 **Kinō koko e kita no wa dare desu ka.**	Who is the one who came here yesterday?
3.	コストの高いハードウエアは作れません。 **Kosuto no takai hādouea wa tsuku-remasen.**	We cannot manufacture high-cost hardware.

4. エクセルを使う<u>の</u>が上手な人を探しています。
Ekuseru o tsukau <u>no</u> ga jōzu na hito o sagashite imasu.

I'm looking for someone who is skilled at using Excel.

5. 英語の<u>できる</u>社員は３人います。
Eigo no <u>dekiru</u> shain wa san-nin imasu.

We have three employees who can speak English.

6. 「あの人は<u>知って</u>いますか。」
"Ano hito wa <u>shitte imasu</u> ka."

"Do you know that person?"

「ちょっと<u>分かりません</u>。」
"Chotto <u>wakarimasen</u>."

"I don't know her."

7. あそこの会社の株は高くなる<u>でしょう</u>。
Asoko no kaisha no kabu wa takaku naru <u>deshō</u>.

The stock value of that company will probably go up.

8. 円高な<u>ので</u>アメリカで買った方がいいですよ。
Endaka na <u>no de</u> Amerika de katta hō ga ii desu yo.

The (Japanese) yen is strong, so it's better to buy it in the U.S.

9. 病気な<u>のに</u>出勤するんですか。
Byōki na <u>no ni</u> shukkin suru n desu ka.

Are you going to work although you are sick?

10. 店で売ら<u>ないで</u>ネットで売るんですか。
Mise de ura<u>nai de</u> netto de uru n desu ka.

Instead of selling them at the store, are we selling them online?

11. 朝ごはんを食べ<u>ないで</u>出勤するんですか。
Asagohan o tabe<u>nai de</u> shukkin suru n desu ka.

Are you going to go to work without eating breakfast?

12. 確認<u>せずに</u>メールを送ってしまいました。
Kakunin <u>sezu ni</u> mēru o okutte shimaimashita.

I sent the email without checking it.

13. ブラウンさんは午後1時に成田に着く<u>はずです</u>。
Buraun-san wa gogo ichi-ji ni Narita ni tsuku <u>hazu desu</u>.

Mr. Brown is supposed to arrive at Narita at 1 p.m.

14. 外国語は若い<u>うち</u>に習った方がいいですよ。 **Gaikokugo wa wakai <u>uchi</u> ni naratta hō ga ii desu yo.**	It's better to learn a foreign language while you are young.
15. この会社に勤める<u>前</u>は何をしていましたか。 **Kono kaisha ni tsutomeru <u>mae</u> wa nani o shite imashita ka.**	What were you doing before you started to work for this company?
16.「仕事が終わった<u>後</u>でちょっといいですか。」 **"Shigoto ga owatta <u>ato</u> de chotto ii desu ka."**	"Do you have a minute after you are done with your work?"
「ええ。今終わった<u>ところ</u>です。」 **"Ē. Ima owatta <u>tokoro</u> desu."**	"Sure. I've just finished."
17. 昨日は遅く<u>まで</u>仕事をしました。 **Kinō wa osoku <u>made</u> shigoto o shimashita.**	I worked until late yesterday.

CULTURE NOTE ▶ **Meishi (Business Cards)**

Japanese business people and professionals almost always exchange their business cards when they introduce themselves. A Japanese business card, called **meishi** in Japanese, can be either horizontal or vertical and includes one's affiliation, title, and contact information. It is very important to handle a business card very respectfully

株式会社　ABC貿易

取締役部長　山田　太郎

110-0011
東京都台東区松井町三丁目三番
TEL: (03)3835-1111
FAX: (03)3835-1234
Mobile: 000-0000-0000
yamada@ABC.co.jp

when you exchange cards. When presenting your business card to someone, hand it over so that it faces him/her. When receiving a business card from someone, use both hands to accept it and bow slightly. Read the information on it carefully, and do not put it away right away. If you are sitting, leave it on the table in front of you while you are talking with the person.

Basic Vocabulary
[cue 05-2]

BUSINESS INSTITUTIONS

会社 **kaisha**	company, firm
店 **mise**	store
事務所 **jimusho**	office
給料 **kyūryō**	salary
時給 **jikyū**	hourly pay
ボーナス **bōnasu**	bonus

PEOPLE

社員 **shain**	staff, company, employee
正社員 **seishain**	full-time employee
派遣社員 **haken shain**	an employee sent from a temporary personnel service
パート **pāto**	part-time job (mostly for housewives)
バイト **baito**	part-time job (mostly for students and young people)
OL **ōeru**	female office workers (office lady)
上司 **jōshi**	boss
マネージャー **manējā**	manager
アシスタント **ashisutanto**	assistant
社長 **shachō**	company president
秘書 **hisho**	secretary

FUNCTIONS

会計士 **kaikeishi**	accountant
プログラマー **puroguramā**	programmer
コンサルタント **konsarutanto**	consultant
アントレプレナー（起業家）**antorepurenā (kigyōka)**	entrepreneur
営業 **eigyō**	sales
生産 **seisan**	production
マーケティング **māketingu**	marketing
プロモーション **puromōshon**	promotion
広告 **kōkoku**	advertisement
輸出 **yushutsu**	export
輸入 **yunyū**	import

DOCUMENTS AND FILES

請求書 **seikyūsho**	invoice
領収書 **ryōshūsho**	receipt
パワーポイント **pawāpointo**	Power Point
エクセル **ekuseru**	Excel
書類 or 文書 **shorui** or **bunsho**	document
ファイル **fairu**	file

ACTIONS

いる・いります **iru/irimasu**	is needed, wanted
借りる・借ります **kariru/karimasu**	borrows
貸す・貸します **kasu/kashimasu**	lends
見つける・見つけます **mitsukeru/mitsukemasu**	finds
探す・探します **sagasu/sagashimasu**	searches
調べる・調べます **shiraberu/shirabemasu**	checks up on
使う・使います **tsukau/tsukaimasu**	uses
作る・作ります **tsukuru/tsukurimasu**	makes, manufactures
売る・売ります **uru/urimasu**	sells
忘れる・忘れます **wasureru/wasuremasu**	forgets
やめる・やめます **yameru/yamemasu**	resigns, ceases it, gives up (doing something)
雇う・雇います **yatou/yatoimasu**	employs
分析する・分析します **bunseki suru / bunseki shimasu**	analyzes
生産する・生産します **seisan suru / seisan shimasu**	produces

ADJECTIVES & ADJECTIVAL NOUNS

多い **ōi**	is much, are many
少ない **sukunai**	is little, are few
忙しい **isogashii**	is busy
暇(だ) **hima (da)**	(is) free, not busy

BUSINESS TRIP

新幹線 **shinkansen**	bullet train
ホテル **hoteru**	hotel
ビジネスホテル **bizinesu hoteru**	business hotel
カプセルホテル **kapuseru hoteru**	capsule hotel

POLITE PHRASES AT THE OFFICE

いつもお世話になっております。 **Itsumo o-sewa ni natte orimasu.**	Thank you for your kindness always./ Thank you for your continued patronage.
外出中でございます。 **Gaishutsu-chū de gozaimasu.**	(He) is out now.
会議中でございます。 **Kaigi-chū de gozaimasu.**	(He) is at the meeting now.
電話中でございます。 **Denwa-chū de gozaimasu.**	(He) is on the phone now.
宜しくお願いいたします。 **Yoroshiku o-negai itashimasu.**	Thank you in advance. (*lit.*, Please take care of my matter favorably.)
お先に。 **O-saki ni.**	Sorry, but I have to get going. Bye. (*lit.*, Ahead.)
お疲れ様。 **O-tsukare-sama.**	Thank you for your work./Good work today. (*lit.*, Your tiredness.)
ご苦労様。 **Go-kurō-sama.**	Thank you for your work. (*lit.*, Your efforts.)

Structure Notes

5.1. Modifiers

In English one noun can modify (restrict the meaning) of another noun just by standing next to it: 'Business Action Plan Objective; Supply Closet Restocking List.' In Japanese, when one noun modifies another, the two are usually connected by the particle **no**. In the case of book titles or names of organizations and institutions, frequently several nouns may be combined to make a COMPOUND NOUN:

基本日本語文法
Kihon-Nihongo-Bunpō
Basic Japanese Language Grammar

日本貿易株式会社
Nippon-Bōeki-Kabushiki-Gaisha
The Japan Trade Co., Inc.

But these are special cases. Ordinarily, modifying nouns are followed by **no**:

日本語の辞書 **Nihongo no jisho** a Japanese (language) dictionary

アメリカのビジネスマン **America no bijinesuman**   an American businessman

昨日の会議 **kinō no kaigi**   yesterday's meeting

私のパソコン **watashi no pasokon**   my PC

大阪の工場 **Ōsaka no kōjō**   the Osaka factory; factories in Osaka

The last noun is often dropped if it is not a person and is understood in the context, as below:

これは日本語の辞書です。あれは中国語のです。
Kore wa Nihongo no jisho desu. Are wa Chūgokugo no desu.
This is a Japanese dictionary. That one is a Chinese one.

Now, in English when a verb or verb phrase modifies a noun, it FOLLOWS the noun and is introduced by a word like *who, which, that,* and *when,* as in 'the man who came yesterday; the book, which is on the table; the movie that I saw; that time when we were in Osaka.' Notice that sometimes the introductory word may be omitted in English: 'the movie I saw, that time we went to Osaka.' Japanese verbs and verb phrases "precede" the noun they modify and have no introductory word or linking particle:

昨日ここへ来た人
kinō koko e kita hito
the man who came here yesterday

机の上にある書類
tsukue no ue ni aru shorui
the documents that are placed on the desk

去年行ったところ
kyonen itta tokoro
the place I went last year

大阪にいた時
Ōsaka ni ita toki
the time we were in Osaka

You have already had expressions like:

行くつもり **iku tsumori**   intention of going

すること **suru koto**   the fact of doing (something) (the act of doing something; doing something)

行ったこと **itta koto**　　　the fact of having gone (the occasion for me to be there)

These are examples of modifier expressions.

The modifying expression preceding a noun phrase may be very short, or it may be quite long. It will always make a complete sentence by itself except that the predicate part is in the plain form, and you would want to change this to the polite form to use as a complete sentence. Notice that the meaning of the juxtaposition between the modifying verb and the noun may be either that of a "subject" or an "object" relationship:

見た人 **mita hito**　　　the man who saw (it)
見た人 **mita hito**　　　the man whom (someone) saw

The relationship is usually made clear by the particles in the rest of the clause:

その映画を見た人 **sono eiga o mita hito**　　　the man who saw that movie
私が見た人 **watakushi ga mita hito**　　　the man I saw

The subject of a modifying clause is never followed by **wa**—that would make it the topic for the entire sentence, not just the modifying clause. It is marked either by **ga** (emphatic) or by **no** (non-emphatic). If you like, you may think of **no** as replacing the particle **wa** in modifying clauses:

あの人はその映画を見ました。
Ano hito wa sono eiga o mimashita.
He saw THAT MOVIE.

あの人の見た映画はそれです。
Ano hito no mita eiga wa sore desu.
THE MOVIE (that) he saw is that one.

あの人がその映画を見ました。
Ano hito ga sono ega omimashita.
HE saw that movie.

あの人が見た映画はそれです。
Ano hito ga mita eiga wa sore desu.
The movie (that) HE saw is that one.

In other words, only sentences have topics; clauses have subjects (or objects). The particle used for the non-emphatic subject of a clause is **no**; the particle used for the emphatic subject is **ga**. If the modifying clause is quite long and the subject is separated from the verb by a number of words, the emphatic subject particle **ga** is usually used.

> 私の行ったゴルフ場は安いところです。
> **Watashi no itta gorufujō wa yasui tokoro desu.**
> The golf course I went to is an inexpensive place.

> 私が加藤部長と先週行ったゴルフ場は結構よかったです。
> **Watashi ga Katō buchō to senshū itta gorufujō wa kekkō yokatta desu.**
> The golf course where I went with Mr. Kato, the division manager, last week was quite good.

When you hear long modifier clauses in actual conversation, you may be confused as to the breaking point where the modifier stops and the part modified begins. Listen for the "plain" imperfect and perfect forms, forms like **suru**, **shita**; **iku**, **itta**; **kuru**, **kita**; **taberu**, **tabeta**: unless followed by a particle like **keredomo** or **kara**, they probably modify the word or phrase that follows. At the breaking point, stick in a 'which,' and then make mental switch of the two parts around to the usual English order. This is just a first-aid measure, of course. After you get used to modifier clauses, you will be putting them in quite naturally like a Japanese, without worrying about the fact that in English you would reverse the order. Remember: everything up to the breaking point modifies the following noun expression. Notice the breaking points (indicated by a forward slash) in the following examples. But try to avoid pausing: the BREAKING POINT is in your head, not on your tongue.

> データ入力とプログラミングのできる / 方を募集しています。
> **Dēta nyūryoku to puroguramingu no dekiru / kata o boshū shite imasu.**
> We are looking for someone who can do data inputting and programming.

> 料理になれていない人が作った / 食べ物はあまり食べたくない。
> **Ryōri ni narete inai hito ga tsukutta / tabemono wa amari tabetaku nai.**
> I don't want to eat dishes prepared by someone who is not used to cooking.

5.2. Modifier clauses made with adjectives

Recall that the full meaning of real adjectives in Japanese is not just 'good, bad, white, red' and the like but 'IS good, IS bad, IS white, IS red' etc.:

いいから **ii kara**	because it's good
悪かったけれども **warukatta keredomo**	it was bad, but
白くていいから **shirokute ii kara**	it's nice and white, so…

Just as verbs can have a subject in Japanese, so can adjectives. And in modifier clauses, the particle that follows the subject is either **ga** (emphatic) or **no** (non-emphatic):

天候が悪いところ
tenkō ga warui tokoro
a place where the WEATHER'S bad

天候の悪いところ
tenkō no warui tokoro
a place where the weather's BAD

Here are some additional examples of adjectives in sentences:

プログラミングの経験のない人は採用しません。
Puroguramingu no keiken no nai hito wa saiyō shimasen.
We are not going to hire people who do not have experience programming.

店は人の多いところにある方がいいです。
Mise wa hito no ōi tokoro ni aru hō ga ii desu.
As for stores, it's better for them to be in a location (that is) heavily trafficked.

カプセル・ホテルは会社が多くて, 駅に近いところに沢山あります。
Kapuseru hoteru wa kaisha ga ōkute, eki ni chikai tokoro ni takusan arimasu.
Capsule hotels are located where there are lots of companies and close to a train station.

5.3. Modifier clauses made with a copula

Something special happens when a copula clause, like **sakka desu** 'he is a writer,' is used as a modifier clause. To mean 'my friend, who is a writer,' they do not say **sakka da tomodachi** but **sakka no tomodachi**. Now, this **no** is not the particle that shows that one noun modifies another—it isn't 'a writer's friend,' it is 'my friend, WHO IS a writer.' This **no** is a special form of the copula, an alternant, or the alternate form, of the word **da** that occurs whenever a copular clause is put in the modifier position before a noun phrase. You can see the difference between the particle **no** and the copula-alternant **no** (= **da**) here:

作家の友達 **sakka no tomodachi**　　　the writer's friend
作家の友達 **sakka no tomodachi**　　　the friend WHO IS a writer

Since the two expressions sound just alike, you have to tell from the context or situation which **no** it is you are hearing. Most of the time, there is little doubt. Here are additional examples:

母親が６０歳以上の学生は全体の３０％だった。
Hahaoya ga rokujus-sai ijō no gakusei wa zentai no sanjup-pāsento datta.
The students whose mothers are over sixty years old constituted 30 percent of entire student body.

うちの会社には出身が九州の男性が３人いる。
Uchi no kaisha ni wa shusshin ga Kyūshū no dansei ga san-nin iru.
There are three men whose birthplace is Kyushu in our company.

5.4. Modifier clauses made with adjectival nouns

In the previous section, you have seen that **no** is an alternant of **da**. However, **no** is not the only alternant of **da**. There is also an alternant **na** that occurs after adjectival nouns. Adjectival nouns are a special sort of nouns that do not often occur before particles like **wa**, **ga**, **o** but occur before some form of the copula (**desu**, **da**, **na**) or before the particle **ni**. When these adjectival noun clauses, like **kirei desu** 'is pretty,' occur in modifier position, the expected form **da** occurs in the alternant form of **na** as in:

きれいな女の人
kirei na onna no hito
women WHO ARE pretty, or pretty women

In citing nouns it is convenient to note the ones that are adjectival nouns by adding in parentheses (**na**). Here are some common ones:

バカ(な) **baka (na)**	fool, foolish
丈夫(な) **jōbu (na)**	strong, rough
綺麗(な) **kirei (na)**	pretty, neat, clean
失礼(な) **shitsurei (na)**	rude
丁寧(な) **teinei (na)**	polite
好き(な) **suki (na)**	liked, likable
大好き(な) **daisuki (na)**	greatly liked
大変(な) **taihen (na)**	terrific, terrible, quite a...
嫌い(な) **kirai (na)**	disliked, dislikable
大嫌い(な) **daikirai (na)**	greatly disliked
素敵(な) **suteki (na)**	excellent, swell
楽(な) **raku (na)**	comfortable
立派(な) **rippa (na)**	splendid, elegant
静か(な) **shizuka (na)**	quiet
結構(な) **kekkō (na)**	excellent, satisfactory
元気(な) **genki (na)**	healthy, good-spirited
上手(な) **jōzu (na)**	skillful, good at
便利(な) **benri (na)**	convenient
下手(な) **heta (na)**	unskillful, poor at
不便(な) **fuben (na)**	inconvenient
有名(な) **yūmei (na)**	famous, well-known
嫌(な) **iya (na)**	unpleasant
にぎやか(な) **nigiyaka (na)**	lively, bustling, gay
変(な) **hen (na)**	queer, odd
大丈夫(な) **daijōbu (na)**	safe

Most nouns belong to the ordinary class that have **no** for the copula alternant (**byōki no hito, puroguramā no Tanaka-san**). Some nouns belong to either class: ordinary **no** or adjectival nouns. An example is **iroiro**: you can say either **iroiro no** or **iroiro na** (commonly pronounced **iron-na**) to mean 'various, of various sorts':

色々の形 **iroiro no katachi**	a variety of shapes
色々な形 **iroiro na katachi**	a variety of shapes

There are a few adjectives that may have **na** instead of the ending **i** when placed before a noun.

小さい部屋 or 小さな部屋	大きい船 or 大きな船
chīsai heya or **chīsa na heya**	**ōkii fune** or **ōki na fune**
a small room	a big ship

When you have two adjectival nouns modifying the same noun phrase, the first takes the gerund of the copula **de** 'is and': **shizuka de kirei na tokoro** 'a place that is quiet and (is) pretty.'

Here are some examples of adjectival nouns in sentences:

大変なことをしてしまいました。
Taihen na koto o shite shimaimashita.
He did something terrible.

この仕事は大変ですよ。
Kono shigoto wa taihen desu yo.
This job is heavy.

パソコン操作が得意な人は有利です。
Pasokon sōsa ga tokui na hito wa yūri desu.
Those who are good at using computers will have some advantage.

きれいでやさしい人は好かれます。
Kirei de yasashii hito wa sukaremasu.
Those who are pretty and kind are liked by others.

働くのが嫌いな人は雇いません。
Hataraku no ga kirai na hito wa yatoimasen.
We will not hire those who do not like to work.

Before the verb **naru** 'becomes,' the particle **ni** occurs just as after any other noun:

病気になりました。
Byōki ni narimashita.
He got sick.

元気になりました。
Genki ni narimashita.
He got his health back.

With other verbs, the particle **ni** makes the meaning of the adjectival noun 'in such a manner':

静かにしてください。
Shizuka ni shite kudasai.
Please be quiet (behave in a quiet way).

毎日元気にしています。
Mainichi genki ni shite imasu.
I'm in good spirits every day (behave in a good-spirited manner).

あの人は英語を上手に話しますね。
Ano hito wa Eigo o jōzu ni hanashimasu ne.
That person speaks English well.

5.5. The noun の *no*

You have seen two kinds of **no**: the particle and the copula-alternant. There is yet a third kind of **no** that is a noun. This noun has two somewhat different meanings, 'one WHO' and 'fact THAT.' In some expressions this word is used much like **hito** 'person':

あそこに座っているのはだれですか。
(or あそこに座っている人はだれですか。)
Asoko ni suwatte iru no wa dare desu ka.
(or **Asoko ni suwatte iru hito wa dare desu ka.**)
Who is the person who is sitting over there?

In some expressions, the noun **no** is used like **koto** 'fact':

アメリカの映画を見るのが好きです。
(or アメリカの映画を見ることが好きです。)
Amerika no eiga o miru no ga suki desu.
(or **Amerika no eiga o miru koto ga suki desu.**)
I like to see American movies.

5.6. ⋯の (ん)です *...n(o) desu*

The noun **no** followed by the copula makes a special expression meaning 'it is a fact that...', but it is not easily translated in English. This is a very common formula in Japanese: it may be tacked on at the end of any sentence (with the verb, adjective, or copula in either plain imperfect or plain perfect), giving an additional refinement. When **no desu** is pronounced softly with a contraction, as in **n desu**, it somewhat softens the directness of the statement, elicits the listener's response and makes the dialog more interactive.

「実は来月結婚するんです。」
"Jitsu wa raigetsu kekkon suru n desu."
"Umm, I'm going get married next month."

「え，だれとですか。」
"E, dare to desu ka."
"What? With whom?"

N(o) desu is somewhat more common when the sentence is not completed but left dangling with a particle like **kedo... (ga...)** 'but...' or **kara...** 'so....'

「あのう，ここでタバコはこまるんですけど。」	「ああ，すみません。」
"Anō, koko de tabako wa komaru n desu kedo."	**"Ā, sumimasen."**
"Umm, smoking here is a bit of problem, but...."	"Oh, sorry."
「ちょっとお願いがあるんですが。」	「何ですか。」
"Chotto onegai ga aru n desu ga."	**"Nan desu ka."**
"I have a favor to ask, but..."	"What is it?"

If uttered with a firm intonation, with or without the contraction, **no desu** makes the expression somewhat more formal.

「毎日3時間は練習するのです。いいですね。」	「はい。」
"Mainichi san-jikan wa renshū suru no desu.	**"Hai."**
Ii desu ne."	"Yes."
"You must practice (at least) for three hours	
every day. Is this understood?"	
「そんなことどこに書いてあるのですか。」	「ええと。」
"Sonna koto doko ni kaite aru no desu ka."	**"Ēto."**
"Such a thing, where is it written?"	"Well..."

Notice the use of the copula forms **datta** and **na** (= **da**). Before the noun **no**, the plain imperfect copula appears in the form **na** regardless of whether preceded by an ordinary noun or an adjectival noun:

前はパートだったんですが，今は正社員なんです。
Mae wa pāto datta n desu ga, ima wa seishain na n desu.
I was a part-time worker but am a full-time employee now.

父はデパートの地下が好きなんです。
Chichi wa depāto no chika ga suki na n desu.
My father loves the basement of a department store.

5.7. Verb + でしょう *deshō*

Many people go a step further and drop the **no** completely from the expressions discussed above: **Doko e iku desu ka?** 'Where's he going?', **Otearai ni itta desu** 'He went to the men's room.' As a general thing, this usage is frowned upon by speakers of Standard Japanese and should perhaps be avoided by the student. However, certain forms that have become a part of Standard Japanese originated in this dropping of the **no**: the polite forms of the adjective **atarashii desu, ii desu** came from the forms **atarashii no desu, ii no desu**. Some older Japanese still consider it poor style to say **atarashii desu, ii desu**, preferring at least **atarashii n desu, ii n desu**—but most people use the forms without even the **n** constantly, so that they are now a part of Standard Japanese. This helps explain the existence of two polite forms for the perfect adjective at one point: **ii deshita** and **yokatta desu**. They come from the expressions **ii no deshita** 'it was a fact that it is good' and **yokatta no desu** 'it is a fact that it was good.' The latter type of phrase, **yokatta desu**, is the currently accepted form.

In a similar way, expressions consisting of imperfect or perfect adjectives plus **no deshō** 'will probably be the fact that...; must be...' created the now Standard forms **ii deshō** 'it must be good' (compare **Tanaka-san deshō** 'It must be Mr. Tanaka') and **yokatta deshō** 'it must have been good' (compare **Tanaka-san datta no deshō** 'it must have been Mr. Tanaka').

There already existed a polite tentative for verbs: **ikimashō, hanashimashō, asobimashō**. These polite tentatives once had the meaning 'will probably do' just as the polite copula **deshō** still has the meaning 'will probably be.' Sometimes the tentatives of verbs are still used with the 'probably' meaning. For example, in modern writings you will see **arō** (= **aru darō**), **narō** (= **naru darō**), **dekiyō** (= **dekiru darō**), **ieyō** (= **ieru darō** 'probably can say') and also tentative adjectives in **-karō** (= **-i darō**) such as **yokarō** (= **ii darō**) and **nakarō** (= **nai darō**).

For the meaning 'probably,' a plain form of the verb is used, either imperfect or perfect, depending on the meaning, followed by the tentative copula **deshō** (from **no deshō** 'it's probably a fact that' with the **no** dropped). This is quite standard usage and often has the flavor of English 'must (be), I bet that..., I'll bet...' Sometimes **kitto** or **tabun** 'no doubt, probably' is added, often at the very beginning of the sentence, just to emphasize the probability. For exmple:

「これから株価が上がるでしょう。」
"Kore kara kabuka ga agaru deshō."
"I guess the stock will go up from now on."

「たぶんそうでしょう。」
"Tabun sō deshō."
"It will probably do so."

5.8. ⋯かね *...ka ne*

The combination of the final particles **ka** and **ne** means something like 'I wonder' or 'is it, do you think.' It is often preceded by a tentative expression:

この企画は成功するでしょうかね。
Kono kikaku wa seikō suru deshō kane.
I wonder whether this project will be successful.

どうして失敗したんでしょうかね。
Dōshite shippai shita n deshō ka ne.
I wonder why it failed.

「たぶんエンジンが悪かったんでしょう。」　　「そうでしょうかね。」
"Tabun enjin ga warukatta n deshō."　　**"Sō deshō ka ne."**
"I guess the engine was bad."　　　　　　　"I wonder whether it is the case."

5.9. ので *no de*

The expression VERB (or ADJECTIVE or COPULA) + **no de** 'it being a fact that; it is a fact that… and' has a special meaning of 'because' or 'since.' This is similar to the meaning of **kara**. In most places **no de** and **kara** seem interchangeable, but there is a slight difference of meaning: **no de** emphasizes the "reason," **kara** emphasizes the "result":

去年は病気でたくさん仕事を休んだので，休暇をとることができませんでした。
Kyonen wa byōki de takusan shigoto o yasunda no de, kyūka o toru koto ga dekimasen deshita.
Because I took many days off due to sickness last year, I could not take vacation.

去年は病気でたくさん休んだから，休暇をとることができませんでした。
Kyonen wa byōki de takusan yasunda kara, kyūka o toru koto ga dekimasen deshita.
I took many days off due to sickness last year, so I could not take vacation.

As in the case of **n(o) desu** discussed in this lesson, the plain imperfect copula appears in the form **na** when followed by **no de**. Here are some additional examples:

私はパートなので週に３日しか働きません。
Watashi wa pāto na no de, shū ni mikka shika hatarakimasen.
Because I'm a part-time employee, I work only three days per week.

あの人はきれいなのでモデルにもなれるでしょう。
Ano hito wa kirei na no de moderu ni mo nareru deshō.
That person is pretty, so she can also be a model.

来月から働くのでスーツを買わなくてはいけません。
Raigetsu kara hataraku no de sūtsu o kawanakute wa ikemasen.
Because I'll start working beginning next month, I need to buy a suit.

ここは禁煙なのでおタバコはご遠慮願います。

Koko wa kin'en na no de otabako wa goenryo negaimasu.

Because it is a non-smoking area, please refrain from smoking.

5.10. のに *no ni*

After a verb in the imperfect mood, the expression **no ni**, literally 'to the fact that, at the fact that,' has two different meanings: 'in the process of doing, for the purpose of doing, in order to do' and 'in spite of the fact that...' The two meanings are distinguished by context. Often the particle **wa** follows **no ni** in the first meaning, and the whole expression is frequently followed by a phrase indicating something is necessary ('in the process of doing something'). Here are some examples of the first meaning 'in the process of':

日本語を勉強するのに(は)いい本が要ります。

Nihongo o benkyō suru no ni (wa) ii hon ga irimasu.

We need a good book in order to study Japanese.

アパートを借りるのに5万円かかります。

Apāto o kariru no ni goman-en kakarimasu.

To rent an apartment costs 50,000 yen.

Here are some examples of the second meaning 'in spite of the fact that':

勉強したのに，いい成績がもらえませんでした。

Benkyō shita no ni, ii seiseki ga moraemasen deshita.

Although I studied, I could not get a good grade.

まずいのに食べるんですか。

Mazui no ni taberu n desu ka.

Are you going to eat it even though it is not delicious?

As in the case of **n(o) desu** discussed in this lesson, the plain imperfect copula appears in the form **na** when followed by **no ni**:

まだ学生なのに高い車を乗り回しているんです。

Mada gakusei na no ni takai kuruma o nori-mawashite iru n desu.

Although he is still a student, he drives an expensive car.

どうして好きなのに好きだって言えないんですか。

Dōshite suki na no ni suki datte ienai n desu ka.

Why can't you say you love her although you love her?

The first meaning of **no ni** 'in the process of, for the purpose of, with the aim of' is usually expressed by the noun **tame** 'sake,' which is often followed by **ni** and sometimes by **wa** or **ni wa**. The expression **tame (ni) (wa)** may be preceded by a plain imperfect verb form or by a NOUN + **no**:

> 日本語を勉強するためにはいい本が要ります。
> **Nihongo o benkyō suru tame ni wa ii hon ga irimasu.**
> We need a good book for studying Japanese.

> 日本語の勉強のためにいい本が要ります。
> **Nihongo no benkyō no tame ni ii hon ga irimasu.**
> We need a good book for the study of Japanese.

> 何のために大阪に行くんですか。
> **Nan no tame ni Ōsaka ni iku n desu ka.**
> Why are you going to Osaka?

The word **tame** is also used after a modifying phrase by many speakers as a virtual equivalent of **kara** 'because':

> 地震があったため電車が遅れた。
> **Jishin ga atta tame densha ga okureta.**
> The train was delayed due to an earthquake.

> 英語ができないため困りました。
> **Eigo ga dekinai tame komarimashita.**
> I had difficulties because I couldn't speak English.

5.11. Plain negative ···ない ...*nai*

The polite negative ends in **-masen** for verbs, as in **hanashimasen** and **ikimasen**, and consists of a special construction for the copula **ja arimasen**, and for adjectives, infinitive (**-ku**) + **arimasen**.

The plain negative of 'exists' is a completely different word, the adjective **nai** 'is non-existent.' The plain negative of the copula is **ja nai**; of adjectives it is **ku nai**. And, in colloquial usage, **(ja) nai desu** is often used for **(ja) arimasen**, **ku nai desu** for **ku arimasen**. The plain negative of every other verb is an adjective made by adding the ending **-(a)nai** to the stem of the verb: add **–anai** to the consonant-ending stem; add **-nai** to the vowel-ending stem.

	Meaning	Plain Affirmative (Imperfect)	Plain Negative (Imperfect)
Vowel Verbs	eats	**tabe-ru**	**tabe-nai**
	sees	**mi-ru**	**mi-nai**
Consonant Verbs	wins	**kats-u**	**kat-anai**
	rides	**nor-u**	**nor-anai**
	buys	**ka-u**	**kaw-anai**
	speaks	**hanas-u**	**hanas-anai**
	writes	**kak-u**	**kak-anai**
	swims	**oyog-u**	**oyog-anai**
	calls	**yob-u**	**yob-anai**
	reads	**yom-u**	**yom-anai**
	dies	**shin-u**	**shin-anai**
Irregular Verbs	comes	**ku-ru**	**ko-nai**
	does	**su-ru**	**shi-nai**

Notice how the 'disappearing' **w** disappears in forms like **kau** but does not disappear in forms like **kawanai**. Also notice the 'appearing' **s** appears in forms like **katsu** but not in forms like **katanai**. Each of the negative verbs is conjugated like any other adjective—for example the adjective **nai** 'is non- existent' or **akai** 'is red':

	Imperfect	Perfect	Gerund	Infinitive
Adjective	**aka-i**	**aka-katta**	**aka-kute**	**aka-ku**
Nai	**na-i**	**na-katta**	**na-kute**	**na-ku**
Vowel Verb	**tabe-na-i**	**tabe-nakatta**	**tabe-na-kute**	**tabe-na-ku**
Consonant Verb	**kaw-ana-i**	**kaw-ana-katta**	**kaw-ana-kute**	**kaw-ana-ku**
Irregular Verb	**ko-na-i**	**ko-na-katta**	**ko-na-kute**	**ko-na-ku**
	shi-na-i	**shi-na-katta**	**shi-na-kute**	**shi-na-ku**

あの製品はあまり売れなかったでしょう。
Ano seihin wa amari urenakatta deshō.
I guess that product did not sell very well.

父が帰って来なくて困っています。
Chichi ga kaette konakute komatte imasu.
I'm troubled because my father hasn't come home.

部長は最近あまりしゃべらなくなりました。
Buchō wa saikin amri shaberanaku narimashita.
The division manager stopped speaking lately.

5.12. Negative infinitive ···ず ...*zu*

In addition to the regular negative infinitive as in **shaberanaku naru** 'gets so he doesn't talk' in the above example, there is a derived adjectival noun with similar meaning but different uses. This form has the ending **-azu**, after a consonant-ending stem, **-zu** after a vowel-ending stem.

	Meaning	Plain Affirmative (Imperfect)	Negative Infinitive with -ku	Negative Infinitive with -(a)zu
Vowel Verbs	eats	**tabe-ru**	tabe-naku	tabe-zu
	sees	**mi-ru**	mi-naku	mi- zu
Consonant Verbs	wins	**kats-u**	kat-anaku	kat-azu
	rides	**nor-u**	nor-anaku	nor-azu
	buys	**ka-u**	kaw-anaku	kaw-azu
	speaks	**hanas-u**	hanas-anaku	hanas-azu
	writes	**kak-u**	kak-anaku	kak-azu
	swims	**oyog-u**	oyog-anaku	oyog-azu
	calls	**yob-u**	yob-anaku	yob-azu
	reads	**yom-u**	yom-anaku	yom-azu
	dies	**shin-u**	shin-anaku	shin-azu
Irregular Verbs	comes	**ku-ru**	ko-naku	ko-zu
	does	**su-ru**	shi-naku	se-zu

Notice that the irregular verbs are **ko-zu** 'not coming' and **se-zu** 'not doing': **ko-zu** is similar in its irregular vowel to **ko-nai**, but **se-zu** is different from **shi-nai**. The appropriate form for **nai** is **arazu**, but it is not used in speech. The **-(a)zu** form is usually limited to a set expression with the particle **ni** meaning either 'instead of doing' or 'without doing,' depending on the context. Here are some examples where **-(a)zu ni** means 'instead':

> 大阪に行かずに岡山に行った。
> **Ōsaka ni ikazu ni Okayama ni itta.**
> Instead of going to Osaka, he went to Okayama.

> クレジットカードを使わずに現金で払います。
> **Kurejitto kādo o tsukawazu ni genkin de haraimasu.**
> Instead of using my credit card, I pay by cash.

(Another way to say 'instead' is to use two full sentences, with the second beginning **sono kawari (ni)** 'instead of that,' as in **Hon wa kawanakatta desu.**

Sono kawari ni zasshi o kaimashita. 'He didn't buy books; instead, he bought magazines.')

Here are some examples where -**(a)zu ni** means 'without':

> 朝ごはんを食べずに家を出た。
> **Asa gohan o tabezu ni ie o deta.**
> He left home without having breakfast.

> よく確認せずに請求書を送ってしまった。
> **Yoku kakunin sezu ni seikyūsho o okutte shimatta.**
> Without checking it carefully, I mailed out the bill.

5.13. Imperfect negative + *de* …ないで …*nai de*

Instead of using -**(a)zu ni** to say 'instead of doing' or 'without doing,' you can use the plain imperfect negative -**(a)nai** + the copula gerund **de** 'being.' This construction is also sometimes used with **kudasai** in direct negative requests: **Amari hanasanai de kudasai** 'Please don't talk too much.'

> 大阪に行かないで岡山に行った。
> **Ōsaka ni ikanai de Okayama ni itta.**
> Instead of going to Osaka, he went to Okayama.

> 朝ごはんを食べないで急いで家を出た。
> **Asagohan o tabenai de isoide ie o deta.**
> He left home in a rush without having breakfast.

> ここでタバコを吸わないでください。
> **Koko de tabako o suwanai de kudasai.**
> Please do not smoke here.

> 運転しなくてはいけないのでお酒を飲まないでおきます。
> **Unten shinakute wa ikenai no de o-sake o nomanai de okimasu.**
> As I have to drive, I won't drink (so I can drive later).

5.14. はず *hazu*

Hazu is a NOUN meaning something like NORMAL EXPECTATION or OBJECTIVE CONCLUSION. Being preceded by a modifier clause and followed by some form of the copula, it means 'is (supposed) to, is expected to,' but not 'supposed to' in the sense of obligation 'ought to.'

Note the **hazu** expresses what is generally expected, and usually refers to what the speaker expects of "other" people or things; it is sometimes close to …**ni chigai nai** 'there is no doubt that.' To make the negative, you usually say **hazu wa nai** (rather than **hazu ja nai**); or, you can make the preceding verb negative: **Tanaka-san wa kuru hazu wa arimasen**, or **...konai hazu desu** 'Mr. Tanaka surely won't come.' Also note that the predicates before **hazu** are in the prenominal form (the form required when placed before a noun) because **hazu** is a noun.

田中さんはしっかりしていますから，きっと確認をとったはずです。
Tanaka-san wa shikkari shite imasu kara, kitto kakunin o totta hazu desu.
Mr. Tanaka is very reliable, so he must have checked it.

あの人はお金をもらうとすぐ使うから，お金があるはずがありません。
Ano hito wa okane o morau to sugu tsukau kara, okane ga aru hazu ga arimasen.
That person uses up all the money he has (each time), so there is no way for him to have money (now).

あの人は生活保護を受けているから収入は高くないはずです。
Ano hito wa seikatsu hogo o ukete iru kara shūnyū wa takaku nai hazu desu.
He is on social welfare, so his income cannot be high.

今，１ドルは８８円のはずです。
Ima, ichi-doru wa hachijūhachi-en no hazu desu.
I suppose a dollar is 88 yen now.

伊藤さんはよく居酒屋に行きますから，お酒が好きなはずです。
Itō-san wa yoku izakaya ni ikimasu kara, o-sake ga suki na hazu desu.
Mr. Ito often goes to *izakaya* bars, so he must like liquor.

来るはずの人が来ないと困ります。
Kuru hazu no hito ga konai to komarimasu.
When people who are expected to come don't come, we get into trouble.

5.15. ところ *tokoro*

The noun **tokoro** 'place' has several special uses. When you speak of going to a person, doing something at a person's (place), coming from a person, in Japanese you usually say 'to, from, or at the PLACE of that person.' In fact **tokoro** is used when you are going to anything that is not itself a place.

クライアントのところまで車で行きました。
Kuraianto no tokoro made kuruma de ikimashita.
I went to my client's place by car.

Tokoro can also refer to time as well as place. It then means 'the time or occasion when something is (was) happening,' and it is followed by the copula or by a particle. Here are some of the expressions that result:

読むところです。
Yomu tokoro desu.
He is (just) about to read.

読むところでした。
Yomu tokoro deshita.
He was (just) about to read.

読んだところです。
Yonda tokoro desu.
He has just (now) read.

読んだところでした。
Yonda tokoro deshita.
He had just (then) read.

読んでいるところです。
Yonde iru tokoro desu.
He is just (now) reading.

読んでいるところでした。
Yonde iru tokoro deshita.
He was just (then) reading.

読んでいたところです。
Yonde ita tokoro desu.
He has just been reading.

読んでいたところでした。
Yonde ita tokoro deshita.
He had just been reading.

Instead of the copula, you can have the particle **e** followed by some clause that INTERRUPTS the action of the clause preceding **tokoro**:

賄賂を受け取ったところをカメラで撮った。
Wairo o uketotta tokoro o kamera de totta.
I took a photo of the moment when he received the bribe.

ネットカフェへ入って行くところを見ました。
Netto kafe e haitte iku tokoro o mimashita.
I saw them enter the Internet café.

弁当を食べているところへ加藤さんが来ました。
Bentō o tabete iru tokoro e Katō-san ga kimashita.
Mr. Kato came just when I was eating my boxed lunch.

There are occasional opportunities for ambiguity. **Jidōsha o tsukutte iru to-koro o mimashita** could mean either 'I saw them making cars' or 'I saw the place where they make cars.'

CULTURE NOTE ▶ Bentō

Bentō is a single-serving meal in a box purchased at a **bentō** shop or prepared at home. Some business people eat lunch at a restaurant near their office, but others bring **bentō** to their office daily. It saves them time and money, and is healthier. There are many cute **bentō** boxes sold in Japan.

5.16. Verbs for leaving

The usual verb for 'leave' is **deru**. There is a compound verb **dekakeru** consisting of the infinitive of **deru (de)** + **-kakeru** 'begins to, starts to.' This is often used when a person leaves on an errand, with the implication that he gets started on his way.

ちょっと出かけてきますね。
Chotto dekakete kimasu ne.
I'll go out (for an errand), okay?

If a person leaves town on a trip, you use a special verb, **tatsu**, which means 'leaves' or 'takes off (airplane),' but you can use **deru** 'leaves' instead. The place you leave is followed by the object particle **o**. The verb for 'arrives' is **tsuku**; the particle for the place is **e** or **ni** 'to.'

新幹線こだま５号が今東京駅を出ました。
Shinkansen Kodama go-gō ga ima Tōkyō eki o demashita.
Shinkansen (bullet train) Kodama #5 has just left Tokyo station.

明日パリへ発ちます。パリに午後３時に着きます。
Ashita Pari e tachimasu. Pari ni gogo sanji ni tsukimasu.
I'll leave for Paris tomorrow. I'll arrive at Paris at three p.m.

5.17. ⋯前に ...*mae ni* and ⋯後で ...*ato de*

To say 'before something happens' or 'before something happened,' you use the imperfect mood followed by **mae ni** 'in front of..., in advance of....' To say 'after something happens' or 'after something happened,' you use the perfect mood followed by **ato ni** 'being after....' Note that **ato ni** can also be substituted by **ato de**. (**Ato de** sounds more colloquial than **ato ni**.)

晩ご飯を食べる前に山田さんに電話をしました。
Bangohan o taberu mae ni Yamada-san ni denwa o shimashita.
Before eating dinner, I called Ms. Yamada.

晩ご飯を食べた後 に/で 映画を見に行きました。
Bangohan o tabeta ato ni/de eiga o mi ni ikimashita.
After eating dinner, I went to see a movie.

Notice that you always use the same mood in front of these two expressions regardless of the English translation:

IMPERFECT + **mae ni**
PERFECT + **ato ni**

The differences of tense in English are mostly conditioned by the tense of the verb in the final clause, and this is all indicated by the mood of the final verb in the Japanese sentence.

Now you have had two ways to say 'after doing something': GERUND (-**te**) + **kara** and PERFECT (-**ta**) + **ato ni/de**. The principal difference of use is that the -**te kara** construction refers to actions IN SEQUENCE (either time sequence or logical sequence), whereas -**ta ato ni** is used for actions not necessarily in immediate sequence, just separated in time. **Gohan o tabete kara, eiga o mi ni iki-mashita**

'I went to see a movie after eating' implies that there is a direct sequence, with nothing else of importance happening between the time I ate and the time I saw the movie: I saw the show right after dinner. **Gohan o tabeta ato ni, eiga o mi ni ikimashita** 'I went to see a movie after I had eaten' does not imply this sequence. Perhaps I did the dishes, studied for a while, and then went for a walk before taking in a late show. Additional examples:

> 新幹線が出る前にホームで駅弁とお茶を買いました。
> **Shinkansen ga deru mae ni hōmu de ekiben to o-cha o kaimashita.**
> I bought a (station) lunchbox and tea at the platform before the train left.

> 会議が終わった後に部長と食事をしました。
> **Kaigi ga owatta ato ni buchō to shokuji o shimashita.**
> After the meeting had ended, I dined with the division manager.

> 仕事が終わってから居酒屋に行きます。
> **Shigoto ga owatte kara izakaya ni ikimasu.**
> I go to *izakaya* after finishing my work.

There are two other things to notice about **mae** and **ato**. **Mae** refers either to space or to time—'before' or 'in front of'. **Ato** usually refers only to time 'after'—for space you ordinarily use **ushiro** 'behind'. The second thing is that **mae** and **ato** are nouns and may be modified by prenouns (**kono, sono, ano**, etc.) or by a noun + the particle **no**. For example: **kono mae** 'before this', **sono ato** 'after that', **sensō no mae** 'before the war', **gohan no ato** 'after the meal'.

> この前にどこにいましたか。
> **Kono mae ni doko ni imashita ka.**
> Where were you before?

> 少し後でいいですか。
> **Sukoshi ato de ii desu ka.**
> Is it all right (if I do it) a little later?

> 後で見てください。
> **Ato de mite kudasai.**
> Please look at it later.

> 前にも後ろにもありますよ。
> **Mae ni mo ushiro ni mo arimasu yo.**
> We have some both in front and behind.

5.18. まで *made* and うち *uchi*

The particle **made** after a noun means 'as far as, up to'; after the imperfect mood of a verb or the infinitive (**-ku**) of some adjectives, it means 'until something happens or is':

次の電車が来るまで駅で待ちましょう。
Tsugi no densha ga kuru made eki de machimashō.
Let's wait at the train station until the next train comes.

次の電車が来るまで駅で待ちました。
Tsugi no densha ga kuru made eki de machimashita.
I waited at the train station until the next train came.

毎日遅くまで仕事をします。
Mainichi osoku made shigoto o shimasu.
I work until very late.

The noun **uchi** means 'interval, inside' (the derived meaning 'house' is a specialized example of this). Following a verb or an adjective in the imperfect mood, it means 'while someone/something is/was doing something or in a certain way.' **Uchi** may be followed by **ni**, **wa**, or **ni wa** and is used when there is a benefit of doing some action in the specified period. In many cases **uchi** and **aida** seem interchangeable, both meaning '(during) the interval.' However, **aida** does not have any implication about the benefit that is implied by **uchi**.

子供が寝ているうちに新聞を読みます。
Kodomo ga nete iru uchi ni shinbun o yomimasu.
While the children are asleep, I'll read a newspaper.

明るいうちに運転しましょう。
Akarui uchi ni unten shimashō.
Let's drive while it is still bright.

若いうちに頑張りなさい。
Wakai uchi ni ganbari nasai.
Work harder while you are young.

After a negative, **uchi** means 'while something (still) doesn't happen; as long as something (still) isn't so,' and this is a common Japanese way to say 'before something happens, before something is so':

忘れないうちに薬を飲みましょう。
Wasurenai uchi ni kusuri o nomimashō.
Let's take medicine before we forget.

警察が来ないうちに逃げよう。
Keisatsu ga konai uchi ni nigeyō.
Let's run away before the police come.

暗くならないうちに帰った方がいいよ。
Kuraku naranai uchi ni kaetta hō ga ii yo.
It's better to go home before it gets dark.

5.19. Verbs meaning 'know'

There are two verbs often translated 'knows': **shiru** and **wakaru**. **Shiru** takes a direct object. When affirmative, it is most often used together with **iru**.

このことを知っていますか。
Kono koto o shitte imasu ka?
Do you know this (fact)?

In the negative, it occurs without the **iru**:

知りません。 **Shirimasen.** I don't know.

This verb is used for knowing specific facts and people:

「小林さんを知っていますか。」
"Kobayashi-san o shitte imasu ka."
"Do you know Ms. Kobayashi?"

「いいえ，知りません。」
"Īe, shirimasen."
"No, I don't know (her)."

「駅前に新しい喫茶店ができたのを知って
いますか。」
**"Eki mae ni atarashii kissaten ga dekita no
o shitte imasu ka."**
"Do you know that a new coffee shop opened
in front of the train station?"

「ええ，知っています。」
"Ē, shitte imasu."
"Yes, I know it."

The verb **wakaru** means 'is distinguished, is understood.' This verb does not take a direct object—the word corresponding to the English object is the subject (just like **eiga ga suki desu** 'I like movies'):

「この言葉の意味が分かりますか。」 「いいえ，分かりませんね。」
"Kono kotoba no imi ga wakari masu ka." **"Ĭe, wakarimasen ne."**
"Do you understand the meaning of this word?" "No, I don't get it."

「日本語が分かりますか。」 「はい。」
"Nihongo ga wakarimasu ka." **"Hai."**
"Do you know (understand) Japanese?" "Yes."

Interestingly, **wakaru** can also be used to mean 'know.'

「田中さんの電話番号は分かります 「すみません。ちょっと分かりません。」
か。」 **"Sumimasen. Chotto wakarimasen."**
"Tanaka-san no denwa bangō "Sorry. I do not know it."
wa wakarimasu ka."
"Do you know Mr. Tanaka's
telephone number?"

「あの人はだれですか。」 「すみません。ちょっと分かりません。」
"Ano hito wa dare desu ka?" **"Sumimasen. Chotto wakarimasen."**
"Who is that person over there?" "Sorry. I don't know."

In addition, **wakaru** can also be used to respond to an instruction.

「この書類をコピーしてください。」 「はい，分かりました。」
"Kono shorui o kopī shite kudasai." **"Hai, wakarimashita."**
"Please make a copy of this document." "Certainly."

5.20. Talking a language

To say 'he speaks English,' you usually say in Japanese 'as for him, English is produced,' using the verb **dekiru**.

あの人は英語ができます。
Ano hito wa Eigo ga dekimasu.

「日本語ができますか。」 「はい，少しできます。」
"Nihongo ga dekimasu ka." **"Hai, sukoshi dekimasu."**
"Do you speak Japanese?" "Yes, a little bit."

日本語があまりできないので 英語でお願いします。
Nihongo ga amari dekinai no de Eigo de onegai shimasu.
I cannot speak/understand Japanese well, so please speak in English with me.

To say 'he understands English,' you can use the verb **wakaru**:

誰か英語が分かる人はいませんか。

Dare ka eigo ga wakaru hito wa imasen ka.

Is there anyone who understands English?

Conversation

[cue 05-3]

Mr. Tanaka, an employee at Yamato Chemical, makes a phone call to Japan Electric.

Receptionist: 日本電気でございます。**Nihon Denki de gozaimasu.**

Japan Electric.

Tanaka: 大和ケミカルの田中ですが，いつもお世話になっております。

Yamato Kemikaru no Tanaka desu ga, itsumo osewa ni natte orimasu.

I'm Mr. Tanaka from Yamato Chemical. Thank you always for your help and kindness.

Receptionist: こちらこそいつもお世話になっております。

Kochira koso itsumo osewa ni natte orimasu.

Likewise, we are indebted to you.

Tanaka: あのう，渡辺部長はいらっしゃいますでしょうか。

Anō, Watanabe buchō wa irasshaimasu deshō ka.

Umm, is Division Chief Watanabe there?

Receptionist: 只今席をはずしておりますが。

Tadaima seki o hazushite orimasu ga.

I'm sorry, but he is away from his desk right now.

Tanaka: ああ，そうですか。じゃあ，また後ほどお電話させていただきます。

Ā, sō desu ka. Jā, mata nochi hodo o-denwa sasete itadakimasu.

Well, I'll call again later.

Receptionist:　申し訳ございません。宜しくお願いいたします。
Mōshiwake gozaimasen. Yoroshiku onegai itashimasu.
Sorry for the trouble. Thank you.

Tanaka:　それでは失礼いたします。**Soredewa shitsurei itashimasu.**
Okay, good-bye.

Receptionist:　失礼いたします。**Shitsurei itashimasu.**
Good-bye.

CULTURE NOTE ▶ Business Telephone Conversations

When you make a phone call or receive one in a business context, talk in slightly higher pitch than usual and use polite language. **Osewa ni natte orimasu** is almost always used at the beginning of a telephone conversation in a business context. **Sewa** means 'care' or 'assistance,' and the phrase literally means that 'I am always being taken care of by you.' It sounds very awkward when translated into English. Japanese tend to be apologetic in phone conversation and email communications in a business context, but it is their way of being extremely courteous. See Lesson 9 about polite language.

Exercises

I. Match the items that form a pair as contrasting or opposite items in the same category.

a. 正社員 **seishain**

b. 輸入 **yunyū**

c. 社長 **shachō**

d. 請求書 **seikyūsho**

i. 領収書 **ryōshūsho**

ii. バイト **baito**

iii. 秘書 **hisho**

iv. 輸出 **yushutsu**

II. Make a grammatical sentence by reordering the items in the parentheses, and translate the sentences.

1. (立って・人・あそこ・いる・に)は田中さんです。
   (tatte, hito, asoko, iru, ni) wa Tanaka-san desu.

2. (食べ物・な・父・好き・の)はすしです。
   (tabemono, na, chichi, suki, no) wa sushi desu.

3. 店は (人・多い・の・ところ) がいいです。
   Mise wa (hito, ōi, no, tokoro) ga ii desu.

4. うちの会社には (いません・が・人・できる・の・英語) 。
   Uchi no kaisha ni wa (imasen, ga, hito, dekiru, no, eigo).

5. (飲んで・の・いる・あの・は・人・が) お酒です。
   (nonde, no, iru, ano, wa, hito, ga) o-sake desu.

III. Fill in the blanks.

1. アイスクリームを_____ところです。
   Aisukurīmu o _____ tokorodesu.

2. アイスクリームを_____ところです。
   Aisukurīmu o _____ tokorodesu.

3. アイスクリームを_____ところです。
   Aisukurīmu o _____ tokorodesu.

IV. Change the form of the underlined part to make the sentence grammatical.

1. 日本に<u>行きます</u>前に日本語を勉強します。
   Nihon ni <u>ikimasu</u> mae ni Nihongo o benkyō shimasu.

2. ご飯を<u>食べます</u>後に電話をします。
   Go-han o <u>tabemasu</u> ato ni denwa o shimasu.

3. 新しい部長はあの人<u>です</u>はずです。
   Atarashii buchō wa ano hito <u>desu</u> hazu desu.

4. 部長はカラオケが好き<u>です</u>はずです。
   Buchō wa karaoke ga suki <u>desu</u> hazu desu.

5. 病気<u>です</u>のに会社に行くんですか。
   Byōki <u>desu</u> no ni kaisha ni iku n desu ka.

6. 私の父はイギリス人<u>です</u>んです。
   Watashi no chichi wa Igirisu-jin <u>desu</u> n desu.

Answers:

I   a-ii, b-iv, c-iii, d-i

II   1. あそこに立っている人は田中さんです。**Asoko ni tatte iru hito wa Tanaka-san desu.** The person who is standing over there is Mr. Tanaka.
2. 父の好きな食べ物はすしです。**Chichi no suki na tabemono wa sushi desu.** The food that my father likes is sushi.
3. 店は人の多いところがいいです。**Mise wa hito no ōi tokoro ga ii desu.** Stores are better (to be) located at heavily trafficked places.
4. うちの会社には英語のできる人がいません。**Uchi no kaisha ni wa eigo no dekiru hito ga imasen.** There is no one who can speak English at our company.
5. あの人が飲んでいるのはお酒です。**Ano hito ga nonde iru no wa osake desu.** The thing that person is drinking is sake.

III   1. たべる **taberu** 2. 食べている **tabete iru** 3. 食べた **tabeta**

IV   1. 行く **iku** 2. 食べた **tabeta** 3. の **no** 4. な **na** 5. な **na** 6. な **na**

LESSON 6 — Going Shopping Again?

また買い物？
Mata Kaimono?

In this lesson you will learn how to describe your experiences about shopping as well as how to express quantities, amounts, and numbers.

Basic Sentences

[cue 06-1]

1.	古本屋でマンガを<u>たくさん</u>買いました。 **Furuhonya de manga o <u>takusan</u> kaimashita.**	I bought a lot of comic books at a used-book store.
2.	りんごを<u>３つ</u>下さい。それから，バナナを<u>３本</u>下さい。 **Ringo o <u>mit-tsu</u> kudasai. Sorekara, banana o <u>san-bon</u> kudasai.**	Please give me three apples. In addition, please give me three bananas.
3.	うちには犬が<u>３匹</u>います。それから，猫が<u>１匹</u>います。 **Uchi ni wa inu ga <u>san-biki</u> imasu. Sorekara, neko ga <u>ip-piki</u> imasu.**	We have three dogs. In addition, we have a cat.

4.	2に3を<u>足す</u>と いくつに なりますか。 **Ni ni san o <u>tasu</u> to ikutsu ni narimasu ka.**	How much is 2 + 3? (When you add 3 to 2, how many does it become?)
5.	9から4を<u>引く</u>と5になります。 **Kyū kara yon o <u>hiku</u> to go ni narimasu.**	9 – 4 is 5. (When you subtract 4 from 9, it becomes 5.)
6.	店員が<u>2, 3人</u>いました。 **Ten'in ga <u>ni san nin</u> imashita.**	There were 2 or 3 salesclerks.
7.	今日は全て<u>3割引き</u>ですよ。 **Kyō wa subete <u>san-wari</u> biki desu yo.**	Today, everything is 30% OFF!
8.	父の生年月日は<u>１９５２年６月２３日</u>です。 **Chichi no seinengappi wa <u>sen kyūhyaku gojū ichi-nen roku-gatsu nijū san-nichi</u> desu.**	My father's date of birth is June 23rd, 1951.
9.	バラ<u>や</u>ゆり<u>など</u>を買いました。 **Bara <u>ya</u> yuri <u>nado</u> o kaimashita.**	I bought roses and lilies and the like.
10.	ほうれん草を１束<u>か</u>２束買いましょう。 **Hōrensō o hitotaba <u>ka</u> futataba kaimashō.**	I guess I'll buy 1 or 2 bunches of Japanese white radishes.
11.	ほうれん草<u>と</u>ねぎを一束<u>ずつ</u>買いました。 **Hōrensō <u>to</u> negi o hitotaba <u>zusu</u> kaimashita.**	We bought one bunch each of spinach and green onions.
12.	「今何<u>時</u>ですか。」 **"Ima nan<u>ji</u> desu ka."**	"What time is it now?"
	「3<u>時</u>４５<u>分</u>です。」 **"San-<u>ji</u> yonjūgo-<u>fun</u> desu."**	"It's 3:45."
13.	田中さん<u>だけ</u>に言いました。 **Tanaka-san <u>dake</u> ni iimashita.**	I only told Mr. Tanaka.
14.	田中さんに<u>しか</u>言いませんでした。 **Tanaka-san ni <u>shika</u> iimasen deshita.**	I only told Mr. Tanaka.
15.	お茶はいかがですか。 **O-cha wa ikaga desu ka.**	How about some tea?
16.	このクラスの<u>四分の三</u>は男子です。 **Kono kurasu no <u>yonbun no san</u> wa danshi desu.**	Three-fourths of (the students in) this class are boys.

Basic Vocabulary

[cue 06-2]

STORES

デパート (or 百貨店) **depāto** (or **hyakkaten**)	department store
スーパー **sūpā**	supermarket
コンビニ **konbini**	convenience store
本屋 (or 書店) **hon'ya** (or **shoten**)	bookstore
レジ **reji**	cashier
店員 **ten'in**	store cleark
店長 **tenchō**	store manager
客 **kyaku**	customers, shoppers

CULTURE NOTE ▸ Convenient *Konbini*

In Japan, convenience stores are called **konbini**. Wherever you are, in Japan, you can see some **konbini** such as 7-Eleven, Lawson, or Family-Mart. In cities, you can find one every few blocks. Like the 7-Elevens in the U.S., **konbini** sell prepared foods, drinks, toiletries, over-the-counter drugs, and stationery, but they offer more. You can buy tickets for shows and sports games, do simple banking, send a fax, make copies, and pay utility bills. **Konbini** stores usually serve as stations for popular delivery services called **takuhaibin**. When you go to an airport, you can drop off your suitcase at a **konbini** on the previous day and have it delivered to the airport when you check in. This is a common practice, because the Japanese do not think it's cool to roll big suitcases in a train station. **Konbini** stores sell popular Japanese-style hot meals, (including **oden**, a Japanese hot-pot), snacks, and cigarettes. Because they are open 24/7, you never have to be hungry or thirsty as long as you have a small amount of money. They also sell magazines and comic books, so you can go there at any time, even at midnight, whenever you feel bored.

THINGS AT THE SUPERMARKET

肉 **niku**	meat
魚 **sakana**	fish
野菜 **yasai**	vegetables
果物 **kudamono**	fruit
牛肉 **gyūniku, bīfu**	beef
鶏肉 **toriniku, chikin**	chicken (meat)
豚肉 **butaniku, pōku**	pork
レタス **retasu**	lettuce
ねぎ **negi**	scallion, green onion
ほうれん草 **hōrensō**	spinach
りんご **ringo**	apple
みかん **mikan**	tangerine
桃 **momo**	peach
キャッシャー **kyasshā**	cashier
買い物かご **kaimono kago**	shopping basket

CULTURE NOTE *Depachika*

If you want to explore Japanese food culture, visit **depachika**, a department store's food floor in its basement. The word **depachika** is an abbreviation of **depāto** 'department store' and **chika** 'basement.' At **depachika**, they usually sell processed, baked, or cooked foods including ham, roasted meat, bento lunch boxes, sushi rolls, pickles, dumplings, and pastries. Most of them are from well-known makers, hotels, or restaurants, and some of them are prepared on-site. They also sell fresh fruit, seafood, and meat from special areas, like Kobe beef and Yubari melon that could cost a fortune. The presentation of foods is done meticulously, with elaborate lighting and showcases. Sales staff are very informative and courteous.

Online shopping

クレジットカード **kurejitto kādo**	credit card
ネットショッピング **netto shoppingu**	Internet shopping
買い物カート **kaimonokāto**	shopping cart
ランキング **rankingu**	rank
ネットオークション **netto ōkushon**	Internet auction
送料無料 **sōryōmuryō**	free shipping
クリック **kurikku**	click
商品 **shōhin**	merchandise, item

ATM terms

ATM **ei tī emu**	ATM
お預入れ **o-azukeire**	deposit
お引き出し **o-hikidashi**	withdrawal
残高照会 **zandakashōkai**	balance inquiry
暗証番号 **anshōbangō**	PIN number
デビットカード **debittokādo**	debit card

Time during the day

朝 **asa**	morning
昼 **hiru**	noon
晩 **ban**	evening
夜 **yoru**	night
夕方 **yūgata**	dusk
明け方 **akegata**	dawn

Adjectives

高い **takai**	is high, is expensive
安い **yasui**	is cheap, is easy
欲しい **hoshii**	is desirable, is wanted
おいしい **oishii**	is delicious
すごい **sugoi**	awesome, wonderful

Fashion

エレガント（だ）**eleganto (da)**	(is) elegant
シック（だ）**shikku (da)**	(is) chic
派手（だ）**hade (da)**	(is) showy

地味（だ）**jimi (da)**	(is) conservative
子どもっぽい **kodomoppoi**	is childish
大人っぽい **otonappoi**	is adult-like
かわいい **kawaii**	is cute
かっこいい **kakkoii**	is cool
きれい（だ）**kirei (da)**	(is) pretty

VERBS

買う・買います **kau/kaimasu**	buys
売る・売ります **uru/urimasu**	sells
数える・数えます **kazoeru/kazoemasu**	counts, enumerates
かかる・かかります **kakaru/kakarimasu**	takes (time, cost); time/cost is taken/required

Structure Notes

6.1. Numerals and numbers

In Japanese there are two classes of words corresponding to English number words: "numerals" and "numbers." A number is a compound word consisting of a numeral (like **ichi** 'one') plus a counter (like **-mai**, the counter for flat, thin objects). You use simple numerals when you are talking about figures in the abstract, as in an arithmetic problem, where you are not counting anything in particular; you use numbers when your figures apply to something more definite, like a certain number of books, pencils, or people, or a certain quantity of water, distance, time, or money. To ask 'how many...,' you attach either **iku-** or (more often) **nan-** to the counter, as in **iku-tsu** 'how many pieces' or **nan-mai** 'how many sheets (of flat items).'

6.2. Other quantity words

In addition to numbers there are some other words that indicate quantity or amount in a more general way. These words are nouns but are often used as adverbs, just like the numbers. Here are some you will find useful:

沢山 **takusan**	lots, much, many
少し **sukoshi**	a little, a few, a bit
大勢 **ōzei**	many (used only for people)
みんな **minna**	all, everything, everybody

The word **minna** only has the meaning 'everybody' when used as a noun with some particle: **Minna ga kimashita** 'Everybody came' or **Minna kimashita** '(They) all came.' When used as an adverb it means 'all' or 'every' and can refer to people or things: **Gakusei ga minna kimashita** 'The students all came.' Here are some examples of these words in sentences:

洋服を沢山買いました。
Yōfuku o takusan kaimashita.
I bought a lot of clothes.

この店は子供服も少しあります。
Kono mise wa kodomo fuku mo sukoshi arimasu.
This store has some children's clothes.

お客さんが大勢来ました。
Okyaku-san ga ōzei kimashita.
Many shoppers came.

この店の漫画はみんな読んだことがあります。
Kono mise no manga wa minna yonda koto ga arimasu.
I have read all the comic books in this store.

6.3. Use of numbers and quantity words

Numbers and quantity words occur as ordinary nouns, connected by **no** to the nouns they modify. They occur also as adverbs without any particle following, and in this case they usually follow the NOUN + PARTICLE expression to which they refer, although sometimes they are put at the very beginning as if modifying the whole sentence, and sometimes you hear them in other positions.

If the particle after the noun is any particle other than **wa**, **ga**, or **o**, the number or quantity word must precede as a regular modifying noun: **futari no hito kara** 'from two people,' **takusan no gakkō e** 'to many schools.' But if the particle after the noun is **wa**, **ga**, or **o**, the number or quantity word can either precede with **no**, or follow as an adverb with no particle at all. There is a slight difference of meaning. If the quantity word or number is used as an adverb, the noun is referred to in an "indefinite" fashion: **enpitsu ga nihon** 'two pencils (some or any two pencils),' **ocha ga sukoshi** 'a little bit of tea.' If the quantity word or number is used as a modifying noun, the reference is more "definite": **nihon no enpitsu ga** 'THE two pencils,' **kono sukoshi no ocha ga** 'this little bit of tea.'

This is about the only place where Japanese maintains the English distinction between 'A man' (**hito wa hitori**) and 'THE man' (**hitori no hito wa**), and it is possible only when the particle involved is **wa**, **ga**, or **o**. When a number or quantity word is used as an adverb with no particle following, it's as if the meaning were 'to the extent of . . .': **tegami o nitsū kakimashita** 'I wrote letters to the extent of two' = 'I wrote two letters'; **tegami o takusan kakimashita** 'I wrote letters to the extent of a lot' = 'I wrote a lot of letters.' Here are more examples:

この二人のアメリカ人は私の友達です。
Kono futari no Amerikijin wa watashi no tomodachi desu.
These two Americans are my friends.

昨晩学生が二人遊びに来ました。
Sakuban gakusei ga futari asobi ni kimashita.
Last night two students came to call on me.

二人の学生は日本語ができますか。
Futari no gakusei wa Nihongo ga dekimasu ka.
Do the two students know Japanese?

日本語が少しできます。
Nihongo ga sukoshi deki masu.
They know a little Japanese.

「何曲ダウンロードしましたか。」 「３曲ダウンロードしました。」
"Nankyoku daunrōdo shimashita ka." **"Sankyoku daunrōdo shimashita."**
"How many pieces of music did you "I downloaded three."
download?"

6.4. Primary and secondary numerals

The numeral system of Japanese includes a primary set, most of which was borrowed from the Chinese—and a secondary set, consisting of early native Japanese elements. The secondary system is used only for counting certain things, and is virtually limited to the first ten number and quantity words. After ten, even those things counted with the secondary set take the primary numerals, and some people use primary numerals for figures lower than ten. A given numeral or number often has variant forms. In the chart on the following page, the more common variant is given first. In certain combinations, only one of the given variants may occur, but in general they are used interchangeably.

6.5. Primary numerals

From one to ten, the digits are simple words. From ten to twenty they are compound words consisting of **jū** 'ten' plus one of the other digits. The even tens (twenty, thirty, forty, etc.) are compound words consisting of one of the digits plus **jū** 'ten.' In other words, the Japanese reads 13 as 'ten-three' and 30 as 'three-ten.' The hundreds and thousands work like the tens: 300 is 3 x 100 (**san-byaku**), 3000 is 3 x 1000 (**san-zen**). You will notice some changes in the pronunciation of the individual elements when they occur in certain compounds. These are summarized below in note 6.8. Other numerals (like 21, 103, 1007, 2326) consist of a phrase of several words: **sanzen sanbyaku sanjū san** '3333'. Here is a list of the primary numerals. Some of the numbers have more than one possible form, as you can see below. The more frequently used one is listed first, but the choice among variants depends on the context and individual preference.

Primary Numerals		
0*	れい; ゼロ	rei; zero
1	いち	ichi
2	に	ni
3	さん	san
4	よん; し	yon; shi
5	ご	go
6	ろく	roku
7	なな; しち	nana; shichi
8	はち	hachi
9	きゅう; く	kyu; ku
10	じゅう	jū
11	じゅういち	jūichi
12	じゅうに	jūni
13	じゅうさん	jūsan
14	じゅうよん; じゅうし	jūyon; jūshi
15	じゅうご	jūgo
16	じゅ.うろく	jūroku
17	じゅうなな; じゅうしち	jūnana; jūshichi
18	じゅうはち	jūhachi
19	じゅうきゅう; じゅうく	jūkyū; jūku
20	にじゅう	nijū
21	にじゅういち	nijū ichi
22	にじゅうに	nijū ni
23	にじゅうさん	nijū san
24	にじゅうよん; にじゅうし	nijū yon; nijū shi
25	にじゅうご	nijū go
26	にじゅうろく	nijū roku
27	にじゅうなな; にじゅうしち	nijū nana; nijū shichi
28	にじゅうはち	nijū hachi
29	にじゅうきゅう;にじゅうく	nijū kyū; nijū ku
30	さんじゅう	sanjū
33	さんじゅうさん	sanjū san

* The number 0 can also be pronounced as **maru**, which literally means a circle.

Primary Numerals		
40	よんじゅう；しじゅう	**yonjū; shijū**
44	よんじゅうよん	**yonjū yon**
50	ごじゅう	**gojū**
55	ごじゅうご	**gojū go**
60	ろくじゅう	**rokujū**
66	ろくじゅうろく	**rokujū roku**
70	ななじゅう	**nanajū**
77	ななじゅうなな	**nanajū nana**
80	はちじゅう	**hachijū**
88	はちじゅうはち	**hachijū hachi**
90	きゅうじゅう	**kyūjū**
99	きゅうじゅうきゅう	**kyūjū kyū**
100	ひゃく	**hyaku**
101	ひゃくいち	**hyaku ichi**
199	ひゃくきゅうじゅうきゅう	**hyaku kyūjū kyū**
200	にひゃく	**nihyaku**
300	さんびゃく	**sanbyaku**
400	よんひゃく	**yonhyaku**
500	ごひゃく	**gohyaku**
600	ろっぴゃく	**roppyaku**
700	ななひゃく	**nanahyaku**
800	はっぴゃく	**happyaku**
900	きゅうひゃく	**kyūhyaku**
1,000	せん	**sen**
2,000	にせん	**nisen**
3,000	さんぜん	**sanzen**
4,000	よんせん	**yonsen**
5,000	ごせん	**gosen**
6,000	ろくせん	**rokusen**
7,000	ななせん	**nanasen**
8,000	はっせん	**hassen**
9,000	きゅうせん	**kyūsen**
10,000	いちまん	**ichiman**
20,000	にまん	**niman**
30,000	さんまん	**sanman**
80,000	はちまん	**hachiman**
100,000	じゅうまん	**jūman**
500,000	ごじゅうまん	**gojūman**
1,000,000	ひゃくまん	**hyakuman**
100,000,000	いちおく	**ichioku**

Primary Numerals		
1,000,000,000	じゅうおく	jūoku
100,000,000,000	いっちょう	itchō
1,000,000,000,000	じゅっちょう	jutchō

6.6. Arithmetic

To ask the price of things, you can say, for example:

いくらですか。 **Ikura desu ka.**   How much is it?

いくらになりますか。 **Ikura ni narimasu ka.**   How much does it become?

いくらしますか。 **Ikura shimasu ka.**   How much does it cost?

To ask the quantity of things, you can say:

いくつですか。 **Ikutsu desu ka.**   How many is it?

いくつになりますか。 **Ikutsu ni narimasu ka.** How many does it become?

Common arithmetic problems are said as follows:

２に３を足すと いくつになりますか。

Ni ni san o tasu to ikutsu ni narimasu ka.

How much is 2 + 3? (When you add 3 to 2, how many does it become?)

９から４を引くと５になります。

Kyū kara yon o hiku to go ni narimasu.

9 – 4 is 5. (When you subtract 4 from 9, it becomes 5.)

８に７を掛けるといくつになりますか。

Hachi ni nana o kakeru to ikutsu ni narimasu ka.

How much is 8 x 7? (When you multiply 8 by 7, how much does it become?)

３６を３で割ると１２になります。

Sanjū roku o san de waru to jūni ni narimasu.

36 ÷ 3 is 12. (When you divide 36 by 3, it becomes 12.)

6.7. Counters

There are three kinds of counters: "unit counters" (like 3 pounds, 2 hours, 4 years), "class counters" (like 400 head of cattle, a loaf of bread, 2 sheets of paper), and "ordinal counters." Unit counters are used to refer to a quantity of something divisible like water, time, money, and distance. Class counters are used for general classes of things that aren't ordinarily divisible, like animals, people, pencils, and books. Ordinal counters are used to specify the place in some order in time, place, and hierarchy.

Here is a list of some common unit counters:

ーグラム **-guramu**	...grams
ーキロ(グラム) **-kiro(guramu)**	...kilograms
ーメートル **-mētoru**	...meters
ーキロ(メートル) **-kiro(mētoru)**	...kilometers
ーセンチ(メートル) **-senchi(mētoru)**	...centimeters
ーミリ(メートル) **-miri (mētoru)**	...millimeters
ーリットル **-rittoru**	...liters
ーマイル **-mairu**	...miles (English)
ーインチ **-inchi**	...inches (English)
ードル **-doru**	...dollars
ー円 **-en**	...yen (Japanese currency unit)
ーポンド **-pondo**	...pounds (English weight or money)
ー時間 **-jikan**	...hours
ー週間 **-shūkan**	...weeks
ーヶ月 **-kagetsu**	...months

Here is a list of some common class counters:

ー台	**-dai**	vehicles, mounted machines
ー杯	**-hai**	containerfuls
ー本	**-hon**	slender objects (pencils, tubes, sticks, cigarettes, bottles, flowers)
ー枚	**-mai**	flat, thin objects (sheets, newspapers, handkerchiefs, dishes)
ー冊	**-satsu**	(bound) volumes (books, magazines)
ー件	**-ken**	buildings
ー通	**-tsū**	letters
ー頭	**-tō**	large animals (horses, cows)
ー匹	**-hiki**	animals, fishes, insects
ー着	**-chaku**	suits, dresses

Here's a list of some commonly used ordinal counters:

ー時	**-ji**	...o'clock
ー階	**-kai**	...th floor
ー月	**-gatsu**	...month names (e.g. January, February)
ーページ	**-pēji**	page ... (e.g. page 46)

6.8. Sound changes

There are a few irregularities when certain numerals are combined with counters. These are summarized below.

1. The last syllable of **ichi** and **hachi** is usually replaced by **p** before **p**, **t** before **t** or **ch**, **s** before **s** or **sh**, and **k** before **k**:

ip-pēji	1 page	**hap-pēji**	8 pages
it-tō	1 animal	**hat-tō**	8 animals
it-tsū	1 letter	**hat-tsū**	8 letters
it-chaku	1 suit	**hat-chaku**	8 suits
is-sai	1 year old	**has-sai**	8 years old
ik-ken	1 building	**hak-ken**	8 buildings

2. The numeral **jū** is usually replaced by **jup** before **p**, **jut** before **t** or **ch**, **jus** before **s** or **sh**, **juk** before **k**. Some speakers use **jip-**, **jit-**, **jis-**, and **jik-** instead of the forms with the vowel **u**.

jup-pēji	10 pages
jut-tō	10 animals
jut-tsū	10 letters
jut-chaku	10 suits
jus-sai	10 years old
juk-ken	10 buildings

3. The numerals **san** and **yon** and the element **nan-**'which, how many' are pronounced as **sam-**, **yom-**, **nam-** before **b**, **p**, or **m** to assimilate the place of articulation. In this book, they are still written with 'n' instead of 'm'. So, **san-pēji** '3 pages' will pronounced as **sam-pēji**. This change to **m** in the spelling works for any **n** before **b**, **p**, or **m** within a word, so **sen** '1,000' becomes **sem-**, **man** '10,000' becomes **mam-**.

4. Before some counters beginning with a voiced sound, the number **yon** '4' appears in the form **yo-**:

4円 **yo-en**	4 yen
4年 **yo-nen**	4 years
4時 **yo-ji**	4 o'clock
4時間 **yo-jikan**	4 hours

Compare **yon-byō** '4 seconds', **yon-jū** '40', **yon-man** '40,000'. For some words, where both forms are heard, the longer is to be preferred: **yo(n)-ban** 'number 4', **yo(n)-retsu** '4 rows'.

5. Counters beginning with **h** or **f** (including the numeral **hyaku** 'hundred' when the second element in a compound numeral) replace this by **p** after **ichi- (ip-)**, **hachi- (hap-)**, **jū (jup-)**. After **san-**, **nan-**, counters change initial **h** to **b**, initial **f** to **p**. After **yon**, a majority of speakers keep the initial **h** intact, but many people say **yon-pun** rather than **yon-fun** '4 minutes'.

	hyaku	hon	hai	hiki	fun
1	--	一本 **ip-pon**	一杯 **ip-pai**	一匹 **ip-piki**	一分 **ip-pun**
8	八百 **hap-pyaku**	八本 **hap-pon**	八杯 **hap-pai**	八匹 **hap-piki**	八分 **hap-pun**
10	--	十本 **jup-pon**	十杯 **jup-pai**	十匹 **jup-piki**	十分 **jup-pun**
3	三百 **san-byaku**	三本 **san-bon**	三杯 **san-bai**	三匹 **san-biki**	三分 **san-pun**
how many	何百 **nan-byaku**	何本 **nan-bon**	何杯 **nan-bai**	何匹 **nan-biki**	何分 **nan-pun**
1,000	--	千本 **sen-bon**	千杯 **sen-bai**	千匹 **sen-biki**	(千分) **(sen-pun)**
4	四百 **yon-hyaku**	四本 **yon-hon**	四杯 **yon-hai**	四匹 **yon-hiki**	四分 **yon-pun**

6. The numerals **roku-** and **hyaku-** become **rop-** and **hyap** before counters beginning with **h** or **f**; the counters replace **h** or **f** by **p**. Some speakers use **rop-** and **hyap-** before counters beginning with a basic **p** also. Some speakers maintain the basic forms **roku-h-** and **roku-f-**, **hyaku-h-** and **hyaku-f-**, insetad of **rop-p-** and **hyap-p-**.

rop-pon, roku-hon	**hyap-pon, hyaku-hon**
rop-pai, roku-hai	**hyap-pai, hyaku-hai**
rop-piki, roku-hiki	**hyap-piki, hyaku-hiki**
rop-pun, roku-fun	**hyap-pun, hyaku-fun**
roku-pēji, rop-pēji	**hyaku-pēji, hyap-pēji**

7. The numerals **roku-** and **hyaku-** become **rok-** and **hyak-** before counters beginning with **k-**: **rok-ken** '6 buildings', **hyak-ken** '100 buildings'.

8. After **san-** '3' and **nan-** 'how many', the elements **-sen** meaning 'thousand', **-kai** 'floor', and **-ken** 'buildings' are respectively **-zen**, **-gai**, and **-gen**.

san-zen 3,000	nan-zen how many thousand
san-gen 3 buildings	nan-gen how many buildings

9. With most counters, either **ku** or **kyū** may be used for '9', either **shichi** or **nana** for '7', either **shi** or **yon (yo-)** for '4'. For some counters only one of the forms occurs: **Shigatsu** 'April', **Shichigatsu** 'July', **Kugatsu** 'September'; **yoji** '4 o'clock', and **kuji** '9 o'clock'.

6.9. Secondary numerals

The secondary set of numerals consists of early native Japanese elements. They run from 1 to 10, and for each digit there are two forms: a long form, used when the numeral is a word by itself, and a short form, used when the numeral is combined with a counter. In addition, there are a few special short forms, used on enumerative occasions, like 'counting off' in gym or in the military.

	As a Word	In a Number	Counting Off
1	ひとつ **hitotsu**	**hito-**	**hi, hī, hito**
2	ふたつ **futatsu**	**futa-**	**fu, fū, futa**
3	みっつ **mittsu**	**mi-**	**mi, mī**
4	よっつ **yottsu**	**yo-**	**yo, yō**
5	いつつ **itsutsu**	**itsu**	**i, ī, itsu**
6	むっつ **muttsu**	**mu-**	**mu, mū**
7	ななつ **nanatsu**	**nana-**	**na, nā, nana**
8	やっつ **yattsu**	**ya-**	**ya, yā**
9	ここのつ **kokonotsu**	**kokono-**	**koko, kono, kō**
10	とお **tō**	**to-, tō-**	**to, tō**
How many?	いくつ **ikutsu**	**iku-**	---

The secondary numerals are used with certain counters. They are also used by themselves to count words that do not take any special counter: **kaban ga hitotsu** 'one suitcase', **futatsu no mado ga** 'the two windows', **mittsu no tsukue** '3 desks'. For counting above 10, the primary numerals can be used by themselves, but they are often followed by the counter **-ko**: **kaban ga jūgo** or **kaban ga jūgo-ko** '15 suitcases'.

The secondary numerals are also commonly used to give ages: **Ano kodomo wa itsutsu deshō** 'That child must be five (years old)'. **Watashi wa kotoshi sanjū desu** 'I'm 30 this year'. **Okāsama wa o-ikutsu desu ka?** 'How old is your mother?' There is a special word for '20 years old', **hatachi**. A somewhat more formal way of stating ages is with the primary numerals + the counter **-sai** 'years of age':

「あなたは何歳ですか。」   「２１歳です。」
"Anata wa nansai desu ka."   **"Nijū-issai desu."**
"How old are you?"   "I'm 21."

6.10. Secondary counters

Here are some counters often used with the secondary numerals. Some speakers use the secondary numerals only for the first few numbers, then switch to the other set; other speakers do not switch to the primary set of numerals until eleven.

一晩	**-ban**	nights
一袋	**-fukuro**	bagfuls
一箱	**-hako**	boxfuls
一部屋	**-heya**	rooms
一切れ	**-kire**	slices, cuts, pieces
一組	**-kumi**	groups, sets (of matched objects)
一間	**-ma**	rooms
一皿	**-sara**	platefuls
一匙	**-saji**	spoonfuls
一揃え	**-soroe**	sets
一束	**-taba**	bunches
一月	**-tsuki**	months (=**-kagetsu** used with primary numerals)

一晩ボストンのホテルに泊まった。
Hitoban Bosuton no hoteru ni tomatta.
I stayed at a hotel in Boston for one night.

このうちには寝室が二間しかない。
Kono uchi ni wa shinshitsu ga futama shika nai.
This house only has two bedrooms.

6.11. Counting people

There are some irregularities in the set of numbers used to count people. Most of the numbers are made up of primary numbers + the counter **-nin**, but there are different forms for 1, 2, and 4. (The expected forms *ichinin, *ninin do occur in some compounds, for example, **ichinin-mae** 'food order for one person.')

1人	**hitori**	1 person
2人	**futari**	2 people
3人	**sannin**	3 people
4人	**yonin**	4 people
5人	**gonin**	5 people
6人	**rokunin**	6 people
7人	**nananin, shichinin**	7 people

8人	**hachinin**	8 people
9人	**kyūnin, kunin**	9 people
10人	**jūnin**	10 people
11人	**jūichinin**	11 people
何人	**nannin**	how many people?
222人	**nihyaku nijū ninin**	222 people

この店には店員が2人います。
Kono mise ni wa ten'in ga futari imasu.
There are two store clerks in this store.

その3人のダンサーはアメリカ人です。
Sono sannin no dansā wa Amerika-jin desu.
Those three dancers are Americans.

6.12. Counting birds

The usual counter for birds, any kinds of bird including sparrows, cranes, ducks, and chickens, is **-wa**, which has the forms **-pa** and **-ba** after certain numerals:

1羽	**ichiwa**
2羽	**niwa**
3羽	**sanba, sanwa**
4羽	**yonwa, yonba**
5羽	**gowa**
6羽	**roppa, rokuwa**
7羽	**nanawa, shichiwa**
8羽	**happa, hachiwa**

９羽	**kyūwa**
１０羽	**juppa, jippa**
何羽 how many birds?	**nanba**

6.13. Counting days

There are a number of irregularities in counting days. The numbers mean either 'so-and-so many days' or 'the so-and-so-many-th day of the month,' except that these two meanings are distinguished for the first number: **ichinichi** '1 day,' **tsuitachi** '1st day.'

１日	**tsuitachi**	1st day
１日	**ichinichi**	1 day
２日	**futsuka**	2 days, 2nd day
３日	**mikka**	3 days, 3rd day
４日	**yokka**	4 days, 4th day
５日	**itsuka**	5 days, 5th day
６日	**muika**	6 days, 6th day
７日	**nanoka**	7 days, 7th day
８日	**yōka**	8 days, 8th day
９日	**kokonoka**	9 days, 9th day
１０日	**tōka**	10 days, 10th day
１１日	**jūichinichi**	11 days, 11th day
１２日	**jūninichi**	12 days, 12th day
１３日	**jūsannichi**	13 days, 13th day
１４日	**jūyokka**	14 days, 14th day
１５日	**jūgonichi**	15 days, 15th day
１６日	**jūrokunichi**	16 days, 16th day
１７日	**jūshichinichi**	17 days, 17th day
１８日	**jūhachinichi**	18 days, 18th day
１９日	**jūkunichi**	19 days, 19th day
２０日	**hatsuka**	20 days, 20th day
２１日	**nijū ichinichi**	21 days, 21st day
２２日	**nijū ninichi**	22 days, 22nd day
２３日	**nijū sannichi**	23 days, 23rd day
２４日	**nijū yokka**	24 days, 24th day
２５日	**nijū gonichi**	25 days, 25th day
２６日	**nijū rokunichi**	26 days, 26th day
２７日	**nijū shichinichi**	27 days, 27th day
２８日	**nijū hachinichi**	28 days, 28th day
２９日	**nijū kunichi**	29 days, 29th day
３０日	**sanjūn ichi**	30 days, 30th day
３１日	**sanjū ichinichi**	31 days, 31st day
何日	**nannichi**	how many days, which day of month?

Most of the numbers are made up of primary numerals + the counter **-nichi** (in rapid speech sometimes pronounced **-nchi**), but the numbers from 2 through 10, 14, 20, and 24 contain elements from the set of secondary numerals + the counter **-ka**.

6.14. Names of the months

The names of the months are made by adding the counter **-gatsu** to the primary numerals:

1 月	**Ichigatsu**	January
2 月	**Nigatsu**	February
3 月	**Sangatsu**	March
4 月	**Shigatsu**	April
5 月	**Gogatsu**	May
6 月	**Rokugatsu**	June
7 月	**Shichigatsu**	July
8 月	**Hachigatsu**	August
9 月	**Kugatsu**	September
1 0 月	**Jūgatsu**	October
1 1 月	**Jūichigatsu**	November
1 2 月	**Jūnigatsu**	December

Notice that the older variants for 4, 7, and 9 (**shi-**, **shichi-**, and **ku-**) are always used in the month names instead of the more common forms **yon-**, **nana-**, and **kyū**. There is also another word for January, **Shōgatsu**. Be sure to differentiate **Nigatsu** '(the second month =) February' from **nikagetsu** 'two months.' To ask 'which month' you say **nangatsu**; to ask 'how many months' you say **nankagetsu**.

6.15. Giving dates

To say which year it is, you attach the counter **-nen** to the appropriate numerals as in **sen kyūhyaku gojū ninen** '1952.' If you add the month, it follows this, and then comes the day of the month—and, if you like, the day of the week and the time of day. For example:

> 1 9 5 2 年 6 月 2 3 日 月曜日午後 3 時
> **sen kyūhyaku gojū ichinen Rokugatsu nijū sannichi getsuyōbi gogo sanji**
> 3 p.m., Monday, 23 June 1951

6.16. Telling time

To say it is such-and-such o'clock, you use a primary numeral + the counter **-ji**: **goji desu** 'it's 5 o'clock.' If you want to say 'it's five minutes past five (5:05)' you say **goji gofun desu** or **goji gofun sugi desu**—the word **sugi** means 'exceeding, more than.' To say 'it's five minutes before five (4:55)' you say **goji gofun mae desu**. **Mae**, of course, means 'before, in front of.' Or you can say **yoji gojūgofun desu** just as you can say 'four fifty-five' in English. To say 'at' a certain time, you use the particle **ni**: **goji ni kimashita** 'he came at five.'

If you want to add 'a.m.' and 'p.m.,' you put the words **gozen** 'before-noon' and **gogo** 'after-noon' in front of the time expression. So 'from 9 a.m. to 9 p.m.' is **gozen kuji kara gogo kuji made**.

To say 'half-past ten' or the like, you just add **-han** 'and a half' at the end of the time expression: **gogo rokuji-han** 'half past six in the evening.'

Notice the difference between **sanji** '(the third hour =) 3 o'clock' and **sanjikan** '3 hours.' To ask 'what time (= which hour, what o'clock)' you say **nanji**. To ask 'how much time, how long (=how many hours)' you say **nanjikan**.

「今何時ですか。」
"Ima nanji desu ka."
"What time is it now?"

「3時45分です。」
"Sanji yonjūgofun desu."
"It's 3:45."

6.17. -ぐらい *-gurai* / -ごろ *-goro*

The particle **gurai** means 'approximate quantity, about so much.' **Gurai** is often written (and sometimes pronounced) **kurai**. There is a related noun **kurai** that means 'position, rank.' Notice also the idioms **kono-kurai** (or **kono-gurai**) and **kore-kurai** (= **kore gurai**) 'this much, to this extent.'

4時間ぐらいかかりました。
Yojikan gurai kakarimashita.
It took me for about four hours.

4時ぐらいに来てくれませんか。
Yoji gurai ni kite kuremasen ka.
Could you come here at around 4 p.m?

これぐらいのことで文句を言ってはいけません。
Koregurai no koto de monku o itte wa ikemasen.
You should not complain about this kind of thing. (It's not a big deal.)

By contrast, the particle **goro** means 'approximate point in time, about then' and cannot be used for quantity. The idiom **kono-goro** means 'recently' (= **chikagoro**). Compare the related noun **koro** 'time, era, period,' as in **ano koro wa** 'at that time (period).'

４時ごろに来てくれませんか。
Yoji goro ni kite kuremasen ka.
Could you come here at around 4 p.m?

あの頃は日本はまだ貧しい国でした。
Ano koro wa Nihon wa mada mazushii kuni deshita.
Japan was still a poor country at that time.

6.18. Particle や *ya*

The particle **ya** is used to make an incomplete enumeration. When you list several things but have not exhausted all the items on your list, you use **ya**. If you do exhaust the list, giving all the items, then you connect the items with the particle **to**. Notice that the particles **to** and **ya** usually occur after every item in the list except the last. After the last item, you use whatever particle is appropriate to show the relationship between the whole phrase and the rest of the sentence.

お酒やビールやワインを買いました。
Osake ya bīru ya wain o kaimashita.
I bought things like sake, beer, and wine.

お酒とビールとワインを買いました。
Osake to bīru to wain o kaimashita.
I bought sake, beer, and wine.

6.19. など *nado,* なんか *nanka*

The particle **nado** is used after a noun, with or without other particles (including **ga**, **o**, and **wa**) following. The English equivalent is often 'and the like, et cetera, and so on, or something of the sort.' The force of the particle is to make the limits of the preceding phrase somewhat more vague. It often occurs after a group of nouns that are usually connected to each other by the particle **ya**, but sometimes the particle is omitted.

Ｔシャツやセーターなどを買いました。
Tīshatsu ya sētā nado o kaimashita.
I bought T-shirts and sweaters and the like.

兄弟と喧嘩なんかしますか。
Kyōdai to kenka nanka shimasu ka.
Do you do such a thing as fight with your siblings.

Occasionally the particle **nado** occurs after a verb or adjective in the plain imperfect or perfect:

イギリスに留学するなどと言っています。
Igirisu ni ryūgaku suru nado to itte imasu.
He's talking of going to study abroad in England and the like.

The particle **nanka** means 'the likes of' with negative or deprecatory implications:

私なんかそんなことはできません。
Watashi nanka sonna koto wa dekimasen
A person like me wouldn't be able to do such a thing.

英語なんか知りません。
Eigo nanka shirimasen.
I don't know any ENGLISH (it's too hard for me)!

6.20. Particle か *ka* meaning 'or'

You have learned the particle **ka** as a sort of audible question mark. It also occurs after a noun with the meaning '(either...) or....' Here are some examples:

本か雑誌を買って読みましょう。
Hon ka zasshi o katte yomimashō.
I guess I'll buy a book or magazine to read.

あしたかあさって行くでしょう。
Ashita ka asatte iku deshō.
I expect he'll go either tomorrow or the next day.

ほうれん草を1束か2束買いましょう。
Hōrensō o hitotaba ka futataba kaimashō.
I guess I'll buy 1 or 2 bunches of spinach.

青木さんか鈴木さんが来ます。
Aoki-san ka Suzuki-san ga kimasu.
Mr. Aoki or Mr. Suzuki (or someone) will come.

Notice the difference in meaning between these two sentences:

お茶かコーヒーは好きですか。
O-cha ka kōhī wa suki desu ka.
Do you like tea or coffee? (either one)

お茶が好きですか。コーヒーが好きですか。
O-cha ga suki desu ka. Kōhī ga suki desu ka.
Do you like tea? Or, do you like coffee? (which one)

6.21. Particles は *wa* and を *o* with いかがですか *ikaga desu ka*

If you want to offer a person some tea, you usually say:

お茶はいかがですか。
O-cha wa ikaga desu ka.
How about some tea?

In this expression, the particle used is **wa**. If you use a quantity word, however, the particle must be **o**.

お茶を一杯いかがですか。
O-cha o ippai ikaga desu ka.
How about a cup of tea?

お茶をもう少しいかがですか。
O-cha o mō sukoshi ikaga desu ka.
How about a little more tea?

6.22. ひとつ *hitotsu*

Sometimes the word **hitotsu** is used, not to mean 'one' of something but to mean 'just,' 'a little,' 'some,' or 'once':

中華料理を一ついかがですか。
Chūka-ryōri o hitotsu ikaga desu ka.
How about some Chinese food?

では，田中さんに一つ協力してみましょう。
Dewa Tanaka-san ni hitotsu kyōryoku shite mimashō.
Okay then, let me collaborate with Mr. Tanaka a little.

6.23. Only: -だけ *-dake* and -しか *-shika*

There are two common ways to say 'only' in Japanese: **dake** and **shika**. **Dake** is a particle that means something like 'to the extent of' and 'to the limit of.' When following a noun that would ordinarily take the particle **ga** or **o**, usually only **dake** occurs; but if the noun is followed by some particle other than **ga** or **o**, then both **dake** and the particle occur—usually in that order. Here are some examples of **dake**:

昨日の晩は私だけ映画を見に行ったんです。
Kinō no ban wa watashi dake eiga o mi ni itta n desu.
Last night I was the only one who went to see the movie.

この雑誌だけ読みませんでした。
Kono zasshi dake yomimasen deshita.
This is the only magazine I didn't read.

これは先生だけに言ってください。
Kore wa sensei dake ni itte kudasai.
Please tell this only to the teacher.

Dake sometimes occurs after a verb or adjective with the meaning 'as much as': **hoshii dake** 'as much as you desire (as is desired),' **dekiru dake** 'as much as possible.' Examples:

できるだけはやく書きました。
Dekiru dake hayaku kaki mashita.
I wrote as fast as I could.

あっただけ食べました。
Atta dake tabemashita.
I ate everything there was.

The other common way to say 'only' is to use the particle **shika** 'but only.' This particle is always followed by the negative; **shika** + the negative has about the same meaning as **dake** + the affirmative: **Kudamono dake kaimashita = Kudamono shika kaimasen deshita** 'I only bought fruit; I bought nothing but fruit.' The basic meaning of **shika** is something like '(nothing) but, except for.' So **Tanaka-san shika kimasen deshita** means something like 'except for Mr. Tanaka (somebody) didn't come,' that is: 'ONLY Mr. Tanaka came.'

The particle **shika**, like the particle **dake**, usually does not occur together with the particles **ga** or **o**. If it occurs with other particles, the others precede **shika**. With **dake** it is more common for the other particles to follow:

先生だけに言いました。
Sensei dake ni iimashita.
I told only the teacher.

先生にしか言いませんでした。
Sensei ni shika iimasen deshita.
I told only the teacher.

If you want to use 'only' + a negative in English ('Only the teacher I didn't tell'), you have to use **dake** in Japanese, since **shika** + the negative would give just the opposite meaning:

先生だけに言いませんでした。
Sensei dake ni iimasen deshita.
The teacher is the only one I didn't tell.

Both **shika** + the negative (but with an affirmative meaning in the English translation) and **dake** with either the negative (with negative meaning in English) or the affirmative are used to translate English 'only' after an ordinary noun. After a number or quantity word, just **shika** + the negative is used to mean 'only'. **Dake** means 'just, neither more nor less than':

十時間かかりました。
Jūjikan kakarimashita.
It took ten hours.

十時間だけかかりました。
Jūjikan dake kakarima shita.
It took just ten hours. (Which seems neither long nor short.)

十時間しかかかりませんでした。
Jūjikan shika kakarimasen deshita.
It took only ten hours. (Which seems short.)

6.24. Approximate numbers

Two consecutive numbers can often be combined to mean 'about 2 or 3, about 3 or 4', etc. These are then added to a single counter.

店員が2, 3人いました。
Ten'in ga ni san nin imashita.
There were 2 or 3 salesclerks.

六, 七年はかかるでしょう。
Rokushichinen wa kakarudeshō.
It will take 6 or 7 years.

Not all possible combinations occur. For instance, none occur with the counter -**ji** 'o'clock' or -**gatsu** 'month'. In such cases, you can use two full words connected by the particle **ka** 'or':

3時か4時に来るでしょう。
Sanji ka yoji ni kuru deshō.
He'll come around 3 or 4 o'clock.

４月か５月でしょう。
Shigatsu ka Gogasu deshō.
It will be April or May.

The secondary numerals usually do not combine in the same way. Instead, the two consecutive numbers are connected by **ka**:

バラを１束か２束買います。
Bara o hitotaba ka futataba kaimasu.
I will buy one or two bunches of roses.

6.25. Fractions

To express ordinary fractions, like 3/4, the Japanese say something like 'three of four parts' using the counter **-bun** 'part.' For 'one-half' there is the special word **hanbun,** and for 'so-many and a half' the regular number takes the suffix **-han** 'and a half:

このクラスの四分の三は男子です。
Kono kurasu no yonbun no san wa danshi desu.
Three-quarters of this class are boys.

武さんはもらったお金の半分を私にくれました。
Takeshi-san wa moratta o-kane no hanbun o watashi ni kuremashita.
Takeshi gave me half of the money he received.

水を３カップ半入れてください。
Mizu o san-kappu han irete kudasai.
Please add 3-1/2 cups of water.

月曜日の朝，11時半にここへ来てください。
Getsuyōbi no asa, jūichiji-han ni koko e kite kudasai.
Please come here at 11:30 a.m. on Monday morning.

２１は６３の三分の一です。
Nijū ichi wa rokujū san no sanbun no ichi desu.
21 is one-third of 63.

6.26. Percentage

The old-fashioned way of expressing percentage in Japanese is to use three different counters: **-rin** '.001 (0.1 percent);' **-bu** '.01 (1 percent);' and **-wari** '.10 (10 percent).' In-between percentages are given by combining these numbers: **niwari sanbu ichirin** '.231 (23.1 percent).' To say '200 is 25 percent of 800' you say **Nihyaku wa happyaku no niwari gobu desu**. However, **pāsento** 'percent' is more commonly used in modern Japanese. For example, the same sentence can be said as:

%

> ２００は８００の２５％です。
> **Nihyaku wa happyaku no nijūgo pāsento desu.**
> 200 is 25 percent of 800.

Other examples:

> 今日は全て3割引きですよ。
> **Kyō wa subete san-wari biki desu yo.**
> Today, everything is 30% OFF!

> この会社の２０パーセントの社員はタバコを吸います。
> **Kono kaisha no nijuppāsento no shain wa tabako o suimasu.**
> Twenty percent of the employees in this company smoke.

6.27. Multiples

To express 'two times (as much or as big, etc., as something else), three times, four times' and so forth, you use the counter **-bai** 'multiple.'

> ６０は２０の3倍です。
> **Rokujū wa nijū no sanbai desu.**
> 60 is 3 times 20.

> これはその２倍です。
> **Kore wa sono nibai desu.**
> This is 2 times (as much as) that.

To state simple multiplication problems, you can say, for example:

> ２０に3を掛けると６０になります。
> **Nijū ni san o kakeru to rokujū ni narimasu.**
> 20 x 3 = 60.

6.28. -ずつ *zutsu*

The particle **zutsu** is placed immediately after a number (numeral + counter) to mean something like 'distributively'. For the English translation you will find its equivalent as 'each, every, at a time, apiece'. The exact reference of the phrase NUMBER + **zutsu** is sometimes in doubt. The sentence **Hitotaba zutsu kaimashita** could mean (1) Everybody bought one bunch; (2) We bought one bunch of each (vegetable); (3) We bought one bunch at a time. The total information actually supplied to us by the sentence is: somebody bought, one bunch was the extent, and there was a distributive relationship between the buying and the one bunch. The NATURE of the relationship of 'each of us', 'each (vegetable)', and 'at a time' has to be inferred from the context or the situation. Often a few additional words in the sentence will help indicate which of the three distributive relationships is referred to:

> みんなが一束ずつ買いました。
> **Minna ga hitotaba zutsu kaimashita.**
> Everybody bought one bunch apiece.

> ほうれん草とねぎを一束ずつ買いました。
> **Hōrensō to negi o hitotaba zusu kaimashita.**
> We bought one bunch each of spinach and green onion.

> 毎朝一束ずつ買いました。
> **Maiasa hitotaba zutsu kaimashita.**
> We bought one bunch (at a time) every morning.

These sentences, too, could be construed with the other meanings, but the additional contexts make the given meanings more probable. There is a similar ambiguity with the English word 'each'. Here are some additional examples of -**zutsu**:

> 昨晩6人の友達に手紙を1通ずつ書きました。
> **Sakuban rokunin no tomodachi ni tegami o ittsū zutsu kakimashita.**
> Last night I wrote each of my six friends a letter.

> 授業時間にことわざを一つずつ習いました。
> **Jugyōjikan ni kotowaza o hitotsu zutsu naraimashita.**
> We learned one proverb in each class.

6.29. ごとに *goto ni,* おきに *oki ni*

The expression **goto ni** is added to a noun or noun phrase to give the meaning 'every so many, each and every': **nijikan goto ni** 'every two hours,' **sannen goto ni** 'every three years.' The expression **oki ni** (from the infinitive of **oku** 'puts aside') means 'regularly skipping': **ichinichi oki ni** 'every other day,' **sangen oki ni** 'every fourth house.'

> 赤ん坊が生まれたら，夜中に２，３時間ごとにおこされた。
> **Akanbō ga umaretara, yonaka ni nisanjikan goto ni okosareta.**
> After the baby was born, I had to wake up every 2 to 3 hours at night.

> ３ヶ月おきに，エンジンオイルを交換します。
> **Sankagetsu oki ni, enjin oiru o kōkan shimasu.**
> I change engine oil every three months.

> １週間ごとに携帯の充電をします。
> **Isshūkan goto ni keitai no jūden o shimasu.**
> I charge my cell phone every week.

6.30. Stores that end in 屋 *ya*

We can refer to some types of stores by a friendly term that ends in **ya**. For example, bookstores are called either **hon'ya** or **shoten**. The former sounds friendly, but the latter sounds formal. In addition, **-ya** can also mean the person who is in the profession in some instances.

本屋 **hon'ya**	bookstore
靴屋 **kutsuya**	shoe store
おもちゃ屋 **omochaya**	toy store
花屋 **hanaya**	flower shop
酒屋 **sakaya**	liquor store
魚屋 **sakanaya**	fish market, fish seller
肉屋 **nikuya**	meat store
飲み屋 **nomiya**	bar
パン屋 **panya**	bakery
電器屋 **denkiya**	electronics store
ラーメン屋 **rāmen'ya**	ramen shop
すし屋 **sushiya**	sushi shop
居酒屋 **izakaya**	Japanese-style bar
焼肉屋 **yakinikuya**	(Korean style) barbecue restaurant

 **Conversation**

[cue 06-3]

Nana (N) and Akiko (A) are talking.

N: 日曜日は何をしましたか。**Nichiyōbi wa nani o shimashita ka.**
    What did you do on Sunday?

A: 渋谷に買い物に行きました。**Shibuya ni kaimono ni ikimashita.**
    I went to Shibuya to shop.

N: 一人でですか。**Hitori de desu ka.** By yourself?

A: いいえ，2人の友達と3人で行きました。
    Īe, futari no tomodachi to sannin de ikimashita.
    No, I went there with two of my friends—three of us went there.

N: 何を買いましたか。**Nani o kaimashita ka.** What did you buy?

A: ショルダーバッグと靴を二足買ったんです。
    Shorudā baggu to, kutsu o nisoku katta n desu.
    I bought a shoulder bag and two pairs of shoes.

N: 安かったんですか。**Yasukatta n desu ka.** Were they cheap?

A: ええ。セールだったんです。すべて５０％オフ！
    Ē. Sēru datta n desu. Subete gojuppāsento ofu.
    Yes. They had a sale. Everything was 50 percent off.

N: 半額ですか。**Hangaku desu ka.** Half price?

A: ええ。友達はドレスや，コートを買っていました。
    Ē. Tomodachi wa doresu ya kōto o katte imashita.
    Yes. My friends were buying dresses, coats, etc.

N: いいですね。**Ii desu ne.** That's great!

A: お昼はイタリア料理のレストランで食べました。
    Ohiru wa Itaria ryōri no resutoran de tabemashita.
    We had lunch at an Italian restaurant.

N: どうでしたか。 **Dō deshita ka.** How was it?

A: まあまあ美味しかったです。 **Māmā oishikatta desu.**
    Yes, it was quite delicious.

Exercises

I. Read the following numbers.

1. 56
2. 397
3. 8,800
4. 1,290
5. 13,500

II. Following the example, say how many items there are.

Example:
バナナ banana (bananas)
バナナが２本あります。 **Banana ga ni-hon arimasu.**

1. りんご **ringo** (apples)

_____

2. 本 **hon** (books)

_____

3. 切手 **kitte** (stamps)

_____

4. ねこ **neko** (cats)

_____

5. 子ども **kokomo** (children)

_____

III. Say the following in Japanese.

1. 3:15 p.m.
2. January 1st
3. Monday, April 9th
4. July 10, 1987
5. September 20, 2012

IV. Choose the appropriate item in the parentheses.

1. ３時（ごろ・など）に来てください。
   Sanji (goro, nado) ni kite kudasai.

2. ５に３を（ひく・たす）といくつですか。
   Go ni san o (hiku, tasu) to ikutsu desu ka.

3. コーヒーを５杯（ごろ・ぐらい）飲みます。
   Kōhī o gohai (goro, gurai) nomimasu.

4. 300円しか（あります・ありません）。
   Sanbyakuen shika (arimasu, arimasen).

5. （２時・２時間）ごとに電車があります。
   (Niji, Nijikan) goto ni densha ga arimasu.

Answers:
I 1. ごじゅうろく **gojūroku** 2. さんびゃくきゅうじゅうなな **sanbyaku kyūjū nana** 3. はっせんはっぴゃく **hassen happyaku** 4. せんにひゃくきゅうじゅう **sen nihyaku kyūjū** 5. いちまんさんぜんごひゃく **ichiman sanzen gohyaku**

II 1. りんごが三つあります。**Ringo ga mittsu arimasu.** 2. 本が二冊あります。**Hon ga nisatsu arimasu.** 3. 切手が四枚あります。**Kitte ga yonmai arimasu.** 4. 猫が三匹います。**Neko ga sanbiki imasu.** 5. 子どもが二人います。**Kodomo ga futari imasu.**

III 1. 午後３時15分 **gogo San-ji jūgo-fun** 2. １月１日 **Ichigatsu tsuitachi** 3. ４月９日月曜日 **Shigatsu kokonoka Getsuyōbi** 4. 1987年７月10日 **sen-kyūhyaku-hachijūnana-nen Shichi-gatsu Tōka** 5. 2012年９月20日 **nisen-jūni-nen Ku-gatsu hatsuka**

IV 1. ごろ **goro** 2. たす **tasu** 3. ぐらい **gurai** 4. ありません **arimasen** 5. ２時間 **nijikan**

Have You Been in a Japanese House?

日本の家に入ったことある？

Nihon no Ie ni Haitta Koto Aru?

In this lesson you will learn vocabulary items that refer to the types, properties, and parts of houses in Japan. You will also learn additional verb forms, particles, and structures so you can express your opinions and convey your understandings more effectively.

Basic Sentences

[cue 07-1]

1.	和室と洋室と，どちらの方が好きですか。 **Washitsu to yōshitsu to, dochira no hō ga suki desu ka.**	Between Japanese-style rooms and Western-style rooms, which ones do you like better?
2.	和室には床の間<u>という</u>ところがあります。 **Washitsu ni wa tokonoma <u>to iu</u> tokoro ga arimasu.**	In the Japanese-style room, there is a place called tokonoma.
3.	床の間にはたいてい掛け軸が<u>掛けてあ</u>ります。 **Tokonoma ni wa taitei kakejiku ga <u>kakete arimasu.</u>**	In the tokonoma a scroll is usually hung.
4.	和室は居間<u>として</u>使えますし，寝室<u>としても使えます。 **Washitsu wa ima <u>to shite</u> tsukaemasu shi, shinshitsu <u>to shite</u> mo tsukaemasu.**	Japanese-style rooms can be used as a living room, and also as a bedroom.

5. 家を建てた<u>ばかり</u>です。
   Ie o tateta <u>bakari</u> desu.

   I just built a house.

6. 今週は住むところを<u>探そう</u>と思っています。
   Konshū wa sumu tokoro o <u>sagasō</u> to omotte imasu.

   I'm thinking of finding a place to live this week.

7. 「うちの中に入るときには，玄関で靴を脱いでください。」
   "Uchi no naka ni hairu toki ni wa, genkan de kutsu o nuide kudasai."

   "When you enter a house, please take off your shoes in the foyer."

   「<u>なるほど</u>。」
   "<u>Naruhodo</u>."

   "Oh, I see."

8. 家賃を払うのを忘れない<u>よう</u>にしてください。
   Yachin o harau no o wasurenai <u>yō</u> ni shite kudasai.

   Try not to forget to pay the rent.

9. 靴を履いた<u>まま</u>家の中に入らないようにしてください。
   Kutsu o haita <u>mama</u> ie no naka ni ikanai yō ni shite kudasai.

   Try not to enter a house with your shoes on.

10. <u>そんな</u>に大変ではありませんから，心配し<u>ないで</u>ください。
    <u>Sonna</u> ni taihen de wa arimasen kara, shinpai shi<u>naide</u> kudasai.

    It's not that hard, so don't worry.

11. トイレは風呂場と<u>同じ</u>ところにありますか。それとも，違うところにありますか。
    Toire wa furoba to <u>onaji</u> tokoro ni arimasu ka. Soretomo, chigau tokoro ni arimasu ka.

    Is the toilet in the same place as the bathroom? Or is it in a different place?

12. 窓から富士山が<u>見えます</u>。
    Mado kara Fujisan ga <u>miemasu</u>.

    We can see Mt. Fuji through the window.

13. 今度遊びに行って<u>みます</u>。
    Kondo asobi ni itte <u>mimasu</u>.

    I'll try visiting there next time.

🎧 Basic Vocabulary

HOUSING

家 **ie**	house
マンション **manshon**	condominium or apartment in neat-looking residential buildings that usually have at least three stories
アパート **apāto**	apartment in residential buildings that usually have one or two stories
社宅 **shataku**	company housing
寮 **ryō**	dormitory

CULTURE NOTE ▶ Manshon

The English word *mansion* refers to a huge, gigantic house like the one that Michael Jackson lived in. However, the Japanese word **manshon** refers to a condominium or an apartment in a relatively neat-looking, new, and tall apartment building. So, anyone with a decent job can rent or buy a **manshon** in Japan. On the other hand, the word **apāto** refers to an apartment in a relatively old and at most two-story building. An **apāto** definitely doesn't have an elevator, whereas a **manshon** usually does have one. The rent for an **apāto** is often much cheaper than that for a **manshon**.

PARTS OF A HOUSE

玄関 **genkan**	entrance, foyer
洋室 **yōshitsu**	Western-style room
和室 **washitsu**	Japanese-style room
寝室 **shinshitsu**	bedroom
キッチン **kitchin**	kitchen
トイレ **toire**	toilet

風呂場 **furoba**	bathing room
窓 **mado**	window
壁 **kabe**	wall
床 **yuka**	floor
ドア **doa**	door
障子 **shōji**	translucent sliding paper doors
襖 **fusuma**	opaque sliding paper doors
床の間 **tokonoma**	raised alcove or recess used for ornamental purposes and as a sort of family shrine

THINGS IN A HOUSE

絵 **e**	paintings, drawings, illustrations
花瓶 **kabin**	vase
スリッパ **surippa**	slippers
電子レンジ **denshi renji**	microwave
洗濯機 **sentakuki**	laundry machine
乾燥機 **kansōki**	dryer
冷蔵庫 **reizōko**	refrigerator

*Also see Basic Vocabulary in Lesson 2.

VERBS

着る・着ます **kiru/kimasu**	puts on, wears (*See Note 7.25.)
履く・履きます **haku/hakimasu**	puts on, wears (*See Note 7.25.)
脱ぐ・脱ぎます **nugu/nugimasu**	takes off
着く・着きます **tsuku/tsukimasu**	arrives
探す・探します **sagasu/sagashimasu**	searches
借りる・借ります **kariru/karimasu**	rents
開ける・開けます **akeru/akemasu**	opens
閉める・閉めます **shimeru/shimemasu**	closes
入る・入ります **hairu/hairimasu**	enters
出る・出ます **deru/demasu**	leaves
座る・座ります **suwaru/suwarimasu**	sits
つける・つけます **tsukeru/tsukemasu**	turns on (e.g. TV, lights)
消す・消します **kesu/keshimasu**	turns off (e.g. TV, lights)
違う・違います **chigau/chigaimasu**	differs
掛ける・掛けます **kakeru/kakemasu**	hangs
掛かる・掛かります **kakaru/kakarimasu**	is hung

ADJECTIVES

広い **hiroi**	is wide, spacious
狭い **semai**	is narrow, not spacious
明るい **akarui**	is bright
暗い **kurai**	is dark
汚い **kitanai**	is dirty
新しい **atarashii**	is new
古い **furui**	is old
うるさい **urusai**	is noisy

ADJECTIVAL NOUNS

静か(だ) **shizuka (da)**	(is) quiet
便利(だ) **benri (da)**	(is) convenient
不便(だ) **fuben (da)**	(is) inconvenient

Structure Notes

7.1. Quotations

When you want to quote what somebody says, asks, thinks, believes, writes, etc., you either do it directly by quoting his exact words, or indirectly by giving the gist of what he says. So you can say either, "Kenji said, 'I'm going to see a movie,'" or "Kenji said that he was going to see a movie." The former is a direct quotation, and the latter is an indirect quotation. The equivalent Japanese sentences are as follows:

> 健二は「映画を見に行く。」と言いました。
> **Kenji wa "Eiga o mi ni iku." to iimashita.**
> Kenji said, "I'm going to see a movie."

> 健二は映画を見に行くと言いました。
> **Kenji wa eiga o mi ni iku to iimashita.**
> Kenji said that he was going to see a movie.

Notice how the tense of English verbs sometimes changes when we shift a direct quotation to an indirect quotation while it doesn't in Japanese, as shown above. The Japanese quotation marks are 「 and 」, but the particle **to** shows that the preceding word, phrase, or clause is a quotation, either direct or indirect.

When the content of a quotation is a question, it ends in **ka**, and the particle **to** is optionally placed after **ka**:

健二は私に映画を見に行くか(と)聞きました。
Kenji wa watashi ni eiga o mi ni iku ka (to) kikimashita.
Kenji asked me if I was going to see the movies.

It is more common to use a PLAIN form before the quoting particle **to**, but sometimes you will hear the POLITE form, especially if the speaker is trying to quote the exact words (direct quote). Sometimes you can't tell how much of the sentence is to be included in the quotation, except by context. The sentence **Watashi wa kyōshi da to iimashita** can mean either 'I said that (somebody) is a teacher' or '(somebody) said that I am a teacher.' Unless the situation indicated otherwise, the topic **watashi wa** would probably be taken to refer both to the subject of the quotation and to the person who said it: 'I said that I was a teacher.'

The quoting particle **to**, not to be confused with the particle meaning 'with' or 'and,' or with the particle meaning 'whenever, if,' is often pronounced with a special high pitch and an abruptly clipped vowel. You will sometimes hear this special high pitch used with other words. It shows that the speaker is injecting an added liveliness, a special color, to his words. Japanese often make a slight pause before, and sometimes after, the quoting particle.

In quoting a question, you use the verb **kiku** 'asks' or the phrase **kiite miru** 'tries asking, asks to see, finds out.' The verb **kiku** also means 'listens, hears':

マネージャーからききました。
Manējā kara kikimashita.
I heard it from the manager.

音楽をききました。
Ongaku o kikimashita.
I listened to music.

お巡りさんにききました。
Omawari-san ni kikimashita.
I asked the police officer.

原さんにききました。
Hara-san ni kikimashita.
I heard from Miss Hara.

The plain copula **da** is usually omitted before **ka**. If you are quoting a question like **shihainin desu ka** 'is it the manager,' which includes the polite copula, instead of replacing **desu** with the plain form **da**, you usually omit the copula altogether: **Shihainin ka to kikimashita** 'He asked if it was the manager.' If an adjective is used, of course, you just put it in the plain form.

建築家です。/建築家だと言いました。
Kenchikuka desu. / Kenchikuka da to iimashita.
He is an architect. / He said that he is an architect.

建築家ですか。/建築家かと聞きました。
Kenchikuka desu ka. / Kenchikuka ka to kikimashita.
Are you an architect? / I asked if he is an architect.

部屋は大きいです。/ 部屋は大きいと言いました。
Heya wa ōkii desu. / Heya wa ōkii to iimashita.
The room is big. / He said the room was big.

部屋は大きいですか。/ 部屋は大きいかと聞きました。
Heya wa ōkii desu ka. / Heya wa ōkii ka to kiki mashita.
Is the room big? / He asked if the room was big.

The meaning of the quotation particle **to** is something like 'close quotes' or 'end of quotation,' but it gets translated various ways in English: he said THAT he'd come, she asked IF there was any, I thought (ZERO) I'd go. Here are some more examples of quotations:

どの建物が郵便局か聞いてみましょう。
Dono tatemono ga yūbinkyoku ka kiite mimashō.
Let's ask which building is the post office.

３０分歩くと疲れると言うんです。
Sanjup-pun aruku to tsukareru to iu n desu.
He says that he gets tired when he walks for a half-hour.

主人は出かけるときに，すぐ帰ると言ったのです。
Shujin wa dekakeru toki ni, sugu kaeru to ittano desu.
My husband said he'd be right back when he went out.

田中さんが来たとき，切符をもう買ったかと聞きましょう。

Tanaka-san ga kita toki, kippu o mō katta ka to kikimashō.

When Mr. Tanaka arrives, let's ask him if he has already bought the tickets.

不動産屋に話すべきだと言いました。

Fudōsanya ni hanasu beki da to iimashita.

He said that I should talk with a real estate agent.

その仕事をしたくないと言った人は解雇されました。

Sono shigoto o shitaku nai to itta hito wa kaiko saremashita.

The people who said that they did not want to do that job were fired.

無駄だと言ったんですが，なんとか家賃を安くできないかと聞いてみると言いました。

Muda da to itta n desuga, nantoka yachin o yasuku dekinai ka to kiite miru to iimashita.

I said that it's useless, but he said that he will ask them if they can do it somehow.

7.2. と言う *to iu*

When a phrase ending in **to iu (to yuu)** modifies a noun, there are several possible meanings. If the noun refers to a message or the like, the part preceding **to iu** may be a quotation or paraphrase of the content.

田中さんが結婚したという噂を聞きました。

Tanaka-san ga kekkon shita to iu uwasa o kikimashita.

I heard the rumor that said that Mr. Tanaka got married.

If the part preceding **to iu** is a name, the expression means 'which is called, which is named':

田中次郎という男の人を知っていますか。

Tanaka Jirō to iu otoko no hito o shitte imasu ka.

Do you know the person named Jiro Tanaka?

妹は高田町という町に住んでいます。

Imōto wa Takada-chō to iu machi ni sunde imasu.

My sister lives in a town called Takada-cho.

花というレストランで食べました。

Hana to iu resutoran de tabemashita.

I ate at a restaurant called Hana.

If the noun modified is **kotoba** 'word,' **sentensu** or **bunshō** 'sentence,' or **ji** 'written character,' the expression **to iu** means something like 'which is said, which is read,' that is, it refers directly to the word, sentence, or character.

> オタクという言葉は今はだれでも知っています。
> **Otaku to iu kotoba wa ima wa dare demo shitte imasu.**
> The word "otaku" is known by everyone now.

> 花よりだんごという諺を聞いたことがありますか。
> **Hana yori dango to iu kotowaza o kiita koto ga arimasu ka.**
> Have you ever heard the proverb "Hana yori dango"? (*Lit.*, "Flowers rather than dumplings.")

> 心という漢字はきれいな形ですね。
> **Kokoro to iu kanji ha kirei na katachi desu ne.**
> The kanji character "kokoro" has such a pretty shape, doesn't it?

To say 'How do you say this word in Japanese?,' you say **Kono kotoba wa Nihongo de nan to iimasu ka**. To say 'How do you say this sentence in Japanese?,' you usually just say **Kore wa Nihongo de dō iimasu ka**. To say 'How do you write this sentence in Japanese?,' you say **Kore wa Nihongo de dō kakimasu ka**.

If the expression is followed by **koto** or **no** 'fact,' the meaning is something like 'the fact that.' This sort of expression is often used with verbs of knowing or informing.

> 家賃が払えないということは，お金がないということですね。
> **Yachin ga haraenai to iu koto wa, okane ga nai to iu koto desune.**
> The fact that you cannot pay the rent means you do not have money, right?

> 母がよく怒るのはストレスのせいだろう。
> **Haha ga yoku okoru no wa sutoresu no sei darō.**
> The fact that my mother often gets angry is due to her stress.

The expression **nan to iu** before a noun sometimes has the flavor of 'just what, just which.' It's a somewhat less specific way to inquire than using **dono** 'which':

> 何という本ですか。 　　　　　どの本ですか。
> **Nan to iu hon desu ka.** 　　　**Dono hon desu ka.**
> Just what book is it? 　　　　　Which book is it?

If you have a certain limited number of possibilities in mind when you ask 'which' or 'what,' you will probably say **dono**, but if the field is wide open for an answer, you are more likely to say **nan to iu**. This expression is sometimes used as a sort of exclamation 'What a...!':

> 何といういいお天気でしょうね。
> **Nan to iu ii otenki deshō nē.**
> My, what a nice day (it seems to be)!

7.3. The plain tentative

When you embed a sentence like **iku deshō** 'he'll probably go' or **itta deshō** 'he probably went,' you usually change the polite tentative copula **deshō** into the corresponding plain form **darō**:

> 行くだろうと思います。
> **Iku darō to omoimasu.**
> I think he'll probably go.

> 行っただろうと思います。
> **Itta darō to omoimasu.**
> I think he must have gone.

The word preceding **darō** may be a verb form, as above, or it may be a noun or an adjective. For instance, to embed the sentence **Kyōshi deshō** 'He must be a teacher,' you say something like **Kyōshi darō to omoimasu** 'I think he must be a teacher.' To embed the sentence **kodomo wa nemui deshō** 'The child is probably sleepy,' you say something like **Kodomo wa nemui darō to omoimasu** 'I think the child is sleepy.' And to embed the sentence **Kodomo wa nemukatta deshō** 'The child must have been sleepy,' you say something like **Kodomo wa nemukatta darō to omoimasu** 'I think the child must have been sleepy.' In rapid speech the form **-katta darō** is usually contracted to **-kattarō**, so you will hear **Kodomo wa nemukattarō to omoimasu**.

Just as there is a form **darō** corresponding to **deshō**, there is a plain tentative form corresponding to the polite tentative form of each verb. The polite tentative forms, you will recall, end in **-mashō**. The plain tentative forms end in **-yō** for vowel verbs, and in **-ō** for consonant verbs. The plain tentative forms for **kuru** and **suru** are irregularly **koyō** and **shiyō**. The plain tentative forms for verbs are also called VOLITIONAL FORMS because they mean 'let's do...' or 'wants and intends to do....' Here are some example verbs in these forms:

	Meaning	Imperfect -(r)u	Plain Tentative (volitional) -(y)ō	Polite tentative -mashō
Vowel Verbs	eats	**tabe-ru**	**tabe-yō**	**tabe-mashō**
	looks at	**mi-ru**	**mi-yō**	**mi-mashō**
Consonant Verbs	returns	**kaer-u**	**kaer-ō**	**kaer-i-mashō**
	wins	**kat(s)-u**	**kat-ō**	**kach-i-mashō**
	talks	**hanas-u**	**hanas-ō**	**hanash-i-mashō**
	buys	**ka(w)-u**	**ka-ō**	**ka-i-mashō**
	writes	**kak-u**	**kak-ō**	**kak-i-mashō**
	swims	**oyog-u**	**oyog-ō**	**oyog-i-mashō**
	calls	**yob-u**	**yob-ō**	**yob-i-mashō**
	reads	**yom-u**	**yom-ō**	**yom-i-mashō**
	dies	**shin-u**	**shin-ō**	**shin-i-mashō**
Irregular Verbs	comes	**kuru**	**koyō**	**kimashō**
	does	**suru**	**shiyō**	**shimashō**

These plain tentative verbs are used when you want to embed a sentence that would, if not embedded, end in the polite tentative with the meaning 'let's do so-and-so' or 'I think I'll do so-and-so.' For example, if a friend says to you **Kōen e sanpo ni ikimashō** 'Let's go to the park for a walk,' you could report his suggestion this way: **Taro wa koen e sanpo ni ikō to iimashita** 'Taro suggested we go to the park for walk.' If you are thinking **Gohan o tabete kara sugu benkyō shimashō** 'I'll study right after eating,' you will probably say **Gohan o tabete kara sugu benkyō shiyō to omoimasu** 'I'll think I'll study right after eating.' Of course, if you're really talking to yourself, you won't use polite forms at all; you'll use plain style instead. Here are some further examples of the plain tentative:

5時半ごろに家へ帰ろうと思っていましたが，帰れませんでした。
Goji-han goro ni uchi e kaerō to omotte imashita ga, kaeremasen deshita.
I was thinking I would return home around half past five, but I couldn't.

あした不動産屋に行ってみようと思います。
Ashita fudōsan'ya ni itte miyō to omoimasu.
I'm thinking of going to the realtor's office tomorrow.

あしたは雨はふらないだろうと言っていました。
Ashita wa ame wa furanai darō to itte imashita.
(He) was saying that it wouldn't rain tomorrow.

田中さんはそんな物は買わなかったろうと思います。
Tanaka-san wa sonna mono wa kawanakatta rō to omoimasu.
I don't think Mr. Tanaka would have bought such a thing.

兄はいっしょにテニスをしようと言いました。
Ani wa issho ni tenisu o shiyō to iimashita.
My brother suggested we play tennis together.

7.4. Tentative (volitional) + とする *to suru*

The plain tentative (or volitional) sometimes occurs followed by the particle **to** and some form of the verb **suru** 'does.' This sort of expression has two different meanings. One meaning is 'is about to do something.' This expression is usually in a non-final clause, followed by a clause that tells of something that happened. For example:

出かけようとしたときに，友達が遊びに来たんです。
Dekakeyō to shita toki ni, tomodachi ga asobi ni kita n desu.
When I was about to go out, a friend dropped in for a visit.

This usage may be combined with the use of **tokoro** to mean 'just':

掃除をしようとしているところです。
Sōji o shiyō to shite iru tokoro desu.
I'm just on the point of cleaning.

掃除をしようとしているところでした。
Sōji o shiyō to shite iru tokoro deshita.
I was just on the point of cleaning.

出かけようとしたところに，友達が遊びに来たんです。
Dekakeyō to shita tokoro ni, tomodachi ga asobi ni kita n desu
Just as I was about to go out, a friend dropped in for a visit.

The other meaning of the tentative + **to suru** is "attempt" with the usual implication that the attempt was unsuccessful.

うそをつこうとしましたが，つけませんでした。
Uso o tsukō to shimashita ga, tsukemasendeshita.
I tried to lie, but I couldn't.

泥棒して逃げようとしたところを警備員に見つかりました。
Dorobō shite nigeyō to shita tokoro o keibiin ni mitsukarimashita.
A security guard found me when I was about to run away after stealing.

(Compare **to suru** (attempt) 'try to do...' with **-te miru** (trial) 'try doing...' discussed in 7.6.)

7.5. Noun + として *to shite* / にして *ni shite*

When a noun is followed by **to shite** or **to shite wa**, the English equivalent is 'as,' 'for,' or 'considered as' in expressions like 'for a renter,' 'as an assistant.' The particle **ni** usually substitutes for **to** when the characteristic is more permanent: 'for an American,' 'as a woman,' 'being a child,' etc.

> マンションの管理人としてここで働いています。
> **Manshon no kanrinin to shite koko de hataraite imasu.**
> I'm working as a caretaker of this *manshon* (apartment building) here.

> 教師としてはこんな映画をクラスで見せるわけにはいきません。
> **Kyōshi to shite wa konna eiga o kurasu de miseru wake ni wa ikimasen.**
> I cannot show such a movie in class as a teacher.

> アメリカの人にしては日本語が上手ですね。
> **Amerika no hito ni shite wa Nihongo ga jōzu desu ne.**
> His Japanese is quite good for an American, isn't it?

> この家賃にしてはこのアパートは悪くありませんね。
> **Kono yachin ni shite wa kono apāto wa waruku arimasen ne.**
> This apartment is not bad for this rent.

7.6. Gerund (*te*-form) + みる *miru*

An expression consisting of the gerund of a verb + some form of the verb **miru** 'sees' has two slightly different meanings: 'does something to see (how it will turn out), 'does something and finds out,' or 'tries to do something (to see how it will turn out).' Compare this with the meaning of the tentative + **to suru** 'tries to do (but doesn't succeed), starts to do' discussed in 7.4.

> あのカラオケボックスに行ってみましょうか。
> **Ano karaoke bokkusu ni itte mimashō ka.**
> Shall we try going to that karaoke box?

> 日本に住んでみたいです。
> **Nihon ni sunde mitai desu.**
> I want to try living in Japan.

> お兄ちゃんに聞いてみるから、ちょっと待ってて。
> **Onīchan ni kiite miru kara, chotto mattete.**
> I'll just find out from my brother, so wait here a minute.

大家さんに頼んでみたんですが，無駄でした。

Ōya-san ni tanonde mita n desu ga, muda deshita.

I tried asking my landlord, but it was in vain.

7.7. Desideratives

To say 'I want to do something,' you use a special kind of adjective that is derived from verb infinitives. The infinitive, you will recall, is the verb form that ends in ZERO for vowel verbs (**tabe, ne, mi**) and in **-i** for consonant verbs (**kaeri, hanashi, oyogi, kaki**) and irregular verbs (**ki, shi**). To this infinitive form you add the ending **-tai**. The resulting form is called a "desiderative" or "desiderative adjective," because it means something is desired to be done.

The final **-i** of the ending **-tai** is itself, of course, the regular adjective ending for the plain imperfect. A desiderative adjective is inflected just like any other adjective. Compare a regular adjective (e.g. **takai** 'expensive') with desiderative adjectives with a verb (e.g. **taberu** 'eats,' and **yomu** 'reads'):

	Adjective	**Vowel Verb**	**Consonant Verb**
Imperfect	takai is expensive	tabe-tai wants to eat	yom-i-tai wants to read
Infinitive	takaku being expensive	tabe-taku wanting to eat	yom-i-taku wanting to read
Gerund	takakute expensive and	tabe-takute wants to eat and	yom-i-takute wants to read and
Perfect	takakatta was expensive	tabe-takatta wanted to eat	yom-i-takatta wanted to read

The understood object can be marked either by **ga** or **o**, although there is a slight difference in meaning. Compare the two sentences below:

ラーメンを食べたいです。

Rāmen o tabetai desu.

I want to eat ramen noodles.

ラーメンが食べたいです。

Rāmen ga tabetai desu.

I want to eat ramen noodles.

The first sentence with **o** is stating what one wants to do, while the second sentence with **ga** is stating what one wants to eat.

The person doing the desiring will be either the topic with the particle **wa** or the emphasized subject with the particle **ga**, depending on the specific emphasis. This sometimes leads to ambiguity. **Tanaka-san wa Nakamurasan ga yobitai desu** can mean either 'Mr. Tanaka wants to invite MR. NAKAMURA' or 'MR. NAKAMURA wants to invite Mr. Tanaka,' since all it tells us literally is 'With Mr. Tanaka for the topic and the emphasis on Mr. Nakamura, somebody wants to invite somebody.' This ambiguity parallels that of **Tarō wa Hanako ga suki desu** ('With Taro for the subject and the emphasis on Hanako, somebody is liked by somebody'), which can mean either 'Taro likes HANAKO' or 'HANAKO likes Taro.' Such ambiguities are straightened out, of course, by the situation and the context. English 'like' (as in 'I like coffee') usually corresponds to Japanese **suki desu**, but in the expression 'I'd like to,' which means 'I want to,' it corresponds to **-tai desu**. 'I think I'd like to go' is **ikitai to omoimasu**. Here are some sentences illustrating the use of desideratives:

ちょっと寝たいと思います。
Nisanjikan netai to omoi masu.
I think I'd like to sleep a bit.

きれいな着物を着たいと言っています。
Kirei na kimono o kitai to itte imasu.
She says she wants to wear a pretty kimono.

今日はちょっと早く帰りたいんですが，いいですか。
Kyō wa chotto hayaku kaeritai n desu ga, ii desu ka.
I want to go home a bit earlier today, but is it okay?

もう２度とあの人に会いたくありません。
Mō nido to ano hito ni aitaku arimasen.
I don't want to see him anymore.

すしが食べたくて，すし屋に行きました。
Sushi ga tabetakute, sushiya ni ikimashita.
I wanted to eat sushi, so I went to a sushi restaurant.

あの大学に入りたかったんですが，入れませんでした。
Ano daigaku ni hairitakatta n desu ga, hairemasendeshita.
I wanted to get into that college, but I couldn't.

7.8. Alternative questions

An alternative question is one in which you give the listener two or more choices for an answer: **Kuruma de ikimashita ka, basu de ikimashita ka, chikatetsu de ikimashita ka?** 'Did you go by car, or by bus, or by subway?' In answer to such a question, the listener picks out the appropriate alternative and replies, perhaps, **Chikatetsu de ikimashita** 'I went by subway.' If the inquirer has omitted the correct alternative in his question, the person answering may say something like **Chigaimasu—densha de ikimashita** 'It's different (from all those)—I went by train.' **Chigau** is a verb meaning 'is different.' The expression **chigaimasu** is often used with about the same meaning as **sō ja arimasen** to inform a person he is mistaken in his assumptions. Do not confuse this verb with the related verb **machigaeru** 'makes a mistake.' **Chigaimashita** means 'it was different (than someone assumed)'; **machigaemashita** means 'I (or he) made a mistake.'

In quoting alternative questions, you usually replace polite verb forms with plain forms, and then follow the entire expression with some verb meaning 'knows, informs, asks, forgets, remembers' or the like. Ordinarily, the quoting particle **to** is omitted. Some examples:

Alternative Question	Quoted Alternative Question
大阪ですか。神戸ですか。 **Ōsaka desu ka. Kōbe desu ka.** Is it Osaka or Kobe?	大阪か神戸か忘れました。 **Ōsaka ka Kōbe ka wasuremashita.** I've forgotten whether it's Osaka or Kobe.
バスで行きましたか。車で行きましたか。 **Basu de ikimashita ka. Kuruma de ikimashita ka.** Did you go by bus or car?	バスで行ったか車で行ったか覚えていますか。 **Basu de itta ka kuruma de itta ka oboete imasu ka.** Do you remember whether he went by bus or by car?
学生でしたか。先生でしたか。 **Gakusei deshita ka. Sensei deshita ka.** Was he a student or a teacher?	学生だったか先生だったか知りません。 **Gakusei datta ka sensei datta ka shirimasen.** I don't know whether he was a student or a teacher.
家賃は高いですか。安いですか。 **Yachin wa takai desu ka. Yasui desu ka.** Is the rent expensive or inexpensive?	家賃は高いか安いか聞いてみましょう。 **Yachin wa takai ka yasui ka kiite mimashō.** Let's find out if the rent is expensive or inexpensive.
500円ですか。1,000円ですか。 **Gohyakuen desu ka. Sen en desu ka.** Is it ¥500 or ¥1,000?	500円か1,000円か教えてください。 **Gohyakuen ka sen'en ka oshiete kudasai.** Please tell (instruct) me whether it's ¥500 or ¥1,000.

Sometimes Japanese add the expression **sore to mo** '(also with that =) or else' like an adverb before the last alternative suggested in an alternative question:

千葉で働いていますか。それとも，東京で働いていますか。
Chiba de hataraite imasu ka. Soretomo, Tōkyō de hataraite imasu ka.
Are you working in Chiba? Or, are you working in Tokyo?

The expression **sore to mo** only emphasizes the fact that you are presenting alternatives—the sentence would mean just about the same without the expression.

Often the last alternative is generalized to just **dō ka** '(or how is it =) or what?,' which seems to correspond to the English translation 'whether...or not.'

車で行ったかどうかわかりません。
Kuruma de itta ka dō ka wakarimasen.
I wasn't sure whether he had gone by car or not.

In this case, **dō ka** might represent **basu de itta ka** 'or went by bus,' **uchi ni ita ka** 'or stayed at home,' or any number of other expressions. When you don't have any particular contrasting alternative to present, in order to say 'whether something happened (or not)' you still use **dō ka**. To say, 'I don't know whether he's arrived yet,' you have to say something like **Mō kita ka dō ka wakarimasen**, that is, 'I don't know whether he's arrived or not.' In English we feel free to drop the 'or not' without changing the meaning, but Japanese almost always put in the **dō ka** to get the meaning 'whether.'

In everyday English we often use 'if' with about the same meaning as 'whether'—'I don't know IF he's come yet.' This IF of course does not mean the same thing as the IF in 'if it rains, I won't go.' We know the two IF's don't mean the same thing, because in the former case we can substitute WHETHER and get the same meaning, but in the latter we cannot. Here are some more examples of alternative questions with **dō ka**:

あの人は赤坂さんかどうか分かりません。
Ano hito wa Akasaka-san ka dō ka wakarimasen.
I don't know whether that person is Ms. Akasaka (or not).

屋根を修理したかどうか覚えていますか。
Yane o shūri shita ka dō ka oboete imasu ka.
Do you remember whether he fixed the roof (or not)?

家賃は高いかどうか調べてみます。
Yachin wa takai ka dō ka shirabete mimasu.
I'll check whether the rent is expensive or not.

7.9. よう *yō*

The adjectival noun **yō**, which is always followed by some form of the copula (**da**, **na**, **desu**, etc.) or by the particle **ni**, has the meaning 'appearance, state, shape, way.' There are several uses of this word, and these are summarized here:

(1) ... *no yō da*

A NOUN PHRASE + **no** + **yō** + COPULA means something is LIKE the noun phrase— it IS (or HAS) the APPEARANCE of the noun phrase. A colloquial synonym of ...**(no) yō (na)** in the meanings 'like' is ...**mitai (na)**. Here are some examples:

> ここはアメリカのようです。(ここはアメリカみたいです。)
> **Koko wa Amerika no yō desu. (Koko wa Amerika mitai desu.)**
> This place is like America.

> その映画の話はまるで私の経験のような話でした。
> **Sono eiga no hanashi wa marude watashi no keiken no yō na hanashi deshita.**
> The story of that movie was just like my own experiences.

(2) ... *no yō ni*

A NOUN PHRASE + **no** + **yō** + **ni** means IN A WAY LIKE the noun phrase, IN A MANNER LIKE the noun phrase.

> 日本人のように話します。
> **Nihonjin no yō ni hanashimasu.**
> He talks like a Japanese.

> あれは老人ホームのように見えました。
> **Are wa rōjin hōmu no yō ni miemashita.**
> That looked like a nursing home.

> 子供のように泣き出しました。
> **Kodomo no yō ni naki dashimashita.**
> He burst into tears like a child.

(3) ...*yō da*

A MODIFYING PHRASE + **yō** + COPULA means it APPEARS or SEEMS that the phrase is so.

> あの人は何か困っているようですね。
> **Ano hito wa nani ka komatte iru yō desu ne.**
> That person seems to be in trouble.

(4) *... yō ni*

A MODIFYING PHRASE + **yō ni** has one of three meanings:

(a) in a way AS IF the modifying phrase is so

> その映画が気に入ったように見ていました。
> **Sono eiga ga ki ni itta yō ni mite imashita.**
> He was watching the movie as if he really liked it.

(b) in a way SO THAT the modifying phrase will be so

> 忘れないようにメモします。
> **Wasurenai yō ni memo shimasu.**
> I will take a memo so I won't forget.

(c) in a way which AGREES WITH or CORRESPONDS TO the modifying phrase

> したいようにしてください。
> **Shitai yō ni shite kudasai.**
> Do as you want to do.

> 好きなようにしてください。
> **Suki na yō ni shite kudasai.**
> Do as you like.

7.10. Quoting requests

The usual way to make a request is to use the GERUND + **kudasai** 'please do (something for me).' To quote such a request in the exact words, you say something like **"Yukkuri hanashite kudasai" to iimashita** 'He said, "Please talk slow." Ordinarily, however, you just give the gist of the request and say **Yukkuri hanasu yō ni (to) iimashita** 'He told me to talk slow.' This is a special use of the expression consisting of a modifying phrase (with a plain imperfect verb) + **yō ni** in the meaning 'so that.' It may be thought of as a sort of shortening of **yō ni shite (kudasai)** '(please) behave in a way so that' or **yō ni suru** '(to) behave in a way so that.' In other words **Yukkuri hanasu yō ni to iimashita** is a sort of shortening of **Yukkuri hanasu yō ni shite kudasai to iimashita** 'He told me to behave in a way so that I talked slow.'

> 子供におもちゃをかたづけるように言いました。
> **Kodomo ni omocha o katazukeru yō ni iimashita.**
> I told my child to put away the toys.

行儀よくするように言います。
Gyōgi yoku suru yō ni iimasu.
I'll tell them to behave.

夜中には大きい音を出さないようにと隣の人にお願いしました。
Yonaka ni wa ōkii oto o dasanai yō ni to tonari no hito ni onegai shimashita.
I asked my next-door neighbor not to make loud noises at night.

The verb 'asks' in English has two different meanings: INQUIRES and RE-QUESTS. When the meaning is INQUIRES, you usually say 'asks if, asks whether.' When the meaning is REQUESTS you usually say 'asks for, asks someone to.' In the meaning INQUIRES, the Japanese equivalent is ...**ka (to) kiku**. In the meaning REQUESTS, the Japanese equivalent is ...**yō ni (to) iu**.

7.11. Particle よ *yo*

The particle **yo** at the end of a sentence gives an INS1STIVE emphasis to what you're saying. It is often used in warnings. The English translation sometimes gives the flavor best by just using an exclamation mark.

ぜんぜん高くありません。安いですよ。
Zenzen takaku arimasen. Yasui desu yo.
It's not expensive at all. It's cheap!

寒いですよ。
Samui desu yo.
It's sure cold!

もう出かけたんですよ。
Mō dekaketa n desu yo.
I tell you they've already gone out!

駄目ですよ。
Dame desu yo.
It's no good (= don't do it; I won't do it).

大丈夫ですよ。
Daijōbu desu yo.
It'll be okay!

「本当ですか。」   「本当ですよ。」
"Hontō desu ka."   **"Hontō desu yo."**
"Are you sure?"   "Sure, I'm sure."

「これを借りてもいいですか。」

"Kore o karite mo ii desu ka."

"Is it okay to borrow this?"

「ええ，いいですよ。」

"Ē, ii desu yo."

"Yes, it is fine."

The meaning of **yo** is in some ways the opposite of that of **ne**. **Yo** means you insist on your statement whatever the other person may say or think; **ne** asks the other person to agree with you, suggests that you think he already knows what you're saying, and implies you might be willing to modify what you've said if you were mistaken about his agreement. If you are not careful, you might sound too pushy when **yo** is not used appropriately. By contrast, the use of **yo** is encouraged when you are giving a compliment or permission to others.

7.12. 見える *mieru* and 聞こえる *kikoeru*

The verb **miru** means 'sees'; the related verb **mieru** means either 'is seen, appears' or 'can see.' The verb **kiku** means 'hears' or 'listens' (**kiku** also means 'asks'); the related verb **kikoeru** means 'is heard, is audible' or 'can hear.' The verbs **miru** and **kiku** may be preceded by an object marked by the particle **o**: **eiga o mimashita** 'I saw a movie,' **rajio o kikimashita** 'I listened to the radio.' The verbs **mieru** and **kikoeru** are never preceded by the particle **o**. Instead, you use the particles **wa** and **ga**, depending on the emphasis. If the meaning is 'can see, can hear,' the person who can see or hear usually takes the particle **wa**, and the thing seen or heard takes the particle **ga**.

> このうちの２階の窓から富士山が見えます。
>
> **Kono uchi no ni-kai no mado kara Fujisan ga miemasu.**
>
> Mt. Fuji is visible from the second-floor windows of this house.

> あの看板の字が見えるんですか。
>
> **Ano kanban no ji ga mieru n desu ka.**
>
> Is it true that you can see the letters on that sign?

> あれ。足音がします。聞こえますか。
>
> **Are. Ashioto ga shimasu. Kikoemasu ka.**
>
> Oh, I can hear footsteps. Can you hear them?

> 聞こえません。もう少し大きい声で話してください。
>
> **Kikoemasen. Mō sukoshi ōkii koe de hanashite kudasai.**
>
> I can't hear you. Could you speak up?

7.13. Prenouns + に *ni*

The prenouns **konna** 'this sort of,' **sonna** 'that sort of,' **anna** 'that-there sort of,' and **donna** 'which sort of' occur before nouns and also before the particle **ni**. In this latter use they have about the same meaning as **kono yō ni, sono yō ni, ano yō ni,** and **dono yō ni** (or **kō, sō, ā,** and **dō**) 'like this, like that, like that-there, and like what' with the emphasis on extent rather than manner.

> どんなに怒ることでしょう。
> **Donna ni okoru koto deshō.**
> I wonder how much he'll be angry.

> そんなに働くと病気になりますよ。
> **Sonna ni hataraku to byōki ni narimasu yo.**
> If you work that hard, you'll get sick!

> こんなにたくさん要りませんね。
> **Konna ni takusan irimasen ne.**
> You see, I don't need this much.

> あんなに静かなところは少ないでしょう。
> **Anna ni shizuka na tokoro wa sukunai deshō.**
> Such quiet places must be rare.

7.14. Gerund (*te*-form) + ある *aru*

The GERUND + the VERB **iru** 'stays, exists' means somebody or something is DO-ING SOMETHING: **hataraite imasu** 'he's working.' If the verb is INTRANSI-TIVE, the meaning may be 'something is in a state as a result of doing or becoming something':

> 晴れています。 **Harete imasu.** It's cleared up.
> 疲れています。 **Tsukarete imasu.** I'm tired.

By contrast, the gerund of a TRANSITIVE verb is used before forms of the verb **aru** 'exists' to mean something is in a state resulting from someone's action on it, in a condition affected by someone's action:

> 手紙は書いてあります。
> **Tegami wa kaite arimasu.**
> The letter is written.

It may help to think of the literal meaning of such a sentence as something like 'as for the letter, somebody writes and—it exists (in the resulting state)' or 'as for the letter, it exists—how?—in a manner such that somebody has written.' Here are some examples of transitive verbs used in simple sentences and then in this special use of GERUND + **aru**:

テーブルの上に花瓶を置きました。/テーブルの上に花瓶が置いてあります。
Tēburu no ue ni kabin o okimashita./Tēburu no ue ni kabin ga oite ari-masu.
I placed the vase on the table./The vase is placed on the table.

封筒に切手を貼りました。/封筒に切手が貼ってあります。
Fūtō ni kitte o harimashita./Fūtō ni kitte ga hatte arimasu.
I pasted a stamp on the envelope./A stamp is pasted on the envelope.

The negative form of a GERUND + **aru** is, of course, the GERUND + **nai**:

テーブルの上には花瓶が置いてありません。
Tēburu no ue ni wa kabin ga oite arimasen.
There is no vase placed on the table.

封筒には切手が貼ってありません。
Fūtō ni wa kitte ga hatte arimasen.
There is no stamp pasted on the envelope.

7.15. The noun 方 *hō*

The word **hō** has the basic meaning 'alternative, choice of one as opposed to another'; it also has the meaning 'direction, side, place.' Both of these meanings seem to be present in expressions like **migi no hō ni** 'on the right (as opposed to the left),' **higashi no hō ni** 'in the east (as opposed to other sections of the country, or as opposed to other directions).' **Watashi no hō** may mean either 'me (as opposed to somebody else)' or 'my direction, my section.' The noun **hō** can be preceded by any noun + the particle **no**. In addition, it may be preceded, just as any other noun, by a modifying expression: a verb, adjective, or copula clause, with the inflected word in a plain form (perfect or imperfect). **Ōkii hō** means 'the big one, as opposed to the little one; the big alternative; the choice of the big one.' **Ginkō de hataraku hō** means 'the choice of working at a bank; working at a bank as opposed to working other places, or to taking a vacation, or doing something.' For a special use of **hō**, in addition to those described in this lesson, see Note 8.13.

7.16. Comparisons

The adjective **ii** just means 'something is good'; the adjective **takai** means 'something is expensive.' To say 'something is BETTER, something is MORE expensive' you also use **ii** and **takai**, but you often add something somewhere in the sentence to bring out the fact that you are making a comparison. Either you're comparing one thing with another with respect to some quality—'this is better (than that), that is more expensive (than this)'—or you are comparing two qualities with respect to one thing: 'this is better (than it used to be), that is more expensive (than it is useful).'

If you only mention the one thing, or the one quality, and leave the other item of comparison implied, you usually add **hō** after the word referring to the stated item of comparison:

> フロアリングの方が好きです。
> **Furoaringu no hō ga suki desu.**
> I prefer wood floor. (as opposed to carpet)

> 地下鉄で行く方がいい。
> **Chikatetsu de iku hō ga ii.**
> It's better to go by subway. (as opposed to going by bus)

> 小さい方を買ったんです。
> **Chīsai hō o katta n desu.**
> I bought the smaller one. (as opposed to the big one)

> 野菜を食べた方がいい。
> **Yasai o tabeta hō ga ii.**
> It's better to eat vegetables. (as opposed to eating no vegetables)

> お酒を飲まない方がいい。
> **O-sake o nomanai hō ga ii.**
> It's better not to drink sake as opposed to drinking it.

Notice the difference of meaning between **hō** 'alternative, choice' and **no** 'one, thing': **chīsai no o katta n desu** 'I bought a small one,' **chikatetsu de iku no ga ii desu** 'it's good to go by subway.'

If you mention both items of comparison, the particle **yori** '(more) than' is used to set off the standard of comparison:

> TYPE 1:
> 犬は馬より小さいです。
> **Inu wa uma yori chīsai desu.**
> Dogs are smaller than horses. (Dogs, more than horses, are small.)

In such a sentence, you do not ordinarily need the noun **hō** 'alternative.' But if you want to emphasize the subject of the comparison, you usually do it by adding not just the emphatic subject particle **ga** but **(no) hō**:

TYPE 2:
犬の方が馬より小さいです。
Inu no hō ga uma yori chīsai desu.
DOGS are smaller than horses.

You can then change the word order around to give a slightly different emphasis:

TYPE 3:
馬より犬の方が小さいです。
Uma yori inu no hō ga chīsai desu.
It's DOGS that are smaller than horses.

You can set off the first expression **uma yori** '(more) than horses' as the topic with the attention-releasing particle **wa**, in order to concentrate the emphasis still more on the subject of the comparison:

TYPE 4:
馬よりは犬の方が小さいです。
Uma yori wa inu no hō ga chīsai desu.
(What are) smaller than horses are dogs.

Actually, all four of these sentences are probably best translated the same way in English 'Dogs are smaller than horses,' since the differences of emphasis in Japanese are more subtle than those in English. But bear in mind that the differences do exist.

Often the particle **yori** is followed by **mo** with only a slight change of emphasis: **Inu wa uma yori mo chīsai desu** 'Dogs are smaller (yet) than horses.'

If, for the items of comparison, instead of nouns you have two adjectives, verbs, or copulas (or their phrases), you can follow the patterns of sentences 2, 3, and 4 above, placing **hō** and **yori** directly after the plain imperfect form. Type 4 is more common for copula phrases. But the pattern of Type 1 above cannot be directly applied, since the particle **wa** does not ordinarily follow the plain imperfect of verb, adjectives, or the copula. Instead you can use the plain imperfect + **no wa**:

TYPE 1:
話すのは書くより簡単でしょう。
Hanasu no wa kaku yori kantan deshō.
(1 think) it would be easier to speak than to write.

広いのは狭いよりいいでしょう。
Hiroi no wa semai yori ii deshō.
I think it's better spacious than small.

静かなのはきれいなより好きです。
Shizuka na no wa kirei na yori suki desu.
I prefer it quiet rather than pretty.

<u>TYPE 2:</u>
話す方が書くより簡単でしょう。
Hanasu hō ga kaku yori kantan deshō.

広い方が狭いよりいいでしょう。
Hiroi hō ga semai yori ii deshō.

静かな方がきれいなより好きです。
Shizuka na hō ga kirei na yori suki desu.

<u>TYPE 3:</u>
書くより話す方が簡単でしょう。
Kaku yori hanasu hō ga kantan deshō.

狭いより広い方がいいでしょう。
Semai yori hiroi hō ga ii deshō.

きれいなより静かな方が好きです。
Kirei na yori shizuka na hō ga suki desu.

<u>TYPE 4:</u>
書くよりは話す方が簡単でしょう。
Kaku yori wa hanasu hō ga kantan deshō.

狭いよりは広い方がいいでしょう。
Semai yori wa hiroi hō ga ii deshō.

きれいなよりは静かな方が好きです。
Kirei na yori wa shizuka na hō ga suki desu.

Sometimes the adjective of comparison is modified by the adverbs **zutto** 'by far' or **chotto (sukoshi)** 'a bit': **Amerika no hō ga zutto ōkii desu** 'America is lots larger.'

Another way to say 'more' when you mean 'more than before' or 'more than now' or the like is to use the adverb **motto**: **Motto hakkiri hanashite kudasai** 'Please talk more clearly,' **Motto yukkuri aruite kudasai** 'Please walk more slowly.' (But **mō sukoshi...** is often better.)

7.17. Questions with comparisons

Sometimes you want to ask a question about WHICH of two or more things is MORE or MOST something, 'Which is bigger, the bank or the theater?,' 'Which is the most expensive, beef, pork, or lamb?' For such questions, in Japanese you first set up the list of things you are going to ask about. This may be done in several ways:

1. AとBとCと(では)
   A to B to C to (de wa)   (as for) A and B and C

2. AとBとCのうち(では)
   A to B to C no uchi (de wa)   (as for) among A and B and C

3. AとBとCで(は)
   A to B to C de (wa)   (as for) being A and B and C

4. AとBとCのうちで(は)
   A to B to C no uchi de (wa)   (as for) being among A and B and C

Note that each of these expressions may or may not be followed by the topic particle **wa**. Now after you've listed the possible items, you ask which one is selected as the more (or most) something-or-other. If there are just two items you ask the question with the word **dochira** (often pronounced **dotchi**) 'which one' or **dochira no hō (dotchi no hō)** 'which alternative':

銀行と映画館ではどちら（の方）が大きいですか。
Ginkō to eigakan de wa dochira (no hō) ga ōkii desu ka.
Which is bigger, the bank or the theater?

健二さんと博さんではどちらが優しいでしょうね。
Kenji-san to Hiroshi-san de wa dochira ga yasashii deshō ne.
Which one is kinder, Kenji or Hiroshi, I wonder.

If you ask about three or more things, the question word is **dore** 'which (of several),' and if the question is about three or more people, it is **dare** 'who.' In addition you add the word **ichiban** 'number one; most of all' before the adjective.

牛肉と豚肉と鶏肉のうちではどれが一番高いですか。

Gyūniku to butaniku to toriniku no uchi de wa dore ga ichiban takai desu ka.

Which is the most expensive—beef, pork, or chicken?

健二さんと博さんと誠さんのうち誰が一番背が高いでしょうかね。

Kenji-san to Hiroshi-san to Makoto-san no uchi dare ga ichiban se ga takai deshō ka ne.

I wonder who would be the tallest, Kenji, Hiroshi, or Makoto.

7.18. 一番 *ichiban*

The counter **-ban** refers to numbers: **ichiban** means 'number one.' Shedding the accent, **ichi-ban** is used as an adverb to mean 'most of all':

日本で一番高い山は富士山です。

Nihon de ichiban takai yama wa Fujisan desu.

The tallest mountain in Japan is Mt. Fuji.

一番好きな食べ物は何ですか。

Ichiban suki na tabemono wa nan desu ka.

What's your favorite food?

7.19. -目 *me* (ordinal numbers)

To say 'first, second, third,' etc., you can add the suffix **-me** to any number: **issatsu-me, nisatsu-me, sansatsu-me** 'the first book, the second book, the third book'; **hitotsu-me, futatsu-me, mittsu-me** 'the first door, the second door, the third door'; **ichinichi-me, futsuka-me, mikka-me** 'the first day, the second day, the third day.' If you mention the noun, this follows the ordinal and is connected to it by the particle **no**: **futatsu-me no heya** 'the second room ,' **nisatsu-me no hon** 'the second book,' **yonin-me no hito** 'the fourth person.'

三つ目の交差点を左に曲がってください。

Mittsu-me no kōsaten o hidari ni magatte kudasai.

Please make a left at the third intersection.

二人目の子どもはよくしゃべる子でした。

Futari-me no kodomo wa yoku shaberu ko deshita.

The second child was a very talkative child.

私の部屋は５階のエレベータから２つ目の部屋です。

Watashi no heya wa gokai no erebētā kara futatsu-me no heya desu.

My room is the second room from the elevator on the fifth floor.

Instead of using a specific ordinal number, you can add **-me** to the numbers made with the counter **-ban**, and use these with any noun: **ichiban-me no heya** 'the first room,' **niban-me no hon** 'the second book,' **sanbam-me no hito** 'the third person.'

Another way to make words meaning 'first, second, third,' etc., is to prefix **-dai** to any primary numeral: **daiichi, daini, daisan, daiyon**, etc. These words are less commonly used than the ones given above with **-me**, but you will often hear **dai-ichi** in proper names: **Daiichi-Hoteru, Daiichi-Birudingu**.

7.20 Particle ほど *hodo*

The particle **hodo** means 'extent, to the extent of, as much as.' It is used in negative comparisons. To say 'I am not as young as he,' a Japanese says **Watashi wa ano hito hodo wakaku arimasen** 'As for me, I'm not young, as much as that person.'

To express 'as much as' in an affirmative sentence, you use either **no yō ni** 'in the manner of, **to onaji yō ni** 'in the same manner as,' or **gurai** 'about (as much as)':

> 東京はマンハッタンのように人が多いですか。
> **Tōkyō wa Manhattan no yō ni hito ga ooi desu ka.**
> Is Tokyo crowded like Manhattan?

> 東京はマンハッタンと同じように人が多いですか。
> **Tōkyō wa Manhattan to onaji yō ni hito ga ōi desu ka.**
> Is Tokyo as crowded as Manhattan?

> 東京はマンハッタンぐらい人が多いですか。
> **Tōkyō wa Manhattan no yō ni hito ga ōi desu ka.**
> Is Tokyo as crowded as Manhattan?

In each case you expect the answer **Hai, sō desu**.

The particles **hodo** as well as **gurai** and **bakari** are used after numbers and quantity words to mean 'about so much.' The following three sentences mean 'It takes about one hour.'

> 一時間ほどかかります。
> **Ichijikan hodo kakarimasu.**

> 一時間ぐらいかかります。
> **Ichijikan gurai kakarimasu.**

> 一時間ばかりかかります。
> **Ichijikan bakari kakarimasu.**

After a noun, verb, or adjective, the particle **hodo** means 'extent':

山ほど本を買いました。
Yama hodo hon o kaimashita.
He bought a mountain of books. (books to the extent of a mountain)

あなたほど日本語が上手な人は見たことがありません。
Anata hodo Nihongo ga jōzu na hito wa mita koto ga arimasen.
I have never seen anyone who is as good in Japanese as you are. (to the extent you are)

夜眠れないほど心配しています。
Yoru nemurenai hodo shinpai shite imasu.
I'm too worried to sleep at night. (to the extent that I can't sleep)

教えられるほど勉強しました。
Oshierareru hodo benkyō shimashita.
I studied enough to be able to teach. (to the extent of being able to teach it to others)

(For another special use of **hodo** see 8.16.)

7.21. なるほど *naruhodo*

From the expression **naru hodo** 'to the extent of becoming or getting to be' comes the adverb **naruhodo** 'just so, quite right, truly, indeed, ever so much, really.' This is often used where we would say, 'Oh, I see.' Japanese will frequently punctuate another person's discourse with **Naruhodo....naruhodo....naruhodo sō desu ne....naruhodo...**, just as we show a running appreciation for information received and presumably understood by saying 'Uh-huh...mmm..., oh, I see...yes...yes...right…, that's right...exactly..., etc.'

7.22. -ばかり *-bakari*

The particle **bakari** means 'just, nothing but.' It is used after the plain forms of the imperfect, perfect, and gerund and also after nouns. When used after nouns, it may be followed by another particle, **haha to bakari** 'only with my mother,' but the particles **o**, **ga**, and **mo** are usually omitted. After gerunds, it means 'does nothing but do....' Here are some examples:

テレビドラマを見てばかりいます。
Terebi dorama o mite bakari imasu.
She does nothing but watch TV dramas.

肉ばかり食べていると太りますよ。
Niku bakari tabete iru to futorimasu yo.
If you eat nothing but meat, you'll gain weight.

居酒屋にばかり行っています。
Izakaya ni bakari itte imasu.
He only goes to *izakaya* bars.

母は姉とばかりしゃべって，私とはしゃべりません。
Haha wa ane to bakari shabette, watashi to wa shaberimasen.
My mother just speaks with my sister, and she does not speak with me.

父は週末は寝てばかりいます。
Chichi wa shūmatsu wa nete bakari imasu.
My father just sleeps on weekends.

After imperfects and perfects, **bakari** is followed by some form of the copula. After imperfects it means 'has only done, has done nothing but,' and after perfects it means 'has just done, has barely finished doing.'

あの人はぜんぜん働きません。文句を言うばかりです。
Ano hito wa zenzen hatarakimasen. Monku o iu bakari desu.
That person does not work. She only complains.

秋葉町のアパートに引っ越したばかりです。
Akibachō no apāto ni hikkoshita bakari desu.
I just moved into an apartment in Akiba town.

家を出たばかりでした。
Uchi o deta bakari deshita.
We had just left the house.

生まれたばかりの赤ちゃんは何も見えません。
Umareta bakari no akachan wa nani no miemasen.
A baby who is just born cannot see anything.

7.23. まま *mama*

The noun **mama** occurs at the end of a phrase, either with the particle **de** following (adverb usage) or with the particle **ni** showing manner, or with some form of the copula. It means 'as, as it is, just as is, intact, just, leaving it as it is.' Here are some examples:

靴を履いたまま（で）家に上がったんですか。
Kutsu o haita mama (de) uchi e agatta n desu ka.
Did he go right in the house with his shoes on?

パジャマを着たまま（で）運転しました。
Pajama o kita mama (de) unten shimashita.
I drove in my pajamas.

手紙を書きかけたままでした。
Tegami o kakikaketa mama deshita.
I had written a letter halfway and left it there.

外国へ行ったまま（で）帰ってきません。
Gaikoku e itta mama (de) kaette kimasen.
He has gone to a foreign country and has not returned (from there).

台所を散らかしたまま（で）出かけました。
Daidokoro o chirakashita mama (de) dekakemashita.
I left (home) with the kitchen still messy.

窓を開けたままにしておきますよ。
Mado o aketa mama ni shite okimasu yo.
I'll leave the window open, okay?

本を借りたままです。すみません。
Hon o karita mama desu. Sumimasen.
I borrowed your book (and have not returned yet). I'm sorry.

7.24. 同じ *onaji*

The word **onaji** 'the same' works both as a noun and as a prenoun. It functions as a noun when followed by the copula: **onaji desu** 'it's the same.' To say 'This is the same as that,' you say **Kore wa sore to onaji desu**. To say 'This is not the same as that,' you say **Kore wa sore to onaji ja arimasen**. To say 'This is different from that,' you say **Kore wa sore to chigaimasu**. Notice that in each of these identifications, the particle used is **to** 'with.'

私の車は山田さんのと同じです。
Watashi no kuruma wa Yamada-san no to onaji desu.
My car is the same as Ms. Yamada's.

人間は犬や猫と同じじゃありません。
Ningen wa inu ya neko to onaji ja arimasen.
People are not the same as dogs, cats, etc.

石田先生と林先生の専門は少し違います。
Ishida sensei to Hayashi sensei no senmon wa sukoshi chigaimasu.
The specialty of Dr. Ishida and the specialty of Dr. Hayashi are slightly different.

Onaji functions as a prenoun when followed by a noun: **onaji hito** 'the same man,' **onaji koto desu** 'it's the same thing.'

田中さんは昨日と同じ服を着ていますね。
Tanaka-san wa kinō to onaji fuku o kite imasu ne.
Mr. Tanaka is wearing the same clothes as yesterday.

私にとって働くことと遊ぶことは同じことです。
Watashi ni totte hataraku koto to asobu koto wa onaji koto desu.
Working and playing are the same thing for me. (Both are fun.)

由美ちゃんと私は同じ学校に行きました。
Yumi-chan to watashi wa onaji gakkō ni ikimashita.
Yumi and I went to the same school.

Many Japanese prefer the expression **onaji gakkō e ikimasu** to **issho no gakkō e ikimasu** 'we go to the same school.' Theoretically, there is a slight difference of meaning: the former could mean 'he goes to the same school as he used to' or 'the same school as the one mentioned in the newspapers' or the like, whereas the latter could only mean 'he goes to the same school as somebody else does.'

7.25. Clothing

Japanese have several different verbs meaning 'puts on (to some part of the body), wears.' To say someone IS WEARING something or WEARS something, you usually use the gerund form of one of these verbs followed by **imasu**:

着物を着ています。
Kimono o kite imasu.
She's wearing a kimono.

Here are the verbs and some of the items of clothing that go with them:

履く **haku** puts on legs or feet, or under waist	靴 **kutsu**	shoes
	スニーカー **sunīkā**	sneakers
	靴下 **kutsushita**	socks
	ズボン **zubon**	trousers
	スカート **sukāto**	skirt

着る **kiru** puts on trunk of body	洋服 **yōfuku**	clothes
	シャツ **shatsu**	shirt
	Tシャツ **tīshatsu**	T-shirt
	セーター **sētā**	sweater
	ジャケット **jaketto**	jacket
	コート **kōto**	coat
	レインコート **reinkōto**	raincoat
	ドレス **doresu**	dress
	着物 **kimono**	kimono
かぶる **kaburu** puts on head	帽子 **bōshi**	hat
かける **kakeru** sets on, hangs on	眼鏡 **megane**	eyeglasses
	サングラス **sangurasu**	sunglasses
する **suru** puts on	ネックレス **nekkuresu**	necklace
	イヤリング **iyaringu**	earrings
	ネクタイ **nekutai**	necktie
	指輪 **yubiwa**	ring
	スカーフ **skāfu**	scarf
	腕時計 **udedokei**	wristwatch
	手袋 **tebukuro**	gloves
	眼鏡 **megane**	eyeglasses

The general verb for removing garments of all sorts is **nugu** 'takes off, gets out of.' But for **megane** 'eyeglasses' and **yubiwa** 'ring,' you use either **hazusu** 'removes' or **toru** 'takes (away).'

 **Conversation**

[cue 07-3]

Alison (A) has been living in Japan for over one year as an intern at an American company in Japan. She sees Bob (B), who is a new intern in the same company. Alison met him at the lobby of the company for the first time, and started to talk with him.

A. いつ日本に来たんですか。**Itsu Nihon ni kita n desu ka.**
   When did you come to Japan?

B. 昨日成田に着いたばかりです。**Kinō Narita ni tsuita bakari desu.**
   I arrived at Narita just yesterday.

A. え。**E.** Oh!

B. 今週は住むところを探そうと思っています。
Konshū wa sumu tokoro o sagasō to omotte imasu.
I'm thinking of finding a place to live this week.

A. ああ，大変ですね。**Ā, taihen desu ne.** Oh, that's a lot of work.

B. マンションとアパートと，どちらの方が家賃が高いですか。
Manshon to apāto to, dochira no hō ga yachin ga takai desu ka.
Which one has a higher rent, *manshons* or apartments?

A. マンションの方が高いでしょう。マンションの方が新しくて，きれいですから。
Manshon no hō ga takai deshō. Manshon no hō ga atarashikute, kirei desu kara.
Manshons are probably more expensive. *Mansons* are newer and prettier, that's why.

B. なるほど。**Naruhodo.** Oh, I see.

Exercises

I. Find an item that does not belong to the words in each set.

1. {靴 **kutsu**, 靴下 **kutsushita**, スカート **sukāto**, ジャケット **jaketto**}
2. {壁 **kabe**, 窓 **mado**, テーブル **tēburu**, 床 **yuka**}
3. {おいしい **oishii**, 広い **hiroi**, 暗い **kurai**, きたない **kitanai**}
4. {入る **hairu**, 着く **tsuku**, 着る **kiru**, 行く **iku**}
5. {マンション **manshon**, 和室 **washitsu**, 洋室 **yōshitsu**, 台所 **daidokoro**}

II. Modify the following direct quotations into indirect quotations.

1. 田中さんは「もうその映画を見ました。」と言いました。
Tanaka-san wa "Mō sono eiga o mimashita." to iimashita.

2. その人は「郵便局はどこですか。」と聞きました。
Sono hito wa "Yūbinkyoku wa doko desu ka." to kikimashita.

3. 父は「もっと早く帰りなさい。」と言いました。

   Chichi wa "Motto hayaku kaerinasai." to iimashita.

4. 「静かにしてください。」とお願いしました。

   "Shizuka ni shite kudasai." to onegaishimashita.

III. Fill in the blanks with either いますimasu or ありますarimasu.

1. 父は今会社で働いて＿＿＿＿＿＿＿＿＿＿＿。

   Chichi wa ima kaisha de hataraite ＿＿＿＿＿＿＿＿＿＿.

2. 今日は晴れて＿＿＿＿＿＿＿＿＿＿＿。

   Kyō wa harete ＿＿＿＿＿＿＿＿＿＿.

3. 壁に絵が掛けて＿＿＿＿＿＿＿＿＿＿＿。

   Kabe ni e ga kakete ＿＿＿＿＿＿＿＿＿＿.

4. 壁に絵が掛かって＿＿＿＿＿＿＿＿＿＿＿。

   Kabe ni e ga kakatte ＿＿＿＿＿＿＿＿＿＿.

5. 猫がテーブルの下に＿＿＿＿＿＿＿＿＿＿＿。

   Neko ga tēburu no shita ni ＿＿＿＿＿＿＿＿＿＿.

6. 花瓶がテーブルの上に＿＿＿＿＿＿＿＿＿＿＿。

   Kabin ga tēburu no ue ni ＿＿＿＿＿＿＿＿＿＿.

7. セーターを着て＿＿＿＿＿＿＿＿＿＿＿。

   Sētā o kite ＿＿＿＿＿＿＿＿＿＿.

IV. Conjugate the verb in the parentheses appropriately.

1. お酒を（飲む）ばかりいます。

   O-sake o (nomu) bakari imasu.

2. ドレスを（着る）みました。

   Doresu o (kiru) mimashita.

3. （寝る）としましたが，寝られませんでした。

   (Neru) to shimashita ga, neraremasen deshita.

4. パジャマを（着る）まま朝ごはんを食べます。
Pajama o (kiru) mama asa-gohan o tabemasu.

5. 今晩はすしが（食べる）たいです。
Konban wa sushi ga (taberu) tai desu.

V. Choose the appropriate item in the parentheses.

1. 兄は田中さんほど背が（高いです・高くありません）。
Ani wa Tanaka-san hodo se ga (takai desu, takaku arimasen).

2. 私の車は山田さんの（と・に）同じです。
Watashi no kuruma wa Yamada-san no (to, ni) onaji desu.

3. 猫と犬と（どちら・どれ・何）が好きですか。
Neko to inu to (dochira, dore, nani) ga suki desu ka.

4. 窓から富士山（を・が）見えます。
Mado kara Fujisan (o, ga) miemasu.

5. スミスさんは日本人のよう（な・に）話します。
Sumisu-san wa Nihonjin no yō (na, ni) hanashimasu.

6. この家が（それ・そんな）に嫌いですか。
Kono ie ga (sore, sonna) ni kirai desu ka.

Answers:
I 1. ジャケット jaketto 2. テーブル tēburu 3. おいしい oishii 4. 着る kiru 5. マンション manshon
II 1. 田中さんはもうその映画を見たと言いました。**Tanaka-san wa mō sono eiga o mita to iimashita.** 2. その人は郵便局はどこか（と）聞きました。**Sono hito wa yūbinkyoku wa doko ka (to) kikimashita.** 3. 父はもっと早く帰るように（と）言いました。**Chichi wa motto hayaku kaeru yō ni (to) iimashita.** 4. 静かにするように（と）お願いしました。**Shizuka ni suru yō ni (to) onegaishimashita.**
III 1. います imasu 2. います imasu 3. あります arimasu 4. います imasu 5. います imasu 6. あります arimasu 7. います imasu
IV 1. 飲んで nonde 2. 着て kite 3. 寝よう neyō 4. 着た kita 5. 食べ tabe
V 1. 高くありません takaku arimasen 2. と to 3. どちら dochira 4. が ga 5. に ni 6. そんな sonna

Let's Keep in Touch!
また連絡してね！
Mata Renraku Shite Ne!

In this lesson, you will learn basic vocabulary for modern methods of communication and sentence structures that are useful for discussing a variety of situations and conditions including permissions and obligations.

🎧 Basic Sentences

[cue 08-1]

1. 「<u>どこか</u>に公衆電話はありませんか。」
    "**<u>Dokoka</u> ni kōshū denwa wa arimasn ka.**"

    "Is there a pay phone somewhere?"

    「この辺では<u>どこにもない</u>と思います。」
    "**Kono hen de wa <u>doko ni mo nai</u> to omoimasu.**"

    "I don't think there's any around here."

2. 「ちょっと電話を借り<u>てもいいですか</u>。」
    "**Chotto denwa o kari<u>te mo ii desu ka</u>.**"

    "Is it okay to use your phone?"

    「はい，いいですよ。どうぞ。」
    "**Hai, ii desu yo. Dōzo.**"

    "Sure, it's fine. Go ahead."

3.	どこにかけても話し中です。 どうすればいいでしょうか。 **<u>Doko</u> ni kake<u>te mo</u> hanashi-chū desu.** **Dō <u>sureba</u> ii deshō ka.**	No matter where I dial, I get a busy signal. What should I do?
4.	よく勉強しなくてはいけません。 **Yoku benkyō shi<u>nakute wa</u> ikemasen.**	I have to study hard.
5.	電車の中では携帯で話し<u>てはいけません。</u> **Densha no naka de wa keitai de hanashi<u>te</u> <u>wa ikemasen</u>.**	You are not allowed to talk on the cell phone in the train.
6.	まだ1時ですから急が<u>なくてもいいです</u>よ。 **Mada ichi-ji desu kara isoga<u>nakute mo ii</u> <u>desu</u> yo.**	It's still one o'clock, so no need to hurry.
7.	「メールアドレスを教えてください。」 **"<u>Mēru adoresu</u> o oshiete kudasai."** 「mori23@ibt.ac.jpです。」 **"mo ri nijūsan atto māku ai bī tī dotto ei shī dotto jei pī desu."**	"Could you let me know your email address?" "It's mori23@ibt.ac.jp."
8.	推薦状は早くお願い<u>した方がいい</u>ですよ。 **Suisenjō wa hayaku onegai shi<u>ta hō ga ii</u> desu yo.**	It's better to request a recommendation letter early.
9.	12月になっ<u>たら</u>年賀状を書か<u>なくてはい</u>けません。 **Jūni-gatsu ni nat<u>tara</u> nengajō o kakana-kute wa ikemasen.**	In December, we have to write New Year's cards.
10.	メールはいつでも送れる<u>し</u>，いつでも読める<u>し</u>，便利です。 **Mēru wa itsu de mo okureru <u>shi</u>, itsu de mo yomeru <u>shi</u>, benri desu.**	Emails are convenient because we can send and read them at any time.
11.	そんなひどいことは私<u>には</u>言えません。 **Sonna hidoi koto wa watashi <u>ni</u> wa iemasen.**	I cannot say such a terrible thing.
12.	今は幼稚園の子どもで<u>さえ</u>簡単にパソコンを使っています。 **Ima wa yōchien no kodomo de <u>sae</u> kantan ni pasokon o tsukatte imasu.**	Nowadays, even kindergarteners use computers with ease.

13. あれこれ考えているうちに嫌になりました。 **Are kore** kangaete iru uchi ni iya ni narimashita.	While I was thinking about it, I started to hate it.
14. 早ければ早いほどいいです。 **Hayakere ba hayai hodo** ii desu.	The sooner, the better.

🎧 Basic Vocabulary

[cue 08-2]

TELEPHONE

電話 **denwa**	telephone
電話番号 **denwa-bangō**	telephone number
携帯(電話) **keitai (denwa)**	cell phone
スマートフォン **sumātofon**	smart phone
公衆電話 **kōshū denwa**	public phone, pay phone
かける・かけます(電話を) **kakeru/kakemasu (denwa o)**	
	makes a phone call
切る・切ります(電話を) **kiru/kirimasu (denwa o)**	(cuts the phone call =) hangs up, ends the call

EMAIL/TEXT

メール **mēru**	email, text
メールする・メールします **mēru suru/mēru shimasu**	sends an email, texts
ログインする・ログインします **roguin suru/roguin shimasu**	
	logs in
ログアウトする・ログアウトします **roguauto suru/roguauto shimasu**	
	logs out
アドレス **adoresu**	(email) address
添付 **tenpu**	attachment

MAIL

郵便 **yūbin**	mail, mailing
郵送する・郵送します **yūsō suru/ yūsō shimasu**	sends something by mail
郵便番号 **yūbin-bangō**	zip code

CULTURE NOTE Nengajō 'New Year's Greeting Cards'

Every year, the Japanese send **nengajō**, a greeting postcard celebrating the new year, to their relatives, friends, bosses, and colleagues. Unlike Christmas cards in the West, which can be mailed and delivered in December, **nengajō** are mailed in December, stocked at the post office, and delivered on January first all at once. It is important to write 年賀 (New Year celebration) in red right below the space for the stamp on the front of the postcard to prevent it from being delivered before January first. Post offices hire numerous part-time workers, mostly students, to sort **nengajō** in December.

Each family receives a bunch of the cards, often more than a hundred. The greeting phrase most commonly written on **nengajō** is **Akemashite omedetō gozaimasu** 'Happy New Year.' The Japanese often print, draw, or stamp the new year's zodiacal animal on the card. **Nengajō** plays an important role in allowing the Japanese to keep in touch with their relatives and friends over the years. As you might suspect, **nengajō** in electronic format are gaining in popularity.

封筒 **fūtō**	envelope
切手 **kitte**	stamp
年賀状 **nengajō**	New Year greeting cards

OTHER COMMUNICATION TOOLS

チャット **chatto**	chat, chatting
ファックス **fakkusu**	fax
ネット **netto**	Internet
ウエブサイト **uebusaito**	Web site
ブログ **burogu**	blog
ソーシャルネットワーク **sōsharunettowāku**	social network
フェイスブック **feisubukku**	Facebook
ツイッター **tsuittā**	Twitter
ツイートする・ツイートします **tsuīto suru/tsuīto shimasu**	tweets
ポストする・ポストします **posuto suru/posuto shimasu**	posts
フォローする・フォローします **forō suru/forō shimasu**	follows
アプリをダウンロードする **apuri o daunrōdo suru**	downloads an app

Bonding

飲み会 **nomikai**	drinking party
カラオケ **karaoke**	karaoke
居酒屋 **izakaya**	Japanese-style (inexpensive) bar

> **CULTURE NOTE** *Izakaya*
>
> An **izakaya** is an inexpensive, casual Japanese-style bar that serves home-style dishes like grilled meat, seafood, and vegetables, edamame, and tofu along with drinks. They often have Japanese-style rooms with a big, long, low tables so a group of friends can sit close together in the same room on tatami mats. Office workers frequently go to **izakaya** after work. The same people who may seem very serious while working at the office during the daytime suddenly become very open, talkative, and cheerful once they enter an **izakaya**. When they drink, they tend to be more frank and honest as well. Accordingly, the **izakaya** is an important place for colleagues to communicate and bond with each other.

Adjectives and adjectival nouns

新しい **atarashii**	is new
古い **furui**	is old
若い **wakai**	is young
難しい **muzukashii**	is difficult
簡単（だ）**kantan (da)**	(is) easy

若い **wakai**

Furui 'is old' is the opposite of **atarashii** 'is new' and does not refer to age. The opposite of **wakai** 'is young' is **toshi ga itte imasu** 'is aged.' To say a person is 'older,' you can say either **toshi ga ue desu** or **toshiue desu**. To say a person is 'younger,' you can say either **toshi ga shita desu** or **toshishita desu**.

Structure Notes

8.1. Interrogatives + も *mo* or か *ka*

An interrogative is a word that asks a question, like **dare** 'who,' **dore** 'which,' **nani** 'what,' **dō** 'how,' **ikura** 'how much,' **ikutsu** 'how many,' **itsu** 'when, what time,' **dono** 'which one,' or **donna** 'what sort of.' These interrogatives can also be followed by the particles **mo** and **ka** with special meanings.

When followed by **mo**, the meaning of the phrase is GENERALIZED, meaning something like 'every, all' if the predicate is affirmative. However, it means 'no, none, not at all, not any' if the predicate is negative. Phrases consisting of INTER-ROGATIVE + **mo** occur more often with the negative than with the affirmative. In the affirmative, phrases of the type INTERROGATIVE + **de** (COPULA GERUND) + **mo** are often used instead. (These are discussed in 8.3.) See the following pairs of examples:

Interrogative + *mo* with an affirmative predicate 'every, all'	Interrogative + *mo* with a negative predicate 'no, none, not at all, not any'
いつも来ます。 **Itsu mo kimasu.** He comes over all the time.	いつも来ません。 **Itsu mo kimasen.** He never comes over.
どのコースも取りました。 **Dono kōsu mo torimashita.** He took every course.	どのコースも取りませんでした。 **Dono kōsu mo torimasen deshita.** He did not take any course.
そんなことはだれもが知っています。 **Sonna koto wa dare mo ga shitte imasu.** Anyone knows this sort of thing.	そんなことはだれも知りません。 **Sonna koto wa dare mo shirimasen.** No one knows such a thing.
何でも食べました。 **Nan de mo tabemashita.** I ate anything.	何も食べませんでした。 **Nani mo tabemasen deshita.** I did not eat anything.
どれも好きです。 **Dore mo suki desu.** I like all of them.	どれも好きじゃありません。 **Dore mo suki ja arimasen.** I like none of them.
どこにもあります。 **Doko ni mo arimasu.** You can find it in everywhere.	どこにもありません。 **Doko ni mo arimasen.** You cannot find it anywhere.

All of the interrogatives except demonstrative adjectives such as **dono** 'which' and **donna** 'what sort of' occur followed by **ka**, and the resulting phrases have an INDEFINITE meaning, something like 'some' and 'any.' For example, **Itsu ka asobi ni kite kudasai** 'Please come to visit us sometime.'

Expressions with **ka** and **mo** are often used with additional particles as well, but the particles **wa**, **ga**, and **o** usually do not occur. The meaning of the **wa**, **ga**, or **o** is carried by the juxtaposition of the phrase with the rest of the sentence and the general context. For the expressions ending in **ka**, any additional particles usually come AFTER the particle **ka**. For the expressions with **mo**, the additional particles usually come BEFORE the particle **mo**. Thus we find **Doko ka e ikimashita** 'He went someplace,' but **Doko e mo ikimasen deshita** 'He didn't go any place.' An exception is the way you say 'in some way,' **dō ni ka**, for this follows the pattern of **dō ni mo** 'in (not) any way, in no way; in every way.' The simple expressions **dō ka** and **dō mo** are not used with these meanings, perhaps because of the existence of the special expressions **dō ka** 'please' (an old-fashioned form of **dōzo**) and **dō mo** 'ever so much, very much' as in **Dō mo arigatō gozaimasu** 'Thank you very much.'

「だれかに言いましたか。」
"Dare ka ni iimashita ka."
"Did you say it to anyone?"

「いいえ, だれにも言いませんでした。」
"Īe, dare ni mo iimasendeshita."
"No, I did not say it to anyone."

「だれか来ましたか。」
"Dare ka kimashita ka."
"Did anyone come?"

「いいえ, だれも来ませんでした。」
"Īe, dare mo kimasen deshita."
"No, no one came."

「ツイッターで誰かをフォローしていますか。」
"Tsuittā de dare ka o forō shite imasu ka."
"Are you following anyone on Twitter?"

「いいえ, 誰もフォローしていません。」
"Īe, daremo forō shite imasen."
"No, I'm not following anyone."

「昨日は何かしましたか。」
"Kinō wa nani ka shimashita ka."
"Did you do anything yesterday?"

「いいえ, 何もしませんでした。」
"Īe, nani mo shimasendeshita."
"No, I did not do anything."

「その中に何かありますか。」
"Sono naka ni nani ka arimasu ka."
"Is there anything in it?"

「いいえ, 何もありません。」
"Īe, nani mo arimasen."
"No, there's nothing."

「夏休みはどこかに行きましたか。」
"Natsu-yasumi wa doko ka ni ikimashita ka."
"Did you go anywhere during summer vacation?"

「いいえ, どこにも行きませんでした。」
"Īe, doko ni mo ikimasen deshita."
"No, I did not go anywhere."

「どれか好きなのはありますか。」
"Dore ka suki na no wa arimasu ka."
Is there any one (of them) you like?"

「いいえ, どれも好きじゃありません。」
"Īe, dore mo suki ja arimasen."
"No, I don't like any one of them."

「どちらか使いますか。」
"Dochira ka tsukaimasu ka."
"Will you use either one of them?"

「いいえ, どちらも使いません。」
"Īe, dochira mo tsukaimasen."
"No, I will use neither one."

Notice that the English translations 'any, anyone, anybody, any time, etc.' correspond to the phrases with **ka** if the English contains an affirmative verb, but to the phrases with **mo** if the English contains a negative verb.

There is a special use of the INDEFINITE EXPRESSIONS in apposition to a noun phrase. An expression like **dare ka** 'somebody, anybody' can be followed immediately by a phrase telling who the somebody is (in general terms):

> 昨日だれか先生のような人が来ましたよ。
> **Kinō dare ka sensei no yō na hito ga kimashita yo.**
> Someone who seemed like a teacher came here yesterday.

> だれか外国為替の仕事の経験がある人を知りませんか。
> **Dare ka gaikoku-kawase no shigoto no keiken ga aru hito o shirimasen ka.**
> Do you know anyone who has experience in foreign-exchange work?

An expression like **doko ka** 'someplace, any place' can be followed immediately by a phrase specifying the sort of place:

> どこか泳ぐことのできるところは近くにありますか。
> **Doko ka oyogu koto no dekiru tokoro wa chikaku ni arimasu ka.**
> Is there any place where we can swim?

> どこかいいレストランは知りませんか。
> **Doko ka ii resutoran wa shirimasen ka.**
> Do you know any good restaurants?

An expression like **itsu ka** 'some time' can be followed immediately by a phrase delimiting the time:

> いつか東京に来る機会があれば電話してください。
> **Itsu ka Tōkyō ni kuru kikai ga are ba denwa shite kudasai.**
> If you have a chance to come to Tokyo sometime, please call me.

And an expression like **nani ka** 'something' can be immediately followed by a phrase limiting the thing:

> 何か部屋の中にあるものですか。
> **Nani ka heya no naka ni aru mono desu ka.**
> Is it something in the room?

> すみません。何か書くものを貸してください。
> **Sumimasen. Nani ka kaku mono o kashite kudasai.**
> Sorry, but could you lend me something that I can write with?

The expressions **ikura ka** and **nan** + COUNTER **ka** are also used this way:

いくらかお金がいります。/お金がいくらかいります。
Ikura ka okane ga irimasu./Okane ga ikura ka irimasu.
I need some (amount of) money.

いくつかスーツケースがありました。/スーツケースがいくつかありました。
Ikutsu ka sūtsukēsu ga arimashita./Sūtsukēsu ga ikutsu ka arimashita.
There were a number of suitcases.

何冊か本を買いました。/本を何冊か買いました。
Nan-satsu ka hon o kaimashita./Hon o nan-satsu ka kaimashita.
I bought some books.

8.2. Gerund + も *mo*

The literal meaning of a GERUND (the **te**-form) + **mo** is something like 'even doing, even being so.' It can often be freely translated 'even if (or though) somebody does something, even if something is so.'

たくさん食べても太りません。
Takusan tabete mo futorimasen.
Even if I eat a lot, I won't gain weight.

オペラを見に行きたくてもお金がありません。
Opera o mini ikitakute mo okane ga arimasen.
Even if I want to see opera, I don't have any money.

母は疲れていても料理をします。
Haha wa tsukarete ite mo ryōri o shimasu.
My mother cooks even if she is tired.

これは犬でも食べませんよ。
Kore wa inu de mo tabemasen yo.
Even a dog would not eat this.

こんな簡単な漢字は子供でも書けますよ。
Konna kantan na kanji wa kodomo demo kakemasu yo.
Even a child can write such an easy kanji character.

The last two examples show a use of the copula gerund **de**. Note that **de mo** often starts a sentence 'But..., Yet...,' as do **shikashi, keredomo** (**keredo, kedo**), and **tokoro ga**.

Sometimes you have two phrases of the pattern GERUND + **mo** with the meaning 'whether someone does one thing or does something else, whether one thing is so or the other is so.' The two gerunds can be either two different verbs, or the same verb in affirmative and negative forms, or the same verb with different objects or modifiers.

お天気がよくても悪くても毎日散歩に行きます。
Otenki ga yokute mo warukute mo mainichi sanpo ni ikimasu.
I go for a walk every day, whether the weather is good or not.

仕事があってもなくても会社に行きます。
Shigoto ga atte mo nakute mo kaisha ni ikimasu.
I go to my office (company) regardless whether there is a job or not.

日本に住んでもアメリカに住んでも同じですよ。
Nihon ni sunde mo Amerika ni sunde mo onaji desu yo.
It's the same regardless of whether you live in Japan or in America.

好きなものは高くても安くても買います。
Suki na mono wa takakute mo yasukute mo kaimasu.
If I like something, I buy it regardless of whether it's expensive or cheap.

肉でも魚でも食べます。
Niku de mo sakana de mo tabemasu.
I even eat meat, and also fish.

Often, the concluding clause consists of the word **kamaimasen** 'it doesn't matter; it makes no difference.' This is a special meaning of the negative form of the consonant verb **kama(w)-u** 'is concerned about, pays attention to, goes to trouble for, takes care of, entertains.' Here are examples:

映画を見に行っても散歩に行っても構いません。
Eiga o mi ni itte mo sanpo ni itte mo kamaima sen.
I don't care whether you go to a movie or go for a walk.

現金で払ってもクレジットカードで払っても構いません。
Genkin de haratte mo kurejitto kādo de haratte mo kamaimasen.
I don't care whether you pay by cash or pay by credit card.

部屋は広くても狭くても構いません。
Heya wa hirokute mo semakukte mo kamaimasen.
It makes no difference whether the room is large or small.

便利でも不便でも構いません。

Benri de mo fuben de mo kamaimasen.

I don't care whether it's convenient or inconvenient.

メールでも電話でも構いません。

Mēru demo denwa demo kamaimasen.

It doesn't matter whether you email me or call me.

8.3. Interrogative + gerund + も *mo*

In an affirmative sentence an INTERROGATIVE + **mo** has a GENERALIZED or IN-CLUSIVE meaning 'everybody, everywhere, everyone.' Usually, however, this expression is expanded to INTERROGATIVE + GERUND + **mo**. If there isn't a modifying verb, then the gerund is that of the copula **de** 'being.' Here are some examples:

彼はどんな仕事をしてもよくできます。

Kare wa donna shigoto o shite mo yoku dekimasu.

No matter what kind of job he undertakes, he does it the best he can.

何を食べても美味しいです。

Nani o tabete mo oishii desu.

No matter what I eat, I feel they are delicious.

私は何でもいいです。

Watashi wa nan de mo ii desu.

Anything is fine with me.

どちらでもいいですよ。

Dochira de mo ii desu yo.

Either one/way is fine with me.

兄はスポーツなら何でもできます。

Ani wa supōtsu nara nan de mo dekimasu.

If it is sports, my brother can do anything.

お金はいくらでもありますから心配しないでください。

Okane wa ikura de mo arimasu kara shinpai shinai de kudasai.

Please do not worry, because I have plenty of money.

いくら勉強しても成績が上がらないんです。

Ikura benkyō shite mo seiseki ga agaranai n desu.

No matter how much I study, my grades do not improve.

アメリカ人ならだれでもその言葉を知っています。
Amerikajin nara dare de mo sono kotoba o shitte imasu.
Any American knows that word.

どの店で買っても値段は同じです。
Dono mise de katte mo nedan wa onaji desu.
It is sold at the same price at any store.

どの店でもクレジットカードは使えます。
Dono mise de mo kurejitto kādo wa tsukaemasu.
You can use your credit card at any store.

いつ地震や台風が来ても準備はしてあります。
Itsu jishin ya taifū ga kite mo junbi wa shite arimasu.
I'm ready regardless of when earthquakes, typhoons, etc. hit us.

いつでも遊びに来てね。
Itsu de mo asobi ni kite ne.
Please come to visit me at any time.

どうしても一度ヨーロッパに遊びに行きたいです。
Dō shite mo ichido Yōroppa ni asobi ni ikitai desu.
I'd like to go to Europe for a visit very much (in every possible way).

どれを使っても構いませんよ。
Dore o tsukatte mo kamaimasen yo.
You may use any one of them.

どの新聞を見てもあのニュースが書いてありました。
Dono shinbun o mite mo ano nyūsu ga kaite arimashita.
No matter which newspaper I read, I could see that news.

8.4. The provisional mood (-れば *-reba*)

The provisional mood has meanings something like 'if something happens (now or in the future); provided something happens.' It is made by adding the following endings to the stems of verbs and adjectives:

Vowel verbs: **-reba**
Consonant verbs: **-eba**
Adjectives: **-kereba**

The provisional of the copula **da** is irregular: **nara** 'if it is, provided it equals.'
The provisionals of **kuru** and **suru** are **kureba** and **sureba**.

	Meaning	Imperfect	Provisional
Vowel verb	eats	**tabe-ru**	**tabe-reba**
	looks at	**mi-ru**	**mi-reba**
Consonant verb	returns	**kaer-u**	**kaer-eba**
	wins	**kats-u**	**kat-eba**
	buys	**ka-u**	**ka-eba**
	lends	**kas-u**	**kas-eba**
	writes	**kak-u**	**kak-eba**
	swims	**oyog-u**	**oyog-eba**
	reads	**yom-u**	**yom-eba**
	calls	**yob-u**	**yob-eba**
	dies	**shin-u**	**shin-eba**
Irregular verbs	comes	**kuru**	**kureba**
	does	**suru**	**sureba**
Adjectives	is expensive	**taka-i**	**taka-kereba**
	is good	**i-i, yo-i**	**yo-kereba**
	wants to eat	**tabeta-i**	**tabeta-kereba**
	wants to go	**ikita-i**	**ikita-kereba**
	does not eat	**tabena-i**	**tabena-kereba**
	does not read	**yomana-i**	**yomana-kereba**
Copula	equals	**da (na, no)**	**nara**

The word **nara** sometimes appears after other inflected forms: **suru nara** (= **suru no nara**) 'if it is a matter of doing,' **shita nara** (=**shita no nara**) 'if it is a case of having done.' The provisional of negative adjectives, **shinakereba** 'if I don't do,' is usually equivalent to English 'unless' + the affirmative:

田中さんがいっしょに来なければ面白くないでしょう。
Tanaka-san ga issho ni konakereba omoshiroku nai deshō.
It won't be any fun unless Mr. Tanaka comes along.

その映画は見なければいいか悪いか分からないでしょう。
Sono eiga wa minakereba ii ka warui ka wakaranai deshō.
We won't know whether the movie's good or bad unless we see it.

Here are some examples of the provisional used in affirmative sentences.

雨が降れば釣りに行きません。
Ame ga fureba tsuri ni ikimasen.
If it rains, I'm not going to go fishing.

日本語で話せばすぐ分かります。
Nihongo de hanaseba sugu wakarimasu.
If you speak in Japanese, they'll understand right away.

フェイスブックにポストすれば人が沢山来るでしょう。
Feisubukku ni posuto sureba hito ga takusan kuru deshō.
Once you post it on Facebook, many people will come.

この薬を飲めばよくなるでしょう。
Kono kusuri o nomeba yoku naru deshō.
I think you'll get better if you take this medicine.

私ならそんなものは買いません。
Watashi nara sonna mono wa kaimasen.
If I were you, I wouldn't buy such a thing.

田舎なら静かなところが多いでしょう。
Inaka nara shizuka na tokoro ga ōi deshō.
If it's the countryside (you're talking about or going to), there are probably lots of quiet places.

そんなに不便ならそこに住みたくありませんよ。
Sonna ni fuben nara soko ni sumitaku arimasen yo.
If it's so inconvenient, I certainly don't want to live there.

8.5. Obligation

For the expression 'someone MUST or HAS TO do something,' Japanese has several equivalents. One of the most common is the use of the provisional form of the negative adjectives derived from the verbs (**yomanakereba** 'if I do not read') + the negative of the verb **naru** (**narimasen** 'it does not become = it won't do'). So, to say 'I must read this book,' you say **Kono hon o yomanakereba narimasen** 'If I do not read this book, it won't do.' Instead of **narimasen**, you can use **dame desu** 'it's no good' or **ikemasen** 'it can't go, it's no good, it won't do.' **Yomanakereba narimasen, yomanakereba dame desu**, and **yomanakereba ikemasen** all mean about the same thing: 'I have to read.' Instead of the provisional of the negative adjective **-(a)nakereba**, you can use the gerund of the negative adjective **-(a)nakute** + the particle **wa**, with a meaning something like '(as for) not doing... (as the topic).' In these expressions of obligation, **yomanakereba** 'if I do not read' and **yomanakute wa** 'as for not reading' are equivalent. So you can say 'I have to read (it)' in any of the following ways:

> 1. 読まなければなりません。**Yomanakereba narimasen.**
> 2. 読まなければ駄目です。**Yomanakereba dame desu.**
> 3. 読まなければいけません。**Yomanakereba ikemasen.**
> 4. 読まなくてはなりません。**Yomanakute wa narimasen.**
> 5. 読まなくては駄目です。**Yomanakute wa dame desu.**
> 6. 読まなくてはいけません。**Yomanakute wa ikemasen.**

The first and last patterns (1 and 6) are more commonly heard than the others. Forms ending **-(a)nakute wa** are often pronounced **-(a)nakucha** in colloquial speech. They can end a sentence with the same meaning as if followed by **ikemasen**.

> もう帰らなくちゃならないんですよ。
> **Mō kaeranakucha naranai n desu yo.**
> I have to go home now.

> もう帰らなくちゃ。
> **Mō kaeranakucha.**
> I have to go home now.

8.6. Permission

To express permission or to say 'someone MAY do something,' the Japanese use the gerund **-te** + the particle **mo** 'even' + some form of the adjective **ii** 'it is good, it is okay.' The expression **-te mo ii desu** means something like 'even doing something is okay.' To say 'You may go home,' you say **Kaette mo ii desu.** Such sentences are often followed by the insistive particle **yo**. Instead of **ii desu**, **kamaimasen** can be used to mean 'okay.'

> 「今日ちょっと早く帰ってもいいですか。」
> **"Kyō chotto hayaku kaette mo ii desu ka."**
> "Is it okay to go home a bit early?"

> 「いいですよ。」
> **"Ii desu yo."**
> "Yes, it's fine."

「この部屋を使ってもいいですか。」
"Kono heya o tsukatte mo ii desu ka."
"Is it okay to use this room?"

「ええ, 構いませんよ。」
"Ē, kamaimasen yo."
"Yes, it's fine."

「携帯に電話してもいいですか。」
"Keitai ni denwa shite mo ii desu ka."
"Is it okay to call your cell phone?"

「もちろん。」
"Mochiron."
"Surely."

8.7. Denial of permission = prohibition

To say 'someone MAY NOT do something,' the Japanese usually use a statement of PROHIBITION, 'someone MUST NOT do something.' This consists of the plain gerund of the affirmative verb **-te** + the particle **wa** + **ikemasen/narimasen/dame desu**. The expression **-te wa ikemasen** means something like 'as for doing something, it's no good,' that is 'don't do it.' You have already had one way to say 'Don't read this book': **Kono hon o yomanai de kudasai**. The use of the PLAIN NEGATIVE + COPULA GERUND + **kudasai** is a rather direct way of OR-DERING someone not to do something. Except when talking to subordinates, Japanese usually prefer a more subtle prohibition. Even the type discussed here is rather strong when talking to an equal or superior; it is better to SUGGEST someone not do something rather than PROHIBIT them from doing it.

Each of the following sentences means 'Don't read this book,' but they would ordinarily be said only to children or one's subordinate, or in making some sort of generalized impersonal statement (like "Keep off the grass!").

1. この本を読んではいけません。 **Kono hon o yonde wa ikemasen.**
2. この本を読んではなりません。 **Kono hon o yonde wa narimasen.**
3. この本を読んでは駄目です。 **Kono hon o yonde wa dame desu.**

Among the above three sentences, **-te wa ikemasen** is most commonly used and **-te wa narimasen** is least commonly used. **-te wa dame desu** is more colloquial than others.

Here are some examples:

「早く帰ってもいいですか。」
"Hayaku kaette mo ii desu ka."
"Is it okay to go home early?"

「いいえ，いけません。」
"Īe, ikemasen."
"No, it's not okay."

「あまり食べすぎてはいけませんよ。」
"Amari tabesugite wa ikemasen yo."
"You should not overeat, okay?"

「はい。気をつけます。」
"Hai, ki o tsukemasu."
"Right. I'll be careful."

カンニングをしてはいけませんよ。
Kanningu o shite wa ikemasen yo.
Don't cheat!

「ここでタバコを吸ってもいいですか。」
"Koko de tabako o sutte mo ii desu ka."
"Is it okay to smoke here?"

「いいえ，ここでは吸わないでください。」
 "Īe, koko de wa suwanai de kudasai."
 "No, please don't smoke here."

And note that **-te wa** is often shortened to **-cha**, **-de wa** to **-ja**.

それ使っちゃ駄目だよ。
Sore tsukatcha dame da yo.
You are not allowed to use that.

あまりお酒を飲んじゃいけませんよ。
Amari osake o nonja ikemasen yo.
You should not drink too much.

マンガばかり読んでちゃ駄目ですよ。
Manga bakari yonde cha dame desu yo.
You should not just read comic books.

8.8. Denial of obligation

To deny obligation or to say 'someone NEED NOT or DOES NOT HAVE TO do something,' you use the gerund of the NEGATIVE ADJECTIVE **-(a)nakute** + **mo** + **ii**. The meaning of this expression is something like 'even not doing it (even if someone doesn't do it), it's okay.' So, to say 'You don't have to read it,' you say **Yomanakute mo ii desu**. If you want to ask 'Do I have to take the medicine?,' you can say either **Kusuri o nomanakereba narimasen ka** if you're just wondering, or, if you're hoping for permission not to take it, you can ask **Kusuri o nomanakute**

mo ii desu ka 'Is it all right even if I don't take the medicine? May I go without the medicine?'

> 「今日買わなくてはなりませんか。」
> **"Kyō kawanakute wa narimasen ka."**
> "Do I have to buy it today?"

> 「いいえ，今日買わなくてもいいですよ。」
> **"Īe, kyō kawanakute mo ii desu yo."**
> "No, you don't have to buy it today."

> 「今日買わなくてもいいですか。」
> **"Kyō kawanakute mo ii desu ka."**
> "Is it okay not to buy it today?"

> 「はい，今日買わなくてもいいですよ。」
> **"Hai, kyō kawanakute mo ii desu yo."**
> "Yes, it is fine even if you don't buy it today."

8.9. Obligation, prohibition, permission: summary

Here is a summary of the forms discussed in the preceding sections.

Obligation 'must, has to'	Denial of Obligation 'need not, doesn't have to'
-(a)nakereba narimasen -(a)nakereba ikemasen -(a)nakereba dame desu ('if does not do, is no good') -(a)nakute wa ikemasen -(a)nakute wa narimasen -(a)nakute wa dame desu ('not doing is no good')	-(a)nakute mo ii desu ('even not doing is okay')
Permission 'may, can'	**Denial of Permission = Prohibition 'may not, must not'**
-te mo ii desu ('even doing is good')	-te wa narimasen -te wa dame desu -te wa ikemasen ('doing is no good')

A confusing point about these expressions is that what looks like the negative equivalent of permission, the form **-(a)nakute mo ii**, is not the denial of permission but the denial of obligation. On the other hand, what looks the affirmative equivalent of the obligation expression, the form **-te wa ikemasen**, is the denial of permission = prohibition. This is just a case of misleading formal similarities. Some students find it easier to remember these expressions as single units: **-(a)nakereba-narimasen** 'must,' **-(a)nakute-wa-ikemasen** 'must,' **-(a)nakute-mo-ii-desu** 'need not,' **-te-mo-ii-desu** 'may,' **-te-wa-ikemasen** 'must not.' However you learn them, remember the following points:

(1)   Japanese often pause within the expression, before the last word: **-(a)na-kereba, narimasen; -(a)nakute wa, ikemasen; -(a)nakute mo, ii desu; -te mo, ii desu.**

(2)   You will also want to learn the less common variants **-(a)nakereba ike-masen, -(a)nakute wa dame desu; -(a)nakute wa narimasen, -(a)na-kute wa dame desu, -(a)nai to dame desu.**

(3)   The final word may be inflected in various ways to fit the whole expression into the sentence properly, as in some of the following examples.

今晩勉強しなければならないので映画は明日にしましょう。
Konban benkyō shinakereba naranai node eiga wa ashita ni shimashō.
As I need to study tonight, let's watch the movie tomorrow.

あんなに働かなければならないのは嫌ですよ。
Anna ni hatarakanakereba naranai no wa iya desu yo.
I sure hate to have to work that much.

これは明日出さなければならない手紙ですから、今晩中に書きます。
Kore wa ashita dasanakereba naranai tegami desu kara, konbanchū ni ka-kimasu.
This is the letter that I have to mail tomorrow, so I'll write it tonight.

医者はもう薬を飲まなくてもいいと言いました。
Isha wa mō kusuri o nomanakute mo ii to iimashita.
The doctor said I didn't have to take the medicine anymore.

明日働かなくてもよければどこかに遊びにいきませんか。
Ashita hatarakanakute mo yokereba dokoka ni asobi ni ikimasen ka.
If you don't have to work tomorrow, why don't we go somewhere for fun?

小さい子どもに見せてもいいアニメですか。
Chīsai kodomo ni misete mo ii anime desu ka.
Is it an anime that we can show to young children?

こんなことはできなくては駄目ですよ。
Konna koto wa dekinakute wa dame desu yo.
You have to be able to do such a thing.

8.10. Conditionals (forms) -たら／-だら *-tara/-dara*

The conditional mood has several meanings: 'if something had happened; supposing something happens; when something happened, when something has happened' and the like. The forms are made by adding **ra** at the end of the verbs, adjectives, and the copula in the perfect form.

		Meaning	Imperfect	Perfect	Conditional
Vowel verb		eats	tabe-ru	tabe-ta	tabe-tara
		looks at	mi-ru	mi-ta	mi-tara
Consonant verb		returns	kaer-u	kaet-ta	kaet-tara
		wins	kats-u	kat-ta	kat-tara
		buys	ka-u	kat-ta	kat-tara
		lends	kas-u	kashi-ta	kashi-tara
		writes	kak-u	kai-ta	kai-tara
		swims	oyog-u	oyoi-da	oyoi-dara
		reads	yom-u	yon-da	yon-dara
		calls	yob-u	yon-da	yon-dara
		dies	shin-u	shin-da	shin-dara
		go	ik-u	it-ta (irregular)	it-tara (irregular)
Irregular verbs		comes	kuru	kita	kitara
		does	suru	shita	shitara
Adjectives		is expensive	taka-i	takakat-ta	takakat-tara
		is good	i-i, yo-i	yokat-ta	yokat-tara
		wants to eat	tabeta-i	tabetakat-ta	tabetakat-tara
		wants to go	ikita-i	ikitakat-ta	ikitakat-tara
		does not eat	tabena-i	tabenakat-ta	tabenakat-tara
		does not read	yomana-i	yomanakat-ta	yomanakat-tara
Copula		equals	da (na, no)	dat-ta	dat-tara

8.11. Conditionals (uses)

In the meaning 'supposing something happens (now or in the future), supposing something is so,' the conditional is very similar to the provisional with its meaning 'provided something happens, provided something is so.' For the meaning 'if,' there are three possibilities: conditional 'supposing that,' provisional 'provided that,' and PLAIN IMPERFECT + PARTICLE **to** 'if = whenever.'

The difference between the conditional and the provisional is often one of explicit doubt. If you use the conditional -**tara** form, you show some doubt as to whether something will happen or not: 'if it should happen (but I doubt it will)'. But if you use the provisional form, you are making a hypothesis without saying anything about the likelihood of its being true: 'if it happens'.

Here are some sentences showing the differences between the conditional and the provisional with the meaning 'if' under a present or future hypothesis. There are also sentences illustrating the particle **to** with the meaning of a repeated or habitual 'if = whenever'.

そのことを日本語で言ったら，すぐ分かるでしょう。
Sono koto o Nihongo de ittara, sugu wakaru deshō.
If you were to say that in Japanese, they'd understand right off.

そのことを日本語で言えば，すぐ分かるでしょう。
Sono koto o Nihongo de ieba, sugu wakaru deshō.
If you say that in Japanese, they'll understand right off.

そのことを日本語で言うと，すぐ分かるでしょう。
Sono koto o Nihongo de iu to, sugu wakaru deshō.
If (whenever) you say that in Japanese, they understand you right off.

天気がよかったら，散歩に行きます。
Tenki ga yokattara, sanpo ni ikimasu.
If the weather is nice, I'll go for a walk.

天気がよければ，散歩に行きます。
Tenki ga yokereba, sanpo ni ikimasu.
If the weather is nice, I'll go for a walk.

天気がいいと，散歩に行きます。
Tenki ga ii to, sanpo ni ikimasu.
If (whenever) the weather is nice, I go for a walk.

日本の映画だったら，見ます。
Nihon no eiga dattara, mimasu.
If it should be a Japanese movie, I will watch it.

日本の映画なら，見ます。
Nihon no eiga nara, mimasu.
If it is a Japanese movie, I'll watch it.

日本の映画だと，見ます。
Nihon no eiga ta to, mimasu.
If (whenever) it is a Japanese movie, I watch it.

In all of the sentences where the conditional forms mean 'if,' it is possible to add the word **moshi** 'supposing, if, say' at the beginning of the sentence. Although the word **moshi** is thus in the same position as the English word 'if,' the meaning of the latter is carried by the conditional form at the end of the clause, and the function of the **moshi** is just to reinforce that meaning and to act as a signal telling the listener to expect a conditional form. So you're more apt to put **moshi** at the beginning if the clause is very long. It is uncommon to use **moshi** with the provisional. Here is an example with **moshi**:

もしインターネットと電話の契約を同じ会社として電話のサービスが嫌いだったら，どうしますか。
Moshi intānetto to denwa no keiyaku o onaji kaisha to shite denwa no sābisu ga kirai dattara, dō shimasu ka.
If you signed a contract with a company for both Internet and telephone and you disliked their phone service, what would you do?

Here are some sentences illustrating the difference between A) the conditional meaning 'when,' with emphasis on what happened at the time; B) plain imperfect or perfect + **toki (ni)** meaning 'when, at the time that,' with emphasis on the time that something happened; and C) plain imperfect + **to** 'whenever,' a general condition, with a repeated or habitual conclusion.

母親が去ったら，子どもは泣きます。
Hahaoya ga sattara, kodomo wa nakimasu.
When (or if) the child's mother leaves, he will cry.

母親が去る時に，子どもは泣きます。
Hahaoya ga saru toki ni, kodomo wa nakimasu.
When the child's mother leaves, he will cry.

母親が去った時に，子どもは泣きます。
Hahaoya ga satta toki ni, kodomo wa nakimasu.
When the child's mother has left, he will cry.

母親が去ると，子どもは泣きます。
Hahaoya ga saru to, kodomo wa nakimasu.
When(ever) the child's mother leaves, he cries.

母親が去ったら，子どもは泣きました。
Hahaoya ga sattara, kodomo wa nakimashita.
When the child's mother left, he cried.

母親が去った時に，子どもは泣きました。
Hahaoya ga satta toki ni, kodomo wa nakimashita.
When the child's mother left, he cried.

母親が去る時に，子どもは泣きました。
Hahaoya ga saru toki ni, kodomo wa nakimashita.
When the child's mother was about to leave, he cried.

母親が去ると，子どもは泣きました。
Hahaoya ga saru to, kodomo wa nakimashita.
When the child's mother left, he cried.

As shown in the above examples, the use of the perfect before **toki ni** is sometimes possible even when the tense of the whole sentence is future.

Here are some more examples of conditional forms with the meaning 'when':

映画館へ行ってみたら，もう見たことのある映画でした。
Eigakan e itte mitara, mō mita koto no aru eiga deshita.
When I went to the theater and looked, it was a film I had already seen.

2時間勉強したら，食事をしましょう。
Nijikan benkyō shitara, shokuji o shimashō.
When we've studied for two hours, let's eat.

8.12. Asking for advice

To ask for advice, use an expression like one of the following:

何をしたらいいでしょうか。
Nani o shitara ii deshō ka.
What should I do? (*lit.*, If I were to do what, would it be good?)

何をすればいいでしょうか。
Nani o sureba ii deshō ka.
What should I do ? (*lit.*, If I do what, will it be good?)

どうしたらいいでしょうか。
Dō shitara ii deshō ka.
What should I do? (*lit.*, If I were to do how, would it be good?)

どうすればいいでしょうか。
Dō sureba ii deshō ka.
What should I do? (*lit.*, If I do how, will it be good?)

こうしたらいいでしょうか。
Kō shitara ii deshō ka.
Should I do like this? (*lit.*, If I were to do like this, would it be good?)

こうすればいいでしょうか。
Kō sureba ii deshō ka.
Should I do like this? (*lit.*, If I do like this, will it be good?)

こうしたらどうでしょうか。
Kō shitara dō deshō ka.
How about doing like this? (*lit.*, If I were to do like this, how would it be?)

こうすればどうでしょうか。
Kō sureba dō deshō ka.
How about doing like this? (*lit.*, If I do like this, how will it be?)

Each expression consists of two parts: a proposed hypothesis (if-clause) with either the conditional or the provisional, since the proposal refers to the future; and a conclusion (then-clause), which asks either how the hypothesis is or whether the hypothesis is all right. The interrogative word may be either in the hypothesis (**dō shitara...**) or in the conclusion (**...dō deshō ka**), but you do not find interrogatives in both the if-clause and the then-clause.

This is the usual polite way of asking and giving directions in Japanese. Notice the difference between the Japanese and English equivalents in this exchange:

ここから高橋病院はどう行ったらいいでしょうか。
Koko kara Takahashi byōin wa dō ittara ii deshō ka.
How can I get to Takahashi Hospital from here?

あのバスに乗ったらいいでしょう。
Ano basu ni nottara ii deshō.
Take that bus.

Here are some more examples of sentences containing advice. The English equivalents contain words like 'should, ought.'

どのバスに乗ったらいいでしょうか。
Dono basu ni nottara ii deshō ka.
Which bus should I take?

これをもう少し勉強すればいいと思います。
Kore o mō sukoshi benkyō sure ba ii to omoimasu.
I think you ought to study this a little more.

値段を比べたらどうでしょうか。
Nedan o kurabetara dō deshō ka.
Should we compare prices?

ローマ字で書けばいいでしょう。
Rōmaji de kakeba ii deshō.
You ought to write it in Roman letters.

だれもいなかったらどうすればいいでしょうか。
Dare mo inakattara dō sure ba ii deshō ka.
If no one is there, what should I do?

　　Sometimes an English equivalent might include the expression 'better' or 'had better,' but this is often closer to the Japanese expression discussed in the next section.

8.13. 'Had better'

One way of giving advice in English is to say things like 'You'd better do like this,' 'I better be there before the teacher arrives.' In such sentences, there is usually the slight implication that a comparison is being made—it would be better to do something than not to do it. The nearest Japanese equivalent is the plain perfect + **hō** 'alternative' + some form of the adjective **ii** 'is good':

ネットで買った方がいいでしょう。
Netto de katta hō ga ii deshō.
I think you'd better buy it online.

できるだけ早く病院に行った方がいいと思いますよ。
Dekirudake hayaku byōin ni itta hō ga ii to omoimasu yo.
I think you'd better go to the hospital as soon as possible.

　　Notice that, for this meaning of 'had better,' the form in front of **hō** is always perfect, regardless of the mood of the final expression. If you use the imperfect mood, the meaning is 'it is better to,' which has a slightly different flavor:

もらうよりやる方がいいです。
Morau yori yaru hō ga ii desu.
It is better to give than to receive.

私が行く方がいいでしょう。
Watashi ga iku hō ga ii deshō.
It would be better for me to go (than for you to, or than for me to stay).

先生になる方がいいです。
Sensei ni naru hō ga ii desu.
It is better (for someone) to become a teacher.

8.14. ···さえ ...*sae*

The particle **sae** 'even, only, just' is more strongly emphatic than **mo** 'even; also.' It singles out a word or phrase for a particularly acute focus of attention. Like **mo**, **sae** follows nouns, nouns + the copula gerund (**de**), and infinitives. Other particles may occur after the noun before **sae** or **de sae**, but ga, o, and of course the focus-shifting **wa** do not ordinarily occur. Here are examples of **mo** and **sae** after nouns, nouns + **de**, and infinitives. After nouns, the translation is often 'just'; after infinitives, 'only.'

子どももできます。
Kodomo mo dekimasu.
Children can do it, too.

子ども(で)さえできます。
Kodomo (de) sae dekimasu.
Even children can do it.

この漢字は日本人(で)さえ分かりません。
Kono kanji wa Nihonjin (de) sae wakarimasen.
Even Japanese people do not know this kanji.

休みさえすれば，よくなります。
Yasumi sae sureba, yoku narimasu.
If you'll just (if you'll only) rest, you'll get better.

安くさえあればどのレストランでもいいです。
Yasuku sae are ba dono resutoran demo ii desu.
If it is cheap, any restaurant is okay.

Notice the patterns VERB-INFINITIVE + **sae sureba** and ADJECTIVE-INFINITIVE + **sae areba**. These are the usual ways to put a clause with the meaning 'if something will ONLY do something or be something,' the actual verb or adjective meaning is carried by the infinitive, and **sureba** and **areba** function as a sort of dummy or auxiliary to carry the provisional ending -(r)eba and the meaning 'if.' The concluding, main clause of the sentence gives the result to be expected, granted 'ONLY' that the provision be so.

8.15. The explicit use of に *ni*

Some expressions that require a verb + a direct object in English are equivalent to Japanese expressions with a subject + a verb:

> フランス語が分かります。 **Furansugo ga wakarimasu.**
> French is clear. = I understand French.
>
> 泳ぐことができます。 **Oyogu koto ga dekimasu.**
> Fact of swimming is possible. = I can swim.
>
> お金が要ります。 **Okane ga irimasu.**
> Money is necessary. = I need money.

The person who understands, is able to do, or needs is usually marked by the particle **wa** as in **Watashi wa Furansugo ga wakarimasu**, **Watashi wa oyogu koto ga dekimasu**, and **Watashi wa okane ga irimasu**. However, you can have the particle **ni**, as you can see in the following sentences.

> 私にはフランス語がわかります。
> **Watashi ni wa furansugo ga wakarimasu.**
> I understand French.
>
> 私には泳ぐことができます。
> **Watashi ni wa oyogu koto ga dekimasu.**
> I can swim.
>
> 私にはお金が要ります。
> **Watashi ni wa okane ga irimasu.**
> I need money.

Following are additional examples where you can see the particle **ni** in a similar context:

> そんなひどいことは私には言えません。
> **Sonna hidoi koto wa watashi ni wa iemasen.**
> I cannot say such a terrible thing.
>
> あの人には友達がいません。
> **Ano hito ni wa tomodachi ga imasen.**
> That person does not have a friend.

眼鏡をかけても父にはこの字は読めません。
Megane o kakete mo chichi ni wa kono ji wa yomemasen.
Even with eyeglasses, my father cannot read this character.

8.16. …ば…ほど … *…ba…hodo* 'the more… the more…'

Sentences like 'the sooner, the better,' 'the more, the merrier,' 'the more I eat fish, the less I like it,' and 'the less I see of him, the better' are the equivalent of a Japanese construction involving one verb or adjective given first in the provisional, then repeated in the plain imperfect + **hodo** 'extent, to the extent that,' followed by the other verb or adjective in a concluding form:

勉強すればするほど分からないことがでてきました。
Benkyō sureba suru hodo wakaranai koto ga detekimashita.
The more I studied, the more questions I came up with.

早ければ早いほどいいです。
Hayakereba hayai hodo ii desu.
The sooner the better.

キッチンは広ければ広いほど便利です。
Kitchin wa hirokereba hiroi hodo benri desu.
The bigger a kitchen is, the more convenient.

8.17. …し *…shi*

The particle **shi** (perhaps derived from the infinitive of **suru**, which is **shi** 'doing') connects clauses with the meaning 'and also.' The verb, adjective, or copula at the end of the clause preceding **shi** is either plain imperfect or perfect. You have already had one way to connect clauses with the meaning 'and,' by using the gerund that means 'does and' or 'is and.' The difference between the use of the gerund and the use of the plain imperfect or perfect + the particle **shi** lies in the tightness of the connection between the two clauses. If there is some sort of sequence in time or logic between the clauses in the order in which they are given, then you use the gerund. However, if you are emphasizing the actions or properties by randomly listing them for making some point, then you use **shi**. When **shi** is used, the concluding phrase is often omitted. It is also common to have only one instance of **shi** in a sentence. Here are some more examples of **shi**.

このアパートは家賃が安いし，静かだし，最高です。
Kono apāto wa yachin ga yasui shi, shizuka da shi, saikō desu.
As for this apartment, the rent is cheap, the place is quiet, so it's just the best.

あの人はかっこいいし，頭がいいし，スポーツもできるし。
Ano hito wa kakkoii shi, atama ga ii shi, supōtsu mo dekiru shi.
That person is cool-looking, smart, can do (all sorts of) sports (...).

もう暗いし，あしたにしましょう。
Mō kurai shi, ashita ni shimashiō.
It's already dark, so let's do it tomorrow.

お金はぜんぜんないし。
Okane wa zenzen nai shi.
I don't have any money... (So what can I do?)

8.18. Correlative compounds

There are a few nouns made up from interrogatives and other correlative words to give a meaning of a non-specific nature:

だれだれ	**daredare**	so-and-so, somebody or other
どこどこ	**dokodoko**	somewhere or other
どこそこ	**dokosoko**	someplace or other
これこれ	**korekore**	such-and-such a one
あれこれ	**arekore**	this or that, one thing or another
かれこれ	**karekore**	about, approximately
あちらこちら（あちこち）	**achira kochira (achikochi)**	here and there

The word **sorezore**, however, has a distributive rather than a non-specific meaning: 'severally, respectively.' Here are a few examples of the use of these words.

どこどこのだれだれがそう言ったとか言っていました。
Dokodoko no daredare ga sō itta toka itte imashita.
He was saying so-and-so in somewhere or other said that or something like that.

あれこれ考えているうちに嫌になりました。
Arekore kangaete iru uchi ni iya ni narimashita.
While I was thinking about this or that, I started to hate (the idea).

このタイプの車は日本でもあちらこちらで見かけられるようになりました。
Kono taipu no kuruma wa Nihon de mo achirakochira de mikakerareru yō ni narimashita.
We started to see this type of car here and there, even in Japan.

この会社ではかれこれ３０年になります。
Kono kaisha de wa karekore sanjūnen ni narimasu.
In this company I have been working about thirty years.

Conversation

[cue 08-3]

Tomomi (T) is on the way to her job interview, but she missed the bus. She calls Yumiko (Y), who lives near the train station.

T. もしもし，由美ちゃん？私。
Moshimoshi, Yumi-chan? Watashi.
Hello, Yumi? It's me.

Y. ああ。友美ちゃん？
Ā, Tomomi-chan?
Oh, Tomomi?

T. うん。**Un.** Yes.

Y. どうしたの。
Dō shita no?
What happened?

T. 3時から面接があるんだけど，電車に乗りおくれちゃって。
San-ji kara mensetsu ga aru n dake do, densha ni nori-okure chatte.
I have a (job) interview at three p.m., but I just missed the train.

Y. 今どこ？**Ima doko?** Where are you now?

T. 駅前。**Ekimae.** In front of the train station.

Y. じゃあ，車で連れて行ってあげるよ。**Jā, kuruma de tsurete itte ageru yo.**
Okay, then I'll take you there by car.

T. ああ，助かる！**Ā, tasukaru!** Oh, that helps!

Y. じゃあ，ロータリーのところで待ってて。**Jā, rōtarī no tokoro de matte te.**
Okay, then, wait for me at the rotary.

T. うん。わかった。ありがとう。**Un. Wakatta. Arigatō.** Okay. Got it. Thanks!

Exercises

I. Fill in the blanks using a question word. If needed, add a particle after it.

1. 「誰か来ましたか。」
   "Dare ka kimashita ka."

   「いいえ，_____来ませんでし
   たよ。」
   "Īe,_____kimasen deshita yo."

2. 「夏休みは_____に行きますか。」
   "Natsu-yasumi wa _____ni
   ikimasu ka."

   「いいえ，どこにも行きません。」
   "Īe, doko ni mo ikimasen."

3. 「日曜日は_____に行きまし
   たか。」
   "Nichiyōbi wa _____ni
   ikimashita ka."

   「渋谷に行きました。」
   "Shibuya ni ikimashita."

4. 「何か要りますか。」
   "Nani ka irimasu ka."

   「いいえ，_____要りません。」
   "Īe, _____irimasen."

5. 「田中さんは_____と話して
   いましたよ。」
   "Tanaka-san wa _____to
   hanashite imashita yo."

   「だれでしょうね。」
   "Dare deshō ne."

6. 姉は_____を食べても太りません。
   Ane wa _____o tabete mo futorimasen.

II. Fill in the blanks appropriately, if necessary. Some sentences may be complete already.

1. 天気が_____ら，公園に行きます。
   Tenki ga _____ra, kōen ni ikimasu.

2. 天気が_____ば，公園に行きます。
   Tenki ga _____ba, kōen ni ikimasu.

3. 日本語で_____ら，すぐ分かります。
   Nihongo de _____ra, sugu wakarimasu.

4. 日本語で_____ば，すぐ分かります。
   Nihongo de _____ba, sugu wakarimasu.

5. 日本の映画＿＿＿＿＿＿＿と必ず見ます。
   Nihon no eiga ＿＿＿＿＿＿＿to kanarazu mimasu.

6. 日本の映画＿＿＿＿＿＿＿なら必ず見ます。
   Nihon no eiga ＿＿＿＿＿＿＿nara kanarazu mimasu.

III. By using all the items in each set, make a sensible sentence. Conjugate verbs and adjectives or add some items if needed.

1. {簡単な **kantan na**, 子ども **kodomo**, 漢字 **kanji**, …さえ **sae**, こんな **konna**}
2. {…に **ni**, お金 **o-kane**, 要ります **irimasu**}
3. {早い **hayai**, …ほど **hodo**, いいです **ii desu**, …ば **ba**}
4. {田中さん **Tanaka-san**, かっこいい **kakko ii**, やさしい **yasashii**, …し **shi**}
5. {ネット **netto**, 買う **kau**, いい **ii**, …方 **hō**}

IV. Complete the following sentences.

1. カンニングを＿＿＿＿は＿＿＿＿よ。**Kanningu o ＿＿＿＿wa ＿＿＿＿yo.**
   Don't cheat!

2. 早く＿＿＿＿＿ですか。**Hayaku ＿＿＿＿＿desu ka.** May I leave early?

3. 私の鉛筆を＿＿＿＿＿いいですよ。**Watashi no enpitsu o ＿＿＿＿＿ii desu yo.** You may use my pencil.

4. まだ３時ですから＿＿＿＿いいですよ。**Mada sanji desu kara＿＿＿＿ii desu yo.** It's still three o'clock, so no need to hurry.

5. 漢字を勉強＿＿＿＿＿いけません。**Kanji o benkyō ＿＿＿＿＿ikemasen.**
   I have to study kanji.

LESSON **9**

In this lesson you will learn a variety of prefixes, suffixes, forms, and words that make your speech very polite.

Be Polite!
礼儀正しく！
Reigi Tadashiku!

Basic Sentences

[cue 09-1]

1.	ご無沙汰いたしております。 **Gobusata itashite orimasu.**	Haven't seen you for a long time! (*lit.*, I have not visited you frequently enough.)
2.	お元気でいらっしゃいますか。 **O-genki de irasshaimasu ka.**	How are you?
3.	はい，お陰さまで。 **Hai, okagesama de.**	I'm fine, thanks to everyone.
4.	お父様はいかがですか。 **Otōsama wa ikaga desu ka.**	How is your father?
5.	父も元気にしております。 **Chichi mo genki ni shite orimasu.**	My father is also fine.
6.	先月田中先生にお会いいたしました。 **Sengetsu Tanaka sensei ni o-ai itashi-mashita.**	Last month I met Professor Tanaka.

7.	どちらでお会いになったんですか。 **Dochira de <u>o-ai ni natta n desu ka</u>.**	Where did you meet him?
8.	博物館でございました。 **Hakubutsukan <u>de gozaimashita</u>.**	It was at the museum.
9.	田中先生にいろいろ教えて頂きました。 **Tanaka sensei ni iroiro <u>oshiete</u> <u>itadakimashita</u>.**	Professor Tanaka taught me a variety of things. (*lit.*, I received a favor of teaching a variety of things from Prof. Tanaka.)
10.	高橋先生はお忙しくていらっしゃいますか。 **Takahashi sensei wa <u>o-isogashikute</u> <u>irasshaimasu ka</u>.**	Is Professor Takahashi busy?
11.	「4月の学会にはおいでにならないのですか。」 **"Shigatsu no gakkai ni wa <u>oide ni naranai</u> <u>no desu ka</u>."**	"You are not going to the conference in April?"
	「はい，参りません。」 **"Hai, <u>mairimasen</u>."**	"Correct, I'm not going."
12.	近いうちにまたお伺いいたします。 **Chikai uchi ni mata <u>o-ukagai itashimasu</u>.**	I'll visit you soon.
13.	他の先生方にも宜しくお伝えください。 **Hoka no sensei-gata ni mo <u>yoroshiku</u> <u>o-tsutae kudasai</u>.**	Please send my best regard to other teachers.

 **Basic Vocabulary**

[cue 09-2]

POLITE PHRASES

お久しぶりです。	**Ohisashiburi desu.**	It's been a long time since I saw you last.
お元気ですか。	**O-genki desu ka.**	How are you?
お陰さまで。	**Okagesama de.**	(I'm fine) thanks to (you and others).
失礼します。	**Shitsurei shimasu.**	(Expression used when one parts. Lit., I'll be rude.)

> **CULTURE NOTE ▶ Bowing**
>
> Bowing plays an important role for communication in Japan. Phrases for gratitude, apology, greeting, and parting are almost always accompanied by bowing. People sometimes bow without saying anything. The deeper the bow, the deeper the respect for the person to whom you are bowing. The bow is called the お辞儀 **ojigi**, or more formally 礼 **rei**. The former is more common because the latter is only one syllable. The deepest bow is called 最敬礼 **saikeirei**. The deep bow, lowering the upper half of the body by 45 degrees, is required if you make a horrible mistake, receive overwhelming kindness, or associate with people to whom you must show serious respect. Otherwise, you don't have to bow very deeply. You can lower your upper body only by about 10–15 degrees, or just tilt your head forward for a moment or two in casual situations. When introductions are being made, Japanese do not shake hands, hug, or kiss, but just bow and smile.
>
>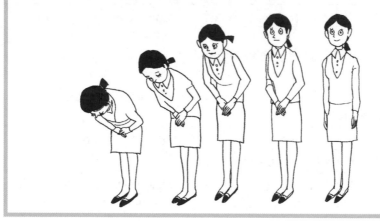

POLITE QUESTIONS

いかがですか。	**Ikaga desu ka.**	How is it?
どなたですか。	**Donata desu ka.**	Who is it?
どちらですか。	**Dochira desu ka.**	Where is it?/Which one is it?
おいくつですか。	**O-ikutsu desu ka.**	How old are you?
おいくらですか。	**O-ikura desu ka.**	How much is it?
どちらからですか。	**Dochira kara desu ka.**	Where are you from?

POLITE PHRASES AT RESTAURANTS

いらっしゃいませ。	**Irasshaimase.**	Welcome!
ご注文は。	**Go-chūmon wa.**	What is your order?
少々お待ちください。	**Shōshō o-machi kudasai.**	Please wait a little bit.
お待たせいたしました。	**O-matase itashimashita.**	Sorry to have kept you waiting.

申し訳ございません。	**Mōshiwake gozaimasen.**	I'm terribly sorry.
ありがとうございました。	**Arigatō gozaimashita.**	Thank you so much!

VERBS OF GIVING AND RECEIVING

あげる・あげます	**ageru/agemasu**	gives
差し上げる・差し上げます	**sashiageru/sashiagemasu**	gives (honorific)
くれる・くれます	**kureru/kuremasu**	gives (to me/us)
下さる・下さいます	**kudasaru/kudasaimasu**	gives (to me/us, honorific)
もらう・もらいます	**morau/moraimasu**	receives
頂く・頂きます	**itadaku/itadakimasu**	receives (honorific)

CULTURE NOTE Gift-giving

The Japanese send gifts to their bosses, clients, former teachers, friends, and relatives. There are two major gift-giving seasons in Japan: one is in summer, and the other is at the end of the year. The summer gift is called **ochūgen**, and the end-of-year gift is called **oseibo**. Popular **ochūgen** and **oseibo** gifts are foods and beverages such as pasta, cheese, seaweed, dried shitake mushrooms, cooking oil, canned foods, beer, sake, cookies, cakes, and items for daily living such as soap and towels. People usually purchase the gifts at a well-known department store and have the store wrap them with the store's wrapping paper and send them directly to their relatives, superiors, and friends. During these seasons, the **ochūgen** and **oseibo** counter at department stores is very crowded with people clutching address books .

Structure Notes

9.1. Status words: humble, neutral, exalted

A word or expression in Japanese may have one of three connotations, indicating its reference to a social status: humble, neutral, and exalted. Many textbooks refer to the exalted forms as "honorific." In this book, honorific is used to refer to BOTH the humble and exalted forms, and to the style of speech in which they usually occur. Most of the words and expressions you have learned so far are neutral. These are used in reference to anyone, provided you are not showing a special deference. Ordinarily, however, Japanese use a more polite level of speech—the

The word **minna** only has the meaning 'everybody' when used as a noun with some particle: **Minna ga kimashita** 'Everybody came' or **Minna kimashita** '(They) all came.' When used as an adverb it means 'all' or 'every' and can refer to people or things: **Gakusei ga minna kimashita** 'The students all came.' Here are some examples of these words in sentences:

洋服を沢山買いました。
Yōfuku o takusan kaimashita.
I bought a lot of clothes.

この店は子供服も少しあります。
Kono mise wa kodomo fuku mo sukoshi arimasu.
This store has some children's clothes.

お客さんが大勢来ました。
Okyaku-san ga ōzei kimashita.
Many shoppers came.

この店の漫画はみんな読んだことがあります。
Kono mise no manga wa minna yonda koto ga arimasu.
I have read all the comic books in this store.

6.3. Use of numbers and quantity words

Numbers and quantity words occur as ordinary nouns, connected by **no** to the nouns they modify. They occur also as adverbs without any particle following, and in this case they usually follow the NOUN + PARTICLE expression to which they refer, although sometimes they are put at the very beginning as if modifying the whole sentence, and sometimes you hear them in other positions.

If the particle after the noun is any particle other than **wa**, **ga**, or **o**, the number or quantity word must precede as a regular modifying noun: **futari no hito kara** 'from two people,' **takusan no gakkō e** 'to many schools.' But if the particle after the noun is **wa**, **ga**, or **o**, the number or quantity word can either precede with **no**, or follow as an adverb with no particle at all. There is a slight difference of meaning. If the quantity word or number is used as an adverb, the noun is referred to in an "indefinite" fashion: **enpitsu ga nihon** 'two pencils (some or any two pencils),' **ocha ga sukoshi** 'a little bit of tea.' If the quantity word or number is used as a modifying noun, the reference is more "definite": **nihon no enpitsu ga** 'THE two pencils,' **kono sukoshi no ocha ga** 'this little bit of tea.'

This is about the only place where Japanese maintains the English distinction between 'A man' (**hito wa hitori**) and 'THE man' (**hitori no hito wa**), and it is possible only when the particle involved is **wa**, **ga**, or **o**. When a number or quantity

	Neutral	**Exalted**
younger brother	弟 **otōto**	弟さん **otōtosan**
younger sister	妹 **imōto**	妹さん **imōtosan**
grandfather	祖父 **sofu**	おじいさん **ojīsan**
grandmother	祖母 **sobo**	おばあさん **obāsan**
uncle	おじ **oji**	おじさん **ojisan**
aunt	おば **oba**	おばさん **obasan**
nephew	甥 **oi**	甥御さん **oigosan**
niece	姪 **mei**	姪御さん **meigosan**
cousin	いとこ **itoko**	おいとこさん **o-itokosan**
relatives	親戚 **shinseki**	ご親戚 **go-shinseki**
husband	主人 **shujin**; 夫 **otto**	ご主人 **go-shujin**
wife	家内 **kanai**; 妻 **tsuma**	奥さん **okusan**
family	家族 **kazoku**	ご家族 **go-kazoku**

The words **ojisan** and **obasan** as well as **ojīsan** and **obāsan** are also used in a general way by young people to refer to anyone of an older generation, for example: **tonari no ojisan** 'the man next door,' **ano obasan** 'that lady,' and **ano obāsan** 'that elderly lady.'

9.3. Other nouns
There are a few other nouns that come in pairs, with one neutral, the other exalted.

	Neutral	**Exalted**
house, home	うち **uchi**; 家 **ie**	お宅 **otaku**
person	人 **hito**; 者 **mono**	方 **kata**
he, she	あの人 **ano hito**	あの方 **ano kata**
how	どう **dō**	いかが **ikaga**
where	どこ **doko**	どちら **dochira**
who	だれ **dare**	どなた **donata**; どちら **dochira**

9.4. Honorific prefixes
There are two common honorific prefixes, **o-** and **go-**. Words containing an honorific prefix may indicate an exaltation of the word itself, on its own merits, as in **watashi no o-tomodachi** 'my friend' and **anata no o-tomodachi** 'your friend,' or it may indicate the relationship between the word and an exalted person, as in

o-niwa 'your garden.' Again, with nouns and verb forms, it may be just generally honorific, used for both humble and exalted situations. With adjective forms, the use of the honorific prefix seems always to indicate an exalted relationship: **oiso-gashii toki** 'at a time when YOU are very busy.'

The prefix **go-** is attached to a number of nouns (often, but not always, of Chinese origin) and to a few verb infinitives: **go-shujin** 'your husband,' **go-yukkuri** 'slowly,' **go-zonji** 'knowing.' The prefix **o-** is more widely used and is attached readily to nouns (including many of Chinese origin: **o-shōyu** 'the soy sauce,' **o-denwa** 'the telephone'), verb infinitives (**o-yasumi**), and many adjectives (**o-isogashii** 'busy').

Some words by convention have the prefixes **o-** and **go-**, particularly in the speech of women and children, regardless of whether the situation calls for an honorific (humble or exalted) form or not. This is an extension of the usage exalting the word itself, on its own merits. Here is a list of some of these words with a conventional honorific prefix:

ご飯 **gohan**	cooked rice, meal, food
お米 **okome**	rice (uncooked, but harvested)
お酒 **osake**	rice wine
ご褒美 **gohōbi**	reward, prize
お盆 **obon**	tray
お茶 **ocha**	tea
お金 **okane**	money
お腹 **onaka**	stomach
お菓子 **okashi**	pastry, sweets
お釣り **otsuri**	change
お湯 **oyu**	hot water

9.5. Honorific suffixes for people's names

There are two honorific suffixes for people's names: **-san** and **-sama**. The latter is a formal variant of the former, usually restricted to certain set expressions. The suffix **-san** is widely used with names (= Mr., Miss, Ms., Mrs.), kinship terms, occupations, and other nouns referring to people. In more formal speech, **-sama** sometimes replaces **-san** in these terms. In more intimate speech, **-chan** is heard.

田中さん **Tanaka-san**	Mr. Tanaka
スミスさん **Sumisu-san**	Mr. Smith
陽子さん **Yōko-san**	Yoko
陽子ちゃん **Yōko-chan**	Yoko
マイケルさん **Maikeru-san**	Michael
社長さん **shachō-san**	president
お客さん **o-kyaku-san** ・ お客様 **o-kyaku-sama**	customer, guest

9.6. Verbs: the honorific infinitive

The humble or exalted equivalent to a simple polite verb of neutral status is often an expression built around the HONORIFIC INFINITIVE. For verbs, this form is usually made by prefixing **o-** to the regular infinitive.

The most common honorific usage for verbs is as follows. For the humble form, use the honorific infinitive plus some form of the neutral verb **suru** 'does' or of the humble verb **itasu** 'does.' The forms with **itasu** show greater deference (= are more humble) than the forms with **suru**:

> お書きいたします。／お書きします。
> **O-kaki itashimasu./O-kaki shimasu.**
> I'll write it.

For the exalted form, use the honorific infinitive + the particle **ni** + some form of the verb **naru** 'becomes.'

> お書きになります。
> **O-kaeri ni narimasu.**
> (He) will write it.

Some verbs such as **kaeru** 'returns' can be used with some form of the copula **da** or of the honorific polite copula **de gozaimasu**, or of the exalted copula **de irassharu**.

> | お帰りです。 **O-kaeri desu.** | (He) is returning. |
> | お帰りでございます。 **O-kaeri de gozaimasu.** | (He) is returning. |
> | お帰りでいらっしゃいます。 **O-kaeri de irasshaimasu.** | (He) is returning. |

Other examples are:

> | お休みでございます。 **O-yasumi de gozaimasu.** | (He) is resting. |
> | お出かけでございます。 **O-dekake de gozaimasu.** | (He) is out. |
> | お探しでございます。 **O-sagashi de gozaimasu.** | (He) is looking (for it). |

9.7. Special honorific verbs

For many common verbs, in addition to (or to the exclusion of) regularly formed exalted and humble forms, Japanese use special verbs or special infinitives for either the exalted or the humble, or for both. In the table of special verbs below, the verbs are arranged in three vertical columns, humble, neutral, and exalted. Where there are blanks in the table, it means there is no special verb for the humble or for the exalted, but that the form can be made in the regular way (HONORIFIC INFINITIVE + **itasu**; HONORIFIC INFINITIVE + **ni naru**, etc.).

	Humble	Neutral	Exalted
I give	差し上げる **sashiageru**	あげる **ageru** やる **yaru**	---
You give or he gives to me or us	---	くれる **kureru**	下さる **kudasaru**
does	致す **itasu**	する **suru**	なさる **nasaru**[1]
says	申す **mōsu**	言う **iu**	おっしゃる **ossharu**[1]
drinks, eats	頂く **itadaku**	飲む **nomu**, 食べる **taberu**	召し上がる **meshiagaru**
receives	頂く **itadaku**	もらう **morau**	---
comes	参る **mairu**	来る **kuru**	いらっしゃる **irassharu**[1]
goes	参る **mairu**[2] 伺う **ukagau**[2]	行く **iku**	いらっしゃる **irassharu**[1]
stays	おる **oru**	いる **iru** (to exist)	いらっしゃる **irassharu**[1]
is, equals	...でござる **de go-zaru**[1,4]	...だ **da**	...でいらっしゃる **de irassharu**[1]
looks	拝見する **haiken suru**[3]	見る **miru**	ご覧になる **go-ran ni naru**
knows	存じる **zonjiru**	知る **shiru**	ご存知だ **go-zonji da**
has	ござる **gozaru**[1,4]	ある **aru**	---
asks	伺う **ukagau**	尋ねる **tazuneru**	---

[1] These verbs are consonant verbs, but り **ri** that appear right before the polite suffix (ます **masu**, ません **masen**, etc.) changes to い **i**.
[2] If the speaker is going to the place of addressee, use 伺う **ukagau** rather than 参る **mairu**.
[3] Use 拝見する **haiken suru** only if the item to be seen belongs to the addressee.
[4] ござる **gozaru** and ...でござる **de gozaru** function either as humble forms or very polite forms.

9.8. 申し上げる *mōshiageru*

The verb **mōshiageru** is used as a humble form for either 'does' or 'says':

またお伺い申し上げます。＝またお伺いいたします。
Mata o-ukagai mōshiagemasu. = Mata o-ukagai itashimasu.
I'll visit you again.

申し上げたいことがございます。 ＝ 申したいことがございます。
Mōshiagetai koto ga gozaimasu. = Mōshitai koto ga gozaimasu.
There's something I want to tell you.

9.9. Inflection of slightly irregular exalted verbs

The verbs **nasaru, irassharu, kudasaru,** and **ossharu** are irregularly inflected in similar ways:

Plain Imperfect	Polite Imperfect	Imperative	Gerund	Plain Perfect
なさる **nasaru** 'does'	なさいます **nasaimasu**	なさい **nasai**	なさって **nasatte**	なさった **nasatta**
いらっしゃる **irassharu** 'comes, goes, is'	いらっしゃい ます **irasshaimasu**	いらっしゃい **irasshai**	いらっしゃって **irasshatte**	いらっしゃった **irasshatta**
くださる **kudasaru** 'gives'	くださいます **kudasaimasu**	ください **kudasai**	くださって **kudasatte**	くださった **kudasatta**
おっしゃる **ossharu** 'says'	おっしゃいます **osshaimasu**	おっしゃい **osshai**	おっしゃって **osshatte**	おっしゃった **osshatta**

For **gozaru (gozaimasu)** see 9.15.

9.10. Special inflections of ます *-masu*

The polite ending **-masu** is really itself a verb that is used only when attached to other verb infinitives. In ordinary polite speech it is inflected only for the imperfect **-masu**, the perfect **-mashita**, and the tentative **-mashō**. But in honorific speech, **-masu** is inflected for all categories except the infinitive. These polite forms are used at the end of sentence fragments, and also in the middle of sentences instead of the usual plain forms, to make the entire expression a bit more honorific:

そこへいらしまして…
Soko e irashimashite...　　　You go there and...

そこへいらしましたら…
Soko e irashimashitara...　　　If you go there ...

そこへいらしてくださいませ。
Soko e irashite kudasaimase.　　　Please go there.

Here are the inflections of the polite verb **-masu**:

Imperfect: **-masu**　　　Perfect: **-mashita**
Tentative: **-mashō**　　　Alternative: **-mashitari** (10.5)

Infinitive: -- Gerund: **-mashite**
Provisional: **-maseba** Conditional: **-mashitara**
Imperative: **-mase**

You may also encounter **deshite**, a polite gerund for the copula 'is and':

スキー王と呼ばれた人でして，関西に初めてスキー場を開いた人でした。
"Sukī-ō" to yobareta hito deshite, Kansai ni hajimete sukī-jō o hiraita hito deshita.
He was the man they called the "Ski King," and the one that opened the first ski resort in Kansai.

9.11. Use of humble verbs

In general, humble verbs are used to denote one's own acts when speaking to persons who are socially superior.

「部長，ちょっとお伺いしても宜しいですか。」 「ええ，何？」
"Buchō, chotto o-ukagai shite mo yoroshii desu ka." **"Ē, nani?"**
"Maneger, is it okay to ask you something?" "Sure, what?"

When two people of approximately equal social status are talking, each may use the exalted forms in reference to the other person, but they generally use just the simple polite forms rather than the humble forms in reference to themselves.

「どこへいらっしゃいますか。」 「銀行へ行きます。」
"Doko e irasshaimasu ka." **"Ginkō e ikimasu."**
"Where are you going?" "I'll go to the bank."

An exception to this occurs when the verb implies participation of the other person or some person of higher social status as fellow-subject, indirect or direct object, possessor of something involved in the action, etc.; in this case, the humble form is customary. Sometimes, however, the humble form may be used by both speakers.

「どこへいらっしゃいますか。」 「田中先生のお宅へ参ります。」
"Doko e irasshaimasu ka." **"Tanaka sensei no otaku e mairimasu."**
"Where are you going?" "I'm going to Professor Tanaka's house."

9.12. Adjectives and adjectival nouns

An adjective used as a modifier before a noun or noun phrase either remains unchanged or just adds the honorific prefix **o-**: **o-isogashii toki** 'a busy time (for you).' When an adjective is used at the end of a sentence as the main predicate, it may be treated in one of two ways: as an exalted expression, or as a general honorific (exalted or humble) expression. It is usually treated as an exalted expression IF THE REFERENCE IS DIRECTLY TO THE PERSON YOU ARE TALKING WITH or TO SOMEONE ELSE OF HIGH SOCIAL STATUS. Otherwise, if the reference is to one of his possessions, or to someone else of equal social status, or to yourself, it is treated as a general honorific.

The exalted expression is made by using the gerund (**-kute**) form of the adjective, with the honorific prefix **o-**, followed by some form of the exalted verb **irassharu** 'stays, exists':

> お忙しくていらっしゃいます。
> **O-isogashikute irasshaimasu.**
> You are busy.

Similarly, adjectival nouns can be preceded by **o** and followed by **de** and **irassharu.**

> 山田さんはいつもおきれいでいらっしゃいますね。
> **Yamada-san wa itsu mo o-kirei de irasshaimasu ne.**
> Ms. Yamada is always pretty.

9.13. Formation of the adjective honorific infinitive

If we include the vowel that appears before the imperfect ending **-i**, Japanese adjectives are of four types: **-ii**, **-ai**, **-oi**, and **-ui** (**ōkii, akai, aoi, warui**). To produce the honorific infinitive form, we have to change not only the ending, but also the vowel before the ending, as follows:

Imperfect	Honorific Infinitive	Neutral Infinitive
-ii	-yū	-iku
-ai	-ō	-aku
-oi	-ō	-oku
-ui	-ū	-uku

Here are some examples of adjective expressions in the plain, polite, and honorific imperfect:

Meaning	Plain	Polite	Honorific
is satisfactory	よろしい **yoroshii**	よろしいです **yoroshii desu**	よろしゅうございます **yoroshū gozaimasu**
is red	あかい **akai**	あかいです **akai desu**	あこうございます **akō gozaimasu**
is early	はやい **hayai**	はやいです **hayai desu**	はようございます **hayō gozaimasu**
is white	しろい **shiroi**	しろいです **shiroi desu**	しろうございます **shirō gozaimasu**
is slow, late	おそい **osoi**	おそいです **osoi desu**	おそうございます **osō gozaimasu**
is thin	うすい **usui**	うすいです **usui desu**	うすうございます **usū gozaimasu**
is good	いい, よい **ii, yoi**	いいです **ii desu**	ようございます **yō gozaimasu**

Note that this form is old-fashioned, and is used only in quite formal contexts or by elderly people.

9.14. Summary of honorific predicates

	Humble	General Honorific	Exalted
Verb	Hon inf + **itasu** Hon inf + **suru** Special Verb	⟷	Hon inf + **ni naru** Hon inf + **nasaru** Special Verb
Verb **aru**	→	**gozaru**	←
Copula	→	**de gozaru**	**de irassharu**
Adjective	→	Hon inf + **gozaru**	Gerund + **irassharu** Gerund + **oide ni naru**

9.15. ござる *gozaru*

The verb **gozaru** is the honorific equivalent of the neutral verb **aru** 'exists'; it is neither specifically humble nor specifically exalted, just generally honorific. In modern speech it never actually occurs in any plain forms—you don't hear **gozaru**. You hear **gozaimasu** in set phrases and within a sentence:

おはようございます。
O-hayō gozaimasu.   Good morning.

ありがとうございます。
Arigatō gozaimasu.   Thank you.

申し訳ございません。
Mōshiwake gozaimasen.
I'm terribly sorry.

お金がございましたら寄付をお願いいたします。
O-kane ga gozaimashitara kifu o o-negai itashimasu.
If you have the money, please donate some for us.

沢山ございますから、どうぞご遠慮なさらないでください。
Takusan gozaimasu kara dōzo go-enryo nasaranai de kudasai.
Because there's lots, please do not feel reserved.

Gozaimasu is also used after the honorific infinitive form of the adjective as in **Takō gozaimasu** 'It is expensive.' (See 9.13)

Just as **gozaimasu (gozaru)** is the general honorific equivalent of the neutral verb **aru**, the expression **de gozaimasu (de gozaru)** is the general honorific equivalent of the copula **da**. For example:

4階でございます。
Yonkai de gozaimasu.
It's the fourth floor.

9.16. いらっしゃる *irassharu*

The exalted verb **irassharu** corresponds to three different neutral verbs: **kuru** 'comes,' **iku** 'goes,' and **iru** 'stays, exists.' As with all homonyms, you can usually tell which meaning is intended by the context:

どちらからいらっしゃいましたか。
Dochira kara irasshaimashita ka.
Where did you come from?

どちらへいらしゃいましたか。
Dochire e irasshaimashita ka.
Where did you go?

お母様はどちらにいらっしゃいますか。
Okāsama wa dochira ni irasshaimasu ka.
Where is your mother?

9.17. おいで *oide*

The expected forms for the honorific infinitives of **kuru** 'comes,' **iku** 'goes,' and **iru** 'stays, exists,' which are **oki, oiki,** and **oi,** rarely occur. Instead, for the exalted form you use either the special exalted infinitive **oide** (+ **ni naru**, etc.) or the exalted verb **irassharu**.

> どちらからおいでになりましたか。
> **Dochira kara oide ni narimashita ka.**
> Where did you come from?

> どちらへおいでになりましたか。
> **Dochire e oide ni narimashita ka.**
> Where did you go?

> お母様はどちらにおいでになりますか。
> **Okāsama wa dochira ni oide ni narimasu ka.**
> Where is your mother?

9.18. Verbs for giving and receiving

The verbs **ageru** and **kureru** both mean to give. The choice between the two depends on how close the speaker feels to the giver and the recipient. The verb **kureru** is used only when the recipient is the speaker's insider, and the recipient is closer to the speaker than the giver. In all other contexts, **ageru** is used. For example, in the following sentences, the recipients are the speaker's "insiders" (the speaker or the speaker's family members), the recipients are closer to the speaker than the giver, and the verb **kureru** is used.

> ジョンさんが私に チョコレートをくれました。
> **Jon-san ga watashi ni chokorēto o kuremashita.**
> John gave me chocolate.

> ジョンさんが母に チョコレートをくれました。
> **Jon-san ga haha ni chokorēto o kuremashita.**
> John gave my mother chocolate.

> 母が私にチョコレートをくれました。
> **Haha ga watashi ni chokorēto o kuremashita.**
> My mother gave me chocolate.

***Watashi ga haha ni chokorēto o kuremashita** 'I gave my mother chocolate' is UNGRAMMATICAL because the recipient is less close to the speaker than the giver, although the recipient is the speaker's insider. Once **kuremashita** is replaced by **agemashita**, as in **Watashi ga haha ni chokorēto o agemashita**, the sentence becomes grammatical. When the giving event takes place among the speaker's insiders, excluding the speaker himself, either **ageru** or **kureru** can be used. If **kureru** is used, it shows that the speaker feels closer to the receiver than to the giver. When the giving event takes place among outsiders, **ageru** is generally used.

The verb **ageru** must be replaced by **sashiageru** when the receiver is socially superior to, and/or distant from, the giver:

> 私は先生にチョコレートを差し上げました。
> **Watashi wa sensei ni chokorēto o sashiagemashita.**
> I gave the teacher chocolate.

> 父は社長にチョコレートを差し上げました。
> **Chichi wa shachō ni chokorēto o sashiagemashita.**
> My father gave the president chocolate.

The verb **kureru** must be replaced by **kudasaru** when the giver is socially superior to, and/or distant from, the receiver.

> 先生は私にチョコレートを下さいました。
> **Sensei wa watashi ni chokorēto o kudasaimashita.**
> The teacher gave me chocolate.

> 社長は父にチョコレートを下さいました。
> **Shachō wa chichi ni chokorēto o kudasaimashita.**
> The president gave my father chocolate.

Note that the verb **kudasaru** is a consonant verb, but its **masu**-form is **kudasaimasu** rather than **kudasarimasu**.

The verb **ageru** can be optionally replaced by **yaru** when the receiver is socially in a lower status than the giver. For example, when you are giving something to your younger siblings, children, or pets, you can use **yaru** instead of **ageru**:

> 子どもにチョコレートをやりました。
> **Kodomo ni chokorēto o yarimashita.**
> I gave chocolate to my children.

For the meaning 'to receive,' you can use **morau** or its honorific version **itadaku**. The receiver must be closer to the speaker than to the giver when using these verbs. The source of receiving is marked by the particle **kara** or **ni**.

> 私は父に時計をもらった。
> **Watashi wa chichi ni tokei o moratta.**
> I received a watch from my father.

母は隣の方からケーキを頂いた。

Haha wa tonari no kata kara kēki o itadaita.

My mother received cakes from our next-door neighbor.

9.19. Favors

When you say 'someone does something FOR someone else,' you are reporting a FAVOR. To do this in Japanese, use the gerund of the verb representing the action of the favor, and then add on the appropriate verb meaning 'gives.' In other words, to say 'I'll write the letter for you,' the Japanese says something like 'I will give you (the favor of) writing the letter,' **Tegami o kaite agemasu.** The person doing the favor is either the topic, followed by the particle **wa**, or the emphatic subject, followed by the particle **ga**. The person for whom the favor is done is indicated by the particle **ni**:

田中さんは中村さんに手紙を書いてあげました。

Tanaka-san wa Nakamura-san ni tegami o kaite agemashita.

Mr. Tanaka wrote the letter to Mr. Nakamura.

The verbs for giving are used just as they would be if you were giving some object instead of a favor. Similarly, the verbs of receiving can also be used for this function. Make sure to mark the recipient of the kind action with the particle **ni**.

兄は私に本を読んでくれました。

Ani wa watashi ni hon o yonde kuremashita.

My brother read a book to me.

先生は私に漢字を教えてくださいました。

Sensei wa watashi ni kanji o oshiete kudasaimashita.

My teacher taught me kanji.

私は犬にセーターを作ってやりました。
Watashi wa inu ni sētā o tsukutte yarimashita.
I made a sweater for my dog.

先生に推薦状を書いていただきました。
Sensei ni suisenjō o kaite itadakimashita.
I had my teacher write a letter of recommendation for me.

9.20. Requests

The Japanese do not use imperative forms as often as we do. There are several ways to make a polite request in Japanese. You can use gerund forms or honorific infinitive along with some forms of verbs of giving and receiving. The expressions ending in a verb of giving (e.g. **kudasai**) are quite straightforward and might be too plain in a polite context. The politeness increases if the expression takes the form of a negative question (**...masen ka**), because this would make it sound more indirect. Furthermore, it sounds more polite if you use a verb of receiving (**morau/ itadaku**) rather than a verb of giving, in the potential form (**moraeru/itadakeru**) in a negative question, as in **moraenai deshō ka**, **itadakemasen ka** or **itadakenai deshō ka**. The following sentences all express the request 'Please read this letter.'

この手紙を読んでください(ませんか)。
Kono tegami o yonde kudasai(masen ka).

この手紙をお読みください。
Kono tegami o o-yomi kudasai.

この手紙を読んでもらえませんか。
Kono tegami o yonde moraemasen ka.

この手紙を読んでいただきたいんですが。
Kono tegami o yonde itadaki-tai n desu ga.

この手紙を読んでいただけないでしょうか。
Kono tegami o yonde itadakenai deshō ka.

Negative requests are not ordinarily made except in the form of prohibitions to inferiors: **Itsu mo okashi o tabete wa ikemasen yo** 'You mustn't eat sweets all the time.' To a social equal or superior, you suggest that 'it would be better not' to do something: **Sore o tabenai hō ga ii deshō** 'It would be better if you didn't eat that.' Or, given two alternatives, you emphasize the positive one: **Sore o tabenai de, kore o tabete kudasai** 'Please eat this one instead of that one.'

9.21. Answers to negative questions

The words **hai** (or **ē**) and **ie** are used to mean 'what you've said is correct' and 'what you've said is incorrect.' So if you state a question in a negative way, the standard Japanese answer turns out to be the opposite of standard English 'yes' and 'no,' which affirm or deny the FACTS rather than the STATEMENT of the facts.

「砂糖はいりませんか。」
"Satō wa irimasen ka."
"Don't you need sugar?"

「はい，いりません。」
"Hai, irimasen."
"Correct, I don't need it."

「バナナはありませんか。」
"Banana wa arimasen ka."
"Do you have no bananas?"

「はい，バナナはありません。」
"Hai, banana wa arimasen."
"Correct, we have no bananas."

Of course, if the negative question is really just an oblique request, then you indicate assent with **hai** and your refusal with **ie**, as you would in English.

「スーツケースを持ってきてください
ませんか。」
**"Sūtsukēsu o motte kite
kudasaimasen ka."**
"Won't you please bring the suitcase
over here?"

「はい，かしこまりました。」
"Hai, kashikomarimashita."
"Yes, gladly.

「もう少し召し上がりませんか。」
"Mō sukoshi meshiagarimasen ka."
"Won't you have a little more (to eat)?"

「いいえ，もう結構です。」
"Īe, mō kekkō desu."
"No, thanks."

9.22. The specific plural

In general, singular and plural are not distinguished in Japanese: **hon** means 'book' or 'books' and **kore** means 'this' or 'these.' There are, however, ways to make specific plurals for certain nouns, and these are in common use, particularly for the equivalents of English pronouns. There is the following set of suffixes:

HUMBLE	NEUTRAL	EXALTED
−ども **-domo**	−たち **-tachi**	−方 **-gata**

These occur in the following combinations:

私たち	**wata(ku)shi-tachi**	we (neutral)
私ども	**wata(ku)shi-domo**	we (honorific = humble)
あなたたち	**anata-tachi**	you all (neutral)
あなた方	**anata-gata**	you all (honorific = exalted)
あの人たち	**ano hito-tachi**	they (neutral)
あの方々	**ano katagata**	they (honorific = exalted)

The suffix -**tachi** is used frequently with nouns indicating people: **gakusei-tachi** 'students', **Tanaka-tachi** 'Tanaka and his group', and **kodomo-tachi** 'children'. Unless used impersonally, such expressions seem rather impolite. They can be made more polite by adding -**san** before -**tachi**, as in **gakusei-san-tachi**, **Tanaka-san-tachi**, **kodomo-san-tachi**. If special deference is shown to the people discussed, the exalted suffix -**gata** is used: **sensei-gata** 'teachers'. Both **hito-tachi** and **hitobito** are used to mean 'people'. Reduplications of the **hitobito** type often include a connotation of variety or respective distribution 'various people'. Other examples are **kuniguni** 'various countries', **shimajima** '(various or numerous) islands, island after island', and **sorezore** 'severally, variously, respectively'.

The words **kore**, **sore**, and **are** refer to both singular and plural, 'this' or 'these', 'that' or 'those'. They can be made specifically plural by adding the suffix -**ra**: **korera** 'these', **sorera** 'these', and **arera** 'those over there'. But in a simple equational sentence like 'These are roses, and those are camellias' you just use the plain forms **Kore wa bara de, sore wa tsuibaki desu**.

Another polite way to say 'you (all)' is **mina-san** or **mina-san-gata**. The word **mina-san** is often heard at the beginning of a public talk, equivalent to English 'Ladies and Gentlemen'. Sometimes it means just 'everybody (at your house)' as in **Mina-san ni yoroshiku** 'Please give my regards to everyone'.

Conversation

[cue 09-3]

Christopher (C) wants to apply for a graduate school in Japan, and he needs a letter of recommendation. He thought of asking his Japanese teacher (T).

C: 来年から大学院で言語学を勉強したいと思っているんです。
Rainen kara daigakuin de gengogaku o benkyō shitai to omotte iru n desu.
I'm thinking of studying linguistics at a graduate school starting next year.

T: ああ，それはいいですね。**Ā, sore wa ii desu ne.** Oh, that's great!

C: はい。それで１つお願いがあるんですが。
Hai. Sore de hitotsu o-negai ga aru n desu ga.
Right. And I have a favor to ask you.

T: はい。何でしょう。**Hai. Nan deshō.** Sure. What's that?

C: 推薦状を書いていただけないでしょうか。
Suisenjō o kaite itadkenai deshō ka.
Could you write a letter of recommendation for me?

T: もちろんいいですよ。**Mochiron ii desu yo.** Of course, I'd be glad to.

C: ああ，どうもありがとうございます。**Ā, dōmo arigatō gozaimasu.**
Oh, thank you so much!

T: いつまでに要りますか。**Itsu made ni irimasu ka.** By when do you need it?

C: 来月の終わりまでにお願いできますでしょうか。
Raigetsu no owari made ni onegai dekimasu deshō ka.
Could you write it by the end of next month?

T: ええ，大丈夫です。**Ē, daijōbu desu.** Sure, no problem.

C: ああ，ありがとうございます。お忙しいところ申し訳ございませんが，
どうぞ宜しくお願いいたします。
**Ā, arigatō gozaimasu. O-isogashii tokoro mōshiwake gozaimasen ga,
dōzo yoroshiku o-negai itashimasu.**
Oh, thank you very much. I'm terribly sorry to ask this when you are busy, but
your help is very much appreciated.

Exercises

I. Fill in the blanks with appropriate verbs of giving or receiving.

1. 私は母にネックレスを_____。
   Watashi wa haha ni nekkuresu o _____.

2. 母は私にTシャツを_____。
   Haha wa watashi ni tīshatsu o _____.

3. 私は母からTシャツを_____。
   Watashi wa haha kara tīshatsu o _____.

4. 私は先生にワインを_____。
   Watashi wa sensei ni wain o _____.

5. 母は隣の方にお菓子を_____。
   Haha wa tonari no kata ni okashi o _____.

6. 田中さんは兄にネクタイを_____。
   Tanaka-san wa ani ni nekutai o _____.

7. 兄は田中さんからネクタイを_____。
   Ani wa Tanaka-san kara nekutai o _____.

II. Match the words in Box A with the words in Box B.

Box A
i. ありました **arimashita**
ii. くれました **kuremashita**
iii. しました **shimashita**
iv. 来ました **kimashita**
v. 言いました **iimashita**

Box B
a. なさいました **nasaimashita**
b. くださいました **kudasaimashita**
c. おっしゃいました **osshaimashita**
d. いらっしゃいました **irasshaimashita**
e. ございました **gozaimashita**

III. Select the best choice.

1. 先生，どうぞ＿＿＿＿＿＿＿＿ください。
   Sensei, dōzo ＿＿＿＿＿＿＿＿ kudasai.

   a. 召し上がって **meshiagatte**
   b. 頂いて **itadaite**
   c. 食べて **tabete**
   d. 食べに **tabeni**

2. 先生，あの本はもう＿＿＿＿＿＿＿＿。
   Sensei, ano hon wa mō ＿＿＿＿＿＿＿＿.

   a. お読みしましたか **o-yomi shimashita ka**
   b. お読みなりましたか **o-yomi narimashita ka**
   c. お読みになりましたか **o-yomi ni narimashita ka**
   d. お読みいたしましたか **o-yomi itashimashita ka**

3. 私が＿＿＿＿＿＿＿＿。
   Watashi ga ＿＿＿＿＿＿＿＿.

   a. お書きします **o-kaki shimasu**
   b. お書きになります **o-kaki ni narimasu**
   c. お書きなさいます **o-kaki nasaimasu**
   d. お書きにいたします **o-kaki ni itashimasu**

4. 僕の＿＿＿＿＿＿＿＿は石田さんの＿＿＿＿＿＿＿＿とよく話します。
   Boku no ＿＿＿＿＿＿＿＿wa Ishida-san no ＿＿＿＿＿＿＿＿to yoku hanashimasu.

   a. 奥さん **okusan**, ご主人 **goshujin**
   b. 主人 **shujin**, 奥さん **okusan**
   c. 家内 **kanai**, 奥さん **okusan**
   d. 家内 **kanai**, 主人 **shujin**

5. この手紙を読んで＿＿＿＿＿＿＿。

   Kono tegami o yonde ＿＿＿＿＿＿＿.

   a. お願いします **onegai shimasu**
   b. いただけませんか **itadakemasen ka**
   c. くださいございます **kudasai gozaimasu**
   d. なさいます **nasaimasu**

What Is Your Take on That?

あれどう思う？
Are Dō Omou?

In this lesson you will learn a variety ways of conveying the speaker's attitude and feelings as well as changing the speaker's perspectives.

Basic Sentences

[cue 10-1]

1.	田中さんは来月結婚する<u>そう</u>です。 **Tanaka-san wa raigetsu kekkon suru <u>sō</u> desu.**	I heard that Mr. Tanaka will get married next month.
2.	雨が降り<u>そう</u>ですね。 **Ame ga furi <u>sō</u> desu ne.**	It looks like (it's going to) rain.
3.	健二さんは陽子さんとつき合っている<u>らしい</u>です。 **Kenji-san wa Yōko-san to tsukiatte iru <u>rashii</u> desu.**	It seems that Kenji is going out with Yoko.
4.	あの人は日本語が上手で日本人の<u>よう</u>です。 **Ano hito wa Nihongo ga jōzu de Nihonjin no <u>yō</u> desu.**	That person speaks good Japanese, and is just like a Japanese.

5.	お酒を飲ん<u>だり</u>，カラオケをし<u>たりし</u> <u>ました</u>。 **O-sake o non<u>dari</u>, karaoke o shi<u>tari</u> <u>shimashita</u>.**	I did such things as drink and sing karaoke.
6.	テレビを見<u>ながら</u>食べます。 **Terebi o mi-<u>nagara</u> tabemasu.**	I eat while watching TV.
7.	私には兄弟が<u>ありません</u>。 **Watashi ni wa kyōdai ga <u>arimasen</u>.**	I don't have siblings.
8.	音楽を専攻する<u>ことにしました</u>。 **Ongaku o senkōsuru <u>koto ni</u> <u>shimashita</u>.**	I decided to major in music.
9.	カメラを壊して<u>しまいました</u>。 **Kamera o kowashite <u>shimaimashita</u>.**	I broke the camera.
10.	母は怒る<u>かもしれません</u>。 **Haha wa okoru <u>ka mo shiremasen</u>.**	My mother might get mad.
11.	こんなことが分からない<u>わけ</u>があり ません。 **Konna koto ga wakaranai <u>wake</u> ga arimasen.**	There is no reason why he cannot do such an easy job.
12.	男性の友達が<u>いないことはありませ</u> <u>ん</u>。 **Dansei no tomodachi ga <u>inai koto wa</u> <u>arimasen</u>.**	It is not that I don't have any male friends.
13.	弟が壊した<u>に違いありません</u>。 **Otōto ga kowashita <u>ni chigai</u> <u>arimasen</u>.**	My little brother must have broken (it).
14.	何について話すの<u>かしら</u>。 **Nani ni tsuite hanasu no <u>kashira</u>.**	I wonder what he is going to talk about.
15.	子どもに野菜を食べ<u>させ</u>ました。 **Kodomo ni yasai o tabe<u>sase</u>mashita.**	I made my child eat vegetables.
16.	弟に先に卒業<u>され</u>ました。 **Otōto ni saki ni sotsugyō <u>sare</u>mashita.**	My little brother graduated before I do.
17.	先生に漢字を１００回<u>ずつ</u>書かされ ました。 **Sensei ni kanji o hyak-kai <u>zutsu</u> kakasaremashita.**	I was made to write kanji characters 100 times each by my teacher.

18. 小さい字が<u>読めません</u>。 **Chīsai ji ga <u>yomemasen</u>.**	I cannot read small letters.
19. 父はゴルフを<u>したがっています</u>。 **Chichi wa gorufu o <u>shitagatte imasu</u>.**	My father wants to play golf.
20. 小さい頃はよく父に叱られた<u>ものです</u>。 **Chīsai koro wa yoku chichi ni shika- rareta <u>mono desu</u>.**	When I was young, I used to stay up all night.

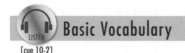

Basic Vocabulary

[cue 10-2]

THINGS TO TALK ABOUT

ニュース **nyūsu**	news
噂 **uwasa**	rumor
悪口 **waruguchi**	gossip
スポーツ **supōtsu**	sports
音楽 **ongaku**	music
ファッション **fasshon**	fashion
卒業 **sotsugyō**	graduation
転職 **tenshoku**	changing jobs
結婚 **kekkon**	marriage
占い **uranai**	fortune-telling

VERBS

叱る・叱ります **shikaru/shikarimasu**	scolds
ほめる・ほめます **homeru/homemasu**	praises
怒る・怒ります **okoru/okorimasu**	gets angry
たたく・たたきます **tataku/tatakimasu**	hits, spanks, slaps
壊す・壊します **kowasu/kowashimasu**	breaks (something)

RESOURCES

検索 **kensaku**	(Internet) search
グーグル **Gūguru**	Google
ヤフー **Yafū**	Yahoo
Wi-Fi（ワイファイ）**waifai**	Wi-Fi

CULTURE NOTE Blood Types and Personality

Many Japanese believe in the correlation between a person's blood type and and his or her personality. Tons of books on blood-type-based fortune-telling have been published during the past several decades. When they meet new people, Japanese often try to guess each other's blood type as they get to know each other, and eventually they will discuss their surmises and their actual blood types: "I thought your blood type was A," "You are a typical B-type person," etc. Here are examples of commonly held views:

Type A: careful, organized, shy
Type B: unique, creative, independent
Type AB: practical, unpredictable, has charac-
teristics of both Type A and Type B
Type O: generous, open-minded, social

CONJUNCTIONS AND ADVERBS

とにかく	**tonikaku**	nevertheless, anyway
ところが	**tokoroga**	however
ところで	**tokorode**	by the way
実は	**jitsu wa**	the fact is, actually

Structure Notes

10.1. Hearsay そうです *sō desu*

When you want to report something you haven't actually witnessed yourself, you usually end the sentence with **sō desu**, which has the meaning 'I hear' or 'I'm given to understand' or 'what I've just said isn't something I myself observed.' The part that goes in front of **sō desu** ends in either the plain imperfect or the plain perfect. If the fact reported were from one's observation or knowledge, there would be no **sō desu** and the sentence would end with a polite form. Here are some examples:

Own Observation	Heard from Someone Else
あそこは天気がいいです。 **Asoko wa tenki ga ii desu.** The weather is good over there.	あそこは天気がいいそうです。 **Asoko wa tenki ga ii sō desu.** The weather is good over there, I hear.
そうです。 **Sō desu.** That's right. It's so.	そうだそうですね。 **Sō da sō desu ne.** So they say (they say it's so).
スミスさんはアメリカへお帰りになります。 **Sumisu-san wa Amerika e okaeri ni narimasu.** Mr. Smith is returning to America.	スミスさんはアメリカへお帰りになるそうです。 **Sumisu-san wa Amerika e okaeri ni naru sō desu.** I hear Mr. Smith is returning to America.
3時に来ると言いました。 **Sanji ni kuru to iimashita.** He said he will come at three p.m.	3時に来ると言ったそうです。 **Sanji ni kuru to itta sō desu.** They say that he said he is coming at three p.m.

10.2. Bound form -そう(な) -sō (na) 'appearance'

There is a form **-sō** added to the infinitive of a verb, the base of an adjective, or an adjectival noun that makes a derived adjectival noun with the meaning 'looking as if, having the appearance of.' The resulting adjectival noun is followed by a form of the copula (**da/na**, etc.) or by the particle **ni**. Here are some examples:

Simple Statement	Looking As If
よく雨が降ります。 **Yoku ame ga furimasu.** It rains often.	雨が降りそうです。 **Ame ga furisō desu.** It looks as if it will rain.
休むことができるところです。 **Yasumu koto ga dekiru tokoro desu.** It's a place where you can rest.	休むことができそうなところです。 **Yasumu koto ga dekisō na tokoro desu.** It's a place where it looks as if you could rest.
このバッグは高いです。 **Kono baggu wa takai desu.** This bag is expensive.	このバッグは高そうです。 **Kono baggu wa takasō desu.** This bag looks expensive.
元気な子どもです。 **Genki na kodomo desu.** He's a lively child.	元気そうな子どもです。 **Genki sō na kodomo desu.** He's a lively-looking child.

To adjectives **ii** 'good' and **nai** 'not exist,' add **-sasō** instead of just **-sō**, as in **yo-sasō** 'looking as if it were good' and **na-sasō** 'looking as if it were non-existent.'

Simple Statement	Looking As If
その魚はいいです。 **Sono sakana wa ii desu.** That fish is good.	その魚はよさそうです。 **Sono sakana wa yosasō desu.** That fish looks as if it were good.
渋滞はありません。 **Jūtai wa arimasen.** There is no traffic jam.	渋滞はなさそうです。 **Jūtai wa nasasō desu.** It looks as if there is no traffic jam.
日本人じゃありません。 **Nihonjin ja arimasen.** He isn't Japanese.	日本人じゃなさそうです。 **Nihonjin ja nasasō desu.** He doesn't look as if he is Japanese.

Notice the difference in meaning between expressions with the form **-sō** (appearance) and expressions ending in **sō desu** (hearsay):

Appearance	Hearsay
雪が降りそうです。 **Yuki ga furisō desu.** It looks as if it were going to snow.	雪が降るそうです。 **Yuki ga furu sō desu.** They say it's going to snow.
お金がなさそうでした。 **O-kane ga nasasō deshita.** It looks as if he did not have money.	お金がなかったそうです。 **O-kane ga nakatta sō desu.** I was given to understand that he did not have money.

10.3. ···らしい *...rashii*

Rashii is added at the end of a sentence and shows that the fact expressed by the sentence is the speaker's objective, logical, careful, and non-intuitive conjecture based on what he or she heard, saw, or read. The verbs and adjectives that precede **rashii** must be in the plain form, except that the **da** that appears at the end of a copula and at the end of an adjectival noun must be deleted.

大川さんのお宅は古いらしいですね。
Ōkawa-san no otaku wa furui rashii desu ne.
Mr. Okawa's house seems to be old.

田中さんは娘さんの結婚式に出なかったそうです。
Tanaka-san wa musumesan no kekkonshiki ni denakatta sō desu.
Mr. Tanaka seems not to have attended his daughter's wedding.

森さんは部長になりたかったらしいです。
Mori-san wa buchō ni naritakatta rashii desu.
Mr. Mori seems to have wanted to become the division manager.

日本ではフェイスブックよりツイッターの方が人気があるらしいです。
Nihon de wa Feisubukku yori Tsuittā no hō ga ninki ga aru rashii desu.
Twitter seems to be more popular than Facebook in Japan.

あのホテルのオーナーは日本人らしいですよ。
Ano hoteru no ōnā wa Nihonjin rashii desu yo.
It seems that the owner of that hotel is Japanese.

あのホテルは静からしいですよ。
Ano hoteru wa shizuka rashii desu yo.
That hotel seems to be quiet.

When **rashii** follows a noun, an additional reading 'is a typical ideal model of' arises. For example, the following sentence has two interpretations, which can be clarified by the context:

あの人は日本人らしいです。
Ano hito wa Nihonjin rashii desu.
That person seems to be a Japanese.
or
That person is the very model of a Japanese.

10.4. Expressions meaning 'like'

There are several ways to say 'A is like B, A looks like B, A resembles B, etc.' Here is a list of some of these expressions:

AはBのようだ。 **A wa B no yō da.**   A is like B.
AはBみたいだ。 **A wa B mitai da.**   A is like B.
AはBに似ている。 **A wa B ni nite iru.**   A resembles B.
AはBと似ている。 **A wa B to nite iru.**   A resembles B.
AとBは似ている。 **A to B wa nite iru.**   A and B are similar.

Here are some example sentences:

陽子さんは天使のようです。
Yōko-san wa tenshi no yō desu.
Yoko is like an angel.

タブレットPCはeリーダーに似ています。
Taburetto PC e-rīdā ni nite imasu.
Tablet PCs are similar to e-book readers.

陽子さんはお母さんと似ています。

Yōko-san wa okāsan to nite imasu.

Yoko resembles her mother.

この双子の姉妹はあまり似ていません。

Kono futago no shimai wa amari nite imasen.

These twin sisters do not look much alike.

10.5. The alternative -たり／-だり *-tari/-dari*

The alternative is a mood indicated by the endings **-tari** or **-dari**. The alternative forms are made in the same way as the perfect or the conditional; but instead of ending in **-ta (-da)** or **-tara (-dara)**, they end in **-tari (-dari)**. For example:

	Meaning	Imperfect	Perfect	Conditional	Alternative
Vowel Verb	eats	**tabe-ru**	**tabe-ta**	**tabe-tara**	**tabe-tari**
	looks at	**mi-ru**	**mi-ta**	**mi-tara**	**mi-tari**
Consonant Verb	returns	**kaer-u**	**kaet-ta**	**kaet-tara**	**kaet-tari**
	wins	**kats-u**	**kat-ta**	**kat-tara**	**kat-tari**
	buys	**ka-u**	**kat-ta**	**kat-tara**	**kat-tari**
	lends	**kas-u**	**kashi-ta**	**kashi-tara**	**kashi-tari**
	writes	**kak-u**	**kai-ta**	**kai-tara**	**kai-tari**
	swims	**oyog-u**	**oyoi-da**	**oyoi-dara**	**oyoi-dari**
	reads	**yom-u**	**yon-da**	**yon-dara**	**yon-dari**
	calls	**yob-u**	**yon-da**	**yon-dara**	**yon-dari**
	dies	**shin-u**	**shin-da**	**shin-dara**	**shin-dari**
	goes	**ik-u**	**it-ta** (irregular)	**it-tara** (irregular)	**it-tari** (irregular)
Irregular Verbs	comes	**kuru**	**kita**	**kitara**	**kitari**
	does	**suru**	**shita**	**shitara**	**shitari**
Adjectives	is expensive	**taka-i**	**takakat-ta**	**takakat-tara**	**takakat-tari**
	is good	**i-i, yo-i**	**yokat-ta**	**yokat-tara**	**yokat-tari**
	wants to eat	**tabeta-i**	**tabetakat-ta**	**tabetakat-tara**	**tabetakat-tari**
	wants to go	**ikita-i**	**ikitakat-ta**	**ikitakat-tara**	**ikitakat-tari**
	does not eat	**tabena-i**	**tabenakat-ta**	**tabenakat-tara**	**tabenakat-tari**
	does not read	**yomana-i**	**yo-manakat-ta**	**yomanakat-tara**	**yo-manakat-tari**
Copula	equals	**da (na, no)**	**dat-ta**	**dat-tara**	**dat-tari**

Some sentences contain one alternative form; others contain several. The most frequent type of sentence using the alternative contains two. The last alternative, or the only one, is always followed by some form of the verb **suru** 'does'—working as a kind of dummy auxiliary.

The meaning of the alternative is either (1) actions in alternation (now doing this, now doing that), (2) simultaneous actions (doing this and that at the same time), or (3) representative or typical actions (doing things like this; doing things like this and that). If there is only one alternative in the sentence, it is a representative or typical action. Here are some examples:

昨日はネットサーフィンをしたりツイッターをしたりしました。
Kinō wa nettosāfin o shitari Tsuittā o shitari shimashita.
I did things like surf the Web and use Twitter.

手紙を書いたり本を読んだりします。
Tegami o kaitari hon o yondari shimasu.
I write letters and read books (in alternation, or typically).

新聞を見たりラジオを聞いたりしていました。
Shinbun o mitari rajio o kiitari shite imashita.
He was looking at the paper and listening to the radio (in alternation, or simultaneously, or typically).

東京へ行くと銀座を散歩したりします。
Tōkyō e iku to Ginza o sanpo shitari shimasu.
When I go to Tokyo, I walk (along) in Ginza (and so on).

この頃はお天気がよかったり悪かったりしますね。
Konogoro wa o-tenki ga yokattari warukattari shimasu ne.
Lately the weather is good one day, bad the next, isn't it?

雨が降ったりやんだりします。
Ame ga futtari yandari shimasu.
It rains intermittently (off and on).

田口さんは新聞記者だったり先生だったりしたことがあります。
Taguchi-san wa shinbun-kisha dattari, sensei dattari shita koto ga arimasu.
Mr. Taguchi has been at various times first a reporter, then a teacher.

ご飯を食べたり食べなかったりすれば病気になりますよ。
Gohan o tabetari tabe nakattari sureba byōki ni narimasu yo.
If you eat irregularly (sometimes eat, sometimes don't eat), you'll get sick.

10.6. ⋯ながら *...nagara*

To describe two simultaneous actions by a single person, you can use the infinitive of a verb + **nagara** 'while ... ing' for the subsidiary action: **Rajio o kikinagara hon o yomimashita** 'I read the book while listening to the radio.' If the two simultaneous actions are performed by different people, you have to say it another way: **Watashi ga rajio o kiite iru aida ni tomodachi wa hon o yomimashita** 'While I was listening to the radio, my friend read a book.'

There is also another possible interpretation for expressions with -**nagara**. Just as English 'while' means either 'during the same time as' or 'although,' Japanese-**nagara** (or -**nagara mo**) sometimes means 'though':

朝ごはんを食べながら宿題をします。
Asagohan o tabe-nagara shukudai o shimasu.
I do my homework while eating my breakfast.

ラジオを聞きながら本を読みました。
Rajio o kiki-nagara, hon o yomimashita.
While I listened to the radio, I also read a book.

本当のことを知っていながら，何も言わなかったんですね。
Hontō no koto o shitte i-nagara, nani mo iwanakatta n desu ne.
Though you knew the truth, you didn't say anything, right?
学生でありながら先生に反論した。
Gakusei de ari-nagara sensei ni hanron shita.
Though only a student, he argued with his teacher.

10.7. ある *aru* with people

The verb **iru** means 'someone (or some animal) stays, someone exists (in a place)' or, after a gerund, 'someone or something is doing something.' The verb **aru** means either 'something exists (in a place)' or 'something or someone exists (as an absolute thing, as a relative, as a role), something or someone is available, we have something or someone.' So, to say 'I have three brothers and sisters,' you can say **Kyōdai ga san-nin arimasu** as well as **Kyōdai ga san-nin imasu**. To say 'My three brothers and sisters are at home,' you say **San-nin no kyōdai ga uchi ni imasu**.

10.8. ⋯ことにする/⋯ことになる *...koto ni suru/...koto ni naru*

After a modifying clause ending in the plain imperfect form, the expression **koto ni suru** means 'decides to (do something'). After a noun, **ni suru** means 'decides on.'

> 映画を見に行くことにしました。
> **Eiga o mi ni iku koto ni shimashita.**
> We decided to go see a movie.

> 映画にしました。
> **Eiga ni shimashita.**
> We decided on the movies.

The expression **koto ni naru** means 'it is decided or settled that'; **koto ni natte iru** means 'it has been decided or settled or arranged that.' After a noun, **ni naru** means 'is decided to be...'

> 英語の教師として日本へ行くことになっています。
> **Eigo no kyōshi to shite Nihon e iku koto ni natte imasu.**
> (It's been decided or arranged that) we are to go to Japan as English teachers.

> 日本になりました。
> **Nihon ni narimashita.**
> It's been decided to be Japan.

> 今日からここで働くことになりました。
> **Kyō kara koko de hataraku koto ni narimashita.**
> It's been decided that I start working here starting today.

> ツイッターでJ–POPの歌手をフォローすることにしました。
> **Tsuittā de J-POP no kashu o forō suru koto ni shimashita.**
> We decided to follow J-POP singers on Twitter.

10.9. …しまう *shimau* and …おく *oku*

The verb **shimau** means 'stores, puts away.' A gerund + **shimau** has the meaning 'finishes up doing, does completely or thoroughly; does and ends up = ends up doing.'

本を読んでしまいました。
Hon o yonde shimaimashita.
I read the entire book.

お金は全部使ってしまいました。
O-kane wa zenbu tsukatte shimaimashita.
I used up the money.

携帯の通話時間の上限を超してしまいました。
Keitai no tsūwa jikan no jōgen o koshite shimaimashita.
I used up my minutes for my cell phone.

うちの犬は長い間病気だったんですが，昨日死んでしまいました。
Uchi no inu wa nagai aida byōki datta n desu ga, kinō shinde shimaimashita.
Our dog was sick for a long time, but yesterday it died.

The verb **oku** means 'puts,' 'places,' or 'puts aside.' A gerund + **oku** has the meaning 'does something and puts it aside; does something in preparation; does something for later on; does something in advance.' The idea is that the action is done and then put to one side, with the expectation of some consequence or result at a later time rather than immediately.

この本を読んでおきましょう。
Kono hon o yonde okimashō.
I'll get this book read (so we can answer questions when the teacher asks us about it).

来週の芝居へ行きたいから，切符を買っておいてください。
Raishū no shibai e ikitai kara, kippu o katte oite kudasai.
I want to go to the play next week, so please buy tickets (in advance).

兄はPCを一日中つけておきます。
Ani wa PC o ichinichijū tsukete okimasu.
My brother leaves his PC on all day.

Notice the difference in meaning between the gerund + **shimau** and the gerund + **oku**: **shimau** suggests completion and thoroughness; **oku** suggests preparatory action in anticipation of later consequences or benefits.

手紙を書いてしまいました。
Tegami o kaite shimaimashita.
I got the letter (all) written. I finished (writing) the letter.

手紙を書いておきました。
Tegami o kaite okimashita.
I got the letter written (so that it would be done, for some later consequence).
I wrote the letter and put it aside. I wrote the letter in advance.

10.10. …わけ …*wake*

The noun **wake** means 'meaning,' 'reason,' 'explanation,' 'case,' or 'special circumstances.' It is often used in explaining a situation.

どういうわけですか。
Dō iu wake desu ka.
What do you mean? What does it mean?

わけを教えてください
Wake o oshiete kudasai.
Please explain the meaning of this.

どういうわけで仕事をやめたんですか。
Dō iu wake de shigoto o yameta n desu ka.
Why (with what reason) did he quit his job?

社長はそんなに忙しいわけはありません。
Shachō wa sonna ni isogashii wake wa arimasen.
There's no reason the president of the firm should be so busy. He can't be so busy.

そういうわけならどうしましょうか。
Sō iu wake nara dō shimashō ka.
If that's the case, what shall we do?

わけが分からない。
Wake ga wakaranai.
I don't know what's what.

そういうわけで行くことができませんでした。
Sō iu wake de iku koto ga dekimasen deshita.
Because of that, I couldn't go.

10.11. Double negatives

In English, we sometimes hear two negative words in a sentence where one would be enough, for example, 'Nobody never does anything' with the same meaning as 'Nobody ever does anything.' In Japanese when two negatives are used, the meaning is always changed. Notice the translations of the following sentences.

靴をはいたままうちに入る人もないことはありません。
Kutsu o haita mama uchi e hairu hito mo nai koto wa arimasen.
It isn't that there aren't also people who enter the house with their shoes on = Some people also enter the house with their shoes on.

日本語ができないわけじゃありません。
Nihongo ga dekinai wake ja arimasen.
It isn't (the case) that I can't speak Japanese.

結婚したくないというわけじゃありません。
Kekkon shitaku nai to iu wake ja arimasen.
It's not that I don't want to get married.

明日までにこの本を返さなければなりません。
Ashita made ni kono hon o kaesanakereba narimasen.
I have to return this book by tomorrow.

10.12. …に違いない *…ni chigai nai*

The noun **chigai** 'discrepancy' or 'error' is made from the infinitive of the verb **chigau** 'is different.' The expression **chigai nai** is based on the construction **chigai wa na**i 'there is no error.' After a noun, an imperfect or perfect verb, or an adjective, the expression **ni chigai nai** means 'without a doubt,' 'no doubt,' 'certainly,' or 'surely.' It is often translated as 'must have done,' 'must be,' etc., but of course this is not the 'must' of obligation (='has to').

パスワードはこれに違いありません。
Pasuwādo wa kore ni chigai arimasen.
The password must be this one. I'm sure this is it.

岡本さんが来るに違いありません。
Okamoto-san ga kuru ni chigai arimasen.
Mr. Okamoto will surely come.

私のパソコンはウイルスに感染したに違いありません。
Watashi no pasokon wa uirusu ni kansen shita ni chigai arimasen.
My PC must have been infected by viruses.

私の主人に違いありません。
Watashi no shujin ni chigai arimasen.
He is surely my husband.

仕事が嫌だったに違いありません。
Shigoto ga iya datta ni chigai arimasen.
He certainly disliked his job.

あんないい家は高いに違いありません。
Anna ii ie wa takai ni chigai arimasen.
Such a nice house must be expensive.

10.13. について *ni tsuite* and によって *ni yotte*

The verb **tsuku** has the basic meaning 'comes in contact with.' The expression
NOUN+ **ni tsuite** mean 'with respect to,' 'regarding,' or 'about.'

ソーシャルネットワーキングについてどう思いますか。
Sōsharu nettowākingu ni tsuite dō omoimasu ka.
What do you think about social networking?

昨日のクラスでは漢字の起源について話しました。
Kinō no kurasu de wa kanji no kigen ni tsuite hanashimashita.
I talked about the origin of kanji in yesterday's class.

The whole expression is usually treated as an adverb, modifying the following
predicate, but it sometimes occurs also as a noun phrase modifying a noun (and
linked to it by the particle **no**). There is no difference in meaning between the following two sentences although they differ in terms of structure:

経済について記事を書きました。
Keizai ni tsuite kiji o kakimashita.
I wrote an article about economics.

経済についての記事を書きました。
Keizai ni tsuite no kiji o kakimashita.
I wrote an article about economics.

The verb **yoru** has the basic meaning 'leans on, relies on.' The expressions
NOUN + **ni yoru to** and NOUN + **ni yoreba** mean 'if you rely on... = according to....'

新聞によると雨がふるそうです。
Shinbun ni yoru to ame ga furu sō desu.
According to the paper, I see it's going to rain.

The expression NOUN + **ni yotte** means 'according to, depending on':

場所によって気候が違います。

Basho ni yotte kikō ga chigaimasu.

The weather varies from place to place. (Depending on the place, the weather is different.)

人によって意見がちがいます。

Hito ni yotte iken ga chigaimasu.

Opinions differ with people. (Different people have different views.)

10.14. Causative, passive, and causative passive verbs

Most Japanese verbs have corresponding CAUSATIVES, PASSIVES, and CAUSATIVE PASSIVES.

The causative verbs are made, for the most part, by adding the ending **-sase-ru** to vowel stems and the ending **-ase-ru** to consonant stems. Some of the meanings of such a verb are 'causes someone to do something; makes someone do something; lets someone do something.' The forms **kosaseru** 'lets/makes someone come' (from **kuru** 'comes') and **saseru** 'lets/makes someone do' (from **suru** 'does') are irregular.

The passive verbs are made by adding the ending **-rare-ru** to vowel stems and the ending **-are-ru** to consonant stems. Some of the meanings are 'is affected by another person's action; undergoes the action; is adversely affected by the action.' Japanese passives can be made both from transitive verbs (those which take a direct object, like **taberu** 'eats') and intransitive verbs (those which do not ordinarily take a direct object, like **shinu** 'dies' and **iru** 'stays'). The forms **korareru** 'has someone come' or 'is affected by someone's coming' and **sareru** 'gets done' or 'is affected by someone's doing' are irregular.

There is also a passive formation made from causatives; this consists of adding the ending **-rare-ru** to the causative stem that ends in -(s)ase-, so that the complete ending for the causative passive is somewhat formidable: **-(s)ase-rare-ru**. There is a shortened form of this ending, alongside the longer form, for consonant verbs that do not end in **su**: **-asare-ru** instead of **ase-rare-ru**. This shortened form may be visualized as **-as(e-r)are-ru**. In other words, the last sound of the causative ending and the first sound of the passive ending are dropped. The meaning of the causative passive is something like 'is made to do' or 'has to do.'

Of course, the final **-ru** in these various endings is just the regular ending for the imperfect mood of vowel verbs. These causatives, passives, and causative passives can be inflected for all the usual moods: **kosaseru, kosaseta, kosaseyō, kosasetara, kosasetari, kosasereba, kosasemasu,** etc.; **sareru, sareta, sareyō, saretara, saretari, sarereba, saremasu,** etc.; **tabesaseru, tabesaseta, tabesaseyō,**

tabesasetara, **tabesasetari**, **tabesasereba**, **tabesasemasu**, etc. Here is a list of some typical verbs together with the causative, passive and causative passive forms. All the forms are imperfect.

		Causative -(s)ase-ru	Passive -(r)are-ru	Passive-Causative Long Form -(s)ase-rare-ru	Passive-Causative Short Form -as-are-ru
Vowel Verb	eats **taberu**	tabesaseru	taberareru	tabesaser-areru	---
	looks at **miru**	misaseru	mirareru	misaserareru	---
Consonant Verb	returns **kaeru**	kaeraseru	kaerareru	kaeraser-areru	kaerasareru
	waits **matsu**	mataseru	matareru	mataserareru	matasareru
	buys **kau**	kawaseru	kawareru	kawaserareru	kawasareru
	speaks **hanasu**	hanasaseru	hana-sareru	hanasaser-areru	---
	writes **kaku**	kakaseru	kakareru	kakaserareru	kakasareru
	swims **oyogu**	oyogaseru	oyogareru	oyogaser-areru	oyogasareru
	reads **yomu**	yomaseru	yomareru	yomaser-areru	yomasareru
	calls **yobu**	yobaseru	yobareru	yobaserareru	yobasareru
	dies **shinu**	shinaseru	shinareru	shinaser-areru	shinasareru
Irregular Verb	comes **kuru**	kosaseru	korareru	kosaserareru	---
	does **suru**	saseru	sareru	saserareru	---

10.15. Use of the causative

The basic meaning of the causative is 'someone causes someone else to do something.' The person who does the causing is indicated by the particle **ga** or **wa**. The person caused to perform the action takes the particle **o** if the verb is intransitive, and the particle **ni** if the verb is transitive. Compare the following:

父は兄を行かせました。
Chichi wa ani o ikasemashita.
My father had my older brother go there.

父は兄に手紙を書かせました。
Chichi wa ani ni tegami o kakasemashita.
My father had my older brother write a letter.

The causative is largely limited to situations in which a person is in a position to order or permit an action on the part of another person. For an act done as a favor, you use an expression with **morau** or **itadaku**. So, while you might say, 'My father had my older brother write the letter' with the causative, you probably wouldn't say my older brother had my father write the letter' with the causative, since the social situation would indicate this was a favor. Compare the above sentence with the following:

兄は父に手紙を書いてもらいました。
Ani wa chichi ni tegami o kaite moraimashita.
My brother had my father write a letter.

Here are some additional examples of uses of the causative:

どんなものを子どもに食べさせますか。
Donna mono o kodomo ni tabesasemasu ka.
What kind of things do you feed the children?

友達を待たせることはよくありませんよ。
Tomodachi o mataseru ko to wa yoku arimasei yo.
It isn't good to keep your friends waiting, you know.

毎日３時間バイオリンを練習させます。
Mainichi san-jikan baiorin o renshū sasemasu.
I make him practice violin for three hours every day.

父は兄に会社のウエブサイトを作らせました。
Chichi wa ani ni kaisha no uebusaito o tsukurasemashita.
My father made my brother create a Web site for his company.

10.16. Uses of the passive

If the underlying verb indicates an action that can be done to a person, the meaning of a passive expression is 'someone has something done to him' or 'someone undergoes the action.' The person undergoing the action is indicated by the particle **wa** or **ga**, and the person responsible for the action (the agent) is indicated by the particle **ni**.

> 子どもが母親にたたかれました。
> **Kodomo ga hahaoya ni tatakaremashita.**
> A child was hit by his mother.

But if the underlying verb indicates some action that can't be done directly to a person, like 'dies,' 'quits,' and 'comes,' the meaning of the passive expression is 'someone is unfavorably affected by another person's action.'

> 山田さんはお子さんに死なれました。
> **Yamada-san wa o-kosan ni shinaremashita.**
> Mrs. Yamada had her child die (suffered the death of her child).

> 私は晩ご飯を食べようとしたときに友達に来られました。
> **Watashi wa bangohan o tabeyō to shita toki ni tomodachi ni koraremashita.**
> Just as I was about to eat dinner, I had a friend drop in on me (unexpectedly).

If the underlying verb takes an object, indicated by the particle **o**, this object may be retained in the passive expression.

> 私はパソコンを盗まれました。
> **Watashi wa pasokon o nusumaremashita.**
> I had my PC stolen.

> 弟にクッキーを全部食べられました。
> **Otōto ni kukkī o zenbu taberaremashita.**
> I had my cookies all eaten up by my little brother.

Inanimate items can be used as the subject of a passive sentence:

> 沢山の国で英語が使われています。
> **Takusan no kuni de eigo ga tsukawareteimasu.**
> English is used in many countries.

> お酒は米から作られます。
> **Osake wa kome kara tsukuraremasu.**
> Sake is made from rice.

The passive is also used just as an EXALTED FORM with no special passive meaning. (See Lesson 9 for a variety of exalted forms.)

日本にはもう行かれましたか。
Nihon ni wa mō ikaremashita ka.
Have you gone to Japan?

ホテルはもう予約されましたか。
Hoteru wa mō yoyaku saremashita ka.
Have you already reserved a hotel room?

Here are some more examples of passives.

猫に魚を食べられました。
Neko ni sakana o taberaremashita
The cat ate our fish up.

学校へ行く途中で雨に降られました。
Gakkō e iku tochū de ame ni furaremashita.
On the way to school, I got rained on.

勉強しているときに友達に来られて困りました。
Benkyō shite iru toki ni tomodachi ni korarete komarimashita.
I had a friend drop in on me in the middle of my studying, darn it.

電車の中でiPodをとられました。
Densha no naka de iPod o toraremashita
I had my iPod swiped on the train.

先生に呼ばれて叱られました。
Sensei ni yobarete shikararemashita.
I was called and scolded by the teacher.

10.17. Use of the causative passive

Expressions with the causative passive mean things like 'someone was made to do something by someone else.' The person made to perform the action is indicated by the particle **wa** or **ga**, the person by whom he is made to perform the action is indicated by the particle **ni**.

私は医者に薬をのませられました。
Watakushi wa isha ni kusuri o nomaserarema shita.
I was ordered to take medicine by the doctor.
(=The doctor had me take medicine.)

先生に漢字を100回ずつ書かせられました。

Sensei ni kanji o hyak-kai zutsu kakaseraremashita.

I was made to write kanji characters 100 times each by my teacher.

日本語のクラスではペアワークやグループワークをさせられます。

Nihongo no kurasu de wa peawāku ya gurūpuwāku o saseraremasu.

In our Japanese class we are made to do pair work and group work.

シンデレラは継母に掃除や洗濯をさせられました。

Shinderera wa mamahaha ni sōji ya sentaku o saseraremashita.

Cinderella was made to do things like clean and do the laundry by her step-mother.

10.18. The potential

Any Japanese verb can be made into a potential verb with the meaning 'is able to be done.' For vowel verbs, the potential is always exactly the same as the passive. **Tabe-rare-ru** means either 'someone gets something eaten on them,' 'someone suffers someone else's eating something' or 'something can get eaten = someone can eat something.' **Ko-rare-ru** means 'someone has someone else come (to their disadvantage)' or 'someone can come.'

私は弟にケーキを食べられた。

Watashi wa otōto ni kēki o taberareta.

My cake was eaten by my brother (and I was upset).

手術の後で食べられないときに、病室で母に弁当を食べられた。
Shujutsu no ato de taberarenai toki ni, byōshitsu de haha ni bentō o tab-erareta.
When I was not allowed to eat after the surgery, my mother ate her boxed lunch in my hospital room (and I was annoyed by it).

大根の葉は食べられる。
Daikon no ha wa taberareru.
The leaves of daikon are edible.

セールスマンにまたうちに来られた。
Sērusuman ni mata uchi ni korareta.
The salesperson came to my house again (and I was not happy).

あしたは7時までに来られますか。
Ashita wa shichiji made ni koraremasu ka.
Can you come here by seven tomorrow?

However, for consonant verbs, the potential form is made by adding **-e-ru** to the stem: **yob-e-ru** 'can be called,' **yom-e-ru** 'can be read,' **aruk-e-ru** 'can walk,' etc. That is, for consonant verbs, their polite forms of the potential differ from their polite forms of the ordinary version only by having the vowel **e** instead of **i** before the endings **-masu, -mashita,**. et cetera, thus it is very important to pronounce these vowels clearly and distinctly so that **kaemasu** 'can buy' will not sound like **kaimasu** 'will buy,' for example. The meaning of the potential verbs is 'something can be done,' and the something itself takes the particle **ga**:

英語が話せます。
Eigo ga hanasemasu.
English can be spoken. = (He) can speak English.

この病院の中では携帯が使えません。
Kono byōin no naka de wa keitai ga tsukaemasen.
Cell phones cannot be used in this hospital.

You're already familiar with this process: **Neko ga suki desu** 'Cats are liked = I like cats.' The person who can do something is marked by either **wa** or **ga** depending on the emphasis; sometimes, the person can be explicitly marked by **ni**:

私(に)は読めません。
Watashi (ni) wa yomemasen.
I cannot read it.

For the potential of **suru** 'does,' the verb **dekiru** 'is possible' is used:

勉強できますか。
Benkyō dekimasu ka.
Can you study?

今朝はログインできませんでした。
Kesa wa roguin dekimasen deshita.
I could not log in this morning.

雨が降ったから散歩できませんでした。
Ame ga futta kara sanpo dekimasen deshita.
It rained, so we couldn't take our walk.

The meaning of any potential is about the same as the meaning of the ordinary verb imperfect + **koto ga dekiru**: **Nihongo ga yomemasu ka** = **Nihongo o yomu koto ga dekimasu ka** 'Can you read Japanese?' Here are additional example sentences:

心配でご飯も食べられません。
Shinpai de gohan mo taberaremasen.
I'm worried about it so much that I cannot even eat meals.

忙しくてメールもチェックできませんでした。
Isogashikute mēru mo chekku dekimasen deshita.
I was so busy and couldn't even check emails.

一人で来られますか。
Hitori de koraremasu ka.
Can you come by yourself?

Instead of **kikeru** and **mirareru** for **kiku** 'hears' and **miru** 'sees,' you often hear the derived verbs **kikoeru** 'is heard, can be heard,' and **mieru** 'is seen, can be seen, appears.'

You will recall that the negative of the potential of **iku** 'goes,' **ikemasen**, is also used with the special meaning 'it's no good, it won't do,' for example, **Nete wa ikemasen** 'You mustn't sleep.' Sometimes it means 'that's too bad,' for example, when someone has told you some ill that has befallen him, you may sympathize with **Sore wa ikemasen deshita ne** 'That was too bad, wasn't it?'

10.19. かもしれない *ka mo shirenai*

The form **shirenai (shiremasen)** is the negative of the potential of **shiru** 'knows', and means 'cannot be known'. **Ka mo shirenai** means something like 'it can't be known even whether', and is added after a predicate in the plain imperfect or perfect or after a noun (with the plain copula **da** dropping before **ka** as usual) with the meaning 'maybe, perhaps, it may be that'. Here are some examples of **ka mo shirenai**:

> あの人は日本人かもしれません。
> **Ano hito wa Nihonjin ka mo shiremasen.**
> He may be Japanese.

> 雨が降るかもしれないから傘を持って行きましょう。
> **Ame ga furu ka mo shirenai kara kasa o motte ikimashō.**
> It may rain, so let's take an umbrella.

> 明日は寒いかもしれませんね。
> **Ashita wa samui ka mo shiremasen ne.**
> It may be cold tomorrow.

> 車より地下鉄の方が便利かもしれませんよ。
> **Kuruma yori chikatetsu no hō ga benri ka mo shiremasen yo.**
> Subways may be more convenient than cars.

> 大阪に行ったら松本さんに会えるかもしれません。
> **Osaka e ittara Matsumoto-san ni aeru ka mo shiremasen.**
> I may be able to see Mr. Matsumoto if I go to Osaka.

> 陽子さんはあまり嬉しくなかったかもしれません。
> **Yōko-san wa amari ureshiku nakatta ka mo shiremasen.**
> Yoko may not have been happy.

10.20. かしら *ka shira*

The expression **ka shira** is added to predicates in the same sort of way as **ka mo shirenai**, but the meaning is a little different: 'I wonder if'. This is very similar to the meaning of **ka ne** at the end of a sentence. The difference is that you are really talking to yourself with **ka shira**, whereas with **ka ne**, you're halfway talking to someone else. Note that **ka shira** is used almost exclusively by women.

> 今晩雨がふるかしら。
> **Konban ame ga furu ka shira.**
> I wonder if it's going to rain tonight.

窓をしめたかしら。
Mado o shimeta ka shira.
I wonder if I closed the windows.

美味しいかしら。
Oishii ka shira.
I wonder if it is delicious.

そんなにお金がほしいかしら。
Sonna ni o-kane ga hoshii ka shira.
I wonder if they want money that much.

10.21. Desiderative verbs ⋯たがる ...*tagaru*

You have learned that each verb can underlie a desiderative adjective with the meaning 'wants to': **taberu** 'eats', **tabetai** 'wants to eat'; **iku** 'goes', **ikitai** 'wants to go.' There is also, for each verb, a DESIDERATIVE VERB made by adding **-ta-gar-u** to the infinitive. So, alongside the adjective **tabetai** 'wants to eat,' we have the verb **tabetagaru** 'is eager to eat, desires to eat.' Alongside the adjective **ikitai** 'wants to go,' we have the verb **ikitagaru** 'is eager to go, desires to go.' (The **-ta-**element is the same in the forms with **-ta-i** and the forms with **-ta-gar-u**.) The desiderative verb is used for third person, and you seldom use them of yourself or for the second person. Notice that the desiderative verbs take direct objects with the particle **o**, although the desiderative adjectives take either direct objects with **o** or emphatic subjects with **ga**.

Here are some examples:

近頃の若者は変な言葉を使いたがります。
Chikagoro no wakamono wa hen na kotoba o tsukaitagarimasu.
Young people nowadays want to use strange words.

陽子さんは英語を習いたがっています。
Yoko-san wa Eigo o naraitagatte imasu.
They're eager to learn English.

うちの犬はアイスクリームを食べたがります。
Uchi no inu wa aisukurīmu o tabetagarimasu.
Our dog wants to eat ice cream.

10.22. ⋯ものです ...*mono desu*

You have learned that the noun **mono** means 'a thing that you can touch or feel,' as contrasted with **koto**, an abstract thing you talk about. It also sometimes means 'guy, fellow,' a slightly less polite term than **hito** 'person.' There is a special use of **mono desu** in which the noun does not have a concrete meaning but means something like 'in the nature of things…,' 'it's characteristic that…,' 'it happens that…,' 'such is life.' Often the adverb **tokaku** 'likely, naturally' (do not confuse with **tonikaku** 'anyway, nevertheless') is added somewhere in the sentence.

> いけないと言うと子どもはとかくやりたがるものです。
> **Ikenai to iu to kodomo wa tokaku yaritagaru mono desu.**
> If you say they mustn't (do something), children always want to do it.

> 年寄りはそんなものを食べたがるものです。
> **Toshiyori wa sonna mono o tabetagaru mono desu.**
> It's natural for old folks to be eager to eat that sort of thing.

When the expression **mono desu** is preceded by the perfect, the meaning is something like 'used to' (that is, it used to be characteristic for someone to do something).

> 東京に住んでいた時にはよく銀座へ遊びに行ったものです。
> **Tōkyō ni sunde ita toki ni wa yoku Ginza e asobi ni itta mono desu.**
> When I was living in Tokyo, I often used to go to the Ginza (for amusement).

> お金がなくて困っていた時にはよく姉のうちへご飯を食べに行ったものです。
> **O-kane ga nakute komatte ita toki ni wa yoku ane no uchi e gohan o tabe ni itta mono desu.**
> When I was in a fix without any money, I used to often go to my sister's house to eat.

> 子どもの頃はよく父に遊んでもらったものです。
> **Kodomo no koro wa yoku chichi ni asonde moratta mono desu.**
> I used to play with my father when I was a child.

10.23. The plain imperative

There is a plain imperative form, but you seldom use it except when showing extreme impatience, or when quoting rather impersonal commands. For vowel verbs, **-ro** is added to the stem. For consonant verbs, **-e** is added to the stem. **Kuru** and **suru** are irregular, and their imperative forms are **koi** and **shiro**, respectively.

行け！ **Ike!**	Go!
気をつけろ！ **Ki o tsukero!**	Be careful!
早く来い！ **Hayaku koi!**	Come here soon!
勉強しろ！ **Benkyō shiro!**	Study!

The plain NEGATIVE imperative is made by adding the particle **na** 'do not!' to the plain imperfect.

来るな！ **Kuru na!**	Don't come!
待つな！ **Matsu na!**	Don't wait!
開けるな！ **Akeru na!**	Don't open it!
負けるな！ **Makeru na!**	Don't lose!
諦めるな！ **Akirameru na!**	Don't give up!

Avoid confusing this with another type of plain command (rather condescending), which consists of the INFINITIVE + **na**, a shortening of **nasai** 'please do,' and often followed by the particle **yo**:

来な（よ）。 **Ki na (yo).**	Come.
待ちな（よ）。 **Machi na (yo).**	Wait.
開けな（よ）。 **Ake na (yo).**	Open it.
しな（よ）。 **Shi na (yo).**	Do it.

 **Conversation**

[cue 10-3]

Mrs. Yamamoto (Y) is talking with Mrs. Haraguchi (H) in front of her house.

Y: 原口さんの息子さんは高校の音楽
の先生になられたそうですね。
Haraguchi-san no musuko-san wa kōkō no ongaku no sensei ni narareta sō desu ne.
Mrs. Haraguchi, I heard that your son became a music teacher at a high school.

H: ええ。バイオリニストになりた
がっていたんですが，教師になり
ました。
Ē. Baiorinisuto ni naritagatte ita n desu ga, kyōshi ni narimashita.
Yes. He wanted to be a violinist, but he became a teacher.

Y: でも，教師の方が楽しいかもしれませんよ。
Demo, kyōshi no hō ga tanoshii kamo shiremasen yo.
But it may be more fun to be a teacher.

H: そうですね。バイオリニストになっていたら，大変でしょうからね。
Sō desu ne. Baiorinisuto ni natte itara, taihen deshō kara ne.
Right. It would be very tough if he had become a violinist.

Y: そうですね。どこの高校で働いているんですか。
Sō desu ne. Doko no kōkō de hataraite iru n desu ka.
Right. Where does he teach?

H: 高木高校で働いています。お宅の息子さんは？
Takagi kōkō de hataraite imasu. Otaku no musuko-san wa?
He is working at Takagi High School. How about your son?

Y: 去年大学を卒業して，今，銀行に勤めています。
Kyonen daigaku o sotsugyō shite, ima, ginkō ni tsutomete imasu.
He graduated from a college last year, and he is working for a bank now.

H: ああ，いいですね。**Ā, ii desu ne.** Oh, that's great.

Y: ええ。でも，毎日お金の計算ばかりさ
せられて，つまらないって言っていま
す。転職するかもしれません。
**Ē. Demo, mainichi o-kane no keisan
bakari saserarete, tsumaranaitte itte
imashita.**
Right. But he has to do calculations all
day long every day, and was saying that
he is bored. He might change his job.

Exercises

I. Make each of the following sentences mean 'I hear that..." or 'They say that...' by changing the predicate (underlined) to the appropriate plain form and adding *sō desu*. Then make each one mean 'It seems that' by adding *rashii desu*.

1. 真弓さんのご主人は<u>イタリア人です</u>。
   Mayumi-san no goshujin wa <u>Itariajin desu</u>.

2. 昨日東京で地震が<u>ありました</u>。
   Kinō Tōkyō de jishin ga <u>arimashita</u>.

3. 川村さんは大きい家に<u>住んでいます</u>。
   Kawamura-san wa ōkii ie ni <u>sunde imasu</u>.

4. 川村さんは子どもが<u>ありません</u>。
   Kawamura-san wa kodomo ga <u>arimasen</u>.

5. 来月ここにレストランが<u>できます</u>。
   Raigetsu koko ni resutoran ga <u>dekimasu</u>.

II. Look at the illustrations and complete the sentences.

1   2   3

1. 猫は魚を_____います。
   Neko wa sakana o _____imasu.

2. 女の子は人形を_____います。
   Onna no ko wa ningyō o _____imasu.

3. 父はゴルフを_____います。
   Chichi wa gorufu o _____imasu.

III. Fill in the blanks appropriately, but creatively.

1. 私は_____ながら勉強します。
   Watashi wa _____nagara benkyō shimasu.

2. 昨日は食べたり, _____しました。
   Kinō wa tabetari, _____shimashita.

3. 来年_____ことにしました。
   Rainen _____koto ni shimashita.

4. 今日から_____ことになりました。
   Kyō kara _____kotoni narimashita.

5. 先生のパソコンを_____しまいました。
   Sensei no pasokon o _____shimaimashita.

6. ビールを_____おきますね。
   Bīru o _____okimasu ne.

7. 雨が_____かもしれません。
   Ame ga _____ka mo shiremasen.

8. 小さい時はよく川で_____ものです。
   Chīsai toki wa yoku kawa de _____mono desu.

9. カフェテリアのメニューは日によって_____ます。
   Kafeteria no menyū wa hi ni yotte _____masu.

10. スミスさんは日本語が_____ません。
    Sumisu-san wa Nihongo ga _____masen.

IV. Pick the most appropriate item in the parentheses.

1. 弟は先生に（a. しかりました, b. しかられました, c. ほめました）。
   Otōto wa sensei ni (a. **shikarimashita**, b. **shikararemashita**,
   c. **homemashita**).

2. 忙しいときに友達に（a. 来ました, b. 行きました, c. 来られました）。
   Isogashii toki ni tomodachi ni (a. **kimashita**, b. **ikimashita**,
   c. **koraremashita**).

3. 母は私に野菜を（a. 食べられました, b. 食べました, c. 食べさせました）。
   Haha wa watashi ni yasai o (a. **taberaremashita**, b. **tabemashita**,
   c. **tabesasemashita**).

4. 妹は母に部屋を掃除（a. しました, b. させました, c. させられました）。
   Imōto wa haha ni heya o sōji (a. **shimashita**, b. **sasemashita**,
   c. **saseraremashita**).

5. 私は弟に先に卒業（a. しました, b. されました, c. させられました）。
   Watashi wa otōto ni saki ni sotsugyō (a. **shimashita**, b. **saremashita**,
   c. **sasararemashita**).

Other Styles of Speech

1. The impersonal style

In lectures, radio announcements, and the like, Japanese often use the impersonal style, which is also encountered in books and articles. Here are the principal ways in which this style differs from the usual polite style of speech:

i. Polite forms are not used. Instead, the plain forms are used even at the end of sentences. Sometimes, however, a Japanese will end his explanatory sentences with **...no de arimasu** instead of **...no de aru** 'it is a fact that...' Here are some examples:

Meaning	Polite	Impersonal
He was born in 1990.	1990-**nen ni umare-mashita.**	1990-**nen ni umareta.**
There is no explanation.	**Setsumei wa arimasen.**	**Setsumei wa nai.**

ii. Colloquial words, lively particles like **yo** and **ne**, and contractions like **ja** for **de wa** and **n** for **no** are avoided.

iii. The copula **da** is replaced by the phrase **de aru** or **de arimasu**. The phrase is inflected just like **aru**:

Imperfect	**de aru**	= **da** [**na, no**]	**de arimasu**	= **desu**
Perfect	**de atta**	= **datta**	**de arimashita**	= **deshita**
Tentative	**dearō**	= **darō**	**de arimashō**	= **deshō**
Gerund	**de atte**	= **de**	**de arimashite**	= **deshite**
Infinitive	**de ari**	= **ni, de**		
Provisional	**de areba**	= **nara**		
Conditional	**de attara**	= **dattara**	**de arimahitara**	= **dehitara**
Alternative	**de attari**	= **dattari**	**de arimashitari**	= **deshitari**

Here are some examples:

Meaning	Polite	Impersonal
China is Japan's neighbor.	**Chūgoku wa Nihon no tonari desu.**	**Chūgoku wa Nihon no tonari de aru.**
That was an earthquake.	**Sore wa jishin deshita.**	**Sore wa jishin de atta.**
Prices have risen.	**Nedan wa agatta n desu.**	**Nedan wa agatta no de aru.**

iv. Instead of a gerund, an infinitive is often used at the end of a clause meaning 'does and, did and' or 'is and, was and.' This is just a stylistic variant of the use of the gerund.

> Japan is an Asian country, and England is a European country.
> **Nihon wa Ajia no kuni de, Igirisu wa Yōroppa no kuni desu.**
> **Nihon wa Ajia no kuni de ari, Igirisu wa Yōroppa no ku ni de aru.**

> The older son became a doctor, and the younger a teacher.
> **Chōnan wa isha ni natte, jinan wa kyōshi ni narimashita.**
> **Chōnan wa isha ni nari, jinan wa kyōshi ni natta (no de aru).**

> They have no money and can't buy food.
> **Okane ga nakute, tabemono o kau koto ga dekimasen.**
> **Okane ga naku tabemono o kau koto ga dekinai.**

v. Nouns are sometimes strung together in a series without a connecting particle (we would expect **to** or **ya** in the polite style). There is often, but not always, a pause after each item except the last, which is usually followed by the appropriate particle to link the entire phrase up with the rest of the sentence.

> Kyoto, Osaka, and Kobe are all in Kansai.
> **Kyōto ya Ōsaka ya Kōbe wa minna Kansai desu.**
> **Kyōto Ōsaka Kōbe wa mina Kansai de aru.**

2. The plain style

The most down-to-earth way of talking in Japanese is that of the plain style (also called the familiar style, the intimate style, the ordinary style). This sort of speech is used among workers, students, club members, and others in a situation where a certain amount of camaraderie is inherent. It is also often used within the family, with truly intimate friends, and in certain set phrases (like proverbs), which are inserted into otherwise polite-style speech. The foreigner seldom has occasion to use much of this style himself, but he hears a good deal of it around him. Here are some of the characteristics of this style of speech:

i. Difference between women's speech and men's speech.

In the polite style, there is very little difference between the way women talk and the way men talk. Women will sometimes choose a more elegant expression, are expected to use the honorific style more than men, and attach the honorific prefix **o-** to nouns more than men do.

Women seem to leave more of their sentences dangling with non-finite verbal expressions than men do, although sentence fragments are widespread in the plain style for both sexes. Japanese often turn a finite verb expression into a noun expression with the noun **no** or **koto** 'fact,' which is frequently followed by the particle **yo**, or just ends the sentence itself: **Iku no yo** 'I'm going.,' **Kore na no yo** 'It's this one,' **Tadaima kita no?** 'Did you just get here?'

Women often use **atashi** for **watashi** or **watakushi** 'I' in plain or sometimes in polite speech, and men often substitute **boku** for it. The explicit plural of **boku** is **bokura**. Men also use **kimi** (explicit plural **kimitachi** or **kimira**) for **anata** 'you.' There are other impolite pronouns such as **ore**, which are considered vulgar; and the condescending word **omae** 'you' is rather insulting.

ii. Use of particles

The particles **wa**, **ga**, and **o** are freely dropped. The question particle **ka** is often dropped. The meaning is carried by the context:

> **Tabako aru (ka)?** = **Tabako ga aru ka?**
> Do you have any cigarettes?

> **Doko iku?** = **Doko e iku ka?**
> Where are you going?

In the speech of men, the question particle **ka** is often replaced by **ka ne** (contraction **kai**) or **da ne** (contraction **dai**). If the sentence contains an interrogative word, **da ne (dai)** is more likely to occur.

> What is it?
> **Nan dai?** = **Nan desu ka?**

> Is it interesting?
> **Omoshiroi kai?** = **Omoshiroi desu ka?**

The plain copula **da** usually drops before **ka**:

Is it your friend?
Tomodachi kai? or **Tomo dachi ka?** = **Tomodachi desu ka?**

The final intensive particle **yo** occurs more commonly in the plain-style for both men and women. Women often end a plain-style sentence with **wa** (or **wa yo!**); you will occasionally hear men use final **wa**, but only after a polite-style sentence. Men sometimes use final **zo!** or **ze!** to be forceful. Both men and (especially) women freely punctuate their relaxed speech with the particle **ne!** ('you see, you know, I mean'). In Tokyo, the more vigorous **sa!** ('I tell you, you see, mind you!') is often used instead.

iii. Use of contractions

Contractions occur in all styles of speech, but they are more common in the plain style. Some contractions are peculiar to individual words—like the women's form **atashi** for **watashi** and **anta** for **anata**. Others are more widespread shortenings or modifications of certain sound sequences.

The topic particle **wa** is often shortened to just **a**. We find **kuruma-a** alongside **kuruma wa** 'as for the car,' and **kinō-a** alongside **kinō wa** 'as for yesterday.' A front vowel—**i** or **e**—at the end of a word preceding **wa** may be replaced by **y**: **kory-a** for **kore wa**, **aky-a** for **aki wa**. Or it may be replaced by nothing: **kor-a** for **kore wa**, **okashi-a** for **okashi wa**. The shortened form of **wa**, **a**, is then sometimes lengthened before a pause to **ā**: **koryā** or **korā**= **kore wa**.

This explains the contraction **ja** (or **jā**) from **de wa**. The sequence **d-y** does not occur in modern Japanese, so **j** is substituted for it. A gerund ending in **-de** followed by the particle **wa** becomes **-ja** in the same way: **Kono mizu o nonja ikenai yo** = **Kono mizu o nonde wa ikenai yo** 'Don't drink this water.' This contraction is paralleled by the contraction of **-cha** (or **-chā**) for **-te wa** (**ch** since the sequence **t-y** does not occur in modern Japanese): **Soko e itcha ikenai yo** = **Soko e itte wa ikenai yo** 'You mustn't go there.' **Mainichi sakana o tabenakucha ike nai** = **Mainichi sakana o tabenakute wa ikenai** 'Every day we have to eat fish.' **Hanashicha dame da** = **Hanashite wa dame da** 'It's no good to talk.'

The provisional endings **-(r)eba** and **-kereba** are often contracted to **-(r)ya** (or **-(r)yā**) and **-kerya**: **Kono kusuri nomanakerya naran** = **Kono kusuri o nomanakere ba naranai** 'I have to take this medicine.' **Kore taberya byōki ni naru yo** = **Kore o tabereba byōki ni naru yo** 'If you eat this, you'll get sick.'

A gerund + the verb **shimau** 'finishes, does completely' is contracted in the following way: **-te shimau** becomes **-chimau** or **-chau**; **-de shimau** becomes **-jimau** or **-jau**. **Shinjimatta** or **Shinjatta** = **Shinde shimatta** 'He died.' **Tabechimatta** or **Tabechatta** = **Tabete shimatta** 'He ate it all up.'

The initial **i** of the verb **iru** 'stays, is ... ing' often drops after a gerund: **Nani shiteru?** = **Nani o shite iru ka?** 'What are you doing?' The final **e** of the gerund form is often dropped before the verb **oku** 'puts away, does for later': **Koko ni oit-oita enpitsu wa doko e itta?** = **Koko ni oite oita enpitsu wa doko e itta ka?** 'Where did the pencil I put here go?' **Kippu katt-oita** = **Kippu o katte oita** 'I bought the tickets (in advance).'

The particle **keredomo** is often shortened to **keredo** or **kedo**. Shortenings of **mono** to **mon** and of **no** to just **n** have already been noted. The use of these, like the use of **ja** for **de wa**, is common in polite speech, too.

The plain negative ending **-(a)nai** is often contracted to **-(a)n**: **Wakaran desu ne** = **Wakaranai desu ne** 'I don't know, you see.' **Wakaran yo** = **Wakaranai yo** 'I don't know.' (The polite negative ending **-masen** also ends in **-n**, as if it were from a form **-masena-i**.)

The word **tte** is said to be a contraction of **to itte** 'saying thus,' but it is perhaps best treated as just another particle. The word has two uses: one is the same as the quoting particle **to** (or **to itte**), the other is the same as the topic particle **wa**. The gerund and conditional forms of the copula, **de** and **nara**, are also often used with about the same meaning as **wa** and **tte**—singling out a topic for consideration:

> This movie'll be OK.
> **Kono eiga nara, ii desu.**
> **Kono eiga de, ii desu.**
> **Kono eiga wa, ii desu.**
> **Kono eiga tte, ii desu.**

> He said good-bye and left.
> **Sayonara tte, itchatta** = **Sayonara to itte, itte shimatta.**

In addition to **tte**, some speakers use **ttara** and **tcha**—from **to ittara**, **to itte wa**—in a similar fashion, as a sort of lively substitute for the drab particle **wa**.

In addition to these and other more-or-less standardized contractions, some speakers tend to underarticulate many of their sounds, particularly certain consonants. The expression **Sō desu ne** 'Let me see now' frequently sounds as if the **d** were completely dropped, and the **e** is also difficult to distinguish: **Sō-s-ne**.

iv. Choice of forms

In the polite style, plain forms of verbs, adjectives and the copula are usual in all positions except at the end of the sentence, and sometimes in the middle before loosely connective particles like **ga** and **keredomo**. Occasionally, polite forms are used within the sentence to give an extra-polite flavor. In plain speech, the plain forms are usual in all positions. The plain copula is often omitted, especially in questions.

v. The plain imperative

In the polite style, you usually make commands in a roundabout way. If a genuine imperative form is used, it is from one of the exalted verbs: **nasai** from **nasaru**, **kudasai** or **kudasaimase** from **kudasaru**. In plain speech, too, oblique commands are common: **Shinbun katte kite kurenai ka** 'Won't you go buy me a newspaper, please?' Often, you use the simple gerund: **Chotto matte (yo)!** 'Wait a minute!'

In addition, there is a plain imperative form, but you seldom use it except when showing extreme impatience, or when quoting rather impersonal commands. The imperative forms are often followed by the particle **yo!** , as in **Ike yo!** 'Go!'

3. The modern literary style

The modern literary style, or **bungo,** is seldom heard except in the form of set expressions quoted, as it were, from written sources. It is not even often used in contemporary writing, but many things written a generation ago were in this style. The grammar of the literary style is different from that of colloquial Japanese in many ways, and its structure should be studied separately. If you are reading something that contains literary passages, the quickest way to understand the material is to get some Japanese to 'translate' the passages into colloquial Japanese.

APPENDIX II
Accent Patterns

The Japanese accent consists of pitch patterns found in words or phrases. In the following discussion, the syllable marked with an acute accent ´ is the LAST SYLLABLE BEFORE A FALL IN PITCH. Japanese words may be divided into TONIC and ATONIC. A tonic word is one that has a basic accent, although this accent may disappear in certain contexts. An atonic word is one with no basic accent, although it may acquire an accent in certain contexts.

An accent may occur on any syllable of a word, from first to last. But within any given word, or any accent phrase, only one accent occurs. When two or more tonic words are said as one accent phrase, the first usually retains its accent, and the following words lose their accents. In Tokyo speech, accent phrases are often quite long, so that many words seem to have lost their accent when you hear them in positions other than near the beginning of a sentence.

Many 4-syllable nouns are atonic (e.g. **yōfuku** [yo-o-fu-ku] 'Western-style clothes' and **tēburu** [te-e-bu-ru] 'table'). A goodly number of 3-syllable nouns are also atonic (e.g. **denwa** [de-n-wa] 'telephone' and **jishin** 'earthquake').

Most nouns of 1, 2, or 3 syllables are unpredictably atonic or tonic, with the accent on any syllable. There are a number of tonic 4-syllable nouns. For nouns of more than 4-syllables, the vast majority are not only tonic but have a THEMATIC accent—one that can be predicted. The rule for the thematic accent is: on the 3rd from the last syllable, unless this is the 2nd vowel in a vowel sequence or is a syllabic consonant—in which cases, on the 4th from the last. Following this rule, we find the following to be examples of thematic accent: **hóteru** 'hotel,' **tatémono** 'building,' **óngaku** 'music,' **chōkyori-dénwa** 'long-distance telephone (call),' **Nippon-Bōeki-Kabushiki-Gáisha** 'The Japan Trade Company, Inc.'

Just as some Americans say "AUtomobile" and others say "automoBILE," or "ICE cream" and "ice CREAM," there are words that will have one accent pattern for some speakers of Standard Japanese and another pattern for other speakers. For 'preacher,' some speakers say **bokushi**, others say **bókushi**. For the masculine 'I, me,' older speakers say **bóku**, younger speakers say **boku**.

APPENDIX III
Verb Forms (Selected)

		Stem	Infinitive	Imperfect	Negative	Perfect	Gerund	Tentative	Imperative	Provisional	Causative	Passive
Vowel Verb	eats	tabe	tabe	taberu	tabenai	tabeta	tabete	tabeyō	tabero	tabereba	tabesaseru	taberareru
	looks at	mi	mi	miru	minai	mita	mite	miyō	miro	mireba	misaseru	mirareru
Consonant Verb	trims	kar	kari	karu	karanai	katta	katte	karō	kare	kareba	karaseru	karareru
	wins	kat	kachi	katsu	katanai	katta	katte	katō	kate	kateba	kataseru	katareru
	buys	kaw	kai	kau	kawanai	katta	katte	kaō	kae	kaeba	kawaseru	kawareru
	lends	kas	kashi	kasu	kasanai	kashita	kashite	kasō	kase	kaseba	kasaseru	kasareru
	writes	kak	kaki	kaku	kakanai	kaita	kaite	kakō	kake	kakeba	kakaseru	kakareru
	smells	kag	kagi	kagu	kaganai	kaida	kaide	kagō	kage	kageba	kagaseru	kagareru
	reads	yom	yomi	yomu	yomanai	yonda	yonde	yomō	yome	yomeba	yomaseru	yomareru
	calls	yob	yobi	yobu	yobanai	yonda	yonde	yobō	yobe	yobeba	yobaseru	yobareru
	dies	shin	shini	shinu	shinanai	shinda	shinde	shinō	shine	shineba	shinaseru	shinareru
Irregular Verb	comes	~	ki	kuru	konai	kita	kite	koyō	koi	kureba	kosaseru	korareru
	does	~	shi	suru	shinai	shita	shite	shiyō	shiro	sureba	saseru	sareru

* The above are all plain forms when relevant.

Glossary
Japanese–English

abura 油 oil

aburu あぶる to roast, to grill

achiragawa あちら側 over there

ago あご chin, jaw

agohige あごひげ beard

ahiru アヒル duck

ai 愛 love

aijō 愛情 affection

aimai na あいまいな vague

airon o kakeru アイロンをかける (服の) to iron (clothing)

aisatsu 挨拶 greetings

aisatsu o suru 挨拶をする to greet

aisukurīmu アイスクリーム ice cream

aisuru 愛する to love

aji 味 taste

ajia アジア Asia

ajike no nai 味気のない dreary

ajimi o suru 味見をする to taste (salty, spicy)

akachan 赤ちゃん baby

akai 赤い red

akari 明かり light (noun)

akarui 明るい bright

akemashite omedetō 明けましておめでとう happy new year!

akeru 開ける to open

aki 秋 autumn, fall (season)

akichi 空き地 field, empty space

akiraka ni suru 明らかにする to reveal (make known)

akubisuru あくびする to yawn

akushū 悪臭 odor, bad smell

akushū o hanatsu 悪臭を放つ to stink

amai 甘い sweet

amari ni~sugiru あまりに～過ぎる too, excessively

amazuppai 甘酸っぱい sweet and sour

ame 飴 candy, sweets

ame 雨 rain

ame ga furu 雨が降る to rain

Amerika アメリカ America

Amerika gasshūkoku アメリカ合衆国 United States

Amerika(jin) no アメリカ(人)の American

ami 網 net

ana 穴 hole

anata あなた you

ani 兄 older brother

anka na 安価な inexpensive

an'naijo 案内所 information booth

an'nainin 案内人 guide, lead

an'naisuru 案内する to guide someone somewhere

anzen na 安全な safe, secure

aoi 青い blue

aoyasai 青野菜 greens (vegetables)

apāto アパート apartment

araarashii 荒々しい fierce

araiotosu 洗い落とす to scrub

arakajime あらかじめ beforehand, earlier

arappoi 荒っぽい rough

arashi 嵐 storm

arau 洗う to wash

arawareru 現れる to appear, to become visible

arawasu 現す to reveal (make visible)

are あれ that

arera あれら those

arigatō ありがとう thank you

arigatō to iu ありがとうと言う to say thank you

aruku 歩く to walk

asa 朝 morning

asai 浅い shallow

asatte 明後日 day after tomorrow

ase o kaku 汗をかく to sweat, to perspire

ashi 足 foot, 脚 leg

ashidori 足取り step

asobu 遊ぶ to play

asu 明日 tomorrow

ataeru 与える to give

atama 頭 head

atarashii 新しい new

atatakai 暖かい warm

atatameru 温める to heat

atsui 厚い thick (of things)

atsui 熱い hot (temperature)

atsukau 扱う to treat

atsumeru 集める to assemble, to gather

atsuryoku 圧力 pressure

au 会う to meet

awaseru 合わせる to join, to go along

ayamaru 謝る to apologize, to say sorry

ayamatta 誤った wrong (false)

aza あざ bruise

azukeru 預ける to deposit (leave behind with someone)

bā バー bar (serving drinks)

baffarō バッファロー buffalo (water buffalo)

bāgen バーゲン sale (reduced prices)

bai 倍 times (multiplying)

baiten 売店 stall (of vendor)

baketsu バケツ bucket

bakkin 罰金 fine (punishment)

banana バナナ banana

bangumi 番組 show (broadcast)

bankai 挽回 recovery

barabara ni suru ばらばらにする to break apart

basha 馬車 cart (horsecart)

basho 場所 place

basu バス bus

basukettobōru バスケットボール basketball

basurōbu バスローブ bathrobe

basutei バス停 bus station

batsu no warui ばつの悪い embarrassed, embarrassing

batā バター butter

beddo ベッド bed

bengoshi 弁護士 lawyer

benkyōzukue 勉強机 desk

benri na 便利な convenient

beruto ベルト belt

besuto ベスト vest

besuto o tsukusu ベストを尽くす to do one's best

betonamu ベトナム Vietnam

betsu no 別の another (different)

bīchi ビーチ beach

bideo dekki ビデオデッキ VCR

bideo kasetto ビデオカセット video cassette

bideo rekōdā ビデオレコーダー video recorder

bikō 鼻腔 nostril

bin 瓶 bottle

binsoku ni 敏速に quickly

bīru ビール beer

Biruma ビルマ(ミャンマーの旧称) Burma

Biruma(jin) no ビルマ(人)の Burmese

bisuketto ビスケット biscuit
biza ビザ visa
bō 棒 stick, pole
bōeki 貿易 trade, exchange
bōgai 妨害 disturbance
bōgyosuru 防御する to defend
bon 盆 tray
bōru ボール ball
bōrugami ボール紙 cardboard
bōrupen ボールペン ballpoint pen
bōshi 帽子(つばの広い) hat
bōto ボート boat
bu 部 department
bubunteki ni 部分的に partly
budō 葡萄 grapes
buhin 部品 part (of machine)
bujoku 侮辱 insult
bujokusuru 侮辱する to insult
buki 武器 arm, weapon
bukkyō 仏教 Buddhism
bukkyōto 仏教徒 Buddhist
bun 文 sentence
bunbōgu 文房具 stationery
bungaku 文学 literature
bunka 文化 culture
bunkatsu 分割 division, split up
bunrui 分類 categorization
buntsūsuru 文通する to correspond (write letters)
burajā ブラジャー bra
burashi ブラシ brush
burausu ブラウス blouse
burei 無礼 impolite
burokkorī ブロッコリー broccoli
burēki ブレーキ brake
burēki o kakeru ブレーキをかける to brake
burīfu ブリーフ(下着) briefs
burīfukēsu ブリーフケース briefcase
burōdobando ブロードバンド broadband
burogu ブログ(= **weburogu** ウェブログ) blog, weblog
buta 豚 pig
butaniku 豚肉 pork
buttai 物体 object, thing
buzoku 部族 tribe
byō 秒 second
byōdō 平等 equality
byōin 病院 hospital
byōki 病気 disease, illness
byōki no 病気の ill, sick
byōshasuru 描写する to describe

cha 茶 tea
chairoi 茶色い brown (adjective)
chakurikusuru 着陸する(飛行機) to land (plane)

chatto チャット chatting, chat
chawan 茶わん cup
chekku チェック checked pattern
chesu チェス chess
chi 血 blood
chichi 父 father
chiiki 地域 area, region
chijoku 恥辱 shame, disgrace
chikaku de 近くで around, nearby
chikara 力 force, power, strength
chikarazuyoi 力強い powerful
chikazuku 近づく(空間、時間) to approach (in space and time)
chikyū 地球 Earth
chīmu チーム team
chingashisuru 賃貸しする to rent out
chingin 賃金 wages
chippu チップ tip (gratuity)
chirakasu 散らかす to make a mess
chiryō 治療(医療) cure (medical)
chiryōsuru 治療する to treat (medically)
chīsai 小さい little, small
chisei 知性 intelligence
chishiki 知識 knowledge
chishiki ga aru 知識がある to know, be acquainted with
chitsu 膣 vagina
chizu 地図 map
chīzu チーズ cheese
chokumensuru 直面する to face
chōbo 帳簿 account book
chōchō 蝶々 butterfly
chōhōkei 長方形 rectangle
chōkakushōgai no 聴覚障害の deaf
chokki チョッキ vest
chōkoku 彫刻 carving, sculpture
chōkokusuru 彫刻する to sculpt
chokorēto チョコレート chocolate
chōrisareta 調理された cooked
chōsasuru 調査する to examine
chōseisuru 調整する to organize, to arrange
chōsen 挑戦 challenge
chōshoku 朝食 breakfast, morning meal
chōshoku o toru 朝食をとる to eat breakfast
chōwa no toreta 調和のとれた harmonious
chūgoku 中国 China
chūi 注意 notice
chūi o harau 注意を払う to pay attention

chūibukai 注意深い cautious
chūmoku 注目 notice
chūmon 注文 order (placed for food, goods)
chūmonsuru 注文する to order (something)
chūō 中央 middle, center
chūsha 注射 injection
chūshasuru 注射する to inject
chūshasuru 駐車する to park (car)
chūshin 中心 center, middle
chūshin no 中心の central
chūshoku 昼食 lunch, midday meal
chūshoku o toru 昼食をとる to eat lunch

daenkei no 楕円形の oval (shape)
dageki 打撃 hit, strike
daiben 大便 feces
daibubun wa 大部分は mostly
daidokoro 台所 kitchen
daigaku 大学 university
daimei 題名(本、映画) title (of book, film)
daisan no 第三の third
daitai だいたい more or less
daitōryō 大統領 president
daiyamondo ダイヤモンド diamond
dakara だから so, because of that
~dake de naku~mo mata ~だけでなく~もまた not only ... but also
damasu だます to cheat, to deceive
dame だめ don't!, no good
danbōru bako 段ボール箱 cardboard box
dango 団子 dumpling
dankotoshita 断固とした determined, stubborn, firm (definite)
dansei 男性 male
dare だれ who
dareka だれか anybody, anyone, somebody, someone
daremo~nai だれも~ない nobody
dāsu ダース dozen
datō na 妥当な adequate
~de ~で in, at
debittokādo デビットカード debit card
detchiageru でっち上げる to make up, invent
deguchi 出口 exit, way out
dekibae できばえ performance
dekigoto 出来事 event, happening, incident

~dekiru ～できる can, be able to

~demonai ～でもない nor, neither

dengon 伝言 message

denki 電気 electricity, light

denki-kiki 電気機器 appliance, electrical

denki no 電気の electric

densetsu no 伝説の legend

densha 電車 train

(denshi) mēru (電子)メール email (system, message)

(denshi) mēru adoresu (電子)メールアドレス email address

(denshi) mēru o okuru (電子)メールを送る to email

denshi no 電子の electronic

denshi shoseki 電子書籍 computer book, digital book, e-book, electronic book

dentō 伝統 tradition

dentōteki na 伝統的な traditional

denwa 電話 telephone

denwa ni deru 電話にでる to answer the phone

denwa o kakeru 電話をかける to dial (telephone)

denwa o suru 電話をする to call on the telephone

denwabangō 電話番号 telephone number

denwa no koki 子機(電話) extension (telephone)

denwasuru 電話する to ring (on the telephone)

depparu 出っ張る to stick out

depāto デパート department store

deru 出る to go out, to exit

~deshō ～でしょう probably

desuku デスク desk

~dewa nai ～ではない no, not

dezāto デザート sweets, dessert

dībuidī ディーブイディー DVD

dō 銅 bronze, copper

dōbutsu 動物 animal

dōbutsuen 動物園 zoo

dochiraka (ippō) no どちらか(一方)の either

dodai 土台 basis

dōgu 道具 tool, utensil, instrument

dōhansuru 同伴する to accompany

dōi 同意 agreement

dōisuru 同意する to agree

dōitashimashite どういたしまして don't mention it! you're welcome!

dōitsu no 同一の identical

dōji ni 同時に at the same time

dojō 土壌 earth, soil

doko どこ where

doko e どこへ to where

dokodemo どこでも everywhere, anywhere

dokoka どこか somewhere

doko nimo~nai どこにも～ない nowhere

doku 毒 poison

dokuritsushita 独立した free, independent

dokusei no 毒性の poisonous

dokushin no 独身の single (not married)

dokutoku no 独特の characteristic

dōkyō 道教 Taoism

domein mei (nēmu) ドメイン名(ネーム) domain-name

donburi どんぶり bowl

don'na どんな what kind of

dono yō ni どのように how

don'yorishita どんよりした(天気) dull (weather)

dore どれ which

doresu ドレス dress, frock

dorobō 泥棒 thief

doryoku 努力 effort

doryokusuru 努力する to make an effort, to try

dote 土手 bank (of river)

dōri ni kanatteiru 道理にかなっている reasonable

dōryō 同僚 co-worker, colleague

dōyara~rashii どうやら～らしい apparently

dōyō ni 同様に alike

dōzo どうぞ(勧めるとき) please (go ahead)

doyōbi 土曜日 Saturday

~e ～へ(場所) to, toward

~e mukau ～へ向かう to head for, toward

~e yōkoso ～へようこそ welcome to

e 絵 picture

eakon エアコン air conditioning

ebi 海老 shrimp, prawn

eda 枝 branch

eien ni 永遠に for ever

eiga 映画 film, movie

eigakan 映画館 cinema, movie house

eikoku 英国 United Kingdom

eikoku(jin) no 英国(人)の British

eikyō 影響 effect, influence

eikyō o ataeru 影響を与える to affect, to influence

eikyū no 永久の permanent

eki 駅 train station

en 円 circle

endōmame エンドウ豆 peas

enjin エンジン motor, engine

enjo 援助 assistance

enkai 宴会 banquet

enkatsu ni susumu 円滑にすすむ to go smoothly

enkishita 延期した postponed, delayed

enkisuru 延期する to postpone, to put off, to delay

enpitsu 鉛筆 pencil

erabu 選ぶ to pick, to choose, to select

erebētā エレベーター lift, elevator

eru 得る to earn

esukarētā エスカレーター escalator

faiāwōru ファイアーウォール firewall

fakkusu ファックス fax (machine)

fakkusu o okuru ファックスを送る to fax

fakkusubun ファックス文 fax (message)

fan ファン fan (admirer)

ferī フェリー ferry

firipin フィリピン Philippines

firumu フィルム film (camera)

fisshingu フィッシング phishing (fraud)

FTP (efutīpī) FTP(エフティーピー) File Transfer Protocol (FTP)

fōku フォーク fork

fuhei 不平 complaint

fuhei o kobosu 不平をこぼす to complain

fuhitsuyō na 不必要な unnecessary

fuhō no 不法の illegal

fujin 婦人 lady

fukai 深い deep

fukanō na 不可能な impossible

fukō 不幸 misfortune

fukō na 不幸な unhappy

fuku 服 clothes, clothing

fuku o nugu 服を脱ぐ to get undressed

fukubu 腹部 abdomen

fukumu 含む to include

fukuzatsu na 複雑な complicated

fumō no 不毛の barren

fun 分 minute

funatabi o suru 船旅をする to sail

funbetsu no aru 分別のある reasonable (sensible)

fune 船 ship

funshitsubutsu 紛失物 lost property

fun'iki 雰囲気 atmosphere, ambience

furikaeru 振り返る to turn around

furo 風呂 bath

furoppīdisuku フロッピーディスク floppy disk

furu 振る to shake, to wave

furui 古い(物) old (of things)

furumau 振舞う to act, to behave

furūto, fue フルート、笛 flute

fusawashii ふさわしい suitable, fitting

fuseikaku na 不正確な inaccurate

fushō 負傷 injury

futa ふた lid

futatabi 再び again

futotta 太った fat, plump

fūtō 封筒 envelope

futsū 普通 normal

futsū wa 普通は normally, usually

futsūyūbin 普通郵便 surface mail

futtōsuru 沸騰する to boil

fuun 不運 bad luck

fuun na 不運な unlucky

fū o suru 封をする to steal

fuyasu 増やす to increase

ga 蛾 moth

~ ga ~が subject marking particle

gatchisuru 合致する to fit

gachō ガチョウ goose

gaido ガイド guide

gaikoku de 外国で abroad

gaikoku no 外国の foreign

gaikokujin 外国人 foreigner

gaitō 外套 coat, overcoat

gakkō 学校 school

gakudō 学童 schoolchild

gakusei 学生 student

gakushūsuru 学習する to study, to learn

gamen 画面 screen (of computer)

ganbō 願望 desire

ganko na 頑固な stubborn, determined

ganryō 顔料 paint

gara 柄 pattern, design

garasu ガラス glass (material)

gasorin ガソリン gasoline, petrol

~gatsu ~月 month

gaun ガウン dressing gown

geijutsu 芸術 art

geijutsuka 芸術家 artist

gekijō 劇場 theater (drama)

gekkei ga aru 月経がある to menstruate

gendai no 現代の modern

gengo 言語 language

genkan 玄関 entrance, way in, front door

genkei no 原型の original

genki 元気 how are you?

genki na 元気な fine, energetic

genki ni naru 元気になる to get better

genkin 現金 cash, money

genshō 減少 reduction

genzai 現在 presently, nowadays

genzai no 現在の current

genzōsuru 現像する to develop (film)

gen'in 原因 cause

getsuyōbi 月曜日 Monday

gimu 義務 duty (responsibility)

gimuteki na 義務的な compulsory

gin 銀 silver

ginkō 銀行 bank (finance)

giri no chichi 義理の父 father-in-law

giri no haha 義理の母 mother-in-law

giri no musuko 義理の息子 son-in-law

giri no musume 義理の娘 daughter-in-law

giron 議論 argument, discussion

gisei 犠牲 sacrifice

gishiki 儀式 ceremony

go 五 five

go 語 word

gochisō ご馳走 treat (something special), delicious meal

gogatsu 五月 May

gogo 午後 p.m.

gohan ご飯(炊いた) rice (cooked)

gōhō no 合法の legal

gojū 五十 fifty

gokai 誤解 misunderstanding

gōkakusuru 合格する(試験) to pass (exam)

gōka na 豪華な luxurious

gōkei no 合計の total

goma ゴマ sesame seeds

goma abura ゴマ油 sesame oil

gomen'nasai ごめんなさい sorry! excuse me!

gomi ごみ garbage

gomu ゴム rubber

goraku 娯楽 pastime

gōru ゴール goal

gorufu ゴルフ golf

gōsei no 合成の synthetic

~goto ni ~毎に each, every

guntai 軍隊 army, troops

gurasu グラス glass (for drinking)

guratsuita ぐらついた loose (wobbly)

gurūpu グループ group

gūzen ni 偶然に accidentally, by chance

gūzō 偶像 idol

gyakkōsuru 逆行する to go backwards

gyanburu ギャンブル gamble

gyōgi no ii 行儀のいい well-behaved

gyōretsu 行列 line (queue)

gyūniku 牛肉 beef

gyūnyū 牛乳 milk

ha 歯 teeth, tooth

ha 葉 leaf

haba 幅 width

habahiroi 幅広い wide

haburashi 歯ブラシ toothbrush

hachi 八 eight

hachi 鉢 pot

hachigatsu 八月 August

hachijū 八十 eighty

hachimitsu 蜂蜜 honey

hada 肌 skin

hadagi 肌着 underwear

hadaka no 裸の naked, nude

hādodisuku ハードディスク hard disk

hae 蝿 fly (insect)

haeru 生える to grow, to come out

hagaki 葉書 postcard

hagane はがね steel

hageshiku utsu 激しく打つ to beat (to strike)

hageta はげた bald

haha 母 mother

hai はい yes

hai 肺 lungs

haibensuru 排便する to defecate

haigūsha 配偶者 spouse

haiiro no 灰色の gray

hairu 入る to enter

haitatsusuru 配達する to deliver

haji 端 tip (end)

hajimari 始まり start, beginning

hajime ni 初めに at first

hajimeru 始める to begin, to start

hajite 恥じて ashamed, embarrassed

haka 墓 grave

hakaisareta 破壊された destroyed, ruined

hakaisuru 破壊する to destroy

hakari はかり scales

hakaru 測る to measure

hakaru 量る to weigh

hakarukoto 計ること measurement

hakidasu 吐き出す to vomit, spit out

hakike ga suru 吐き気がする to feel sick

hakkā ハッカー hacker, hack

hakkensuru 発見する to discover

hako 箱 box

hakobu 運ぶ to carry

haku 掃く to sweep

hakusai 白菜 Chinese cabbage

hamabe 浜辺 beach

hamaki 葉巻 cigar

hamigakiko 歯磨き粉 toothpaste

hana 花 flower

hana 鼻 nose

hanabi 花火 fireworks

hanamuko 花婿 groom

hanashi 話 story (tale)

hanashichū 話し中(電話) busy, engaged (telephone)

hanasu 話す to speak, to talk, to tell

hanayome 花嫁 bride

hanbun 半分 half

hankagai 繁華街 downtown, center (of city)

hankyōsuru 反響する to reflect

han'nō 反応 reaction, response

han'nōsuru 反応する to react

hansamu ハンサム handsome

hantai no 反対の opposed, opposite

hantaisuru 反対する to object, to protest, to oppose

hanzaisha 犯罪者 criminal

hara 腹 stomach, belly

harau 払う to pay

hareta 晴れた(天気) clear (of weather)

hari 針 needle

haru 春 spring (season)

hasami はさみ scissors

hashi 橋 bridge

hashi 端 edge, end (tip)

hashi 箸 chopsticks

hashigo 梯子 ladder

hashira 柱 post, column, pillar

hashiru 走る to run

hata 旗 flag

hatasu 果たす to fulfill

hatsugen 発言 utterance

hatsumei 発明 invitation

hatsumeisuru 発明する to invent

hatsunetsu 発熱 fever

hatsuonsuru 発音する to pronounce

hatten 発展 development

hattensuru 発展する to develop

hayai 速い fast, rapid

hazukashii 恥ずかしい embarrassing

hebi 蛇 snake

heibon na 平凡な plain (not fancy)

heikin 平均 average (numbers)

heisa 閉鎖(道) closed (road)

heitai 兵隊 soldier

heitan na 平坦な flat, smooth

heiten 閉店(店) closed (shop)

heiwa 平和 peace

heiwa na 平和な peaceful

hen na 変な strange

henji 返事 answer, response (spoken), reply

henji o suru 返事をする to answer, to reply

henshin 返信 answer, response (written)

henshinsuru 返信する to answer, to respond (written)

hentō 返答 response

hentōsuru 返答する to reply (in speech), to respond

herasu 減らす to reduce

heru 減る to decrease

heya 部屋 room

hi ga tsuku 火がつく to be caught on fire

hiatari ga ii 日当たりがいい sunny

hidarigawa 左側 left-hand side

hidoi ひどい terrible

higashi 東 east

hiji ひじ elbow

hijō ni 非常に very, extremely

hikaeme na 控えめな modest

hikakusuru 比較する to compare

hikaru 光る to shine

hikidashi 引き出し drawer

hikō 飛行 flight

hikōki 飛行機 airplane

hiku 引く to pull, to draw

hikui 低い low, short (not tall)

himitsu 秘密 secret

himitsu o mamoru 秘密を守る to keep a secret

himo 紐 string

hinan 非難(言葉で) attack (with words), blame

hinode 日の出 sunrise

hinoiri 日の入 sunset

hinpan ni 頻繁に frequently

hiraiteiru 開いている open

hiroba 広場 square, town square

hirobiroshita 広々した spacious

hiroi 広い broad, spacious, large

hiroma 広間 hall

hishaku ひしゃく dipper, ladle

hisho 秘書 secretary

hissu no 必須の compulsory

hitaru 浸る to soak

hīta 引いた less, minus

hito 人 person

hitobito 人々 people

hitokire 一切れ piece, portion

hitonami 人並み average (so-so, just okay)

hitori de ひとりで alone, on one's own

hitsuji 羊 sheep

hitsuyō na 必要な necessary

hitsuyōsei 必要性 necessity

hiyasareta 冷やされた chilled

hiyoku na 肥沃な fertile

hiyō 費用 cost (expense)

hiza 膝 knee

hizashi 日差し sunlight

hizuke 日付 date (of the month)

hō 頬 cheek

hōgen 方言 dialect

hogoku 保護区(動物) reserve (for animals)

hoka no ほかの different, other

hokansuru 保管する to leave behind for safekeeping

hoken 保険 insurance

hokori 誇り pride

hokori 埃 dust

hokōkyori 歩行距離 distance that one walks

hon 本 book

hone 骨 bone

honkon 香港 Hong Kong

honō 炎 fire

hontō 本当 really, truth

hontō ni 本当に really, truly

hontō no 本当の true

hon'yaku 翻訳 translation

horaana 洞穴 cave

horu 彫る to carve

hoshi 星 star

hoshōsho 保証書 guarantee

hoshōsuru 保証する to guarantee

hosoi 細い slender, slim

hoteru ホテル hotel

hotondo ほとんど almost, most (the most of), nearly

hotondo~nai ほとんど~ない hardly, seldom

hōhō 方法 method, way

hōki ほうき broom

hōkisuru 放棄する to desert, to abandon

hōkoku 報告 report

hōkokusuru 報告する to report

hōkō 方向 direction

hōrensō ほうれん草 spinach

hōritsu 法律 laws, legislation

hōsekirui 宝石類 jewelry

hōshi 奉仕 service
hōsō 放送 broadcast
hōsōsuru 放送する to broadcast
hōtai 包帯 bandage
hyakkaten 百貨店 department store
hyaku 百 hundred
hyakubunritsu 百分率 percent, percentage
hyakuman 百万 million
hyō 表 list
hyōmen 表面 surface
hyōshiki 標識 sign, signpost

ichi 一 one
ichiba 市場 market
ichiban no 一番の first
ichibu 一部 part (not whole)
ichido 一度 once
ichigatsu 一月 January
ichihōkō o shimesu 位置方向を示す point out the position/direction
ichijiteki na 一時的な temporary
ichimai no kami 一枚の紙 a sheet of paper
ichiman 一万 ten thousand
idaku 抱く to embrace
ido 井戸 well (for water)
idōsuru 移動する to move
ie 家 home, house
igaku no 医学の medical
igirisu イギリス England, UK
igirisu(jin) no イギリス(人)の English, British
ijiwarui 意地悪い mean (cruel)
ika イカ squid
ikari 怒り anger
iken 意見 opinion
ikinobiru 生延びる to survive
ikite 生きて alive
ikiteiru 生きている living
ikko no 一個の a piece of
iku 行く to go
ikuradesuka いくらですか how much?
ikutsudesuka いくつですか how old?, how many?
ikutsuka no いくつかの several, some
ima 今 now
imi 意味 meaning
imisuru 意味する to mean (word)
imōto 妹 younger sister
inaka 田舎 country (rural area)
inazuma 稲妻 lightning
Indoneshia インドネシア Indonesia
ine 稲 rice (plant)
ingenmame インゲン豆 kidney beans
inoru 祈る to pray

insatsusuru 印刷する to print
inshōzukeru 印象付ける to make an impression
intaishita 引退した retired
intānetto インターネット Internet
intānetto kafe インターネットカフェ (= **netto kafe** ネットカフェ) Internet Café, Net café (Internet)
inu 犬 dog
ippai no いっぱいの full of
ippakusuru 一泊する to stay overnight
ippan ni 一般に generally
ippanteki na 一般的な general, all-purpose
irai 以来 since then
iraisuru 依頼する to ask for, to request
irekawaru 入れ替わる to replace
iriguchi 入り口 entrance, way in
iro 色 color
irui 衣類 garment
isamashii 勇ましい brave, daring
iseki 遺跡 remains (historical)
isha 医者 doctor
ishi 石 rock, stone
isogashii 忙しい busy (doing something)
isoide 急いで in a hurry
isshō 一生 lifetime
issō いっそう even (also)
isu 椅子 chair, seat
Isuramu no イスラムの Islamic
Isuramukyō no イスラム教(徒)の Muslim
IT (aitī) IT(アイティー) information technology (computer)
itai 痛い sore, painful
itamu 痛む to ache
itazura na いたずらな naughty
ito 意図 intention
ito 糸 thread
itosareta 意図された intended for
itsu いつ when
itsudemo いつでも whenever
itsumo いつも always, every-time
itsumo no いつもの usual
ittsui no 一対の a pair of
iu 言う to say
iwau 祝う to celebrate
iyakuhin 医薬品 medicine
iyaringu イヤリング earrings
izen ni 以前に before (in time)
izonsuru 依存する to depend on

jagaimo ジャガイモ potato
jaketto ジャケット coat, jacket
jama 邪魔 hindrance
jamu ジャム jam
janguru ジャングル jungle

jibun no 自分の own, personal
jidōsha 自動車 automobile, car
jidōsha-shūrikōjō 自動車修理工場 garage (for repairs)
jijitsu 事実 fact
jiin 寺院 temple
jikaku 自覚 awareness
jikakusuru 自覚する to be conscious of
jikan 時間 hour, time
jikandōri ni 時間どおりに punctual, on time
jiken 事件 incident
jiko 事故 accident
jikokuhyō 時刻表 timetable
jikoshōkaisuru 自己紹介する to introduce oneself
jimen 地面 ground, earth
jimi na 地味な simple, plain (modest)
jimusho 事務所 office
jinkō 人口 population
jinkō no 人工の artificial
jinrui 人類 human
jinzō 腎臓 kidney
jishin 自信 confidence
jishin 自身 self
jishin 地震 earthquake
jishin o motsu 自信を持つ to have confidence
jisho 辞書 dictionary
jisonshin 自尊心 pride
jissai ni 実際に actually, really (in fact)
jiten 時点(時間) point (in time)
jitensha 自転車 bicycle
jitsugyōka 実業家 businessperson
jiyū 自由 freedom
jōdan 冗談 joke
jogen 助言 advice
jogensuru 助言する to advise
jōhō 情報 information
jōi no 上位の ranked higher
jojo ni 徐々に gradually
jōken 条件 condition (pre-condition)
jōki 蒸気 steam
jōku ジョーク joke
jōkyaku 乗客 passenger
jōkyō 状況 condition (status), situation, how things are
joō 女王 queen
jōryūshu 蒸留酒 spirits, hard liquor
josei 女性 female, woman
jōsharyōkin 乗車料金 fare
jōshasuru 乗車する to get on, to ride, to board
jōshi 上司 boss
jōshō 上昇 rise, ascendance
jōzai 錠剤 pills, tablets

jū 十 ten
jūbun na 十分な enough
jūgatsu 十月 October
jūgo 十五 fifteen
jugyō 授業 lesson, class
jūhachi 十八 eighteen
jūichi 十一 eleven
jūichigatsu 十一月 November
jūjun na 従順な obedient, tame
jukurenshita 熟練した skillful
jukushita 熟した ripe
jukyō 儒教 Confucianism
jūkyū 十九 nineteen
jūman 十万 hundred thousand
jūnana 十七 seventeen
junban 順番 order, sequence
junbisuru 準備する to prepare, to make ready
junchō na 順調な smooth, normal
jūni 十二 twelve
jūnigatsu 十二月 December
jūnin 住人 resident, inhabitant
junjo 順序 sequence, order
junsui na 純粋な pure
jūoku 十億 billion
juritsusuru 樹立する to establish, to set up
jūroku 十六 sixteen
jūsan 十三 thirteen
jūshichi 十七 seventeen
jūsho 住所 address
jūsu ジュース juice
jūtan 絨毯 carpet
jūyaku 重役(会社の) director (of company)
jūyon 十四 fourteen
jūyō na 重要な major (important)
jūyō sa 重要さ importance

ka 蚊 mosquito
kaban 鞄 bag
kabe 壁 wall
kabi カビ mold, mildew
kabin 花瓶 vase
kachi 価値 value (cost)
kado 角 corner
kaeru 変える to change
kaesu 返す to return, to give back
kagaku 科学 science
kagami 鏡 mirror
kage 陰 shade
kage 影 shadow
kagee 影絵 shadow play
kagi 鍵(部屋) key (to room)
kago かご basket
kagu 家具 furniture
kai 階(建物) storey (of a building)
kaichō 会長 president

kaichūdentō 懐中電灯 flashlight, torch
kaidan 階段 steps, stairs
kaifukushita 回復した recovered, cured
kaiga 絵画 painting
kaigai no 海外の overseas
kaigō 会合 meeting
kaihatsu 開発 development
kaiin 会員 member
kaiketsusuru 解決する(問題) to resolve, to solve (a problem)
kaikosuru 解雇する to fire (lay off) someone
kaikyō 海峡 strait
kaikyū 階級 rank, station in life
kaimono o suru 買い物をする to go shopping, to shop
kairomō 回路網 network
kaisanbutsu 海産物 seafood
kaisha 会社 company
kaiwa 会話 conversation
kaji o toru かじをとる to steer
kajū 果汁 juice
kakaku 価格 price
kakegoto 賭け事 gamble
kaketeiru 欠けている lacking
kaki 牡蠣 oyster
kakikomu 書き込む to fill out (form)
kakitome 書留 registered post
kakitomeru 書き留める to note down
kakōsuru 下降する to descend, to go/come down
kaku 書く(手紙、本、音楽) to write (letters, books, music)
kaku 描く(絵) to paint (a painting)
kakuchōsuru 拡張する to enlarge
kakudaisuru 拡大する to expand, to grow larger
kakureta 隠れた hidden
kakushin 確信 conviction
kakusu 隠す to hide
kakuteishita 確定した definite
kamaboko かまぼこ fish paste
kamado かまど cooker
kamera カメラ camera
kami 紙 paper
kami 神 God
kami 髪 hair
kamikazari 髪飾り hair ornaments
kaminari 雷 thunder
~kamoshirenai ～かもしれない maybe
kamu 噛む to bite, to chew
kan 缶 can, tin
kanari かなり quite (fairly)
kanashii 悲しい sad, unhappy

kanashimi 悲しみ sorrow
kanban 看板 signboard
kanbatsu 干ばつ drought
Kanbojia カンボジア Cambodia
kanchisuru 完治する to fully recover
kandai na 寛大な generous
kandai sa 寛大さ generosity
kane 金 money
kanemochi 金持ち rich person
kangae 考え idea
kangaeru 考える to ponder, to think
kani 蟹 crab
kanja 患者 patient (doctor's)
kanji 感じ feeling
kanjiru 感じる to feel
kanjō 感情 emotion
kanjō o gaisuru 感情を害する to hurt one's feeling
kankinsuru 換金する to exchange (money)
kankitsurui かんきつ類 citrus fruit
Kankoku 韓国 South Korea
kankō 観光 sightseeing
kankōkyaku 観光客 tourist
kankyō 環境 environment, surroundings
kanningu カンニング cheating
kanō na 可能な possible
kanō ni suru 可能にする to make possible
kanojo 彼女 she, her, girlfriend
kanpai 乾杯 cheers!
kanpeki na 完璧な complete (thorough)
kanrinin 管理人 custodian
kanseishita 完成した complete (finished)
kanshasuru 感謝する to be grateful, to thank
kansōshita 乾燥した(天気) dry (weather)
kantan na 簡単な simple (easy)
kanyoshita 関与した involved
kanzei 関税 duty (import tax)
kanzen na 完全な whole, complete
kanzen ni 完全に completely, entirely
kanzō 肝臓 liver
kao 顔 face
kao o shikameru 顔をしかめる to frown
~kara ～から from
kara no 空の empty
karada 体 body
karai 辛い hot (spicy)
kare 彼 he, him, boyfriend
karera 彼ら they, them

kareshi 彼氏 boyfriend
kari ga aru 借りがある to owe
karifurawā カリフラワー cauliflower
kariru 借りる to borrow
karōjite かろうじて barely
karui 軽い light (not heavy)
kasa 傘 umbrella
kashi 菓子 confectionery
kashikoi 賢い clever, smart
kashitsu 過失 fault
kasu 貸す to lend, to rent
kata 肩 shoulder
katachi 形 form, shape, style
katachizukuru 形作る to form, to shape
katagaki 肩書き(人) title (of person)
katai 堅い stiff
katai 固い hard (solid)
katai 硬い(マットレス) firm (mattress)
katami-chikippu 片道切符 one-way ticket
katazukeru 片付ける to tidy up
katei shitemiru 仮定してみる to hypothesize
kāten カーテン curtain
kāto カート(手押し) cart (push-cart)
katsudō 活動 activity
katsuryoku 活力 energy
katsute かつて in the past
kau 買う to buy
kauntā カウンター counter (for paying, buying tickets)
kawa 川 river
kawa 革 leather
kawaii かわいい cute
kawairashii かわいらしい(女性) pretty (of women)
kawaita 乾いた dry
kawakasu 乾かす to dry
kawaru 変わる(状況が) to change (conditions, situations)
kawase-sōba 為替相場 exchange rate
kawaserēto 為替レート rate of exchange (for foreign currency)
kayōbi 火曜日 Tuesday
kazan 火山 volcano
kazaru 飾る to decorate
kaze 風邪 cold, flu
kazoeru 数える to count
kazoku 家族 family
kazu 数 number
~ka~ ～か～ or
kega 怪我 wound
keihi 経費 expenses
keikaku 計画 plan, schedule
keikakusuru 計画する to plan
keiken 経験 experience

keikensuru 経験する to experience, to undergo
keikoku 警告 warning
keikokusuru 警告する to warn
keimusho 刑務所 jail, prison
keisanki 計算機 calculator
keisansuru 計算する to calculate
keisatsukan 警察官 police officer
keisatsu 警察 police
keitaidenwa 携帯電話 cell phone
keizai 経済 economy
keizaiteki na 経済的な economical
keizokusuru 継続する to continue
kekka 結果 result
kekkonshiki 結婚式 wedding
kekkonsuru 結婚する to marry, to get married
kemuri 煙 smoke
ken 券(娯楽) ticket (for entertainment)
ken 腱 tendon
kenchiku 建築 architecture
ken'i 権威 authority (person in charge)
kenka けんか fight, quarrel
kenkōteki na 健康的な healthy
kenkyū 研究 research
kenkyūsuru 研究する to research
kenri 権利 rights
kenryoku(sha) 権力(者) authority (power)
kensakusuru 検索する(本を) to look up (find books)
ken'okan 嫌悪感 hatred
ken'osuru 嫌悪する to hate
keshiki 景色 scenery, view, panorama
keshita 消した off (turned off)
kesseki no 欠席の missing, absent
kesshin 決心 decision
kesshite~nai 決して～ない never
kesu 消す to turn off
kesu 消す(火、ろうそく) to put out (fire, candle)
ketten 欠点 defect
ki 木 tree, wood
kī キー(コンピューター) key (computer)
ki o tsukete 気をつけて take care
kibin na 機敏な quick
kibishii きびしい severe, strict
kibō 希望 desire
kībōdo キーボード(コンピューター) keyboard (of computer)
kichintoshita きちんとした neat, orderly

kigaeru 着替える to change clothes
kigan(suruhito) 祈願(する人) prayer
kigen 起源 origin
kigyō 企業 firm, company
kihon 基本 basic
kiji 記事 article (in newspaper)
kikai 機会 chance, opportunity
kikai 機械 machine
kikairui 機械類 machinery
kikan 期間 period (of time)
kiken 危険 danger
kiken na 危険な dangerous
kikō 気候 climate
kiku 聴く to listen
kiku 聞く to hear
kikyōsuru 帰郷する to return to one's town
kimeru 決める to decide, to fix
kimi 君 you (male)
kinben na 勤勉な hardworking, industrious
kinchōshita 緊張した tense
kinenhi 記念碑 monument
ki ni iru 気に入る to suit one's taste
ki ni naru 気になる to be anxious
ki ni shinaide 気にしないで never mind!
kinjirareta 禁じられた forbidden
kinkyūjitai 緊急事態 emergency
kinkyū no 緊急の urgent
kin'niku 筋肉 muscle
kinō 昨日 yesterday
kinoko きのこ mushroom
kinōsuru 機能する to function, to work
kinshisuru 禁止する to forbid
kinu 絹 silk
kinyōbi 金曜日 Friday
kioku 記憶 memories
kippu 切符(乗り物) ticket (for transport)
kirei na きれいな clean, beautiful
kirei ni suru きれいにする to clean
kiri 霧 fog, mist
kirisutokyō キリスト教 Christianity
kiroguramu キログラム kilogram
kīroi 黄色い yellow (adjective)
kiromētā キロメーター kilometer
kiru 切る to cut
kiru 着る to get dressed, to wear, to put on
kisetsu 季節 season
kisha 記者 journalist
kiso 基礎 base, foundation
kisoku 規則 rules
kisu キス kiss
kita 北 north

kitachōsen 北朝鮮 North Korea

kitai o motte 期待をもって hopefully

kitakusuru 帰宅する to go home

kitanai 汚い dirty

kitsui きつい close together, tight

kitte 切手(郵便) stamp (postage)

kiwifurūtsu キーウィフルーツ kiwi fruit

kiyomeru 清める to purify

kizamu 刻む to engrave

kizuiteiru 気づいている aware

kizuku 気づく to notice

kizutsuku 傷つく to get hurt/injured

kodai no 古代の ancient

kōdō 行動 action

kodomo 子ども(子孫/若い人一般) child (offspring/young person)

koe 声 voice

kōen 公園 garden, park

kōen 公演 performance

kōfunshita 興奮した on (turned on), excited

kōgaku no 高額の expensive

kogatana 小刀 knife

kōgei 工芸 crafts

kōgeika 工芸家 craftsperson

kōgeki 攻撃(戦争) attack (in war)

kōgi 講義 lecture

kogirei na こぎれいな(場所、物) neat (of places, things)

kogitte 小切手 check (bank)

kōhei na 公平な just, fair

kōhī コーヒー coffee

koi 濃い thick (of liquids)

koishikuomou 恋しく思う to miss (loved one)

koji 古寺 ancient temple

kojinteki na 個人的な private

kōjō 工場 factory

kōka 硬貨 coin

kōkai 後悔 regret

kōkaisuru 後悔する to regret

kōkan 交換 exchange

kōkansuru 交換する to switch, to change

kokka 国家 country (nation)

kokku コック cook (person)

kokkyō 国境 border (between countries)

koko ここ here

kokochiyoi 心地良い comfortable

kokonattsu ココナッツ coconut

kokoromi 試み attempt

kokoromiru 試みる to attempt

kokorozuke 心付け tip (gratuity)

kōkūbin 航空便 airmail

kokusaiteki na 国際的な international

kokuseki 国籍 nationality

kōkyō no 公共の public

kome 米(穀物) rice (uncooked grains)

komichi 小道 alley, lane

kōmon 肛門 anus

komugiko 小麦粉 flour

konagona ni kowareta 粉々に壊れた broken, shattered

konagona ni suru 粉々にする to shatter

konban 今晩 tonight

konchū 昆虫 insect

kone コネ contact, connection

kongansuru 懇願する to plead

kongōshita 混合した mixed

kon'nan na 困難な hard (difficult)

kon'nan 困難 trouble, difficulty

kon'nichi de wa 今日では nowadays

kon'nichiwa こんにちは hello, hi

kono この this (adjective)

konomanai 好まない to dislike

konomi ni urusai 好みにうるさい fussy

konomu 好む to prefer

kononde 好んで fond of

konpyūtā コンピューター computer

konpōbako 梱包箱 crate

konranshita 混乱した confused

konro コンロ stove

kontei 根底 bottom (base)

konwakuseru 困惑させる to confuse

kon'yakuchū no 婚約中の engaged (to be married)

kon'yakusha 婚約者 fiancé, fiancée

konzatsushita 混雑した crowded

koppu コップ cup

kopī コピー photocopy

kopīsuru コピーする to photocopy

korera no これらの these (adjective)

koriandā コリアンダー(香草) cilantro, coriander

kōri 氷 ice

kōritsuku 凍りつく to freeze

korobu 転ぶ to fall over

korosu 殺す to kill, to murder

kōryosuru 考慮する to consider (to think over)

kōsaisuru 交際する to associate

kosame 小雨 shower (of rain)

kōsaten 交差点 intersection

kosei 個性 personality

kōshi 講師(大学の) lecturer (at university)

koshikake 腰掛 stool

kōshiki no 公式の official, formal

kōshinryō 香辛料 spices

koshōsuru 故障する to break down (car, machine)

kōsui 香水 perfume

kotai no 固体の solid

kōtta 凍った frozen

koteisareta 固定された fixed, won't move

koto こと (intangible) thing, matter

kōto コート coat, overcoat

kotowaru 断る to decline (refuse)

kottōhin 骨董品 antiques

kōtsū 交通 traffic

kōun 幸運 lucky

kōun o inoru 幸運を祈る good luck!

kōun nimo 幸運にも fortunately

kowagatte 恐がって afraid

kowareta 壊れた broken, does not work, spoiled

koya 小屋 hut, shack

koyū no 固有の indigenous, peculiar

kozeni 小銭 small change

kōzui 洪水 flood

kozutsumi 小包 package, parcel

kubi 首 neck

kubikazari 首飾り necklace

kuchi 口 mouth

kuchibiru 唇 lips

kuchihige 口ひげ moustache

kudaketa 砕けた cracked

kudamono 果物 fruit

kūfuku no 空腹の hungry

kugatsu 九月 September

kugi 釘 nail (spike)

kujō 苦情 complaint

kūkan 空間 room, space

kūki 空気 air

kukkī クッキー cookie

kūkō 空港 airport

kumiawaseru 組み合わせる to assemble, to put together

kumotta 曇った cloudy

kuni 国 nation, country

kuni no 国の national

kunren 訓練 training

kurai 暗い dark

kurakkā クラッカー cracker

kurasu クラス class

kurikaesu 繰り返す to repeat

kuroi 黒い black

kurokoshō 黒胡椒 pepper, black

kuromame 黒豆 black beans

kuru 来る to come
kurubushi くるぶし ankle
kuruma ni noseru 車に乗せる (人を) to pick up (someone)
kurushimi 苦しみ suffering
kurushimu 苦しむ to suffer
kurutta 狂った crazy
kusa 草 grass
kusai 臭い smelly
kusatta 腐った rotten, spoiled
kushami くしゃみ sneeze
kushi 櫛 comb
kūsō 空想 fancy, fantasy
kūsōsuru 空想する to daydream
kusuri 薬 drug (medicine)
kutōten 句読点 commas and periods
kutsu 靴 shoes
kutsurogu くつろぐ to relax
kutsushita 靴下 socks
kuwaete 加えて in addition
kyabetsu キャベツ cabbage
kyaku 客 guest, customer
kyodai na 巨大な huge
kyoka 許可 permit, license
kyokasuru 許可する to let, to allow, to permit
kyokutan ni 極端に extremely
kyori 距離 distance
kyō 今日 today
kyōbai ni kakeru 競売にかける to auction
kyōdai きょうだい sibling, brothers
kyōdōkeieisha 共同経営者 partner (in business)
kyōhakusuru 脅迫する to threaten
kyōiku 教育 education
kyōikusuru 教育する to educate
kyōkai 教会 church
kyōkaisen 境界線 boundary, border
kyōki no 狂気の insane
kyōmi bukai 興味深い interesting
kyōsō 競争 competition
kyōsōaite 競争相手 rival
kyōsōsuru 競争する to compete
kyozetsu 拒絶 refusal
kyū 九 nine
kyū ni 急に suddenly
kyūji 給仕 waiter, waitress
kyūjitu 休日 day off
kyūjosuru 救助する to rescue
kyūjū 九十 ninety
kyūka 休暇 holiday (vacation)
kyūri キュウリ cucumber
kyūryō 給料 salary

ma ni awase no 間に合わせの makeshift

matchi マッチ matches
machi 町 town
machigaerareta 間違えられた mistaken
machigai 間違い error
machigatta 間違った wrong (mistaken)
mada まだ still, even now
madadesu まだです not yet
mada~nai まだ~ない not yet
~made ~まで until
~mae ni ~までに by (deadline)
mae ni 前に before, in the past
maebaraisuru 前払いする to pay in advance
maemotte 前もって earlier, beforehand
magaru 曲がる to turn, to make a turn
magirawashii 紛らわしい confusing
mago 孫 grandchild
magomusuko 孫息子 grandson
magomusume 孫娘 granddaughter
mahishita 麻痺した numb
maikurobasu マイクロバス minibus
mainichi no 毎日の daily
maishū no 毎週の weekly
mājan 麻雀 mahjong
majime na まじめな serious (not funny)
makeru 負ける to lose, to be defeated
makura 枕 pillow
mame 豆 bean
mamoru 守る to guard, to protect
mangō マンゴー mango
manzokusaseru 満足させる to satisfy
manzokushita 満足した pleased, satisfied
mare ni まれに occasionally
Marēshia マレーシア Malaysia
marui 丸い round (shape)
massāji マッサージ massage
massugu mae ni 真っ直ぐ前に straight ahead
massugu na 真っ直ぐな straight (not crooked)
masuku マスク mask
maton マトン mutton
matsu 待つ to wait for
matsuri 祭り festival
matto マット mat
mattoresu マットレス mattress
mausu マウス(コンピューター) mouse (of computer)
mayaku 麻薬 drug, narcotic
mayonaka 真夜中 midnight

mayotta 迷った(道に) lost (can't find way)
mayuge 眉毛 eyebrow
mazaru 混ざる to mix
mazushii 貧しい poor
me 目 eye
megami 女神 goddess
megane めがね eyeglasses, spectacles
me ga sameru 目が覚める wake up
mei 姪 niece
meirei 命令 command, order
meiwaku 迷惑 bother, nuisance
meiwaku mēru 迷惑メール (= **supamu mēru** スパムメール) e-mail spam, junk mail
meiwakusuru 迷惑する to be annoyed
memo メモ note (written)
men 綿 cotton
mendō na 面倒な troublesome
menkyo 免許 permit, license
menkyoshō 免許証(運転) license (for driving)
menrui 麺類 noodles
menyū メニュー menu
meron メロン melon
meshitsukai 召使 servant
mezameru 目覚める to wake up
mezurashii 珍しい rare (scarce)
mibōjin 未亡人 widow
miburi 身振り gesture
miburuisuru 身震いする to shiver
michi 道 road, street
michibiku 導く to lead, to guide
midori no 緑の green
migaku 磨く to brush, to polish
migigawa 右側 right-hand side
migoto na 見事な great, impressive
migurushii 見苦しい ugly
miharu 見張る to watch over, to guard
mihon 見本 sample
mijikai 短い brief, short
mikake 見かけ appearance, looks
mikata 見方 viewpoint
mimi 耳 ear
minami 南 south
minamoto 源 source
minato 港 harbor, port
miru 観る to watch (show, movie)
miru 見る to watch, to look, to see
miryokuaru 魅力ある attractive
mise 店 shop, store
miseijuku no 未成熟の unripe
miseru 見せる to show
mitasu 満たす to fill

mitomeru 認める to recognize
mitsukeru 見つける to find
mitsumoru 見積もる to estimate
mitsurin 密林 jungle
mitsuyunyūsuru 密輸入する to smuggle
mizu 水 water
mizugi 水着 swimming costume, swimsuit
mizusashi 水差し jug, pitcher
mizushibuki 水しぶき splash
mizutama no 水玉の spotted (pattern)
mizuumi 湖 lake
mochiageru 持ち上げる(物を) to pick up, to lift (something)
mochidasu 持ち出す(話題を) to bring up (topic)
mochigome もち米 glutinous rice, sticky rice
mochiron もちろん certainly!, of course
modoru 戻る to return, to go back
moetsukita 燃え尽きた burned down
mōfu 毛布 blanket
mōhitotsu no もうひとつの another
moji 文字 character (written)
mokugekisha 目撃者 witness
mokugekisuru 目撃する to witness
mokuhyō 目標 goal
mokusei no 木製の wooden
mokuteki 目的 purpose
mokutekichi 目的地 destination
mokuyōbi 木曜日 Thursday
~mo mata ～もまた as well, too, also
momo もも thigh
~mo~mo~nai ～も～も～ない neither ... nor
mōmoku 盲目 blindness
mon 門 gate
mondai 問題 matter, issue, problem
mondainai 問題ない no problem
monitā モニター(コンピューター) monitor (of computer)
mono 物 thing
moreguchi 漏れ口 leak
mori 森 forest
moshi もし if
mōshikomu 申し込む to apply
moshimoshi もしもし hello (on phone)
mosuku モスク mosque
mōtā モーター motor, engine
moto ni shita 基にした based on
motomeru 求める to seek
mottekuru 持ってくる to bring

mottomo 最も most (superlative)
moyō 模様 pattern, design
moyōshi 催し show (live performance)
muchi no 無知の ignorant
mueki na 無益な useless
mugon no 無言の silent
muimi na kotoba 無意味な言葉 nonsense
mukashi 昔 old times, past
mukashi no 昔の past, former
mukatsukuyō na むかつくような disgusting
muku 剥く to peel
mune 胸 chest (breast)
mura 村 village
murasaki no 紫の purple (adjective)
muryō de 無料で free of charge
musareta 蒸された steamed
museigen ni 無制限に free of restraints
mushisuru 無視する to ignore
musubu 結ぶ to tie
musuko 息子 son
musume 娘 daughter
muzukashii 難しい difficult
Myanmā ミャンマー Myanmar
myōji 苗字 surname

na 名(姓に対する名) given name
nabe 鍋 pan
nagai 長い(距離、時間) long (length, time)
nagaisu 長いす couch, sofa
nagasa 長さ length
nageru 投げる to throw
naibu 内部 inside
naifu ナイフ knife
nairon ナイロン nylon
nakaniwa 中庭 courtyard
naku 泣く to cry, to weep
nama no 生の raw, uncooked, rare
namae 名前 name
namayake no 生焼けの rare (half- cooked)
nameraka na なめらかな smooth, glassy
nameru 舐める to lick
nami 波 wave (in sea)
namida 涙 tears
nan no tame ni 何のために what for
nana 七 seven
nanajū 七十 seventy
nani 何 what
naniga okita 何が起きた what happened
nanika 何か anything, something

nanimo~nai 何も～ない nothing
nanji 何時 what time
nanjūbaimo no 何十倍もの tens of, multiples of ten
naosu 直す to mend
narabu 並ぶ to line up
narasu 鳴らす(ベルを) to ring (bell)
narau 習う to learn
nareteiru 慣れている to be used to, to be accustomed
~nashi ni ～なしに without
nasu ナス aubergine, eggplant
natsu 夏 summer
naze なぜ why
nazenara なぜなら because
ne 根(植物) root (of plant)
nebanebashita ねばねばした sticky
nedan 値段 price
neko 猫 cat
nekutai ネクタイ necktie
nemaki 寝巻き pajamas
nemui 眠い sleepy
nemutte 眠って asleep
nenchō no 年長の elder
neru 寝る to go to bed, to sleep
netto ginkō ネット銀行 Internet bank, Web bank (Internet)
netto kafe ネットカフェ(= **intānetto kafe** インターネットカフェ) Internet café
nesoberu 寝そべる to lie down
nezumi ねずみ mouse, rat
~ni ～に on, at, in
~ni hanshite ～に反して contrary to
~ni kanshite ～に関して concerning, regarding
~nimo kakawarazu ～にもかかわらず in spite of
~ni tsuite ～について about (regarding)
~ni yoruto ～によると according to
~ni yotte ～によって(作者、芸術家) by (author, artist)
ni 二 two
nibai no 二倍の double
nitchū 日中 daytime
nichiyōbi 日曜日 Sunday
nigai 苦い bitter
nigatsu 二月 February
nigeru 逃げる to run away
nigiyaka na にぎやかな busy, lively (crowded), cheerful
Nihon 日本 Japan
Nihon(jin) no 日本(人)の Japanese
nijū 二十 twenty
nikki 日記 diary, journal
nikomi 煮込み stew

nikudango 肉団子 meatball
ninjin 人参 carrot
ninki no aru 人気のある popular
ninmeisuru 任命する to appoint
nin'niku にんにく garlic
niru 煮る to boil
niru 似る to resemble
nise no 偽の false (imitation)
ninshinsuru 妊娠する to get pregnant
nintai no aru 忍耐のある patient (calm)
nishi 西 west
niwa 庭 garden, yard
niwatori 鶏 chicken, rooster
~no ～の of, from
~no aida ～の間(時間、年) in (time, years), during
~no aida ni ～の間に among, while, during, between
~no atode ～のあとで after
~no kawari ni ～の代わりに instead of
~no kekkatoshite ～の結果として as a result of
~no mae ni ～の前に before
~no mae ni ～の前に in front of
~no mukai ni ～の向かいに across from
~no naka ni ～の中に inside of, into
~no saichū ～の最中に in the middle of
~no shita ni ～の下に under
~no soba ni ～のそばに near
~no soto ni ～の外に outside of
~no ue ni ～の上に on, above
~no ushiro ni ～の後ろに behind
~no yō na ～のような like, as, such
nō 脳 brain
noberu 述べる to express, to state, to mention
noboru 登る to go up, to climb
nodo のど throat
nodo no kawaita のどの渇いた thirsty
nokkusuru ノックする to knock
nokori 残り left, remaining, rest, remainder
nokorimono 残り物 remainder, leftover
nokoru 残る to stay, to remain
nomikomu 飲み込む to swallow
nomimono 飲み物 drink, beverage
nomu 飲む to drink
norimono 乗り物 vehicle
noriokureru 乗り遅れる(バス、飛行機) to miss (bus, flight)
noru 乗る(動物) to ride (animal)

noseru 乗せる(車) to give a lift
nōto ノート notebook
nozoite 除いて except
nozomi 望み desire, hope
nugu 脱ぐ(服) to take off (clothes)
nukumori ぬくもり warmth
nuno 布 cloth, fabric, textile
nureta 濡れた wet
nuu 縫う to sew
Nyūjīlando ニュージーランド New Zealand
nyūsu ニュース news
nyūyokusuru 入浴する to bathe, to take a bath

~o ～を object marking particle
o 尾 tail
oba おば aunt
obake お化け ghost
obieta おびえた scared
oboeteiru 覚えている to remember
oboreru おぼれる to drown
ōbun オーブン oven
ochiru 落ちる to fall
odayaka na 穏やかな calm, mild (not severe)
odeko おでこ forehead
odori 踊り dance
odoroku 驚く to be surprised
odorokubeki 驚くべき surprising
odoru 踊る to dance
ofisu オフィス office
ōfukukippu 往復切符 return ticket
ōgon 黄金 gold
oi 甥 nephew
oiharau 追い払う to chase away, to chase out
oikakeru 追いかける to chase
oishii おいしい delicious, tasty
oiteiku 置いていく leave behind on purpose
oji おじ uncle
oka 丘 hill
okashii おかしい funny
okidokei 置き時計 clock
ōkii 大きい big
ōkikunaru 大きくなる to grow larger
okiru 起きる to get up (from bed)
okiwasureru 置き忘れる to leave behind by accident, to lose, to mislay
okō お香 incense
okoru 起こる to happen, to occur
okoru 怒る to get angry
okosu 起こす to wake someone up

okotta 怒った cross, angry
oku 置く to place, to put
okureru 遅れる to be delayed
okurimono 贈り物 present (gift)
okurimono o suru 贈り物をする to present
okuru 送る to send
omedetō おめでとう congratulations!
omo ni 主に mainly
omosa 重さ weight
omocha おもちゃ toy
omoi 重い heavy
omoidasaseru 思い出させる to remind
omoshiroi おもしろい humorous
omou 思う to consider (to have an opinion), to think
onajitakasa no 同じ高さの of the same level (height)
onaji yō ni 同じように likewise
onaka ga ippai no お腹がいっぱいの full, eaten one's fill
ondo 温度 degrees (temperature)
onegaishimasu お願いします(何かを依頼する時) please (request for something)
oneuchi お値打ち good value
ongaku 音楽 music
oniai no お似合いの suitable, fitting, compatible
on'na no ko 女の子 girl
onrain gēmu オンラインゲーム online game
onryō no aru 音量のある loud
onsen 温泉 hot spring
orenji オレンジ orange (citrus)
orenjiiro no オレンジ色の orange-colored (adjective)
oreru 折れる(骨など) to be broken, snapped (of bones, etc.)
orimono 織り物 weaving
oroka na 愚かな stupid
oru 織る to weave
oru 折る to fold
osaeru 抑える to restrain
ōsama 王様 king
oshieru 教える to teach, to tell, to let know
oshikumo 惜しくも regrettably
osoi 遅い late, slow
osokutomo 遅くとも at the latest
osoraku おそらく perhaps, probably
osore 恐れ fear
osu 押す to press, to push
ōsugiru 多過ぎる too much
Ōsutoraria オーストラリア Australia
oto 音 sound, noise
ōtobai オートバイ motorcycle

otoko no hito 男の人 man
otoko no ko 男の子 boy
otōto 弟 younger brother
ototoi 一昨日 day before yesterday
otto 夫 husband
ōu 覆う to cover
owari 終わり end (finish)
owaru 終る to end
owatta 終った finished, gone, over
oyogu 泳ぐ to bathe, to swim
ōyoso おおよそ approximately, roughly
ōyoso no おおよその approximate, rough

pai パイ pie
painappuru パイナップル pineapple
pajama パジャマ pajamas, pyjamas
pan パン bread
panorama パノラマ panorama
pantsu パンツ(下着) shorts (underpants)
pantī パンティー panties
papaiya パパイヤ papaya
pāsento パーセント percent, percentage
pasupōto パスポート passport
pātī パーティー party (event)
pechikōto ペチコート slip
pēji 頁 page
pen ペン pen
penki ペンキ paint
penki o nuru ペンキを塗る(家、家具) paint, to (house, furniture)
petto ペット pet animal
pīnattsu ピーナッツ peanut
pinku no ピンクの pink (adjective)
pittarishita ぴったりした tight-fitting
poketto ポケット pocket
ponpu ポンプ pump
puragu プラグ plug (electric)
puramu プラム plum
purasuchikku プラスチック plastic
purotokoru プロトコル protocol
pūru プール swimming pool

raichi ライチ lychee
raimu ライム lime
rainen 来年 next year
raishū 来週 next week
raitā ライター lighter
rajio ラジオ radio
ramu ラム lamb
ranpu ランプ lamp
rasenjō no らせん状の spiral

rei 例 example
reigitadashii 礼儀正しい polite
reizōko 冷蔵庫 refrigerator
rekishi 歴史 history
remon レモン lemon (citrus)
remongurasu レモングラス(香草) lemongrass
reinen no 例年の annual
renketsusuru 連結する to connect together
renrakusuru 連絡する to contact, to get in touch with
renshūsuru 練習する to practise
repōtā レポーター reporter
reshipi レシピ recipe
ressun レッスン lesson
resutoran レストラン restaurant
retsu 列 queue, line
retsu o tsukuru 列をつくる to queue, to line up
ribon リボン ribbon
rieki 利益 profit
rikaisuru 理解する to understand
rikonsuru 離婚する to divorce
ringo りんご apple
rinjin 隣人 neighbor
rinkaku 輪郭 border, edge
rishi 利子 interest
riyū 理由 reason
rō ロウ wax
rojji ロッジ lodge, small hotel
rōka 廊下 corridor
roku 六 six
rokugasuru 録画する to videotape
rokugatsu 六月 June
rokujū 六十 sixty
rōpu ロープ rope
rōsoku ろうそく candle
ruiji 類似 resemble
ruijin'en 類人猿 ape
ruijishita 類似した similar
rusuban-denwa 留守番電話 answering machine, voicemail
ryō 量 amount
ryō 寮 dormitory
ryōgae 両替 exchange
ryōhō 両方 both
ryoken 旅券 passport
ryōkin 料金 fee
ryokō suru 旅行する to travel
ryokōan'nai 旅行案内 guidebook
ryokōsha 旅行者 traveler
ryōri 料理 cooking, cuisine, dish (particular food)
ryōrinin 料理人 cook (person)
ryōrisuru 料理する to cook
ryōshin 両親 parents
ryōshūsho 領収書 receipt
ryūchō na 流暢な fluent

sabaku 砂漠 desert (arid land)
sabishii 寂しい lonely
sāfin サーフィン surf
sagasu 探す to look for, to search for
sagi 詐欺 fraud
~sai ～歳 ~ years old
sai 差異 difference (discrepancy in figures)
saifu 財布 wallet, purse
saigo 最後 last
saigo ni 最後に finally
saigo no 最後の final, last
saijitsu 祭日 holiday (festival)
saikō no 最高の best
sain サイン signature
sainan 災難 disaster
saishō no 最小の smallest
saizu サイズ size
saka 坂 slope
sakaba 酒場 bar (serving drinks)
sakana 魚 fish
sakasama 逆さま upside down
sakasama no 逆さまの reversed, backwards
sake 酒 alcohol, liquor, sake
sakebu 叫ぶ to cry out, to shout, to yell
sakka 作家 writer
sakkā サッカー soccer
saku 柵 fence
sakuhin 作品 composition, writings
sakunen 昨年 last year
sakuya 昨夜 last night
samasu 冷ます to cool
samatageru 妨げる to disturb, to hinder, to prevent
same 鮫 shark
samui 寒い cold
san 三 three
sanchō 山頂 summit
sandaru サンダル sandals
sangatsu 三月 March
sangoshō さんご礁 coral reef
sanjū 三十 thirty
sankaku 三角 triangle
sankasuru 参加する to go along, to join in, to participate
sanpo ni iku 散歩に行く to go for a walk
sara 皿 dish, platter, plate
sara ni 更に also
sararīman サラリーマン businessperson
saru 猿 monkey
sashikomi 差込(電気) plug (electric)
sashō 査証 visa
sasou 誘う to invite (ask along)
sassoku 早速 immediately

satoru 悟る to realize, to be aware of

satō 砂糖 sugar

satōkibi サトウキビ sugarcane

sayōnara さようなら goodbye

sebone 背骨 spine

seibetsu 性別 sex, gender

seifu 政府 government

seiji 政治 politics

seijin no 成人の adult

seikaku 性格 character (personality)

seikaku na 正確な correct, exact

seikatsu 生活 life

seiketsu 清潔 cleanliness

seiki 世紀 century

seikō 成功 success

seikōsuru 成功する to succeed

seikyūsho 請求書 bill

seiri 生理 period (menstrual)

seiridansu 整理だんす chest (box)

seisansuru 生産する to produce

seishin no 精神の mental

seito 生徒 pupil, student

seitonsuru 整頓する to tidy up

seiyōjin 西洋人 westerner

seizōsuru 製造する to manufacture

sekai 世界 world

seki 咳 cough

sekikomu 咳きこむ to cough

sekinin 責任 responsibility

sekinin o motsu 責任を持つ to be responsible

sekken 石鹸 soap

semai 狭い narrow

semeru 責める to blame

sen 千 thousand

sen 栓(風呂) plug (bath)

sen 線 line (mark)

senaka 背中 back (part of body)

senkyo 選挙 election

senmonka 専門家 expert

senpūki 扇風機 fan (for cooling)

senro 線路 railroad, railway

sensei 先生 teacher

senshū 先週 last week

sensō 戦争 war

sentaku 選択 choice

sentensu センテンス sentence

sentō 戦闘 battle

senzai 洗剤 detergent

senzo 先祖 ancestor

serori セロリ celery

setsumeisuru 説明する to explain

setsuzokusuru 接続する to join together

sewa o suru 世話をする to take care of, to look after

shakkin 借金 debt

shako 車庫 garage (for parking)

shakushi 杓子 ladle, dipper

shanpū シャンプー shampoo

sharin 車輪 wheel

shasen 車線(高速道路) lane (of a highway)

shashin 写真 photograph

shashin o toru 写真を撮る to photograph

shatsu シャツ shirt

shawā シャワー shower (for washing)

shawā o abiru シャワーを浴びる to take a shower

shi 市 city

shi 死 death

shiai 試合 match, game

shiawase 幸せ happiness

shibashiba しばしば often

shibō no ōi 脂肪の多い fatty, greasy

shichakusuru 試着する(服) to try on (clothes)

shichi 七 seven

shichigatsu 七月 July

shichū シチュー stew

shīdī シーディー CD

shīdī romu シーディーロム CD-ROM

shidōsha 指導者 leader

shigatsu 四月 April

shigeki no nai 刺激のない dull, monotonous

shigoto 仕事 job, work, occupation

shigoto o suru 仕事をする to work

shiharai 支払い payment

shihei 紙幣 note (currency)

shiiru 強いる to force, to compel

shijisuru 指示する to instruct, to tell to do something

shijisuru 支持する to back up

shikaku 資格 qualification

shikakui 四角い square (shape)

shikashi しかし however

shikashinagara しかしながら however, nevertheless

shiken 試験 exam, test

shikin 資金 funds, funding

shikke no aru 湿気のある damp, humid

shikō 思考 thoughts

shikyū 子宮 uterus

shima 島 island

shima no aru 縞のある striped

shimai 姉妹 sister

shimaru 閉まる to close

shimatta 閉まった shut, closed

shimi しみ stain

shimin 市民 citizen

shinbun 新聞 newspaper

shinda 死んだ dead

shindai 寝台 bed

Shingapōru シンガポール Singapore

shingurui 寝具類 bedding, bedclothes

shinjiru 信じる to believe

shinju 真珠 pearl

shinkōsuru 信仰する to worship

shin'nen 信念 belief, faith

shinpaisuru 心配する to worry

shinraisuru 信頼する to trust

shinsei na 神聖な holy, sacred

shinseki 親戚 relatives

shinsen na 新鮮な fresh

shinshitsu 寝室 bedroom

shintō 神道 Shinto

shinu 死ぬ to die

shinwa 神話 myth

shinzō 心臓 heart

shio 塩 salt

shiokarai 塩辛い salty

shippai 失敗 failure

shippaisuru 失敗する to fail

shippo しっぽ tail

shiraseru 知らせる to inform

shiri 尻 bottom (buttocks)

shiriai 知り合い acquaintance

shiro 城 castle

shiro 白 white (noun)

shiru 知る to learn, to realize

shiryo no aru 思慮のある sensible

shisai 司祭 priest

shisan 資産 property, assets

shishoku o suru 試食をする to taste (sample)

shishū 刺繍 embroidery

shishunki no kodomo 思春期の子供(13〜19歳) teenager

shishū no 刺繍の embroidered

shison 子孫 descendant

~shitai 〜したい to want

~shitakoto ga aru 〜したことがある have done something

~shitemoyoi 〜してもよい can, may

shita 舌 tongue

shita e 下へ down, downward

shitagau 従う to obey

shitagi 下着 underwear

shītsu シーツ bedsheet, sheet

shitsubōsuru 失望する to be disappointed

shitsugyōchū no 失業中の unemployed

shitsumon 質問 question

shitsurei 失礼 impoliteness

shitsurei na 失礼な rude, impolite

shitteiru 知っている to know

shitto 嫉妬 jealousy
shittobukai 嫉妬深い jealous
~shiyō ～しよう(提案) let's (suggestion)
shiyōdekiru 使用できる available
shizen 自然 nature
shizen no 自然の natural
shizuka na 静かな still, quiet
shō ショー show (live performance)
shōbai 商売 trade, business
shōchishita 承知した OK, all right!
shōdō o karitateru 衝動を駆り立てる urge, to push for
shōga 生姜 ginger
shōgai 障害 handicap, obstacle
shōgo 正午 midday, noon
shohōsen 処方箋 prescription
shōjiki na 正直な honest
shojisuru 所持する to own
shōkaisuru 紹介する to introduce someone
shokki o arau 食器を洗う wash the dishes
shokkidana 食器棚 cupboard
shōko 証拠 proof, evidence
shokubutsu 植物 plant
shokugyō 職業 occupation, profession
shokuji 食事 meal
shokuniku 食肉 meat
shomei 署名 signature
shōmei 照明 lighting
shōmeisuru 証明する to prove
shomeisuru 署名する to sign
shōrai 将来 in future
shōronbun 小論文 essay
shorui 書類 document
shōsan 賞賛 praise
shōsansuru 賞賛する admire, praise
shōsetsu 小説 novel
shōsho 証書 certificate
shōshō omachikudasai 少々お待ちください Please wait for a moment
shōtaisuru 招待する to invite (formally)
shotei no 所定の set
shōtotsu 衝突 collision
shōtotsusuru 衝突する to collide
shōtsu ショーツ shorts (short trousers)
shōyu しょう油 soy sauce
shoyūbutsu 所有物 belongings
shoyūken 所有権 the right of ownership
shoyūsuru 所有する to have, to own, to possess
shozokusuru 所属する to belong to

shū 週 week
shūchūsuru 集中する to concentrate
shuhin 主賓 guest of honor
shujin 主人 host
shūkan 習慣 custom, practice
shūkinsuru 集金する to collect money
shukōgei 手工芸 handcraft
shukuhakujo 宿泊所 accommodation
shukuhakushisetsu 宿泊施設 accommodations, facilities
shūyō 宗教 religion
shūhen ni 周辺に around (surrounding)
shūmatsu 週末 weekend
shumi 趣味 hobby
shunkan 瞬間 moment (instant)
shuppansuru 出版する to publish
shuppatsu 出発 departure
shuppatsusuru 出発する to leave, to depart
shūrisuru 修理する to fix (repair)
shurui 種類 kind, type, sort
shushō 首相 prime minister
shussekisuru 出席する to attend
shuyō na 主要な main, most important
sō 層 layer
sobo 祖母 grandmother
sōchō ni 早朝に early in the morning
sōdai na 壮大な grand, great
sōdansuru 相談する to consult, to talk over with
sodateru 育てる(子供) to raise, to bring up (child)
sodatsu 育つ(子供) to grow up (child)
sofā ソファー couch, sofa
sofu 祖父 grandfather
sofubo 祖父母 grandparents
sōkan 壮観 spectacles
soketto ソケット(電気の) socket (electric)
sokkuri no そっくりの exactly like
soko de そこで there
sokonau 損なう to damage
soko ni そこに there
songai 損害 damage
sonkei 尊敬 respect
sonkeisuru 尊敬する to respect
sono go その後 afterwards, later, after that
sono hito その人 that person
sono kekka その結果 therefore
sono ta no その他の the other

sono tōri その通り exactly! just so!
sono ue その上 besides, further, additional
sono yō ni そのように like that
sonzaisuru 存在する to exist
sora 空 sky
sore それ that one/matter
soredewa mata それではまた see you later!
sore nimo kakawarazu それにもかかわらず nevertheless
soreyue それゆえ therefore
soru 剃る to shave
sōshiki 葬式 funeral
sōshokuhin 装飾品 ornament
sosogu 注ぐ to pour
sōsu ソース sauce
sotogawa 外側 outside
sōzōsuru 想像する to imagine
su 酢 vinegar
su 巣 nest
subarashii すばらしい wonderful
~subeki de aru ～すべきである ought to, should
subesubeshita すべすべした smooth (of surfaces), glossy
subete 全て all
sugu ni すぐに in a moment, right now, immediately
sugusoba no すぐそばの close to, nearby
suitchi スイッチ switch
suijun 水準 level (standard)
suika スイカ watermelon
suisokusuru 推測する to guess
suiyōbi 水曜日 Wednesday
sūji 数字 figure, number
sukkari すっかり completely
sukoshi 少し bit (slightly)
sukunai 少ない few, little (not much)
sukunakunaru 少なくなる to lessen, to reduce
sukunakutomo 少なくとも at least
sukurīn スクリーン(コンピューター) screen (of computer)
sukāto スカート skirt
sumasu 済ます to finish off
sumāto na スマートな slender
sumi 墨 ink
sumimasen すみません excuse me!
sumu 住む to live (stay in a place)
suna 砂 sand
sumu 済む to be completed
sūpā スーパー supermarket
supamu mēru スパムメール(= **meiwaku mēru** 迷惑メール) spam e-mail, spam mail, e-mail spam

supai wea スパイウェア spyware
supīchi スピーチ speech
supīchi o suru スピーチをする to make a speech
supīdo スピード speed
suponji スポンジ sponge
supōtsu スポーツ sports
suppai すっぱい sour
supuringu スプリング spring (metal part)
supurē スプレー spray
sūpu スープ broth, soup
supūn スプーン spoon
suri すり pickpocket
surimu スリム slim
surippa スリッパ slippers
surippu スリップ slip
suru する to do, to perform an action, to play
suru する to pickpocket
surudoi 鋭い sharp
~surukoto ga dekiru ～することができる to be able to do...
~suru tame ni ～するために in order to do...
~suru toki ～する時 when doing
~suru tsumori ～するつもり to intend to do...
~suru yoyū ga aru ～する余裕がある to afford to do...
susumeru 勧める to recommend
sutaffu スタッフ staff
sutanpu スタンプ stamp (ink)
suteki na 素敵な lovely, nice
suteru 捨てる to throw away, to throw out
sutoraiki o suru ストライキをする to go on strike
sūtsu スーツ business suit
sūtsukēsu スーツケース suitcase
suu 吸う to suck, to smoke
suwaru 座る to sit down, to sit
suzushii 涼しい cool

tabako タバコ cigarette
tabako o suu タバコをすう to smoke (tobacco)
tabemono 食べ物 food
taberu 食べる to eat
tabi 旅 trip, journey
tabun 多分 perhaps
tachiagaru 立ち上がる to stand up
tadashii 正しい right, correct
Tai タイ Thailand
taido 態度 attitude
taifū 台風 typhoon
taiju ga heru 体重が減る to lose weight
taijū ga fueru 体重が増える to gain weight

taikakusen no 対角線の diagonal
taikōsha 対抗者 opponent
taikutsu na 退屈な dull (boring)
taiman na 怠慢な lazy
taipusuru タイプする to type
taira na 平らな level, plain (even, flat)
tairiku 大陸 continent
taishi 大使 ambassador
taishikan 大使館 embassy
taishitakotonai 大したことない minor (not important)
taisho 対処 dealing
taiyō 太陽 sun
taizai 滞在 visit
takai 高い high, tall
takameru 高める to lift, to raise
takarakuji 宝くじ lottery
takasa 高さ height
taki 滝 waterfall
takusan no たくさんの lots of, many, much
takushī タクシー taxi
takuwae 蓄え store, reserve
tamago 卵 egg
tamanegi 玉葱 onion
tamerau ためらう to hold back, to hesitate
tamesu 試す to test
tamotsu 保つ to keep, to save
tanbo 田んぼ rice fields
tane 種 seed
tani 谷 valley
tanjikan 短時間 short time, a moment
tanjōbi 誕生日 birthday, date of birth
tanmatsu 端末 computer terminal
tan ni 単に merely
tanomu 頼む to request
tanoshimeru 楽しめる enjoyable
tanoshimi 楽しみ pleasure, delight
tanoshimu 楽しむ to enjoy oneself, to have fun
tanpan 短パン shorts
tansha 単車 motorcycle
taoru タオル towel
tashika ni 確かに indeed, surely
tashikameru 確かめる to check, to verify
tasseisuru 達成する to attain, to reach
tasukeru 助ける to assist, to help
tasukete 助けて help!
tatemono 建物 building
tateru 建てる to build
tatoeba 例えば such as, for example

tatsu 立つ to stand
tatta hitotsuno たった一つの sole, only
tatta ima たった今 just now
tatta no たったの just, only
tatta~dake たった～だけ only
tazuneru 尋ねる to ask about, to enquire
tazuneru 訪ねる to go around, to visit, to stop by, to pay a visit
te 手 hand
tēburukurosu テーブルクロス tablecloth
tēburumatto テーブルマット tablemat
tegami 手紙 letter
tegoro na 手ごろな（値段） reasonable (price)
tehai 手配 arrangements, planning
teian 提案 suggestion
teiansuru 提案する to suggest
teido 程度 degree, level
teikyō 提供 offering
teikyōsuru 提供する to offer, to suggest
teiryūjo 停留所（バス、電車） stop (bus, train)
teiseisuru 訂正する to correct
teishutsu 提出 handing out, submission
teki 敵 enemy
tekisetsu na 適切な appropriate, fitting, suitable
tekubi 手首 wrist
ten 点 point, dot
tenimotsu 手荷物 baggage, luggage
ten'in 店員 sales assistant, shopkeeper
tenisu テニス tennis
tenji 展示 display
tenjisuru 展示する to display
tenjō 天井 ceiling
tenkeiteki na 典型的な typical
tenkensuru 点検する to inspect
tenki 天気 weather
tenpi 天火 oven
tēpu no rokuon テープの録音 tape recording
terebi テレビ TV, television
tesūryō 手数料 fee
tetsu no 鉄の iron
tīshatsu ティーシャツ teeshirt
~to ～と and, with
~to hanarete ～と離れて apart from
~to hikakusuru ～と比較する compared with
~to omowareru ～と思われる to seem
~to onaji ～と同じ same as

~to~ryōhō 〜と〜両方 both ... and

to 戸 door

tō 党（政治的な） party (political)

tō 塔 tower

toboshii 乏しい scarce

tobu 跳ぶ to jump

tōchaku 到着 arrival

tōchakusuru 到着する to arrive, to reach, to get to

tochi 土地 land

tochū de 途中で on the way

tōfu 豆腐 beancurd, tofu

tōgarashi 唐辛子 chilli pepper

tōgarashisōsu 唐辛子ソース chilli sauce

toho de 徒歩で on foot

tōhyōsuru 投票する to vote

tōi 遠い far

toire トイレ toilet, restroom

tojiru 閉じる to shut

tokidoki 時々 from time to time, sometimes

tokoro de ところで by the way

tokoya 床屋 barber

toku ni 特に particularly, especially

tokubetsu na 特別な special

tokubetsu no 特別の extra

tokuchō 特徴 characteristics

tokei 時計 clock, watch

tomato トマト tomato

tomaru 止まる to stop (by itself)

tomeru 止める to stop (something)

tomo ni 共に together

tomodachi 友達 friend

tomonau 伴う to involve, to be accompanied by

tōmorokoshi トウモロコシ corn, grain

tonari ni 隣に next to

tora トラ tiger

toraeru 捕らえる to capture

torakku トラック truck

toranpu トランプ cards

tori 鳥 bird

torikesu 取り消す to cancel

tōrikosu 通り越す to pass, to go past

toriniku 鶏肉 poultry

torinozoku 取り除く to remove

tōrinukete 通り抜けて through, past

tōrokusuru 登録する to register

toshi 都市 city

toshi 年 age, year

toshi no 都市の urban

toshitotta 年取った（人） old (of persons)

toshokan 図書館 library

totemo とても very

totonoeru 整える to arrange

totte 取っ手 handle

tōtte 通って via

tsugi ni 次に next, secondly

tsugi no 次の next (in line, sequence), the following

tsuiyasu 費やす to spend

tsūjō no 通常の regular, normal

tsūka 通貨 currency

tsukaeru 仕える to serve

tsukaifurushita 使い古した（服、機械） worn out (clothes, machine)

tsukamaeru 捕まえる to catch

tsukamu つかむ to hold, to grasp

tsukarekitta 疲れ切った burned down, exhausted

tsukareta 疲れた weary, worn out, tired

tsukau 使う to use

tsukeru つける to switch on, to turn (something) on

tsuki 月 moon

tsukitōshita 突き通した pierced, penetrated

tsukue 机 table

tsukue o naraberu 机を並べる to lay the table

tsukuru 作る to create, to make

tsumaranai つまらない boring

tsumasaki つま先 toe

tsume 爪（手、足） nail (finger, toe)

tsumikomu 積み込む to load up

tsumini 積み荷 load

tsureai つれあい partner (spouse)

tsuru 釣る to fish

tsute つて contact, connection

tsutsumi 包み pack, wrap

tsūyakusha 通訳者 interpreter

tsuyoi 強い strong

tsuzuru 綴る to spell

uchiakeru 打ち明ける to admit, to confess

uchikatsu 打ち勝つ to overcome

uchimakasu 打ち負かす to beat (to defeat)

uchiwa うちわ fan (hand-held, for cooling)

uchiyoseru nami 打ち寄せる波 surf

ude 腕 arm

udedokei 腕時計 watch (wristwatch)

udewa 腕輪 bracelet

ue no 上の top

ue no hō e 上のほうへ up, upward

ueru 植える to plant

ugoki 動き movement, motion

ugoku 動く to move

uketoru 受け取る to accept, to get, to receive

uma 馬 horse

umareru 生まれる to be born

umi 海 ocean, sea

umigame 海ガメ sea turtle

umu 産む to give birth

un 運 luck

un'eisuru 運営する to manage, to run

untensuru 運転する（車） to drive (a car)

uragaesu 裏返す over, to turn over

urareta 売られた sold

urayamashii 羨ましい envious

ureshiku omou うれしく思う to be glad

urikire 売り切れ sold out

urimono 売りもの for sale

uru 売る to sell

urusai うるさい noisy

ushi 牛 cow

ushinatta 失った lost (missing)

ushiro 後ろ back, rear, tail

ushiromuki ni 後ろ向きに backward

uso o tsuku 嘘をつく to lie, to tell a falsehood

uta 歌 song

utagau 疑う to doubt, to suspect

utau 歌う to sing

utsu 撃つ to shoot

utsu 打つ to strike, to hit

utsukushii 美しい beautiful

utsushi 写し copy

uttaeru 訴える to accuse, to sue

uwabaki 上履き slippers

wadai 話題 topic

wai-fai ワイ・ファイ (= **musen-ran** 無線LAN） Wi-Fi, wireless LAN

wakai 若い young

wakamono 若者 youth (young person)

wakareta 分かれた separate

wakasa 若さ youth (state of being young)

wakemae 分け前 portion, share

wakeru 分ける to separate

wakimizu 湧き水 spring (of water)

wakkusu ワックス wax

wakuwakusaseru わくわくさせる exciting

wakuwakushita わくわくした excited

wan 湾 bay

wanpaku na 腕白な naughty

warau 笑う to laugh, to smile

wareware no 我々の our
waribiki 割引 discount
warui 悪い bad, wicked, wrong (morally)
warukunatte 悪くなって off (gone bad)
wasureru 忘れる to forget
watashi no 私の my, mine
watashi 私 I, me
watasu 渡す to hand over
wazuka わずか bit (part)
wazuka ni わずかに slightly
wazuka no わずかの a little, slight
weburogu ウェブログ(= **burogu** ブログ) weblog, blog
webusaito ウェブサイト website

yaburu 破る to tear, to rip
yagi 山羊 goat
yakedo 火傷 burn (injury)
yakeru 焼ける to burn
yakigushi 焼き串 skewer
yakkyoku 薬局 drugstore, pharmacy
yaku 焼く to bake, to fry, to grill
yaku 約 about (approximately)
yakudatsu 役立つ to be useful
yakusokusuru 約束する to promise
yakuwari 役割 role
yama 山 mountain
yameru やめる to stop, to cease, to quit
yamete やめて don't! stop it!
yane 屋根 roof
yasai 野菜 vegetable
yasashii やさしい gentle, kind
yaseta やせた(人) thin (of persons)
yashinau 養う to grow, to cultivate
yasui 安い cheap
yasumu 休む to rest, to relax
yasuuri 安売り sale (reduced prices)
yasuurisuru 安売りする to bargain
yatō 雇う to hire
yawarakai やわらかい soft
yoake 夜明け dawn
yōbi 曜日 day of the week
yobidasu 呼び出す to call, to summon
yobōsesshu 予防接種 vaccination
yobun no 余分の extra
yōgosuru 擁護する defend
yoi 良い well, good
yōisuru 用意する to arrange, to prepare
yoitabi o 良い旅を bon voyage!

yokinsuru 預金する to deposit (put money in the bank)
yokisuru 予期する to expect
yokodaoshi ni suru 横倒しにする to lay sideways
yoko 横 side
yokogiru 横切る to cross, to go over
yokogitte 横切って across
yōkoso ようこそ welcome!
yoku dekimashita よくできました well done!
yokuaru よくある common, frequent
yoku hi no tōtta よく火の通った well-cooked, well-done
yokushitsu 浴室 bathroom
yoku~shitamonoda よく〜したものだ used to do something
yōkyūsuru 要求する to demand
yōmō 羊毛 wool
yomu 読む to read
yon 四 four
yonjū 四十 forty
yopparau 酔っ払う to get drunk
~yori 〜より than
yori warui より悪い worse
yori yoi よりよい better
yoroppa ヨーロッパ Europe
yoru 夜 night
yoru ni 夜に at night
yoru no 夜の of the night
yoruosoku 夜遅く late at night
yōsai 要塞 fortress
yōshi 用紙 form (to fill out)
yosoou 装う to pretend
yotei 予定 program, schedule, plan
yowai 弱い weak
yoyaku 予約 reservation, booking
yoyakusuru 予約する to reserve (ask for in advance)
yubi 指 finger
yūbin 郵便 post, mail
yūbinbutsu 郵便物 mail, post
yūbinkyoku 郵便局 post office
yubiwa 指輪 ring (jewelry)
yūfuku na 裕福な well off, wealthy
yūga na 優雅な elegant
yūgata 夕方 evening
yūguredoki 夕暮れ時 dusk
yuiitsu no 唯一の single (only one)
yuka 床 floor
yukai na 愉快な amusing, comical
yuki 雪 snow
yuki ga furu 雪が降る to snow
yukkuri ゆっくり slowly
yūkō na 有効な valid, effective

yukuefumei 行方不明 missing (lost person)
yūkyū no 有給の paid
yume 夢 dream
yume o miru 夢を見る to dream
yūmei na 有名な famous
yūnō na 有能な capable
yunyū 輸入 to import
yunyūsuru 輸入する to import
yuri ugokasu 揺り動かす to swing
yurui ゆるい loose, not tight
yurusu 許す to forgive
yūshoku 夕食 dinner, evening meal
yūshōsha 優勝者 champion
yūshū na 優秀な excellent
yushutsu 輸出 export
yushutsusuru 輸出する to export
yūsō 郵送 mailing
yūzai 有罪 guilty (of a crime)

zaiakukan o kanjiru 罪悪感を感じる to feel guilty
zairyō 材料 material, ingredient
zankoku na 残酷な cruel
zan'nen 残念 what a shame!
zan'nen da 残念だ what a pity!
zan'nen nagara 残念ながら unfortunately
zasshi 雑誌 magazine
zenbu de 全部で altogether, in total
zenkei 全景 panorama
zenmen 前面 front
zenpō ni 前方に forward, in front
zenshinsuru 前進する to advance, to go forward
zenshu no 全種の every kind of
zentaikara mite 全体から見て on the whole
zentai no 全体の entire
zero 零 zero
zō 象 elephant
zō 像 statue
zōge 象牙 ivory
zōka 増加 rise, increase
zubon ズボン pants, trousers
zuga 図画 drawing
zuibun ずいぶん quite (very)
zuii no 随意の optional
zungurishita ずんぐりした stout, chubby

English–Japanese

able to ~surukoto ga dekiru ～することができる

about (approximately) yaku 約, ōyoso おおよそ

about (regarding) ~ni tsuite ～について

above ~yori ue ni ～より上に

abroad gaikoku de 外国で

absent kesseki 欠席

accept, to uketoru 受け取る

accident jiko 事故

accidentally gūzen ni 偶然に

accommodation shukuhakujo 宿泊所

accompany, to dōhansuru 同伴する

according to ~ni yori ～により

accuse, to uttaeru 訴える

ache itami 痛み

ache, to itamu 痛む

acquaintance shiriai 知り合い

acquainted, to be ~o shitteiru ～を知っている

across yokogitte 横切って

across from ~no mukai ni ～の向かいに

act, to furumau 振る舞う

action kōdō 行動

activity katsudō 活動

actually jissai ni 実際に

add, to kuwaete 加えて

address jūsho 住所

admire, to shōsansuru 賞賛する

admit, to uchiakeru 打ち明ける

adult seijin no 成人の

advance, to (go forward) zenshinsuru 前進する

advance money (deposit) maebaraisuru 前払いする

advice jogen 助言

advise, to jogensuru 助言する

affect, to eikyō o ataeru 影響を与える

affection aijō 愛情

afford, to ~suru yoyū ga aru ～する余裕がある

afraid kowagatte 恐がって

after ~no ato de ～のあとで

afternoon (3 pm to dusk) gogo 午後(午後三時から夕暮れ)

afternoon (midday) shōgo 正午

afterwards (then) sonogo その後

again futatabi 再び

age toshi 年

ago mae ni 前に

agree, to dōisuru 同意する

agree to do something, to ~surukoto o shōdakusuru ～することを承諾する

agreed! shōchishita 承知した

agreement dōi 同意

air kūki 空気

air conditioning eakon エアコン

airmail kōkūbin 航空便

airplane hikōki 飛行機

airport kūkō 空港

a little wazuka no わずかの

a lot takusan たくさん

alcohol (liquor) sake 酒

alike dōyō ni 同様に

alive ikite 生きて

all subete 全て

alley komichi 小道

allow, to kyokasuru 許可する

allowed to ~surukoto o kyokasareru ～することを許可される

almost hotondo ほとんど

alone hitori de ひとりで

already sude ni すでに

also sara ni 更に

altogether zenbu de 全部で

although keredomo けれども

always itsumo いつも

ambassador taishi 大使

ambience fun'iki 雰囲気

America amerika アメリカ

American amerika(jin) no アメリカ(人)の

among ~no naka ni ～の中に

amount ryō 量

ancestor senzo 先祖

ancient kodai no 古代の

and ~to ～と, ~oyobi~ ～及び～

anger ikari 怒かり

angry okkotta 怒った

animal dōbutsu 動物

ankle kurubushi くるぶし

annoyed meiwakushita 迷惑した

another (different) betsu no 別の

another (same again) mōhitotsu no もうひとつの

annual reinen no 例年の

answer (spoken) henji 返事

answer (written) henshin 返信

answer, to (spoken) henji o suru 返事をする

answer, to (written) henshinsuru 返信する

answer the phone, to denwa ni deru 電話にでる

answering machine rusuban-denwa 留守番電話

antiques kottōhin 骨董品

anus kōmon 肛門

anybody, anyone dareka だれか

anything nanika 何か

anywhere dokoka ni どこかに

ape ruijin'en 類人猿

apart hanarete 離れて

apartment apāto アパート

apologize, to ayamaru 謝る

apparently dōyara~rashii どうやら～らしい

appear, to arawareru 現れる

appearance mikake 見かけ

apple ringo りんご

appliance denki-kiki 電気機器

apply, to mōshikomu 申し込む

appointment ninmei 任命

approach, to (in space and time) chikazuku 近づく(空間、時間)

appropriate tekisetsu na 適切な

approximately ōyoso おおよそ

April shigatsu 四月

architecture kenchiku 建築

area chiiki 地域

argue, to gironsuru 議論する

argument giron 議論

arm ude 腕, buki 武器

armchair hijikakeisu ひじ掛け椅子

army guntai 軍隊

around (approximately) ōyoso おおよそ

around (nearby) chikaku de 近くで

around (surrounding) shūhen ni 周辺に

arrange, to totonoeru 整える, yōisuru 用意する

arrangements (planning) tehai 手配

arrival tōchaku 到着

arrive, to tōchakusuru 到着する

art geijutsu 芸術

article (in newspaper) kiji 記事

artificial jinkō no 人工の

artist geijutsuka 芸術家

as well ~mo mata ～もまた

ashamed hajite 恥じて

Asia ajia アジア

ask about, to tazuneru 尋ねる

ask for, to iraisuru 依頼する

asleep nemutte 眠って

assemble, to (gather) atsumeru 集める

assemble, to (assemble) kumiawaseru 組み合わせる

assist, to tasukeru 助ける

assistance enjo 援助

at ~de ～で, ~ni ～に

at home ie de 家で

at night yoru ni 夜に

at once sugu ni すぐに

atmosphere fun'iki 雰囲気

attack (in war) kōgeki 攻撃(戦争)

attack (with words) hinan 非難 (言葉で)

attain, to tasseisuru 達成する

attempt kokoromi 試み

attempt, to kokoromiru 試みる

attend, to shussekisuru 出席する

at the latest osokutomo 遅くとも

attitude taido 態度

attractive miryokuaru 魅力ある

aubergine nasu ナス

auction, to kyōbai ni kakeru 競売にかける

auctioned off kyōbai ni kaker-areta 競売にかけられた

August hachigatsu 八月

aunt oba おば

Australia ōsutoraria オーストラリア

authority (person in charge) ken'i 権威

authority (power) kenryokusha 権力者

automobile jidōsha 自動車

autumn aki 秋

available shiyōdekiru 使用できる

available, to make kanō ni suru 可能にする

average (numbers) heikin 平均

average (so-so, just okay) hiton-ami 人並み

awake me ga samete 目が覚めて

awake, to sameru 覚める

awaken, to okosu 起こす

aware kizuiteiru 気づいている

aware: to be aware of satoru 悟る

awareness jikaku 自覚

baby akachan 赤ちゃん

back (part of body) senaka 背中

back (rear) ushiro 後ろ

back, to go modoru 戻る

back up, to shijisuru 支持する

backward ushiromuki ni 後ろ向きに

bad warui 悪い

bad luck fuun 不運

bag kaban 鞄

baggage tenimotsu 手荷物

bake, to yaku 焼く

baked yakareta 焼かれた

bald hageta はげた

ball bōru ボール

ballpoint pen bōrupen ボールペン

banana banana バナナ

bandage hōtai 包帯

bank (finance) ginkō 銀行

bank (of river) dote 土手

banquet enkai 宴会

bar (blocking way) kōshi 格子

bar (serving drinks) bā バー, sakaba 酒場

barber tokoya 床屋

barely karōjite かろうじて

bargain yasuuri 安売り

barren fumō no 不毛の

base (foundation) kiso 基礎

based on ~o moto ni shita ～を基にした

basic kihon 基本

basis dodai 土台

basket kago かご

basketball basukettobōru バスケットボール

bath furo 風呂

bathe, to (swim) oyogu 泳ぐ

bathe: to take a bath nyūyokusuru 入浴する

bathrobe basurōbu バスローブ, yukata 浴衣

bathroom yokushitsu 浴室

battle sentō 戦闘

bay wan 湾

be, to (exist) sonzaisuru 存在する

be able to ~dekiru ～できる

beach bīchi ビーチ, hamabe 浜辺

bean mame 豆

beancurd tōfu 豆腐

beard agohige あごひげ

beat, to (to defeat) uchimakasu 打ち負かす

beat, to (to strike) hageshiku utsu 激しく打つ

beautiful kirei na きれいな, utsu-kushii 美しい

because nazenara なぜなら

become, to ~ni naru ～になる

become visible, to arawareru 現れる

bed beddo ベッド, shindai 寝台

bedroom shinshitsu 寝室

bedsheet shītsu シーツ

beef gyūniku 牛肉

beer bīru ビール

before (in front of) ~no mae ni ～の前に

before (in time) izen ni 以前に

begin, to hajimeru 始める

beginning hajime 始め

behave, to furumau 振る舞う

behind ~no ushiro ni ～の後ろに

belief (faith) shin'nen 信念

believe, to shinjiru 信じる

belly hara 腹

belongings shoyūbutsu 所有物

belong to, to shozokusuru 所属する

below (downstairs) kaika ni 階下に

belt beruto ベルト

beside ~no toko ni ～の横に

besides sonoue その上

best saikō no 最高の

best wishes gotakō o inorimasu ご多幸を祈ります

better yoriyoi よりよい

better (improve) genki ni naru 元気になる, yokunaru よくなる

between ~no aida ni ～の間に

bicycle jitensha 自転車

big ōkii 大きい

bill seikyūsho 請求書

billion jūoku 十億

bird tori 鳥

birth, to give umu 産む

birthday tanjōbi 誕生日

biscuit (cookie) bisuketto ビスケット, kukkī クッキー

biscuit (cracker) kurakkā クラッカー

bit (part) wazuka わずか

bit (slightly) sukoshi 少し

bite, to kamu 噛む

bitter nigai 苦い

black kuroi 黒い

black beans kuromame 黒豆

blame, to semeru 責める

bland onwa na 温和な

blanket mōfu 毛布

blind mōmoku no 盲目の

blood chi 血

blouse burausu ブラウス

blue aoi 青い

board, to (bus, train) jōshasuru 乗車する(バス、電車)

boat bōto ボート, kobune 小船

body karada 体

boil, to futtōsuru 沸騰する

boiled nita 煮た

bone hone 骨

book hon 本

border (between countries) kokkyō 国境

border (edge) rinkaku 輪郭

bored taikutsushita 退屈した

boring tsumaranai つまらない

born, to be umareru 生まれる

borrow, to kariru 借りる

boss jōshi 上司

both ryōhō 両方

both ... and ~to~ryōhō ～と～両方

bother, to jamasuru 邪魔する

bottle bin 瓶

bottom (base) kontē 根底

bottom (buttocks) shiri 尻

boundary kyōkaisen 境界線

bowl donburi どんぶり

box hako 箱

box (cardboard) danbōrubako 段ボール箱

boy otoko no ko 男の子

boyfriend kareshi 彼氏

bra burajā ブラジャー

bracelet udewa 腕輪

brain nō 脳

brain (mind) chiryoku 知力

brake burēki ブレーキ

brake, to burēki o kakeru ブレーキをかける

branch eda 枝

brave (daring) isamashii 勇ましい

bread pan パン

break, to konagona ni suru 粉々にする

break apart, to barabara ni suru ばらばらにする

break down, to (car, machine) koshōsuru 故障する

breakfast chōshoku 朝食

breakfast, to eat chōshoku o toru 朝食をとる

breasts mune 胸

bride hanayome 花嫁

bridegroom hanamuko 花婿

bridge hashi 橋

brief mijikai 短い

briefcase burīfukēsu ブリーフケース

briefs burīfu ブリーフ（下着）

bright akarui 明るい

bring, to mottekuru 持ってくる

bring up, to (children) sodateru 育てる（子供を）

bring up, to (topic) mochidasu 持ち出す（話題を）

broad (spacious) hiroi 広い

broadcast, to hōsōsuru 放送する

broken (does not work) kowareta 壊れた

broken (of bones, etc.) oreta 折れた（骨など）

broken (shattered) konagona ni kowareta 粉々に壊れた

broken off ~kara hazureta ~からはずれた

bronze dō 銅

broom hōki ほうき

broth sūpu スープ

brother (older) ani 兄

brother (younger) otōto 弟

brown chairoi 茶色い

bruise aza あざ

brush burashi ブラシ, hake はけ

brush, to migaku 磨く

bucket baketsu バケツ

Buddhism bukkyō 仏教

Buddhist bukkyōto 仏教徒

build, to tateru 建てる

building tatemono 建物

burn (injury) yakedo 火傷

burn, to yakeru 焼ける

burned down/out moetsukita 燃え尽きた, tsukarekitta 疲れ切った

bus basu バス

bus station basutei バス停

business shōbai 商売

busy (crowded) nigiyaka na にぎやかな

busy (doing something) isogashii 忙しい

but demo でも

butter batā バター

butterfly chōchō 蝶々

buttocks shiri 尻

buy, to kau 買う

by (author, artist) ~ni yotte ~によって（作者、芸術家）

by means of ~no hōhō de ~の方法で

by the way tokorode ところで

cabbage kyabetsu キャベツ

cabbage, Chinese hakusai 白菜

cake (pastry) kēki ケーキ, pai パイ

calculate, to keisansuru 計算する

calculator keisanki 計算機

call, to yobidasu 呼び出す

call on the telephone, to denwa o suru 電話をする

called yobareteiru 呼ばれている

calm odayaka na 穏やかな

camera kamera カメラ

can ~dekiru ~できる

can (may) ~shitemoyoi ~してもよい

can (tin) kan 缶

cancel, to torikesu 取り消す

candle rōsoku ろうそく

candy ame 飴

capable of yūnō na 有能な

capture, to toraeru 捕らえる

car jidōsha 自動車

cardboard bōrugami ボール紙

cards (game) toranpu トランプ

care for, to konomu 好む

care of, to take sewa o suru 世話をする

careful! ki o tsukete 気をつけて

carpet jūtan 絨毯

carrot ninjin 人参

carry, to hakobu 運ぶ

carve, to horu 彫る

carving chōkoku 彫刻

cash genkin 現金

cash a check, to kogitte o kankinsuru 小切手を換金する

cat neko 猫

catch, to tsukamaeru 捕まえる

cauliflower karifurawā カリフラワー

cause gen'in 原因

cautious chūi bukai 注意深い

cave horaana 洞穴

CD shīdī シーディー

CD-ROM shīdī romu シーディーロム

ceiling tenjō 天井

celebrate, to iwau 祝う

celery serori セロリ

cell phone keitai denwa 携帯電話

center (of city) hankagai 繁華街（町の）

center chūshin 中心

central chūshin no 中心の

century seiki 世紀

ceremony gishiki 儀式

certain tashika na 確かな

certainly! mochiron もちろん

certificate shōsho 証書

chair isu 椅子

challenge chōsen 挑戦

champion yūshōsha 優勝者

chance kikai 機会

chance, by gūzen ni 偶然に

change kozeni 小銭

change, to (clothes) kigaeru 着替える

change, to (conditions, situations) kawaru 変わる（状況が）

change, to (money) kankinsuru 換金する

change one's mind, to kangae o kaeru 考えを変える, ki ga kawaru 気が変わる

character (personality) seikaku 性格

character (written) moji 文字

characteristic dokutoku no 独特の

chase, to oikakeru 追いかける

chase away/out oiharau 追い払う

cheap yasui 安い

cheat peten ぺてん

cheat, to damasu だます

cheating (in a test/exam) kanningu カンニング

check, to tashikameru 確かめる

cheek hō 頬

cheers! kanpai 乾杯

cheese chīzu チーズ

chess chesu チェス

chest (box) seiridansu 整理だんす

chest (breast) mune 胸

chew, to kamu 噛む

chicken niwatori 鶏

child (offspring) kodomo 子供（子孫）

child (young person) kodomo 子供（若い人一般）

chilled hiyasareta 冷やされた

chin ago あご

China chūgoku 中国

chocolate chokorēto チョコレート

choice sentaku 選択

choose, to erabu 選ぶ

chopsticks hashi 箸

Christian kirisutokyō(to) no キリスト教(徒)の

Christianity kirisutokyō キリスト教

church kyōkai 教会
cigarette tabako タバコ
cinema eiga(kan) 映画(館)
circle en 円, maru 丸
citizen shimin 市民
citrus kankitsurui かんきつ類
city toshi 都市, machi 町, shi 市
class (category) bumon 部門
classes (at university) kurasu ク
ラス(大学の), jugyō 授業
clean kirei na きれいな
clean, to kirei ni suru きれいにする
cleanliness seiketsu 清潔
clear (of weather) hareta 晴れた
(天気)
clever kashikoi かしこい
climate kikō 気候
climb onto, to yojinoboru よじ
登る
climb up, to (hills, mountains)
noboru 登る(丘, 山)
clock okidokei 置き時計
close, to shimaru 閉まる
close to sugusoba no すぐそばの
close together kitsui きつい
closed (door) shimatta 閉まった
(ドア)
closed (road) heisa 閉鎖(道)
closed (shop) heiten 閉店(店)
cloth nuno 布
clothes, clothing fuku 服
cloudy (overcast) kumotta 曇った
co-worker dōryō 同僚
coat (jacket) jaketto ジャケット,
uwagi 上着
coat (overcoat) kōto コート, gaitō
外套
coconut kokonattsu ココナッツ
coffee kōhī コーヒー
coin kōka 硬貨
cold samui 寒い
cold (flu) kaze 風邪
colleague dōryō 同僚
collide, to shōtotsusuru 衝突する
collision shōtotsu 衝突
color iro 色
comb kushi 櫛
come, to kuru 来る
come back fukki 復帰
come in, to ~ni hairu ～に入る
come on sā ikō さあ行こう
comfortable kokochi yoi 心地良い
command (order) meirei 命令
command, to meireisuru 命令する
common yokuaru よくある
company kaisha 会社, kigyō 企業
compare, to hikakusuru 比較する
compared with ~to hikakushite
～と比較して
compel, to shiiru 強いる
compete, to kyōsōsuru 競争する
competition kyōsō 競争

complain, to fuhei o kobosu 不
平をこぼす
complaint fuhei 不平, kujō 苦情
complete (finished) kanseishita
完成した
complete (thorough) kanpeki na
完璧な
complete (whole) subete sorotta
全てそろった
complete, to kanzen ni suru 完
全にする
completely kanzen ni 完全に
complicated fukuzatsu na 複雑な
compose, to (letters, books,
music) kaku 書く(手紙, 本, 曲)
composition sakuhin 作品
compulsory hissu no 必須の,
gimuteki na 義務的な
computer konpyūta コンピューター
concentrate, to shūchūsuru 集中
する
concerning ~ni kanshite ～に関して
condition (pre-condition) jōken
条件
condition (status) jōkyō 状況
confectionery kashi 菓子
confess, to uchiakeru 打ち明ける
confidence jishin 自信
confidence, to have jishin o
motsu 自信を持つ
Confucianism jukyō 儒教
confuse, to konwakusaseru
困惑させる
confused (in a mess) konranshita 混乱した
confused (mentally) konwaku-
shita 困惑した
confusing magirawashii 紛らわしい
congratulations! omedetō おめで
とう
connect together, to renketsusuru 連結する
conscious of, to be jikakusuru
自覚する
consider, to (to think over)
kōryosuru 考慮する
consult, to sōdansuru 相談する
contact, connection kone コネ,
tsute つて
contact, to renrakusuru 連絡する
continent tairiku 大陸
continue, to keizokusuru 継続する
convenient benri na 便利な
conversation kaiwa 会話
cook (person) kokku コック,
ryōrinin 料理人
cook, to ryōrisuru 料理する
cooked chōrisareta 調理された
cooker (stove) konro コンロ
cookie (sweet biscuit) kukkī ク
ッキー, bisuketto ビスケット
cooking ryōri 料理

cool suzushii 涼しい
cool, to samasu 冷ます
copper dō 銅
copy utsushi 写し
corner kado 角
correct seikaku na 正確な
correct, to teiseisuru 訂正する
correspond, to (write letters)
buntsūsuru 文通する
corridor rōka 廊下
cost (expense) hiyō 費用
cost (price) kakaku 価格
cotton men 綿
couch sofā ソファー, nagaisu 長いす
cough seki 咳
cough, to sekikomu 咳きこむ
could hyottoshitara ~kamoshire-
nai ひょっとしたら～かもしれない
count, to kazoeru 数える
counter (for paying, buying
tickets) kauntā カウンター,
kanjōdai 勘定台
country (nation) kokka 国家
country (rural area) inaka 田舎
courtyard nakaniwa 中庭
cover, to ōu 覆う
cow ushi 牛
cracked kudaketa 砕けた
cracker kurakkā クラッカー
crafts kōgei 工芸
craftsperson kōgeika 工芸家
crazy kurutta 狂った
create, to tsukuru 作る
criminal hanzaisha 犯罪者
cross, to (go over) yokogiru
横切る
crowded konzatsushita 混雑した
cruel zankoku na 残酷な
cry, to naku 泣く
cry out, to sakebu 叫ぶ
cucumber kyuuri キュウリ
culture bunka 文化
cup koppu コップ, chawan 茶わん
cupboard shokkidana 食器棚,
todana 戸棚
cure (medical) chiryō 治療(医療)
cured hozonsareta 保存された
currency tsūka 通貨
curtain kāten カーテン
custom shūkan 習慣, dentō 伝統
cut (slice) kireme 切れめ
cut, to kiru 切る
cute (appealing) kawaii かわいい

daily mainichi no 毎日の
damage songai 損害
damage, to ~o sokonau ～を損なう
damp shikke no aru 湿気のある
dance odori 踊り
dance, to odoru 踊る
danger kiken 危険
dangerous kiken na 危険な

dark kurai 暗い
date (of the month) hizuke 日付
date of birth tanjōbi 誕生日
daughter musume 娘
daughter-in-law girino musume 義理の娘
dawn yoake 夜明け
day hi 日
day after tomorrow asatte 明後日
day before yesterday ototoi 一昨日
day of the week yōbi 曜日
day off kyūjitu 休日
daydream, to kūsōsuru 空想する
dead shinda 死んだ
deaf chōkakushōgai no aru 聴覚障害のある
death shi 死
debt shakkin 借金
deceive, to damasu だます
December jūnigatsu 十二月
decide, to kimeru 決める
decision kesshin 決心
decline, to (get less) kakōsuru 下降する
decorate, to kazaru 飾る
decrease, to heru 減る
deep fukai 深い
defeat, to uchimakasu 打ち負かす
defect ketten 欠点
defend, to (in war) bōgyosuru 防御する(戦争)
defend, to (with words) yōgosuru 擁護する(言葉で)
definite kakuteishita 確定した
degree (level) teido 程度
degrees (temperature) ondo 温度
delay okure 遅れ
delayed okureta 遅れた
delicious oishii おいしい
deliver, to haitatsusuru 配達する
demand, to yōkyūsuru 要求する
depart, to shuppatsusuru 出発する
department bu 部, ka 課
department store hyakkaten 百貨店, depāto デパート
departure shuppatsu 出発
depend on, to izonsuru 依存する
deposit, to (put money in the bank) yokinsuru 預金する
descendant shison 子孫
describe, to byōshasuru 描写する
desert (arid land) sabaku 砂漠
desert, to (abandon) hōkisuru 放棄する
desire kibō 希望, ganbō 願望
desire, to nozomu 望む
desk desuku デスク, benkyōzukue 勉強机
dessert dezāto デザート
destination mokutekichi 目的地
destroy, to hakaisuru 破壊する
detergent senjōzai 洗浄剤

determined dankotoshita 断固とした
develop, to (happen) hattensuru 発展する
development hatten 発展, kaihatsu 開発
dial, to (telephone) denwa o kakeru 電話をかける
dialect hōgen 方言
diamond daiyamondo ダイヤモンド
diary nikki 日記
dictionary jisho 辞書
die, to shinu 死ぬ
difference (discrepancy in figures) sai 差異
difference (in quality) sōi 相違
different (other) hoka no ほかの
difficult muzukashii 難しい
dinner yūshoku 夕食
dinner, to eat yūshoku o toru 夕食をとる
direction hōkō 方向
director (of company) jūyaku 重役(会社の)
dirty kitanai 汚い
disappointed shitsubōshita 失望した
disaster sainan 災難
discount waribiki 割引
discover, to hakkensuru 発見する
discuss, to gironsuru 議論する
discussion giron 議論
disease byōki 病気
disgusting mukatsukuyō na むかつくような
dish sara 皿
dish (particular food) ryōri 料理
dislike, to konomanai 好まない, kirau 嫌う
display tenji 展示
display, to tenjisuru 展示する
distance kyori 距離
disturb, to samatageru 妨げる
disturbance bōgai 妨害
divide, to bunkatsusuru 分割する
divided by ~de warareta 〜で割られた
divorce, to rikonsuru 離婚する
divorced rikonshita 離婚した
do, to (perform an action) ~suru 〜する
do one's best besuto o tsukusu ベストを尽くす
doctor isha 医者
document shorui 書類
do(es) not work (spoiled) kowareta 壊れた
dog inu 犬
done (cooked) yoku hi no tōtta よく火の通った
done (finished) sunda 済んだ

door to 戸, doa ドア
double nibai no 二倍の
doubt, to utagau 疑う
down, downward shita e 下へ
downstairs kaika e 階下へ
downtown hankagai 繁華街
dozen dāsu ダース
draw, to hiku 引く
drawer hikidashi 引き出し
drawing zuga 図画
dream yume 夢
dream, to yume o miru 夢を見る
dress doresu ドレス
dressed, to get kiru 着る
drink nomimono 飲み物
drink, to nomu 飲む
drive, to (a car) untensuru 運転する(車)
drought kanbatsu 干ばつ
drown, to oboreru おぼれる
drug (medicine) kusuri 薬
drugstore yakkyoku 薬局
drunk yopparatta 酔っ払った
dry kawaita 乾いた
dry (weather) kansōshita 乾燥した(天気)
dry, to kawakasu 乾かす
duck ahiru アヒル
dull (boring) taikutsu na 退屈な
dull (weather) don'yorishita (tenki) どんよりした(天気)
dumpling dango 団子
during ~no aida ni 〜の間に
dusk yūgure doki 夕暮れ時
dust hokori 埃
duty (responsibility) gimu 義務
DVD dībuidī ディーブイディー

each ~goto ni 〜毎に
ear mimi 耳
earrings iyaringu イアリング
earlier maemotte 前もって
early hayai 早い
early in the morning sōchō ni 早朝に
earn, to eru 得る
earth dojō 土壌
Earth chikyū 地球
earthquake jishin 地震
east higashi 東
easy kantan na 簡単な
eat, to taberu 食べる
economical keizaiteki na 経済的な
economy keizai 経済
edge hashi 端
educate, to kyōikusuru 教育する
education kyōiku 教育
effect eikyō 影響
effort doryoku 努力
effort: to make an effort doryokusuru 努力する
egg tamago 卵

eggplant nasu ナス
either dochiraka ippō no どちらか一方の
elbow hiji ひじ
elder nenchō no 年長の
election senkyo 選挙
electric denki no 電気の
electricity denki 電気
electronic denshi no 電子的の
elegant yūga na 優雅な
elephant zō 象
elevator erebētā エレベーター
else: anything else sonota no その他の
else: or else ~de nakereba ～でなければ
email (message) denshi mēru 電子メール（メッセージ）
email, to denshi mēru o okuru 電子メールを送る
email address denshi mēru adoresu 電子メールアドレス
embarrassed batsu no warui ばつの悪い
embarrassing hazukashii 恥ずかしい
embassy taishikan 大使館
embrace, to idaku 抱く
emergency kinkyūjitai 緊急事態
Emoticon (computer) kaomoji 顔文字, emōtikon エモーティコン
emotion kanjō 感情
empty kara no 空の
end (finish) owari 終わり
end (tip) hashi 端
end, to owaru 終る
enemy teki 敵
energy katsuryoku 活力
engaged (to be married) kon'yakuchū no 婚約中の
engine enjin エンジン
England igirisu イギリス
English igirisu(jin) no イギリス（人）の
enjoy oneself, to tanoshimu 楽しむ
enjoyable tanoshii 楽しい
enough jūbun na 十分な
enter, to hairu 入る
entire zentai no 全体の
entirety zentai 全体
entrance genkan 玄関, iriguchi 入口
envelope fūtō 封筒
envious urayamashisō na 羨ましそうな
environment kankyō 環境
envy urayamashi sa 羨ましさ
equal dōtō na 同等の
error machigai 間違い
escalator esukarētā エスカレーター
especially toku ni 特に
establish, to setsuritsusuru 設立する, juritsusuru 樹立する

essay shōron 小論, essē エッセー
estimate, to mitsumoru 見積もる
even (also) issō いっそう
even (smooth) nameraka na なめらかな
evening yūgata 夕方
evening meal yūshoku 夕食
event dekigoto 出来事
ever katsute かつて
every (all) subete no 全ての
every (each) ~goto ni ～毎に
every kind of zenshu no 全種の
every time itsumo いつも
everybody, everyone subete no hito 全ての人, ban'nin 万人
everything subete no mono 全ての物
everywhere dokodemo どこでも
exact, exactly seikaku na 正確な
exactly! sonotōri その通り
exam shiken 試験
examine, to chōsasuru 調査する
example rei 例
example, for tatoeba 例えば
excellent yūshū na 優秀な
except ~o nozoite ～を除いて
exchange, to (money) kankinsuru 換金する
exchange rate kawase-sōba 為替相場
excited wakuwakushita わくわくした
exciting wakuwakusaseru わくわくさせる
excuse me! (apology) gomennasai ごめんなさい（謝罪）
excuse me! (attracting attention) sumimasen すみません（注目を引くとき）
excuse me! (getting past) sumimasen すみません（通り抜けるとき）
exist, to sonzaisuru 存在する
exit, to (go out) deru 出る
exit deguchi 出口
expand, to kakudaisuru 拡大する
expect, to yokisuru 予期する
expense hiyō 費用, shuppi 出費
expensive kōgaku no 高額の, takai 高い
experience keiken 経験
expert senmonka 専門家
explain, to setsumeisuru 説明する
export yushutsu 輸出
export, to yushutsusuru 輸出する
express, to noberu 述べる
extension (telephone) denwa no koki 電話の子機, naisen 内線（電話）
extra yobun no 余分の, tokubetsu no 特別の
extremely kyokutan ni 極端に
eye me 目

eyebrow mayuge 眉毛
eyeglasses megane めがね

fabric (textile) nuno 布
face kao 顔
face, to chokumensuru 直面する
Facebook (internet) feisubukku フェイスブック
fact jijitsu 事実
factory kōjō 工場
fail, to shippaisuru 失敗する
failure shippai 失敗
fall (season) aki 秋
fall, to ochiru 落ちる
fall over, to korobu 転ぶ
false (imitation) nise no にせの
false (not true) fuseikaku na 不正確な
family kazoku 家族
famous yūmei na 有名な
fan (admirer) fan ファン
fan (for cooling) senpūki 扇風機, uchiwa うちわ
fancy kūsō 空想
far tōku e 遠くへ, tōi 遠い
fare jōsharyōkin 乗車料金
fast (rapid) hayai 速い
fast, to danjikisuru 断食する
fat (grease) shibō 脂肪
fat (plump) futotta 太った
father chichi 父
father-in-law giri no chichi 義理の父
fault kashitsu 過失
fax, to fakkusu o okuru ファックスを送る
fear osore 恐れ
February nigatsu 二月
fee ryōkin 料金, tesūryō 手数料
feed, to tabemono o ataeru 食べ物を与える
feel, to kanjiru 感じる
feeling kanji 感じ
female josei 女性
fence saku 柵
ferry ferī フェリー, watashibune 渡し舟
fertile hiyoku na 肥沃な
festival matsuri 祭り
fetch, to tottekuru 取ってくる
fever hatsunetsu 発熱
few sukunai 少ない
fiancé kon'yakusha 婚約者(男性)
fiancée kon'yakusha 婚約者(女性)
field (empty space) akichi 空き地
fierce araarashii 荒々しい
fight, to (physically) kenka けんか
fight over, to ~de kenkasuru ～で喧嘩する
figure (number) sūji 数字
fill, to mitasu 満たす

fill out, to (form) kakikomu 書き込む
film (movie) eiga 映画
final saigo no 最後の
finally saigo ni 最後に
find, to mitsukeru 見つける
fine (healthy) genki na 元気な
fine (punishment) bakkin 罰金
finger yubi 指
finish saigo 最後
finish off, to sumasu 済ます
finished (complete) kanseishita 完成した
finished (none left) owatta 終った
fire honō 炎
fire someone, to kaikosuru 解雇する
fireworks hanabi 花火
firm (definite) dankotoshita 断固とした
firm (mattress) katai 硬い(マットレス)
firm (company) kigyō 企業
first ichiban no 一番の
first mazu まず, hajime ni 初めに
fish sakana 魚
fish, to tsuru 釣る
fit, to gatchisuru 合致する
fitting (suitable) tekisetsu na 適切な
fix, to (a time, appointment) kimeru 決める(時間、約束)
fix, to (repair) shūrisuru 修理する
flag hata 旗
flashlight kaichūdentō 懐中電灯
flat (apartment) apāto アパート
flat (smooth) heitan na 平坦な
flight hikō 飛行
flood kōzui 洪水
floor yuka 床
flour komugiko 小麦粉
flower hana 花
flu kaze 風邪, infuruenza インフルエンザ
fluent ryūchō na 流暢な
flute furūto フルート, fue 笛
fly (insect) hae 蝿
fly, to tobu 飛ぶ
fog kiri 霧
fold, to oru 折る
follow along, to ~ni tsuzuku ~に続く
follow behind, to ushirokara tsuitekuru 後ろからついてくる
following tsugi no 次の
fond of ~o kononde ~を好んで
food tabemono 食べ物
foot ashi 足
for ~surutame no ~するための
for ever eien ni 永遠に
forbid, to kinshisuru 禁止する

forbidden kinjirareta 禁じられた
force chikara 力
force, to shiiru 強いる
forehead odeko おでこ
foreign gaikoku no 外国の
foreigner gaikokujin 外国人
forest mori 森
forget, to wasureru 忘れる
forget about, to ~ni tsuite wasureru ~について忘れる
forgive, to yurusu 許す
forgiveness kandai sa 寛大さ
forgotten wasurerareta 忘れられた
fork fōku フォーク
form (shape) katachi 形
form (to fill out) yōshi 用紙
fortress yōsai 要塞
fortunately kōun nimo 幸運にも
forward zenpō ni 前方に
free (independent) dokuritsushita 独立した
free of charge muryō de 無料で
freedom jiyū 自由
freeze kōritsuku 凍りつく
frequent hinpan na 頻繁な
fresh shinsen na 新鮮な
Friday kin'yōbi 金曜日
fried yakareta 焼かれた
friend tomodachi 友達
friendly (outgoing) shakōteki na 社交的な
frightened odoroita 驚いた
from ~kara ~から
front zenmen 前面
front: in front of ~no mae ni ~の前に
frown: with a frown kao o shikameta 顔をしかめた
frown, to kao o shikameru 顔をしかめる
frozen kōtta 凍った
fruit kudamono 果物
fry, to yaku 焼く
fulfill, to hatasu 果たす
full ippai no いっぱいの
full (eaten one's fill) onaka ga ippai no お腹がいっぱいの
fun: to have fun tanoshimu 楽しむ
function, to (work) kinōsuru 機能する
funds, funding shikin 資金
funeral sōshiki 葬式
funny okashii おかしい
furniture kagu 家具
further (additional) sonoue その上
fussy konomi ni urusai 好みにうるさい
future shōrai 将来

gamble kakegoto 賭け事, gyanburu ギャンブル

game shiai 試合
garage (for parking) shako 車庫
garage (for repairs) jidōsha-shūrikōjō 自動車修理工場
garbage gomi ごみ
garden (yard) niwa 庭
garden (park) kōen 公園
garlic nin'niku にんにく
garment irui 衣類
gasoline gasorin ガソリン
gasoline station kyūyujo 給油所
gate mon 門
gather, to atsumeru 集める
gender seibetsu 性別
general (all-purpose) ippanteki na 一般的な
generally ippan ni 一般に
generous kandai na 寛大な
gentle yasashii やさしい
gesture miburi 身振り
get in touch with, to (contact) renrakusuru 連絡する
get, to (receive) uketoru 受け取る
get off, to (transport) kōshasuru 降車する
get on, to (transport) jōshasuru 乗車する
get up, to (from bed) okiru 起きる
get well soon hayaku naotte 早く治って
ghost obake お化け
gift okurimono 贈り物
ginger shōga 生姜
girl on'na no ko 女の子
girlfriend kanojo 彼女
give, to ataeru 与える
given name na 名(姓に対する名)
glad ureshii うれしい
glass (for drinking) gurasu グラス
glass (material) garasu ガラス
glasses (spectacles) megane めがね
glutinous rice mochigome もち米
go, to iku 行く
go along, to (join) sankasuru 参加する
go around, to (visit) tazuneru 訪ねる
go back modoru 戻る
go for a walk, to sanpo ni iku 散歩に行く
go home, to kitakusuru 帰宅する
go out (fire, candle) kieru 消える (火、ろうそく)
go out, to deru 出る
go over, to yokogiru 横切る
go to bed, to neru 寝る
go up, to (climb) noboru 登る
goal gōru ゴール, mokuhyō 目標
goat yagi 山羊
God kami 神
god gūzō 偶像, kami 神

goddess megami 女神
gold ōgon 黄金
golf gorufu ゴルフ
gone (finished) owatta 終った
good yoi 良い
good luck! kōun o inoru 幸運を祈る
goodbye sayōnara さようなら
goodness! aramā あらまあ
government seifu 政府
gradually jojo ni 徐々に
grand sōdai na 壮大な
granddaughter magomusume 孫娘
grandfather sofu 祖父
grandmother sobo 祖母
grandparents sofubo 祖父母
grandson magomusuko 孫息子
grapes budō 葡萄
grass kusa 草
grateful kanshashita 感謝した
grave haka 墓
gray haiiro no 灰色の
great (grand) sōdai na 壮大な
great (impressive) migoto na 見事な
green midori no 緑の
greens (vegetables) aoyasai 青野菜
greet, to aisatsu o suru 挨拶をする
greetings aisatsu 挨拶
grill, to yaku 焼く
ground jimen 地面
group gurūpu グループ, atsumari 集まり
grow: to be growing (plant) haeru 生える(植物)
grow, to (cultivate) yashinau 養う
grow larger, to ōkikunaru 大きくなる
grow up, to (child) sodatsu 育つ (子供)
guarantee hoshōsho 保証書
guarantee, to hoshōsuru 保証する
guard, to mamoru 守る
guess, to suisokusuru 推測する
guest kyaku 客
guide gaido ガイド, an'nainin 案内人
guidebook ryokōan'nai 旅行案内
guilty (of a crime) yūzai 有罪
guilty, to feel zaiakukan o kanji-ru 罪悪感を感じる

hair kami 髪
half hanbun 半分
hall hiroma 広間, genkan 玄関
hand te 手
hand out, to teishutsusuru 提出する
hand over, to watasu 渡す
handicraft shukōgei 手工芸
handle totte 取っ手
handsome hansamu ハンサム
hang, to kakeru 掛ける
happen, to okoru 起こる

happened, what nani ga okita 何が起きた
happening dekigoto 出来事
happy shiawase na 幸せな
happy birthday! tanjōbi omedetō 誕生日おめでとう
happy new year! akemashite omedetō 明けましておめでとう
harbor minato 港
hard (difficult) kon'nan na 困難な
hard (solid) katai 固い
hard disk hādodisuku ハードディスク
hardly hotondo~nai ほとんど~ない
hardworking kinben na 勤勉な
harmonious chōwa no toreta 調和のとれた
hat bōshi 帽子(つばの広い)
hate, to ken'osuru 嫌悪する
hatred ken'okan 嫌悪感
have, to shoyūsuru 所有する
have already katsute かつて
have to ~nakute wa ikenai ~なくてはいけない
head atama 頭
head for, to (toward) ~e mukau ~へ向かう
headdress kamikazari 髪飾り
healthy kenkōteki na 健康的な
hear, to kiku 聞く
heart shinzō 心臓
heat, to atatameru 温める
heavy omoi 重い
height takasa 高さ
hello! (on phone) moshimoshi もしもし
hello, hi kon'nichiwa こんにちは
help! tasukete 助けて
help, to tasukeru 助ける, tetsudau 手伝う
here koko ここ
hidden kakureta 隠れた
hide, to kakusu 隠す
high takai 高い
hill oka 丘
hinder, to samatageru 妨げる
hire, to yatou 雇う
history rekishi 歴史
hit (strike) dageki 打撃
hobby shumi 趣味
hold, to (grasp) tsukamu つかむ
hold back, to tamerau ためらう
hole ana 穴
holiday (festival) saijitsu 祭日
holiday (vacation) kyūka 休暇
holy shinsei na 神聖な
home, house ie 家
honest shōjiki na 正直な
honey hachimitsu 蜂蜜
hope, to nozomu 望む
hopefully kitai o motte 期待をもって

horse uma 馬
hospital byōin 病院
host shujin 主人
hot (spicy) karai 辛い
hot (temperature) atsui 熱い
hot spring onsen 温泉
hotel hoteru ホテル
hour jikan 時間
house ie 家
how? dono yō ni どのように
how are you? genkidesuka 元気ですか
however shikashinagara しかしながら
how long? donokurai どのくらい (時間)
how many? donokurai どのくらい (数)
how much? ikura いくら(価格)
how old? ikutsu いくつ(年齢)
huge kyodai na 巨大な
human jinrui 人類
humid shikke no aru 湿気のある
humorous omoshiroi おもしろい
hundred hyaku 百
hundred thousand jūman 十万
hungry kūfuku no 空腹の
hurry up! isoide 急いで
hurt (injured) kizutsuita 傷ついた
hurt, to (cause pain) kizutsuku 傷つく
husband otto 夫

ice kōri 氷
ice cream aisukurīmu アイスクリーム
idea kangae 考え
identical dōitsu no 同一の
if moshi もし
ignore, to mushisuru 無視する
ignorant muchi no 無知の
illegal fuhō no 不法の
ill byōki no 病気の
illness byōki 病気
imagine, to sōzōsuru 想像する
immediately sassoku 早速
impolite shitsurei na 失礼な, burei na 無礼な
import, to yunyūsuru 輸入する
importance jūyō sa 重要さ
important jūyō na 重要な
impossible fukanō na 不可能な
impression: to make an impression inshōzukeru 印象付ける
impressive migoto na みごとな
in, at (space) ~ni ~に, ~de ~で (空間)
in (time, years) ~no aida ~の間, ~ni ~に(時間、年)
in addition ~ni kuwaete ~に加えて
in order that tame ni ために, yō ni ように
incense okō お香

incident jiken 事件
included, including ~o fukumete ～を含めて
increase zōka 増加
increase, to fuyasu 増やす
indeed! tashika ni 確かに
indigenous koyū no 固有の
industrious kinben na 勤勉な
inexpensive yasui 安い, anka na 安価な
influence eikyō 影響
inform, to shiraseru 知らせる
information jōhō 情報
information booth an'naijo 案内所
inhabitant jūnin 住人
injection chūsha 注射
injured kizutsuita 傷ついた
injury fushō 負傷
ink sumi 墨
inquire, to tazuneru 尋ねる
insane kyōki no 狂気の
insect konchū 昆虫
inside naibu 内部
inside of ~no naka ni ～の中に
inspect, to tenkensuru 点検する
instead of ~no kawari ni ～の代わりに
instruct, to shijisuru 指示する
instrument dōgu 道具
insult bujoku 侮辱
insurance hoken 保険
intend, to ~surutsumoridearu ～するつもりである
intended for itosareta 意図された
intention ito 意図
interest kyōmi 興味, rishi 利子
interested in ~ni kyōmi ga aru ～に興味がある
interesting kyōmi bukai 興味深い, omoshiroi 面白い
international kokusaiteki na 国際的な
Internet intānetto インターネット
interpreter tsūyakusha 通訳者
intersection kōsaten 交差点
into ~no naka ni ～の中に
introduce oneself, to jikoshōkaisuru 自己紹介する
introduce someone, to shōkaisuru 紹介する
invitation hatsumei 発明
invite, to (ask along) sasou 誘う
invite, to (formally) shōtaisuru 招待する
invoice shikirijō 仕切り状
involve, to tomonau 伴う
involved kan'yoshita 関与した
Ireland airurando アイルランド
iron tetsu no 鉄の
iron, to (clothing) airon o kakeru アイロンをかける(服の)

Islam isuramu イスラム
island shima 島
item (individual thing) hinmoku 品目
ivory zōge 象牙

jacket jaketto ジャケット, uwagi 上着
jail keimusho 刑務所
jam jamu ジャム
January ichigatsu 一月
Japan nihon 日本
Japanese nihon(jin) no 日本(人)の
jaw ago あご
jealous shittobukai 嫉妬深い
jealousy shitto 嫉妬
jewelry hōsekirui 宝石類
job shigoto 仕事
join in, to sankasuru 参加する
join, to awaseru 合わせる
join together, to setsuzokusuru 接続する
joke jōku ジョーク, jōdan 冗談
journalist kisha 記者, jānarisuto ジャーナリスト
journey tabi 旅
juice jūsu ジュース, kajū 果汁
July shichigatsu 七月
jump, to tobu 跳ぶ
June rokugatsu 六月
jungle janguru ジャングル, mitsurin 密林
just (fair) kōhei na 公平な
just (only) tatta no たったの
just now tatta ima たった今
just so! sonotōri その通り

keep, to tamotsu 保つ
key (computer) kī キー(コンピューター)
key (to room) kagi 鍵(部屋)
keyboard (of computer) kībōdo キーボード(コンピューターの)
kill, to korosu 殺す
kilogram kiroguramu キログラム
kilometer kiromētā キロメーター
kind (of persons) yasashii やさしい(人)
kind (type) shurui 種類
king ōsama 王様
kiss kisu キス
kitchen daidokoro 台所
knee hiza 膝
knife kogatana 小刀, naifu ナイフ
knock, to nokkusuru ノックする
know (be acquainted with) chishikiga aru 知識がある
know, to shitteiru 知っている
knowledge chishiki 知識
Korea, North kitachōsen 北朝鮮
Korea, South kankoku 韓国

lacking kaketeiru 欠けている
ladder hashigo 梯子
ladle shakushi 杓子
lady fujin 婦人
lake mizuumi 湖
lamb hitsujiniku 羊肉, ramu ラム
lamp ranpu ランプ, shōmei 照明
land tochi 土地
land, to (plane) chakurikusuru 着陸する(飛行機)
lane komichi 小道
lane (of a highway) shasen 車線(高速道路)
language gengo 言語
large hiroi 広い, ōkii 大きい
last saigo no 最後の
last night sakuya 昨夜
last week senshū 先週
last year sakunen 昨年
late osoi 遅い
late at night yoruosoku 夜遅く
later sono go その後, ato de 後で
laugh, to warau 笑う
laugh at, to ~o warau ～を笑う
laws (legislation) hōritsu 法律
lawyer bengoshi 弁護士
layer sō 層
lazy taiman na 怠慢な
lead, to (to guide someone somewhere) an'naisuru 案内する
lead, to (as a leader) michibiku 導く
leader shidōsha 指導者
leaf ha 葉
leak, to moreru 漏れる
learn, to narau 習う
least (smallest amount) saishō no 最小の
least: at least sukunakutomo 少なくとも
leather kawa 皮
leave, to shuppatsusuru 出発する
leave behind by accident, to okiwasureru 置き忘れる
lecture kōgi 講義
lecturer (at university) kōshi 講師(大学の)
left (remaining) nokori 残り
left-hand side hidarigawa 左側
leg ashi 脚
legal gōhō no 合法の
legend densetsu 伝説
lemon remon レモン
lend, to kasu 貸す
length nagasa 長さ
less (smaller amount) yori sukunaku より少なく
less (minus) ~o hiita ～を引いた
lessen, to sukunakunaru 少なくなる
lesson ressun レッスン, jugyō 授業
let, to kyokasuru 許可する

let someone know, to shiraseru しらせる
let's (suggestion) ~shiyō 〜しよう
let's go sā ikō さあ行こう
letter tegami 手紙
level (even, flat) taira na 平らな
level (height) onajitakasa no 同じ高さの
library toshokan 図書館
license (for driving) menkyoshō 免許証(運転)
lick, to nameru 舐める
lid futa ふた
lie, to (tell a falsehood) uso o tsuku 嘘をつく
lie down, to nesoberu 寝そべる
life seikatsu 生活
lifetime isshō 一生
lift, to (something) mochiageru 持ち上げる(物を)
lift, to (ride in car) noseteageru (車に)乗せてあげる
lift, to (raise) takameru 高める
light (bright) akarui 明るい
light (lamp) shōmei 照明
light (not heavy) karui 軽い
lightning inazuma 稲妻
like (as) ~no yōna 〜のような
like (be pleased by) ki ni iru 気に入る
likewise onaji yō ni 同じように
lime (citrus) raimu ライム
line (mark) sen 線
line (queue) gyōretsu 行列
line up, to narabu 並ぶ
lips kuchibiru 唇
liquor sake 酒
list hyō 表
listen, to kiku 聴く
listen to ~o kiku 〜を聴く
literature bungaku 文学
little (not much) sukunai 少ない
little (small) chiisai 小さい
live, to (be alive) ikiteiru 生きている
live, to (stay in a place) sumu 住む
load tsumini 積み荷
load up, to tsumikomu 積み込む
located, to be ichisuru 位置する
lock jō 錠
lock, to jō o kakeru 錠を掛ける
lonely sabishii 寂しい
long (length) nagai 長い(距離)
long (time) nagai 長い(時間)
look! mite 見て
look, to ~no yō ni omoeru 〜のように思える
look after, to sewa o suru 世話をする
look at, to miru 見る
look for, to sagasu 探す
look like, to ~no yō ni mieru 〜のように見える

look out! ki o tsukete 気をつけて
looks mikake 見かけ
look up, to (find in book) kensakusuru (本を)検索する
loose (not in packet) tabanete inai 束ねていない
loose (wobbly) guratsuita ぐらついた
lose, to (be defeated) makeru 負ける
lose, to (mislay) okiwasureru 置き忘れる
lose money, to kane o nakusu 金をなくす
lost (can't find way) mayotta (道に)迷った
lost (missing) ushinatta 失った
lots of takusan no たくさんの
lottery takarakuji 宝くじ
loud onryō no aru 音量のある
love ai 愛
love, to aisuru 愛する, konomu 好む
lovely suteki na 素敵な
low hikui 低い
luck un 運
lucky kōun 幸運
luggage tenimotsu 手荷物
lunch chūshoku 昼食
lunch, to eat chūshoku o toru 昼食をとる
luxurious gōka na 豪華な

machine kikai 機械
machinery kikairui 機械類
magazine zasshi 雑誌
mail (post) yūbinbutsu 郵便物
mail, to yūsōsuru 郵送する
main (most important) shuyō na 主要な
mainly omo ni 主に
major (important) jūyō na 重要な
make, to tsukuru 作る
make up, to (invent) detchiageru でっち上げる
makeshift maniawase no 間に合わせの
male dansei 男性
man otoko no hito 男の人
manage, to (run) un'eisuru 運営する
manager manējā マネージャー
manufacture, to seizōsuru 製造する
many takusan no たくさんの
map chizu 地図
March sangatsu 三月
market ichiba 市場
married kekkonshita 結婚した
marry: to get married kekkonsuru 結婚する
mask masuku マスク
massage massāji マッサージ
mat matto マット

match (game) shiai 試合
material (ingredient) zairyō 材料
matter (issue) mondai 問題
matter, it doesn't dōdemoii どうでもいい
mattress mattoresu マットレス
May gogatsu 五月
may ~kamoshirenai 〜かもしれない
maybe tabun 多分
meal shokuji 食事
mean (cruel) ijiwarui 意地悪い
mean, to (intend) ~surutsumori 〜するつもり
mean, to (word) imisuru 意味する
meaning imi 意味
meanwhile sono aida ni その間に
measure, to hakaru 計る
measurement sokutē 測定
measure out, to hakari wakeru 計り分ける
meat shokuniku 食肉
medical igaku no 医学の
medicine iyakuhin 医薬品
meet, to au 会う
meeting kaigō 会合
melon meron メロン
member kaiin 会員
memories kioku 記憶
mend, to naosu 直す
mental seishin no 精神の
mention, to noberu 述べる
menu menyū メニュー
merely tan ni 単に
mess: in a mess chirakari 散かり
message dengon 伝言
method hōhō 方法
midday shōgo 正午
midday meal chūshoku 昼食
middle (center) chūō 中央
middle: be in the middle of doing ~no saichū 〜の最中
midnight mayonaka 真夜中
might moshikashitara ~kamoshirenai もしかしたら〜かもしれない
mild (not severe) odayaka na 穏やかな
mild (not spicy) amakuchi no 甘口の
milk gyūnyū 牛乳
million hyakuman 百万
mind (brain) chiryoku 知力
mind, to (be displeased) ki ni naru 気になる
minor (not important) taishita koto nai 大したことない
minus ~o hiita 〜を引いた
minute fun 分
mirror kagami 鏡
misfortune fukō 不幸
miss, to (bus, flight) noriokureru (バス、飛行機に)乗り遅れる

miss, to (loved one) koishiku omou 恋しく思う

missing (absent) kesseki no 欠席の

missing (lost person) yukue-fumei 行方不明

mist kiri 霧

mistake machigai 間違い

mistaken machigae rareta 間違えられた

misunderstanding gokai 誤解

mix, to mazaru 混ざる

mixed kongōshita 混合した

mobile phone keitaidenwa 携帯電話

modern gendai no 現代の

modest (simple) hikaeme na 控えめな

moment: in a moment, just a moment sugu ni すぐに, shōshō omachi kudasai 少々お待ちください

moment (instant) shunkan 瞬間

Monday getsuyōbi 月曜日

money okane お金

monitor (of computer) monitā （コンピューターの）モニター

monkey saru 猿

month tsuki 月

monument kinenhi 記念碑

moon tsuki 月

more (comparative) ~yori ōku ～より多く

more of (things) ~yori ōku no ～より多くの

more or less daitai だいたい

morning asa 朝

morning meal chōshoku 朝食

most (superlative) mottomo 最も

most (the most of) hotondo ほとんど

mostly daibubun wa 大部分は

mother haha 母

mother-in-law girinohaha 義理の母

motor, engine motā モーター, enjin エンジン

motor vehicle dōryokusha 動力車

motorcycle ōtobai オートバイ, tansha 単車

mountain yama 山

mouse (computer) mausu マウス （コンピューター）

mouth kuchi 口

move, to ugoku 動く

movement (motion) ugoki 動き

movie eiga 映画

movie house eigakan 映画館

much takusan no たくさんの

murder, to korosu 殺す

muscle kin'niku 筋肉

mushroom kinoko きのこ

music ongaku 音楽

Muslim isuramukyō(to) no イスラム教(徒)の

must ~nakutewaikenai ～なくてはいけない

mustache kuchihige 口ひげ

my, mine watashi no 私の

myth shinwa 神話

nail (finger, toe) tsume 爪(手、足)

nail (spike) kugi 釘

naked hadaka no 裸の

name namae 名前

narrow semai 狭い

nation (country) kuni 国

national kuni no 国の

nationality kokuseki 国籍

natural shizen no 自然の

nature shizen 自然

naughty itazura na いたずらな, wanpaku na 腕白な

nearby sugusoba no すぐそばの

nearly hotondo ほとんど

neat (orderly) kichintoshita きちんとした

necessary hitsuyō na 必要な

neck kubi 首

necklace kubikazari 首飾り

necktie nekutai ネクタイ

need hitsuyō 必要

need, to hitsuyō de aru 必要である

needle hari 針

neighbor rinjin 隣人

neither ~de nai ～でない

neither ... nor ~mo~mo~nai ～も～も～ない

nephew oi 甥

nest su 巣

net ami 網

Netbook (computer) Netto-bukku ネットブック

Netizen (internet) netto-shimin ネット市民 (from internet + citizen)

network hōsōmō 放送網, kairomō 回路網

never kesshite~nai 決して～ない

never mind! ki ni shinaide 気にしないで

nevertheless sore nimo kakawarazu それにもかかわらず

new atarashii 新しい

New Zealand nyūjīrando ニュージーランド

news nyūsu ニュース

newspaper shinbun 新聞

next (in line, sequence) tsugi no 次の

next to tonari ni 隣に

next week raishū 来週

next year rainen 来年

nice suteki na 素敵な

niece mei 姪

night yoru 夜

no, not (with nouns) ~dewa nai ～ではない（名詞につく）

no, not (with verbs and adjectives) ~nai ～ない, ~dewanai ～ではない（動詞と形容詞につく）

nobody daremo~nai 誰も～ない

noise oto 音

noisy urusai うるさい

nonsense muimi na kotoba 無意味な言葉, nansensu ナンセンス

noodles menrui 麺類

noon shōgo 正午

nor ~demo nai ～でもない

normal futsū no 普通の

normally futsū wa 普通は

north kita 北

nose hana 鼻

nostril bikō 鼻腔

not ~dewa nai ～ではない

not only ... but also ~dake de naku~mo mata ～だけでなく～もまた

not yet madadesu まだです

note (written) memo メモ

note down, to kaki tomeru 書き留める

notebook nōto ノート

nothing nani mo~nai 何も～ない

notice chūmoku 注目, chūi 注意

notice, to kizuku 気づく

novel shōsetsu 小説

November jūichigatsu 十一月

now ima 今

nowhere doko nimo~nai どこにも～ない

nude hadaka 裸

numb mahishita 麻痺した

number kazu 数

o'clock ~ji ～時

obedient jūjun na 従順な

obey, to shitagau 従う

object (thing) buttai 物体

object, to (protest) hantaisuru 反対する

occasionally tama ni たまに

occupation shokugyō 職業

occur, to okoru 起こる

ocean umi 海

October jūgatsu 十月

odor (bad smell) akushū 悪臭

of (from) ~no ～の, ~kara ～から

of course mochiron もちろん

off (turned off) keshita 消した, tomatta 止まった

off: to turn something off keshita 消した

offend, to kanjō o gaisuru 感情を害する

offer, to (suggest) teikyōsuru 提供する

offering teikyō 提供

office jimusho 事務所, ofisu オフィス

official (formal) kōshiki no 公式の

often shibashiba しばしば, yoku よく

oil abura 油

okay ii いい, ōkē オーケー

old (of persons) toshitotta 年取った(人)

old (of things) furui 古い(物)

older brother chōkei 長兄

older sister chōshi 長姉

on (of dates) ~ni ~に, ~no toki ni ~の時に

on (turned on) haitta 入った

on (at) ~no ue ni ~の上に, ~ni ~に

on: to turn something on tsuketa 点けた

on board ~ni notte ~に乗って

on fire hi ga tsuita 火がついた

on foot toho de 徒歩で

on the way tochū de 途中で

on time jikan dōri ni 時間通りに

once ichido 一度

one ichi 一

one-way ticket katamichi-kippu 片道切符

onion tamanegi 玉葱

only ...shika (...nai) ...しか(...ない)

open hiraiteiru 開いている

open, to akeru 開ける

opinion iken 意見

opponent taikōsha 対抗者

opportunity kikai 機会

oppose, to hantaisuru 反対する

opposed, in opposition hantai no 反対の

opposite (contrary) ~ni hanshite ~に反して

opposite (facing) hantai gawa no 反対側の

optional zuii no 随意の

or ~ka~ ~か~

orange (color) orenjiiro オレンジ色

orange (citrus) orenji オレンジ

order (command) meirei 命令

order (placed for food, goods) chūmon 注文(食べ物や物)

order (sequence) junban 順番

order, to (command) meireisuru 命令する

order something, to chūmonsuru 注文する

orderly (organized) seitonsareta 整とんされた

organize, to chōseisuru 調整する

origin kigen 起源

original genkei no 原型の

originate, to (come from) ~kara okoru ~から起こる

ornament sōshokuhin 装飾品

other hoka no 他の

ought to ~subeki de aru ~すべきである

out ~no soto e ~の外へ

outside sotogawa 外側

outside of ~no soto ni ~の外に

oval (shape) daenkei 楕円形

oven tenpi 天火, ōbun オーブン

over (finished) owatta 終った

over: to turn over uragaesu 裏返す

over there achira gawa あちら側, asoko あそこ

overcast (cloudy) kumotta 曇った

overcome, to uchikatsu 打ち勝つ

overseas kaigai no 海外の

owe, to kari ga aru 借りがある

own, to shojisuru 所持する

own (personal) jibun no 自分の

own: on one's own hitori de 独りで

pack, package tsutsumi 包み

page pēji 頁

paid yūkyū no 有給の

pain itami 痛み

painful itai 痛い

paint, to (a painting) kaku 描く(絵)

paint, to (house, furniture) penki o nuru ペンキを塗る(家、家具)

painting kaiga 絵画

pair of, a ittsui no 一対の

pajamas nemaki 寝巻き, pajama パジャマ

palace kyūden 宮殿

pan nabe 鍋

panorama zenkei 全景, panorama パノラマ

panties pantī パンティー

pants zubon ズボン

paper kami 紙

parcel kozutsumi 小包

parents ryōshin 両親

park kōen 公園

park, to (car) chūsha suru 駐車する

part (not whole) ichibu 一部

part (of machine) buhin 部品

participate, to sankasuru 参加する

particularly toku ni 特に

partly bubunteki ni 部分的に

partner (in business) kyōdō keieisha 共同経営者

partner (spouse) tsureai つれあい

party (event) pātī パーティー(催し)

party (political) tō 党(政治的な)

pass, to (exam) gōkakusuru 合格する(試験)

pass, to (go past) tōrikosu 通り越す

passenger jōkyaku 乗客

passport ryoken 旅券, pasupōto パスポート

past: go past tōrikosu 通り越す

past (former) mukashi no 昔の

pastime goraku 娯楽

patient (calm) nintai no aru 忍耐のある

patient (doctor's) kanja 患者

pattern (design) moyō 模様, gara 柄

pay, to harau 払う

pay attention chūi o harau 注意を払う

payment shiharai 支払い

peace heiwa 平和

peaceful heiwa na 平和な

peak (summit) sanchō 山頂, chōten 頂点

pearl shinju 真珠

peel, to muku 剥く

pen pen ペン

pencil enpitsu 鉛筆

people hitobito 人々

pepper (black) kurokoshō 黒胡椒

pepper (chilli) tōgarashi 唐辛子

percent, percentage hyakubun-ritsu 百分率, pāsento パーセント

performance kōen 公演, dekibae 出来映え

perfume kōsui 香水

perhaps (maybe) tabun 多分

period (menstrual) seiri 生理

period (of time) kikan 期間

permanent eikyū no 永久の

permit (license) menkyo 免許

permit, to (allow) kyokasuru 許可する

person hito 人

personality kosei 個性, seikaku 性格

perspire, to ase o kaku 汗をかく

pet animal aigandbutsu 愛玩動物, petto ペット

pharmacy yakkyoku 薬局

photocopy kopī コピー

photocopy, to kopīsuru コピーする

photograph shashin 写真

photograph, to shashin o toru 写真を撮る

pick, to (choose) erabu 選ぶ

pick up, to (someone) kuruma ni noseru 車に乗せる(人を)

pick up, to (something) mochiageru 持ち上げる(物を)

pickpocket suri すり

picture e 絵

piece (item) ikko 一個

piece (portion, section) hitokire ひと切れ

pierce, to tsukitōsu 突き通す

pig buta 豚

pillow makura 枕

pills jōzai 錠剤

pink pinku no ピンクの

pitcher mizusashi 水差し
pity: what a pity zan'nen da 残念だ
place basho 場所
place, to oku 置く
plain (level ground) taira na 平らな
plain (not fancy) heibon na 平凡な
plan keikaku 計画
plan, to keikakusuru 計画する
plane hikōki 飛行機
plant shokubutsu 植物
plant, to ueru 植える
plastic purasuchikku プラスチック
plate sara 皿
play, to ~suru ～する
play around, to asobimawaru 遊びまわる
plead, to kongansuru 懇願する
pleasant kanjinoii 感じのいい
please (go ahead) dōzo どうぞ(勧めるとき)
please (request for help) onegai shimasu お願いします(助けを依頼する時)
please (request for something) onegai shimasu お願いします(何かを依頼する時)
pleased manzokushita 満足した
plug (bath) sen 栓(風呂)
plug (electric) sashikomi 差込, puragu プラグ(電気)
plus tsukekuwawatta 付け加わった, purasu プラス
pocket poketto ポケット
point (in time) jiten 時点(時間)
point (dot) ten 点
point out shitekisuru 指摘する
poison doku 毒
police keisatsu 警察
police officer keisatsukan 警察官
polish, to migaku 磨く
politics seiji 政治
polite reigitadashii 礼儀正しい
poor mazushii 貧しい
popular ninki no aru 人気のある
population jinkō 人口
pork butaniku 豚肉
port minato 港
portion (serve) wakemae 分け前
possess, to shoyūsuru 所有する
possessions shoyūbutsu 所有物
possible kanō na 可能な
possibly osoraku~darō おそらく～だろう
post (mail) yūbin 郵便
postcard hagaki 葉書
postpone, to enkisuru 延期する
post office yūbinkyoku 郵便局
pot hachi 鉢
potato jagaimo ジャガイモ
pour, to sosogu 注ぐ
power chikara 力

powerful chikarazuyoi 力強い
practice shūkan 習慣, renshū 練習
practice, to renshūsuru 練習する
praise shōsan 賞賛
praise, to shōsansuru 賞賛する
pray, to inoru 祈る
prayer kigan(suruhito) 祈願(する人)
prefer, to konomu 好む
pregnant ninshinshita 妊娠した
prepare, to (make ready) junbisuru 準備する
prepared (ready) yōi ga dekiteiru 用意ができている
prescription shohōsen 処方箋
present (gift) okurimono 贈り物, purezento プレゼント
present, to be (here) koko ni iru ここにいる
present, to okurimono o suru 贈り物をする
present: at the present moment genzai 現在
presently (nowadays) genzai 現在
preserved hozonsareta 保存された
president daitōryō 大統領, kaichō 会長, shachō 社長
press (journalism) shinbun 新聞
press, to osu 押す
pressure atsuryoku 圧力
pretend, to ~o yosoou ～を装う
pretty (of places, things) utsukushii 美しい, kogirei na こぎれいな(場所、物)
pretty (of women) kawairashii かわいらしい(女性)
pretty (very) totemo とても
prevent, to samatageru 妨げる
price nedan 値段
pride hokori 誇り, jisonshin 自尊心
priest shisai 司祭
print, to insatsusuru 印刷する
prison keimusho 刑務所
private kojinteki na 個人的な
probably osoraku おそらく
problem mondai 問題
produce, to seisansuru 生産する
profession shokugyō 職業
profit rieki 利益
program (schedule) yotei 予定
promise, to yakusokusuru 約束する
pronounce, to hatsuonsuru 発音する
proof shōko 証拠
property shisan 資産
protest, to hantaisuru 反対する
proud hokori ni omou 誇りに思う
prove, to shōmeisuru 証明する
public kōkyō no 公共の
publish, to shuppansuru 出版する
pull, to hiku 引く
punctual jikandōri no 時間どおりの
pupil seito 生徒

pure junsui na 純粋な
purple murasaki 紫
purpose mokuteki 目的
purse (for money) saifu 財布(お金)
push, to osu 押す
put, to (place) oku 置く
put off (delay) enkisuru 延期する
put on (clothes) kiru 着る(服を)
put together, to kumiawaseru 組み合わせる

qualification shikaku 資格
queen joō 女王
question shitsumon 質問
quick kibin na 機敏な, hayai 速い
quickly binsoku ni 敏速に
quiet shizuka na 静かな
quite (fairly) kanari かなり
quite (very) zuibun ずいぶん

radio rajio ラジオ
railroad, railway senro 線路, tetsudo 鉄道
rain ame 雨
rain, to ame ga furu 雨が降る
raise, to (children) sodateru 育てる(子供)
raise, to (lift) ageru あげる
rapid hayai 速い
rare (scarce) mezurashii 珍しい
rare (half-cooked) namayake no 生焼けの
rarely, seldom mare ni まれに
rate (tariff) ryōkin 料金
rate of exchange (for foreign currency) kawase rēto 為替レート
rather than ~yori mushiro ～よりむしろ
raw (uncooked) nama no 生の
reach, to (get to) tōchakusuru 到着する
react, to han'nōsuru 反応する
read, to yomu 読む
ready yōidekita 用意できた
ready: to get/make ready junbisuru 準備する
realize, to satoru 悟る
really (in fact) jissai ni 実際に
really (truly, honestly) hontō ni 本当に
really? hontō 本当
rear (tail) ushiro 後ろ
reason riyū 理由
reasonable (price) tegoro na 手ごろな(値段)
reasonable (sensible) funbetsu no aru 分別のある
receipt ryōshūsho 領収書
receive, to uketoru 受け取る
recipe reshipi レシピ
reckon, to kazoeru 数える
recognize, to mitomeru 認める

recommend, to susumeru 勧める
recovered (cured) kaifukushita 回復した
rectangle chōhōkei 長方形
red aka 赤
reduce, to herasu 減らす
reduction genshō 減少
reflect, to hankyōsuru 反響する
refreshment (drink) nomimono 飲み物
refrigerator reizōko 冷蔵庫
refusal kyozetsu 拒絶
refuse, to kotowaru 断る
regarding ~ni kanshite ～に関して
region chiiki 地域
register, to tōrokusuru 登録する
registered post kakitome 書留
regret, to kōkaisuru 後悔する
regrettably oshikumo 惜しくも
regular (normal) tsūjō no 通常の
relatives shinseki 親戚
relax, to kutsurogu くつろぐ
release, to hanasu 放す
religion shūkyō 宗教
remainder (leftover) nokori-mono 残り物
remember, to oboeteiru 覚えている
remind, to omoidasaseru 思い出させる
rent, to kasu 貸す
repair, to shūrisuru 修理する
repeat, to kurikaesu 繰り返す
replace, to irekawaru 入れ替わる
reply (response) henji 返事
reply, to (in speech) hentōsuru 返答する
reply, to (in writing) henji o kaku 返事を書く
report hōkoku 報告
report, to hōkokusuru 報告する
reporter repōtā レポーター
request, to (formally) iraisuru 依頼する(公式に)
request, to (informally) tanomu 頼む(非公式に)
rescue, to kyūjosuru 救助する
research kenkyū 研究
research, to kenkyūsuru 研究する
resemble ruijisuru 類似する
reservation yoyaku 予約
reserve, to (ask for in advance) yoyakusuru 予約する
resident jūnin 住人
resolve, to (a problem) kaiketsusuru 解決する(問題)
respect sonkei 尊敬
respect, to sonkeisuru 尊敬する
respond, to hentōsuru 返答する
response (reaction) hentō 返答, han'nō 反応

responsibility sekinin 責任
responsible, to be sekinin o motsu 責任を持つ
rest (remainder) nokori 残り
rest, to (relax) yasumu 休む
restaurant resutoran レストラン
restrain, to osaeru 抑える
restroom tearai 手洗い
result: as a result, resulting from ~no kekkatoshite ～の結果として
result kekka 結果
result (effect) eikyō 影響
retired intaishita 引退した
return, to (give back) kaesu 返す
return, to (go back) modoru 戻る
return ticket ōfuku-kippu 往復切符
return to one's home town, to kikyōsuru 帰郷する
reveal, to (make known) akiraka ni suru 明らかにする
reveal, to (make visible) arawa-su 現す
reverse, to (go backwards) gyakkōsuru 逆行する
ribbon ribon リボン
rice (cooked) gohan ご飯(炊いた)
rice (plant) ine 稲
rice (uncooked) kome 米
rice fields tanbo 田んぼ
rich kanemochi no 金持ちの
rid: get rid of torinozoku 取り除く
ride, to (in car, on an animal) noru (車、動物に)乗る
ride, to (transport) jōshasuru (乗り物に)乗車する
right (correct) tadashii 正しい
right-hand side migigawa 右側
right now sugu ni すぐに
rights kenri 権利
ring (jewelry) yubiwa 指輪
ring, to (bell) narasu (ベルを)鳴らす
ring, to (on the telephone) denwasuru 電話する
ripe jukushita 熟した
rise (ascendance) jōshō 上昇
rise (increase) zōka 増加
river kawa 川
road michi 道
roast, to (grill) aburu あぶる, yaku やく
rock ishi 石
role yakuwari 役割
roof yane 屋根
room (in hotel/house) heya 部屋 (ホテル/家)
room (space) kūkan 空間
root (of plant) ne 根(植物)
rope rōpu ロープ, nawa 縄
rotten kusatta 腐った
rough arappoi 荒っぽい

roughly (approximately) ōyoso おおよそ
round (shape) marui 丸い
rubber gomu ゴム
rude shitsurei na 失礼な
ruined hakaisareta 破壊された
rule kisoku 規則
run, to hashiru 走る
run away, to nigeru 逃げる

sacred shinēs na 神聖な
sacrifice gisei 犠牲
sacrifice, to gisei ni suru 犠牲にする
sad kanashii 悲しい
safe anzen na 安全な
sail, to funatabi o suru 船旅をする
salary kyūryō 給料
sale, for urimono 売りもの
sale (reduced prices) yasuuri 安売り, bāgen バーゲン
sales assistant ten'in 店員
salt shio 塩
salty shiokarai 塩辛い
same onaji 同じ
sample mihon 見本
sand suna 砂
sandals sandaru サンダル
satisfied manzokushita 満足した
satisfy, to manzokusaseru 満足させる
Saturday doyōbi 土曜日
sauce sōsu ソース
save, to tamotsu 保つ
say, to iu 言う
say hello, to kon'nichiwa to iu こんにちはと言う, yoroshiku よろしく
say goodbye, to sayōnara to iu さようならと言う
say sorry, to ayamaru 謝る
say thank you, to arigatō to iu ありがとうと言う
scarce toboshii 乏しい
scared obieta おびえた
schedule kēkaku 計画
school gakkō 学校
schoolchild gakudō 学童
science kagaku 科学
scissors hasami はさみ
screen (of computer) gamen 画面, sukurīn スクリーン(コンピューター)
scrub, to araiotosu 洗い落とす
sculpture chōkoku 彫刻
sea umi 海
seafood kaisanbutsu 海産物
search for, to ~o sagasu ～を探す
season kisetsu 季節
seat isu 椅子
second byō 秒, daini no 第二の
secret himitsu 秘密
secret: to keep a secret himitsu o mamoru 秘密を守る

secretary hisho 秘書
secure anzen na 安全な
see, to miru 見る
seed tane 種
seek, to motomeru 求める
seem, to ~to omowareru ～と思われる
see you later! soredewa mata それではまた
seldom hotondo~nai ほとんど～ない
select, to erabu 選ぶ
self jishin 自身
sell, to uru 売る
send, to okuru 送る
sensible shiryo no aru 思慮のある
sentence bun 文, sentensu センテンス
separate wakareta 分かれた
separate, to wakeru 分ける
September kugatsu 九月
sequence (order) junjo 順序
serious (not funny) majime na まじめな
serious (severe) hidoi ひどい
servant meshitsukai 召使
serve, to tsukaeru 仕える
service hōshi 奉仕
set shotei no 所定の
set up, to setsuritsusuru 設立する, juritsusuru 樹立する
several ikutsuka no いくつかの
severe kibishii きびしい
sew, to nu'u 縫う
sex (gender) seibetsu 性別
shade kage 陰
shadow kage 影
shadow play kagee 影絵
shake, to furu 振る
shall ~deshō ～でしょう
shallow asai 浅い
shame (disgrace) chijoku 恥辱
shame: what a shame! zan'nen 残念
shampoo shanpū シャンプー
shape katachi 形
shape, to (form) katachizukuru 形作る
shark same 鮫
sharp surudoi 鋭い
shatter, to konagona ni suru 粉々にする
shave, to soru 剃る
sheet (for bed) shītsu シーツ
sheet (of paper) ichimai no kami 一枚の紙
Shinto shintō 神道
shiny hikaru 光る
ship fune 船
shirt shatsu シャツ
shiver, to miburuisuru 身震いする
shoes kutsu 靴

shoot, to utsu 撃つ
shop, to (go shopping) kaimono o suru 買い物をする
shop mise 店
shopkeeper ten'in 店員
short (concise) mijikai 短い
short (not tall) hikui 低い
short time (a moment) tanjikan 短時間
shorts shōtsu ショーツ, tanpan 短パン
shoulder kata 肩
shout, to sakebu 叫ぶ
show (broadcast) bangumi 番組
show (live performance) shō ショー, moyōshi 催し
show, to miseru 見せる
shower (for washing) shawā シャワー
shower (of rain) kosame 小雨
shower: to take a shower shawā o abiru シャワーを浴びる
shrimp ebi 海老
shut shimatta 閉まった
shut, to tojiru 閉じる
sick byōki no 病気の
sick, to be (vomit) hakike ga suru 吐き気がする
side yoko 横
sightseeing kankō 観光
sign (symbol) hyōshiki 標識
sign, to shomei suru 署名する
signature shomei 署名, sain サイン
silent mugon no 無言の
silk kinu 絹
silver gin 銀
similar ruijishita 類似した
simple (uncomplicated, modest) jimi na 地味な
simple (easy) kantan na 簡単な
since irai 以来
sing, to utau 歌う
single (not married) dokushin no 独身の
single (only one) yuiitsu no 唯一の
sir (term of address) kika 貴下 （男性への敬称）
sister shimai 姉妹
sit, to suwaru 座る
sit down, to suwaru 座る
situated, to be ~no jōtai ni aru ～の状態にある
situation (how things are) jōkyō 状況
size saizu サイズ
skillful jukurenshita 熟練した
skin hada 肌
skirt sukāto スカート
sky sora 空
sleep, to neru 寝る
sleepy nemui 眠い

slender hosoi 細い, sumāto na スマートな
slight wazuka na わずかな
slightly wazuka ni わずかに
slim surimu na スリムな, hosoi 細い
slip surippu スリップ, pechikōto ペチコート
slippers surippa スリッパ, uwabaki 上履き
slope saka 坂
slow osoi 遅い
slowly yukkuri ゆっくり
small chīsai 小さい
small change kozeni 小銭
smart kashikoi 賢い
smartphone sumātofon スマートフォン
smell (bad odor) akushū 悪臭
smell, to niou 臭う
smile, to warau 笑う
smoke kemuri 煙
smoke, to (tobacco) tabako o suu タバコをすう
smooth (of surfaces) subesubeshita すべすべした
smooth (to go smoothly) enkatsu ni susumu 円滑にすすむ
smuggle, to mitsuyunyūsuru 密輸入する
snake hebi 蛇
sneeze kushami くしゃみ
sneeze, to kushami o suru くしゃみをする
snow yuki 雪
snow, to yuki ga furu 雪が降る
so (therefore) sorede それで, soreyue それゆえ
so (very) totemo とても
so that dakara だから, ~suru tame ni ～するために
soak, to hitaru 浸る
soap sekken 石鹸
socket (electric) soketto ソケット, ukeguchi 受け口（電気の）
socks kutsushita 靴下
sofa sofā ソファー
soft yawarakai やわらかい
soil tsuchi 土
sold urareta 売られた
sold out urikire 売り切れ
soldier heitai 兵隊
sole (only) tatta hitotsu no たったひとつの
solid kotai no 固体の
solve, to (a problem) kaiketsusuru 解決する（問題を）
some ikutsuka no いくつかの
somebody, someone dareka 誰か
something nanika 何か
sometimes tokidoki 時々

somewhere dokoka どこか
son musuko 息子
son-in-law giri no musuko 義理の息子
song uta 歌
soon sugu ni すぐに
sore, painful itai 痛い
sorrow kanashimi 悲しみ
sorry gomen'nasai ごめんなさい
sorry, to kōkaisuru 後悔する
sort (type) shurui 種類
sort out, to taishosuru 対処する
sound oto 音
soup (clear) sūpu スープ
soup (spicy stew) shichū シチュー, nikomi 煮込み
sour suppai すっぱい
source minamoto 源
south minami 南
souvenir miyagemono みやげ物
space kūkan 空間
spacious hirobiroshita 広々した
speak, to hanasu 話す
special tokubetsu na 特別な
speech supīchi スピーチ
speed supīdo スピード
spell, to tsuzuru 綴る
spend, to tsuiyasu 費やす
spicy karai 辛い
spinach hōrensō ほうれん草
spine sebone 背骨
spiral rasenjō no らせん状の
spoiled (of food) kusatta 腐った（食べ物）
spoon supūn スプーン
sponge suponji スポンジ
sports supōtsu no スポーツの, undōyō no 運動用の
spray supurē スプレー
spring (of water) wakimizu 湧き水
spring (season) haru 春
split up, to bunkatsusuru 分割する
spouse haigūsha 配偶者
square (shape) shikakui 四角い
square (town square) hiroba 広場
squid ika イカ
staff sutaffu スタッフ, ichiin 一員
stain shimi しみ
stairs kaidan 階段
stall, to (car) shissoku saseru 失速させる（車）
stamp (ink) kokuin 刻印, sutanpu スタンプ
stamp (postage) kitte （郵便）切手
stand, to tatsu 立つ
stand up, to tachiagaru 立ち上がる
star hoshi 星
start (beginning) hajimari 始まり
start, to hajimeru 始める
state, to noberu 述べる
stationery bunbōgu 文房具
statue zō 像

stay, to (remain) nokoru 残る
stay overnight, to ippakusuru 一泊する
steal, to nusumu 盗む
steam jōki 蒸気
steamed musareta 蒸された
steel hagane はがね
steer, to kaji o toru かじをとる
step ashidori 足取り, ippo 一歩
steps, stairs kaidan 階段
stick (pole) bō 棒
stick out, to depparu 出っ張る
sticky nebanebashita ねばねばした
sticky rice mochigome もち米
stiff katai 堅い
still (even now) mada まだ
still (quiet) shizuka na 静かな
stink, to akushū o hanatsu 悪臭を放つ
stomach hara 腹
stone ishi 石
stool koshikake 腰掛, benki 便器
stop (bus, train) teiryūjo 停留所, eki 駅（バス、電車の）
stop, to (cease) yameru やめる
stop, to (halt) tomeru 止める
stop by, to (pay a visit) tazuneru 訪ねる
stop it yamete やめて
store (saving) takuwae 蓄え
store, shop mise 店
storm arashi 嵐
story (of a building) kai 階（建物）
story (tale) hanashi 話
stout zungurishita ずんぐりした
stove (cooker) konro コンロ, kamado かまど
straight (not crooked) massugu na 真っ直ぐな
straight ahead massugu mae ni 真っ直ぐ前に
strange hen na 変な
stranger shiranai hito 知らない人
street michi 道, tōri 通り
strength chikara 力
strict kibishii 厳しい
strike, to (hit) utsu 打つ
strike: to go on strike sutoraiki o suru ストライキをする
string himo 紐
strong tsuyoi 強い
stubborn (determined) ganko na 頑固な
stuck (won't move) koteisareta 固定された
student gakusei 学生
study, to gakushūsuru 学習する
stupid oroka na 愚かな
style katachi 形
succeed, to seikōsuru 成功する
success seikō 成功

such as ~no yōna 〜のような, tatoeba 例えば
suck, to suu 吸う
suddenly kyū ni 急に
suffer, to kurushimu 苦しむ
sugar satō 砂糖
sugarcane satōkibi サトウキビ
suggest, to teian suru 提案する
suggestion teian 提案
suit (business) sūtsu スーツ
suitable fusawashii ふさわしい, oniai no お似合いの
suitcase sūtsukēsu スーツケース
summer natsu 夏
summit (peak) sanchō 山頂
summon, to yobidasu 呼び出す
sun taiyō 太陽
Sunday nichiyōbi 日曜日
sunlight hizashi 日差し
sunny hiatari ga ii 日当たりがいい
sunrise hinode 日の出
sunset hinoiri 日の入
supermarket sūpāmāketto スーパーマーケット
suppose, to ~dato omou 〜だと思う
sure kakushinshita 確信した
surf uchiyoseru nami 打ち寄せる波, sāfin サーフィン
surface hyōmen 表面
surface mail futsūyūbin 普通郵便
surname myōji 苗字
surprised odoroita 驚いた
surprising odorokubeki 驚くべき
surroundings kankyō 環境
survive, to ikinobiru 生き延びる
suspect, to utagau 疑う
suspicion kengi 嫌疑
stubborn dankotoshita 断固とした
swallow, to nomikomu 飲み込む
sweat hakkan 発汗
sweat, to ase o kaku 汗をかく
sweep, to haku 掃く
sweet amai 甘い
sweet and sour amazuppai 甘酸っぱい
sweets (candy) ame 飴
swim, to oyogu 泳ぐ
swimsuit mizugi 水着
swing, to yuri ugokasu 揺り動かす
switch suitchi スイッチ
switch, to (change) kōkansuru 交換する
switch, to (clothes) kigaeru 着替える
switch on, to tsukeru 点ける

table tsukue 机, tēburu テーブル
tablecloth tēburukurosu テーブルクロス
tablemat tēburumatto テーブルマット

tail o 尾, shippo しっぽ
take, to (remove) motteiku 持っていく
take care of, to sewa o suru 世話をする
take off, to (clothes) nugu 脱ぐ (服)
talk, to hanasu 話す
talk about, to ~ni tsuite hanasu ～について話す
tall takai 高い
tape, adhesive setchaku tēpu 接着テープ
taste aji 味
taste, to (sample) shishoku o suru 試食をする
taste, to (salty, spicy, etc.) ajimi o suru 味見をする
tasty oishii おいしい
taxi takushī タクシー
tea cha 茶
teach, to oshieru 教える
teacher sensei 先生
team chīmu チーム
tear, to (rip) yaburu 破る
tears namida 涙
teenager shishunki no kodomo 思春期の子供(13～19歳)
teeshirt tyīshatsu ティーシャツ
teeth ha 歯
telephone denwa 電話
telephone number denwabangō 電話番号
television terebi テレビ
tell, to (a story) hanasu 話す
tell, to (let know) oshieru 教える
temperature ondo 温度
temple (ancient) koji 古寺
temple jiin 寺院, tera 寺
temporary ichijiteki na 一時的な
ten thousand ichiman 一万
tennis tenisu テニス
tens of (multiples of ten) nanjūbaimono 何十倍もの
tense kinchōshita 緊張した
terrible hidoi ひどい
test shiken 試験, tesuto テスト
test, to tamesu 試す
than ~yori ～より
Thailand tai タイ
thank, to kanshasuru 感謝する
thank you arigatō ありがとう
that (introducing a quotation) ~to (iu) ～と(言う)
that person sono hito その人
that are あれ
that thing sore それ
theater (drama) gekijo 劇場
then sono go その後, sorekara それから
there soko ni そこに, soko de そこで

there is/are ~ga aru ～がある, ~ga iru ～がいる
therefore sono kekka その結果
these korera no これらの
thick (of liquids) koi 濃い
thick (of things) atsui 厚い
thief dorobō 泥棒
thin (of liquids) usui 薄い(液体)
thin (of persons) yaseta やせた(人)
thing mono 物
think, to (have an opinion) omou 思う
think, to (ponder) kangaeru 考える
third daisan no 第三の
thirsty nodo no kawaita のどの渇いた
this kono この
those arera あれら
though ~nimo kakawarazu ～にもかかわらず
thoughts shikō 思考
thousand sen 千
thread ito 糸
threaten, to kyōhakusuru 脅迫する
throat nodo のど
through (past) ~o tōrinukete ～を通り抜けて
throw, to nageru 投げる
throw away/out, to suteru 捨てる
thunder kaminari 雷
Thursday mokuyōbi 木曜日
thus (so) shitagatte 従って
ticket (for entertainment) ken 券, chiketto チケット(娯楽)
ticket (for transport) kippu 切符 (乗り物)
tidy sētonsareta 整頓された
tidy up, to sētonsuru 整頓する
tie (necktie) nekutai ネクタイ
tie, to musubu 結ぶ
tight pittarishita ぴったりした, kitsui きつい
time jikan 時間
time: from time to time tokidoki 時々
times (multiplying) bai 倍
timetable jikokuhyō 時刻表
tiny totemo chīsa na とても小さな
tip (end) hashi 端
tip (gratuity) chippu チップ, kokorozuke 心付け
tired (sleepy) nemui 眠い
tired (worn out) tsukareta 疲れた
title (of book, film) daimei 題名 (本、映画)
title (of person) katagaki 肩書き (人)
to (a person) ~e ～へ, ~no hō ni ～の方に(人)
to (a place) ~e ～へ, ~no hōkō ni ～の方向に(場所)

toasted aburareta あぶられた
today kyō 今日
toe tsumasaki つま先
tofu tōfu 豆腐
together tomo ni 共に, issho ni 一緒に
toilet tearai 手洗い, toire トイレ
tomato tomato トマト
tomorrow asu 明日
tongue shita 舌
tonight konban 今晩
too (also) ~mo mata ～もまた
too (excessive) amari ni~sugiru あまりに～過ぎる
too much ōsugiru 多過ぎる
tool dōgu 道具
tooth ha 歯
toothbrush haburashi 歯ブラシ
toothpaste hamigakiko 歯磨き粉
top ue 上
topic wadai 話題
total gōkei (no) 合計(の)
touch, to fureru 触れる
tourist kankōkyaku 観光客
toward ~no hōe ～の方へ
toward, to ~e mukau ～へ向かう
towel taoru タオル
tower tō 塔
town machi 町
toy omocha おもちゃ
trade (business) shōbai 商売
trade (exchange) bōeki 貿易
tradition dentō 伝統
traditional dentōteki na 伝統的な
traffic kōtsū 交通
train densha 電車
train station eki 駅
training kunren 訓練
translate, to hon'yakusuru 翻訳する
travel, to ryokō o suru 旅行をする
traveler ryokōsha 旅行者
tray bon 盆
treat (something special) tanoshimi 楽しみ, gochisō ご馳走
treat, to (deal with) atsukau 扱う
treat, to (medically) chiryōsuru 治療する
tree ki 木
triangle sankaku 三角
tribe buzoku 部族
trip (journey) tabi 旅
trouble kon'nan 困難
troublesome mendō na 面倒な
trousers zubon ズボン
truck torakku トラック
true hontō no 本当の
truly hontō ni 本当に
trust, to shinraisuru 信頼する
try, to doryokusuru 努力する
try on, to (clothes) shichakusuru 試着する

Tuesday kayōbi 火曜日
turn: to make a turn magaru 曲がる
turn around, to furikaeru 振りかえる
turn off, to kesu 消す
turn on, to tsukeru 点ける
TV terebi テレビ
Tweet (internet) (tsuittā de) tsubuyaku (ツイッターで)つぶやく
Twitter (internet) tsuittā ツイッター
type (sort) shurui 種類
type, to taipusuru タイプする
typhoon taihū 台風
typical tenkeiteki na 典型的な

ugly migurushii 見苦しい
umbrella kasa 傘
uncle oji おじ
uncooked nama no 生の
under ~no shita ni ～の下に
undergo, to keikensuru 経験する
underpants pantsu パンツ
undershirt hadagi 肌着
understand, to rikaisuru 理解する
underwear shitagi 下着
undressed, to get fuku o nugu 服を脱ぐ
unemployed shitsugyōchū no 失業中の
unfortunately zan'nen nagara 残念ながら
unhappy fukō na 不幸な
United Kingdom eikoku 英国
United States amerika gasshūkoku アメリカ合衆国
university daigaku 大学
unless ~de nai kagiri ～でない限り
unlucky fuun na 不運な
unnecessary fuhitsuyō na 不必要な
unripe miseijuku no 未成熟の
until ~made ～まで
up, upward ue no hōe 上のほうへ
upset dōyōshita 動揺した
upside down sakasama 逆さま
upstairs jōkai e 上階へ
urban toshi no 都市の
urge, to (push for) shōdō o karitateru 衝動を駆り立てる
urgent kinkyū no 緊急の
urinate, to shōben o suru 小便をする
use, to tsukau 使う
used to (accustomed) nareteiru 慣れている
used to do something yoku ~shitamonoda よく～したものだ
useful yakudatsu 役立つ
useless mueki na 無益な
usual itsumo no いつもの

usually taitei たいてい
utensil dōgu 道具

vacation kyūka 休暇
vaccination yobōsesshu 予防接種
vague aimai na あいまいな
valid yūkō na 有効な, datō na 妥当な
valley tani 谷
value (cost) kachi 価格
value (good) oneuchi お値打ち
vase kabin 花瓶
VCR bideo dekki ビデオデッキ
vegetable yasai 野菜
vehicle norimono 乗り物
verify tashikameru 確かめる
very (extremely) hijō ni 非常に
via ~o tōtte ～を通って
video recorder bideo rekōdā ビデオレコーダー
videotape, to rokugasuru 録画する
Vietnam betonamu ベトナム
view (panorama) keshiki 景色
viewpoint mikata 見方
village mura 村
vinegar su 酢
visa biza ビザ, sashō 査証
visit taizai 滞在
visit: pay a visit to tazuneru 訪ねる
voice koe 声
voicemail rusuban-denwa 留守番電話
volcano kazan 火山
vomit, to haku 吐く
vote, to tōhyōsuru 投票する

wages chingin 賃金
wait for, to ~o motsu ～を待つ
waiter, waitress kyūji 給仕
wake someone up, to okosu 起こす
wake up, to mezameru 目覚める
walk, to aruku 歩く
wall kabe 壁
wallet saifu 財布
want, to ~ga hoshii ～が欲しい, ~shitai ～したい
war sensō 戦争
warm atatakai 暖かい
warmth nukumori ぬくもり
warn, to kēkokusuru 警告する
warning kēkoku 警告
wash, to arau 洗う
wash the dishes, to shokki o arau 食器を洗う
watch (wristwatch) udedokei 腕時計
watch, to miru 見る
watch, to (show, movie) miru 観る

watch over, to (guard) miharu 見張る
water mizu 水
waterfall taki 滝
watermelon suika スイカ
wave (in sea) nami 波
wave, to furu 振る
way (method) hōhō 方法
way: the way of ~suru hōhō ～する方法
way in iriguchi 入口
way out deguchi 出口
weak yowai 弱い
wealthy yūfuku na 裕福な
weapon buki 武器
wear, to kiru 着る
weary tsukarekitta 疲れ切った
weather tenki 天気
weave, to oru 織る
website webusaito ウェブサイト
wedding kekkonshiki 結婚式
Wednesday suiyōbi 水曜日
week shū 週
weekend shūmatsu 週末
weekly maishū no 毎週の
weep, to naku 泣く
weigh, to hakaru 量る
weight omosa 重さ
weight, to gain taijū ga fueru 体重が増える
weight, to lose taiju ga heru 体重が減る
welcome! yōkoso ようこそ
welcome to ~e yōkoso ～へようこそ
well (for water) ido 井戸
well (good) yoi 良い
well done! yoku dekimashita よくできました
well off (wealthy) yūfuku na 裕福な
well-behaved, well-mannered gyōgi no ii 行儀のいい
well-cooked, well-done yoku hi no tootta よく火の通った
west nishi 西
westerner seiyōjin 西洋人
wet nureta 濡れた
what nani 何
what for nan no tame ni 何のために
what happened nani ga okitano 何が起きたの
what kind of don'na どんな
what time nanji 何時
wheel sharin 車輪
when itsu いつ
when (at the time) ~suru toki ～する時
whenever itsudemo いつでも
where doko どこ
where to doko e どこへ

which dore どれ
while (during) ~no aida ni 〜の間に
white shiro 白
who dare だれ
whole (all of) subete no 全ての
whole (to be complete) kanzen na 完全な
why naze なぜ
wicked warui 悪い
wide habahiroi 幅広い
width haba 幅
widow mibōjin 未亡人
will ~deshō 〜でしょう
with ~to 〜と
within reason dōri ni kanatteiru 道理にかなっている
without ~nashi ni 〜なしに
witness mokugekisha 目撃者
witness, to mokugekisuru 目撃する
woman josei 女性
wonderful subarashii すばらしい
wood ki 木
wooden mokusei no 木製の

wool yōmō 羊毛
word go 語, kotoba 言葉
work (occupation) shigoto 仕事
work, to shigoto o suru 仕事をする
work, to (function) kinōsuru 機能する
world sekai 世界
worn out (clothes, machine) tsukaifurushita 使い古した（服、機械）
worn out (tired) tsukarekitta 疲れ切った
worry, to shinpaisuru 心配する
worse yori warui より悪い
worship, to shinkōsuru 信仰する
worst mottomohidoi 最もひどい
worth, to be kachigaaru 価値がある
wound kega 怪我
wrap, to tsutsumu 包む
wrist tekubi 手首
write, to kaku 書く
writer sakka 作家
wrong (false) ayamatta 誤った

wrong (mistaken) machigatta 間違った
wrong (morally) warui 悪い（道徳的に）

yawn, to akubisuru あくびする
year toshi 年
years old ~sai 〜歳
yell, to sakebu 叫ぶ
yellow kīro 黄色
yesterday kinō 昨日
yet: not yet mada~nai まだ〜ない
you're welcome dōitashimashite どういたしまして
young wakai 若い
younger brother otōto 弟
younger sister imōto 妹
youth (state of being young) wakasa 若さ
youth (young person) wakamono 若者

zero zero 零
zoo dōbutsuen 動物園

Illustration Credits

The line drawings throughout the text are by Akiko Saito.

The credits for the photographs are as follows:

ayustety (http://www.flickr.com/photos/ayustety/12482886/)/Wikimedia Commons:153, *depachika* at Lotte Department Store

Bobby (http://flickr.com/photos/84468390@N00)/Wikimedia Commons: 13, bookshelves with manga

Dorregaray/Dreamstime.com: 125, capsule hotel

Eriko Sato: 140, bento boxes

Radzian/Dreamstime.com: 78, Akihabara

Taeko Kamei: 39, *netto kafe*; 52, fast-food restaurants; 152, *konbini*

Tsuneomp/Dreamstime.com: 189, tatami room

List of Culture Notes

NOTE

Practice your Japanese with the included MP3 audio files!

This CD contains MP3 audio files.

You can play MP3 files on your computer (most computers include a default MP3 player); in your portable MP3 player; on many mobile phones and PDAs; and on some newer CD and DVD players.

You can also convert the MP3 files and create a regular audio CD, using software and a CD writing drive.

To play your MP3 files:

1. Open the CD on your computer.

2. Click on the MP3 file that you wish to play, to open it. The file should start playing automatically. (If it doesn't, then perhaps your computer does not have an MP3 player; you will need to download one. There are dozens of players available online, and most of them are free or shareware. You can type "mp3 player" or "music downloads" into your search engine to find some.)